AF512671

Armed Conflict and Peace Process in Nepal

The Maoist insurgency, past negotiations, and opportunities for conflict transformation

Armed Conflict and Peace Process in Nepal

The Maoist insurgency, past negotiations, and opportunities for conflict transformation

BISHNU RAJ UPRETI, PhD

ADROIT PUBLISHERS

Published by
ADROIT PUBLISHERS
4675/21, Ganpati Bhawan, Ansari Road,
Daryaganj, New Delhi-110 002
Phone : 011-23266030

Distributors
AKHIL BOOK DISTRIBUTORS
e-mail: akhilbooks@yahoo.com
akhilbooks@hotmail.com

All rights reserved

© *Author, 2006*
Reprint 2010

No part of this publication may be reproduced or transmitted in any form or by any means, electronic or mechanical, including photocopying, recording, or any information storage and retrieval system, without permission in writing from the publisher & author.

Requests for permission to make copies of any part of the work should be mailed to:

Copyrights & Permissions Department
ADROIT PUBLISHERS

ISBN: 81-87392-74-6

Printed in India on behalf of M/s Adroit Publishers
by Arpit Printographers • E-mail: arpitprinto@yahoo.com

Dedicated to:

People struggling to turn the Nepalese crisis into opportunities for a democratic, prosperous and inclusive nation.

Preface

Nepal is a confusing state at the crossroad, which can either take a path of more peaceful, democratic modern Nepal or to a path of failed state with anarchy and chaos. Which path to opt mainly depends upon the king, the Maoists and the political parties? They have only two choices. If they opt for anarchy, history will besieged them, and regret, humiliation and worthlessness will be in their share. Nepalese rulers and elite never learnt lessons from mistakes they made in the past and the mistake the world made in its modern history. They never feel time and context is far stronger than their feudal thinking and unrealistic ambitions. Despite its rich natural resources, honest and hardworking people, exotic tourist destination, huge hydro-power potential, geo-strategically important position, Nepalese rulers never attempt to capitalise these advantages and exploit for the benefit of people. Instead, they barely engage in power struggle, grabbing nation's resources and exploitation of people. Consequently, this country is facing this unprecedented crisis manifested in the form of the armed insurgency and the post 1st February autocracy. Suspicion, mistrust, allegations, shifting blames and counter blames are becoming common social characteristics of Nepalese ruling elites. The current crisis is the precise outcome of their failure. They abuse civil institutions, captured state resources, constrained social formation for their vested interests, suppress ethnic, linguistic, cultural and religious diversities, which became breeding grounds for the armed conflict and political crisis. International relations were focused to fulfil vested interests of rulers, which further exacerbated instability and isolation.

However, Nepal cannot remain the same. It may enter into a horrible confrontation between progressive forces who want to change Nepal as an inclusive, modern democratic nation and regressive forces who want to obstruct state restructuring process and progressive change. At the end, progressive force will prevail and this country will emerge as modern democratic country. Nevertheless, cost of confrontational transformation will be unbearably high. Therefore, the best option would be a 'negotiated settlement' with an agreement with a radical state reform, addressing all structural causes of conflict and crisis.

While examining the present Nepalese crisis, the important questions are how and why the Maoist insurgency was emerged? Why the past two negotiations were failed? Why and how the king opted for 1st February coup? What are the initiatives taken so far by political parties, civil society, and media in resolving this crisis and what are the opportunities for conflict transformation? Attempts have been made to answer these questions in this book. My conclusion is that the time for 'ripeness for resolution' of the current crisis is approaching, which either would be more confrontational or compromise.

It gives me pleasure to introduce my perspective, thinking, and opinions in the form of book entitled 'Armed Conflict and Peace Process in Nepal: The Maoist Insurgency, Past Negotiations and Opportunities for Conflict transformation'. The contents of this book are the reflections of my engagement in research, studies and teaching in conflict related subjects for more than nine years. My engagement in generating, processing and disseminating knowledge is guided by the principle of 'honourable living of Nepalese people with human dignity' which involves fairness, empathy and integrity that is very much lacking in present Nepal.

Bishnu Raj Upreti, PhD

The Kathmandu Metropolitan City
Ward No -35 Koteshwor
P.O. Box 12709, Kathmandu, Nepal
March 2006

Acknowledgement

Many people have contributed to bring this book in this form and I must sincerely apologise for not being able to mention their name in this volume. However, I express my sincere thanks to all of them. I should thank Mr. Dev Raj Dahal, Mr. Laxman Aryal, Mr. Padma Ratna Tuladhar, Mr. Daman Nath Dhungana, Mr. Madhav Kumar Nepal, Mr. Keshav Badal, Mr. Jhala Nath Khanal, Mr. Arjun Narsingh KC, Mr. Daman Dhoj Chand, Dr. Minendra Rijal, Mr. Gauri Pradhan, Mr. Anand Aditya Mr. Shankar Pokharel, Dr. Sundar Mani Dixit, Mr. Sambhu Thapa, Mr. Gopal Thapaliya, Prof. Krishna Khanal, Prof. Dhruba Kumar, Mrs. Sobha Gautam, Mr. Himalaya Samser Rana, Mr. Sailendra Kumar Upadhaya, Mrs. Rita Thapa, Mr. Janak Raj Joshi, Mr. Vidya Dhar Mallik, Mr. Arjun Kumar Mainali, Dr. Prem Singh Basnyet, Dr. Rabi Aryal, Mr. Likhat Pandey, Mr. Saroj Upreti, Mr. John Howel, Mr. Shankar Upreti, Mr. Dan Huntington, Mr. Shiva Prasad Upreti, Mr. Jerry Burton, Mr Achut Luintel, Mr. Mark Harvey, Mr. Martin Hermann, Mr. Tanka Prasad Upreti, Dr Snimer Shani, Dr Susanne Nagel, Mr Sandesh Hamal, Mrs, Marge Tsitouris, Mr Govinda Gyawali, Dr. Netra Timsina, Mr. Uttam Upreti, Mr. Ishwor Chandra Shivakoti, Mr. Kul Prasad Adhikari, Mr. Tirtha Gyawali, Dr. Rohit Kumar Nepali, Mrs Shova Shrestha, Dr Karna Bahadur Thapa, Mr. Shyam Basnet, Mr. Bhawani Prasad Kharel, Mr Laxmi Nath Upreti, Prof. Chuda Raj Upreti, Dr. Ananda Prasad Shrestha, Dr. David Gelner, Prof. Kapil Shrestha, Mr. Nayan Bahadur Khatri, Dr. Gopal Krishna Shivakoti, Mr. Gopal Shivakoti Chintan, Ms. Nirmala Sharma, Dr. Poorna Kanta Adhikari, Dr. Krishna Prasad Oli, Mr. Yuba Raj Shangraula, Mr. Bishnu Pukar Shrestha, Mr. Thakur Dhakal, Prof. Birendra Prasad Misra, Dr. Jaganath Adhikari, Prof. David Seddon,

Dr. Günther Bächler, Mr. Walton McCaslin, Dr. Shambhu Ram Simkhada, Prof. Shridhar Khatri and Dr. Prakash Chandra Lohani for their encouragement, direct and or indirect inputs in terms of comments, suggestions, sharing of opinions and materials.

I would like to extend my sincere thanks to those people in the villages who participated in meetings and discussions, gave us valuable first hand information during my field visits to collect primary data.

I express my sincere gratitude to Asian Development Bank, Care International Nepal; Department for International Development of British Government, WSP International and Royal Danish Embassy for giving me responsibility to analyse conflict from which I draw lot of materials to prepare this book. A dedicated team of researchers collected empirical and qualitative information form Doti, Achham, Kaski, Lamjung, Dolakha, Ramechhap, Bara, Parsa and Surkehet to furnish the required content. I would like to thank all of them.

I would also like to thank Mr D.K. Sharma, Adroit Publishers, New Delhi. Last but not least, I am grateful to my family members, especially loving son Ayush and daughter Asmita, caring wife and professional colleague Yamuna, and respected mother Shanta Kumari Upreti and father-in-law Mr Kabi Ghale, and nephew Sharmila Shivakoti. Without their understanding, cooperation and full support I could have never succeeded in publishing this book. Time reserved for my family is fully consumed in writing this book.

This book is the product of collective efforts of many people who gave me valuable information, inputs comments and suggestions. However, I remain solely responsible for any errors and shortcomings. Constructive comments and suggestions form the readers are highly appreciated.

Koteshwor
March 2006

Bishnu Raj Upreti, PhD

Contents

Abbreviations

ACCORD	African Centre for Constructive Resolution of Disputes
ADB/N	Agricultural Development Bank of Nepal
AI	Amnesty International
AIN	Association of INGOs
AMARC	World Association of Community Radio Broadcasters,
BATNA	Best Alternatives to Negotiated Agreement
BBC	Beyond Beijing Committee
BHCT	Berghof Handbook of Conflict Transformation
BJP	Bharatiya Janata Party
BOGs	Basic Operating Guidelines
CA	Conflict Analysis
CBOs	Community Based Organisations
CBS	Central Bureau of Statistics
CCOMPOSA	Coordination Committee of Maoist Parties and Organisations in South Asia
CCS	Creation of Creative Society
CDO	Chief District Officer
CEFJAR	Christian Community in Nepal for Peace, Justice and Reconciliation
CIAA	Commission for Investigation of Abuse of Authority
CIDA	Canadian International Development Agency
CiSoPD	Civil Society for Peace and Development
CM	Conflict Management
CoC	Code of Conduct
COCAP	Collective Campaign for Peace
CoCMC	Code of Conduct Monitoring Committee

CPJ	Committee to Protect Journalists
CPN (M)	Communist Party of Nepal (Maoist)
CPN (UC)	Communist Party of Nepal (Unity Centre)
CPN-ML	Communist Party of Nepal Marxist-Leninist
CPN-UML	Communist Party of Nepal United Marxist-Leninist
CRA	Conflict Risk Assessment
CSP	Civil Solidarity for Peace
CVICT	Centre for Victim of Torture
CWIN	Child Workers in Nepal
DDC	District Development Committee
DFID	Department for International Development of UK
ELN	National Liberation Army of Columbia
ETNA	Estimated Alternative to Negotiated Agreement
FARC	Revolutionary Armed Force of Columbia
FCO	Foreign and Common Wealth Office of UK
FFP	Friends for Peace
FNCCI	Federation of Nepalese Chambers of Commerce and Industries
GDP	Gross Domestic Products
GTZ	German Development Organisation
HimRights	Himalayan Human Rights Monitor
ICG	International Crisis Group
ICJ	International Commission of Jurists
ICRC	International Committee of Red Cross and Red Crescent
IDD	Inter Agency Internal Displacement Division
IDPs	Internally Displaced Persons
IFJ	International Federation of Journalists,
IHDP	Integrated Hill Development Project
IHF	International Helsinki Federation of Human rights
IMS	International Media Support,
INGOs	International Non-Governmental Organisations
INSEC	Informal Sector Service Centre
INTERPOL	International Police
IPI	International Press Institute,
IRD	Integrated Rural Development
IRDP	Integrated Rural Development Project
JRPC	Joint Revolutionary People's Council
KHARDP	Koshi Hill Area Rural Development Project
KLO	Kamtapur Liberation Organisation of India
KTWR	Koshi Tappu Wildlife Reserve

LACC	Legal Aid and Consultancy Centre
LTTE	Liberation Tigers of Tamil Elem
MPPRPC	Minimum Policy and Programme of Revolutionary People's Council
MRD	Movement for Restoration of Democracy
NC	Nepali Congress
NC-D	Nepali Congress-Democratic
NDF	National Development Forum
NHRC	National Human Rights Commission
NPC	National Planning Commission
NSP	Nepal Sadbhawana Party
OAS	Organisation of American States
OCHA	The United Nations Office for the Coordination of Humanitarian Affairs
OHCHR	Office of the High Commissioner for Human Rights of United Nations
PAPAD	Professional Alliance for Peace and Development
PCIA	Peace and Conflict Impact Assessment
PLA	People's Liberation Army
PRA	Participatory Rural Appraisal
PWG	People's War Group
RCCC	Royal Commission for Corruption Control
RNA	Royal Nepal Army
RRA	Rapid Rural Appraisal
RSF	Reporters sans Frontières,
SAFMA	South Asian Free Media Association
SALW	Small Arms and Light Weapons
SDC	Swiss Agency for Development and Cooperation
SLC	School Leaving Certificate
SNV	Netherlands Development Organisation
SoE	State of Emergency
SPDI	Support for Peace and Development Initiative
TADO	Terrorist and Destructive Activities Control and Punishment Ordinance
TMI	The Mountain Institute
ULFA	United Liberation Front of Assam
UMN	United Mission to Nepal
UN	United Nations
UNDP	United Nations Development Programme
UNESCO	United Nations Educational, Scientific and Cultural

	Organization,
UNICEF	United Nations Children Education Fund
UNTAC	United Nations Transitional Authority in Cambodia
UPF	United People's Front
URPC	United Revolutionary People's Council
USAID	United State Agency for International Development
VDC	Village Development Committee
WAN	World Association of Newspapers
WGEID	UN Working Group on Enforced or Involuntary Disappearances
WOREC	Women Rehabilitation Centre
WTO	World Trade Organisation

CHAPTER 1

Armed Conflict in Nepal: An Overview

1.1. INTRODUCTION

There is a fairly large amount of publications and documents available about the analysis of the causes of the armed conflict in Nepal. Some books have been written by Nepalese and foreign scholars (e.g, Karki and Seddon, 2003; Upreti, 2004, Raj, 2003; Thapa, 2003; Thapa and Sijapati, 2003; Muni, 2003: Bhattarai, 2003; Shrestha and Upreti, 2002, etc.); many research papers have been prepared by various researchers and several conflict assessment documents are produced by donor agencies and INGOs/NGOs. However, there is a dearth of publications on documentation of peace process and negotiations, local approach of conflict management, civil society initiatives on conflict transformation and peace building, human rights approach of dealing with conflict and impacts of armed conflict. This book attempts to fill this gap.

The first chapter of this book deals with the general overview of the Maoist armed conflict in Nepal, its causes and consequences. Governance failure, development failure, the experiment failure of the Royal Palace and the 1st February Royal takeover, ideological dimension, and constitutional causes have been identified as some of the major causes of the Maoist insurgency. The chapter examines relations between empowerment and conflict. It further sheds light on triggers and catalysts of the armed conflict. Some of the major triggers are the coercive approach taken by the previous and present governments, Royal massacre of 1st June 2001, terrorist attack in New York and Washington on 11 September 2001, role of media and role of the Election Commission. The chapter also discusses some issues related to erosion of trust, social psyche and the roles of the international community particularly the USA, India, the UK, some other bilateral countries and INGOs in the escalation and de-escalation of the armed conflict in Nepal. One of the main features of the present armed conflict is the triangular power struggle.

The aim of the Second chapter is to offer a proper theoretical and conceptual understanding to analyse the peace process and negotiation of Nepal's ongoing armed conflict. Therefore a comprehensive conceptual framework presented in this chapter is used to shape the analysis of other chapters of the book.

The Third chapter deals with local approaches of conflict management in Nepal. In this chapter, different traditional approaches used by the Nepalese people since centuries, a brief comparison between traditional (or informal) systems and formal systems of conflict resolution, assessment of potential of traditional approaches to resolved armed conflict, religious approach of dealing with conflict, different approaches used by civil society and business community, conflict settlement approaches of Maoists in their influence areas. The chapter concludes that the state is not able to use potentials of different approaches in resolving the ongoing armed conflict in Nepal.

Chapter Four is specifically devoted to reviewing the formal peace talks and negotiation of 2001 and 2003. It identifies the causes of the failure of negotiation in the 2001 and 2003 peace talks. It examines the role of the state, the political parties, and the Maoists in the light of the past two formal peace talks.

Chapter Five examines the efforts and contributions of civil society, political parties and media in Nepal's peace process in general by comparing them with the efforts of different conflict-ridden countries of the world. This chapter further explores the engagement of civil society in different elements of peace process (such as peace awareness, protection of human rights, trust building and reconciliations, disarmament, demobilisation, reconstruction, rehabilitation, reintegration and creation of peace zones, citizen's diplomacy and media monitoring, among others). A brief description of some of the leading organisations has been presented to give a glimpse of how civil society organisations are engaged in the conflict. Initiatives of major political parties: Communist Party of Nepal United Marxist-Leninist, Nepali Congress Party, Rastrya Prajatantra Party, Samyukta Janamorcha, Nepali Congress (Democratic), Nepal Sadbhawana Party and Communist Party of Nepal Marxist-Leninist, agenda of five and seven party alliances formed to fight against the regression have also been dealt with in this chapter. The role of media in conflict transformation has been discussed as one of its central themes.

The Sixth chapter devotes considerable space to discussion of dialogue as one of the most suitable approaches of resolving the armed conflict in Nepal and suggests a step-wise procedure, not as a recipe but as a broad framework. This chapter also discusses the historical perspective and Nepal's contribution to third party mediation in Chinese and British conflict. It explores the potential and constraints/limitations of third party mediation of Nepal's armed conflict, examines the interests and intentions of the government and the insurgents regarding the involvement of third party negotiation. Potentials of bilateral, inter-governmental and non-governmental organisations in mediating the armed conflict have been discussed. A short analysis of assumptions and risks of involving third party mediators has been presented. The chapter argues that it is late for Nepal to involve a third party in facilitating negotiation between the state and the Maoists as it is extremely difficult to overcome deep mistrust and antagonism between the state and insurgents. The chapter concludes that the UN is one of the best few third parties who could positively influence conflict dynamics.

Chapter Seven highlights the importance of a human rights approach to settle the worst conflicts. Different factors (psychological factors, strategies of warring parties, etc) affecting violation of human rights have been highlighted. International concerns (by the UN, International Commission of Jurists, the USA, India, and other organisations have been presented. This chapter concludes that violation of human rights complicates the negotiation process.

The Eighth chapter is devoted to the impacts of armed conflict, highlighting social impacts (such as migration and internal displacement; social crimes, etc.), economic impacts (shift of financial resource flow from development to security budget and increasingly weakened economy, market and employment), political impacts, security impacts, environmental, developmental and international impacts. It also explores the risk and effects of landmine explosives and discusses physical damage of infrastructures.

The Ninth chapter discusses conditions and structures required to make the negotiation successful. The chapter argues that alteration or polarisation of existing power relations, trust building and rising level of confidence, people's participation in peace process, mobilisation of external support, learning from past experiences and mistakes, developing long- and medium term strategies are some of the essential conditions for making the future negotiation successful. Furthermore, different steps and phases of negotiation have been highlighted. Finally, some structures necessary for the successful negotiation of the armed conflict such as a national peace commission, peace secretariat, ceasefire monitoring committee, negotiation coordination committee, establishment of conflict transformation departments in political parties, formation of a reconciliation commission, creation of donors' Nepal helping group, judicial or constitutional court, human rights monitoring committee, and media monitoring committee are presented.

The Tenth chapter critically examines the possible future political scenarios and conflict situation. This chapter argues that Nepal is at a crossroads and it can turn to any direction (worst autocracy, compromise in independence, radical communist rule, power sharing arrangement with accepting existence of all political forces, democratic republic, etc.). In-depth discussion on the 1st February royal takeover and consequent power struggle between the constitutional force and undermining of democratic process by the extremist thinking and action of the hardliner ex-panchas, international response to the king's takeover, changing power relations and allies have been presented in this chapter. The last chapter presents synthesis of the book in the form of conclusion.

1.2 METHODOLOGICAL NOTE

This book is the outcome of the active engagement of author in:

1. International and national-level meetings, discussions and debate with leaders of political parties, diplomats, foreign missions and delegates coming Nepal to help in resolving the ongoing armed conflict, civil society leaders and human rights activists, government officials, experts working in the field of conflict transformation and peace building, international relations and political science and constitutionalism, as well as informal sharing, training as a resource person on conflict transformation;
2. Presentation of papers on different dimensions of the ongoing armed conflict at local, national and international workshops, seminars and meetings, and preparing journal articles and

chapters of edited books;

3. Review of literature related to theory and practice of conflict transformation and peace building both general and Nepal-specific (including impact assessments, political analysis, etc.);
4. Information collected from the field. The author was visited 14 districts of different parts of the country (Bhojpur, Sankhuwasawa, Dhankuta, Morang, Jhapa, Susari, Saptari, Surkhet, Banke, Bardiya, Kailali, Dadeldhura, Doti, Achham) and research assistants collected information from additional 6 districts (Dolakha, Ramechhap, Bara, Parsa, Lamjung, Kaski) to prepare this book.

During the field visit to the villages and districts, there were in-depth discussions with local people (both male and female), internally displaced persons and other conflict victims, security forces, local leaders of different political parties, Maoist local leaders workers and sympathisers, regional administrators and security commanders, NGO workers and development staff of INGOs and bilateral donors, nominated DDC-executive members, representatives of business, human rights activists, etc. The primary information collected from these sources has been used in discussion and analysis. Some of the selected papers presented by the author in various workshops-seminars have been revised, updated and used in different chapters of the book.

1.3 AN OVERVIEW OF THE ARMED CONFLICT

On the fourth of February 1996, the UPF submitted a 40-point demand to the Prime Minister Ser Bahadur Deuba of the Nepali Congress government. They declared that they would wage a 'people's war' if the government did not respond to these demands within 15 days. Unfortunately, the Deuba government did not take the demands seriously. Prime Minister Deuba went to India on an official visit, ignoring the deadline. The UPF (Maoist[1]) started a people's war on 13 February 1996, three days before the given deadline, attacking police post at Holeri (Rolpa) and Thibsikot (Rukum).

Since then, Nepal has been facing an unprecedented crisis. The 'people's war' waged by a radical Communist Party of Nepal-Maoists (hereinafter referred as Maoists or insurgents) has not only taken lives of more than 13,000 people and billions of rupees of property but also challenged a centuries-old authoritarian political regime. The circumstances in the current Nepalese polity are pushing to demonstrate a 'failed-state syndrome' (i.e., sustained military conflict between insurgents and government to displace the regime, sustained policy of protagonists that results in the death of large number of people and an adverse and disruptive regime transfer with a major abrupt shift in patterns of governance leading towards authoritarian rules, collapse of economy, dysfunctional bureaucracy, erosion of trust on government, etc.).

Three communist parties, believers of Mao's ideology, policy and programmes, had formed CPN-Unity Centre (CPN-UC), as a 'political front' to join the 1990's popular movement for the restoration of democracy (MRD). They wanted more radical change from the MRD and to decide the issues of 'constitution' and 'monarchy' through a constituent assembly election. However, major MRD forces (Nepali Congress Party and United Leftist Front[2]) rejected these issues (decision of 'constitution' and 'monarchy' through a constituent assembly election) raised by CPN (UC). Negotiation between the king and the major MRD forces was made through a compromise with a power-sharing arrangement. Though disappointed, the CPN (UC) did participate in the 1991 national election, won 9 out of 205 parliamentary seats and became the third largest party of Nepal. Their decision to participate in the parliamentary election was based on a tactic to expose 'the contradictions and limits of the parliamentary system' (Misra, 2004). CPN (UC) wanted to implement political programme within the strict framework of Marxist, Leninist and Maoist ideology specific to Nepalese political, economic and cultural conditions. After one year of underground preparation of programme and organisation for the 'people's war', it declared the formation of the Communist Party of Nepal-Maoist (CPN-M) in 1995 and the 'people's war' was initiated on 13 February 1996 (Philipson, 2002; Nickson, 2003; Thapa, and Sijapati, 2003; Upreti, 2004a). By now, this armed conflict had severely shaken the existing political structures and governance system established by the 1990's political change.

Three domestic power centres in addition to an international power are the key players in the Nepalese conflict. The invisible force is directly or indirectly engaged in sustaining or escalating the crisis. The giant arm traders, smugglers or foreign political masterminds are most probably sponsoring this invisible force (Kumar, 2004; Upreti, 2004a). Before 4th October 2002, there were only two visible power centres in the conflict (i.e., constitutional force - the king/parliamentary parties, and the Maoists in the domestic arena). However, the invisible force successfully managed the ambitions of the king to separate constitutional force and create a tripartite conflict. Consequently, the Maoists gained much from the changing power equation, as parliamentary parties and the Maoists are willy-nilly moving closer and the palace is distancing itself from its legitimate traditional allies. Consequently, systematically raised by the Maoists from the beginning of their insurgency is now increasingly becoming a centre of debate in the street when the students and other political activists start to chant the republican slogan. Though the 1st February takeover was not an overnight decision but the outcome of more than three years of calculated and planned moves, the outcome became counterproductive to the king. Many of the assumptions of king at the time of the royal takeover [for example, continued support will obtain from the international community, particularly from those who were providing military aids if the Maoists are presented as 'terrorists' to the international community, political parties will collapse when presented as solely responsible for the all ills of the country, and will get strong support from civil society[3] and ordinary people, full support of military (that assumption proved right)] became wrong . Hence, the royal takeover was vehemently opposed both at national and international levels. Recruitment of hardline ex-panchas, convicted criminals, and bank loan defaulters in the cabinet and regional/zonal administration, censorship in media, curtailing civil rights of people, arresting and detaining political leaders and restricting movement of civil society leaders and politicians resulted in a direct confrontation between the major political parties and the king. Still, political parties were hoping to reconcile with the king but the constant and continuous undermining democratic values and process and sideling major political parties betrayed them with the king and they have started to change their twin-pillar theory of democracy (i.e., multiparty democracy and constitutional monarchy), opting for democratic republic (Nepali Congress removed 'constitutional monarchy' from its constitution and Communist Party of Nepal (UML) decided to go for a democratic republic political set-up of the country. Many other communist parties were in favour of the republic system. This situation will virtually lead to heavy confrontations between the palace (by using its traditional force, i.e., RNA) and political parties working for a democratic republic set-up. Therefore, the conflict between the state and the Maoists has been shifted to a wider political crisis between the traditional autocratic force and progressive force fighting for democracy.

1.4 CAUSES OF THE CONFLICT

Nepal was a monolithic, feudalistic, autocratic, authoritarian, centralised and closed state for centuries (Thapa, 2003; Karki and Seddon, 2003; Misra, 2004; Kumar, 2004; Upreti, 2004a). The state governing system in the entire history of modern Nepal was orchestrated by cajoling, threat of suppression and use of coercive power by the state (Hutt, 2004; Kumar, 2004). Such characteristics of the state consequently excluded a vast majority of Nepalese people from the nation-building process (Upreti, 2005b; Thapa, 2003, Raj, 2004). This became virtually a breeding ground of insurgency in Nepal. Rampant poverty, abject destitution, systematic and deliberate exclusion, severe caste, gender, and ethnic discriminations, and greater injustice have been identified by many researchers and analysts (Thapa, 2003; Karki and Seddon, 2003; Misra, 2004, Rana and Sharma, 2004; Upreti, 2004a; Raj, 2004) as structural causes of the ongoing armed conflict. Similar observations were made by the Dhami (1997) and Deuba (2000) Commissions, which were constituted by the government to recommend ways of resolving the conflict. The Maoists started their 'people's war' to dismantle the existing feudal socio-political structures of production relations. Babu Ram Bhattarai, senior leader of the Maoists, has vividly explained his perspective on the socio-political structures of society as the core of the problem of Nepal, which is acknowledged in the theoretical documents of Maoists (Bhattarai, 2004). According to the Maoists, 'the principal objective of the people's war is thus to develop the social productive forces and create a higher form of society through a continuous revolution... by putting 'politics in command' " (Kumar, 2004). Therefore, the Maoists argue that they are not the problem but the solution of the problem facing the nation for a long time[4]. Though political conflicts are an integral part of state governance system and management process (Pahari, 2003; Kumar, 2004), opportunity for state reform and progressive change and welfare of its citizens, failure of managing such conflict in a constructive way leads to crisis, as observed in Nepal.

The Maoist insurgency is not the sole product of the failure of multiparty democracy, rather, the cumulative effects of 30 years of an autocratic Panchayat system and beyond. The post-1990 governance failure provided the space for conflict escalation because of: (a) its inability to fulfil people's expectations, degenerating into malgovernance and (b) the freedom it offered. People were frustrated with the Panchayat regime and looking for a change. Consequently, people widely supported the democratic movement of the 1990 and the multiparty democracy was restored.

In a context of complex conflict like the Maoist insurgency in Nepal, it is very hard to identify and separate causes and effects, as causes become effects and effects turn into causes. For example, poverty is a cause of conflict but it turned out to be its consequence when local food security and production system wa s severely disturbed by the insurgency. However, the following categories of interrelated causes can help to analyse the Maoist conflict in Nepal and the consequence thereof.

1.4.1 Governance failure to address structural causes of conflict

Century-old production relations, social structures and governance system maintained by status quo, severely skewed resource distribution and control, injustice, racial, ethnic, geographical, gender and social discriminations, rampant poverty and unemployment have contributed to igniting and expanding the insurgency (Thapa, 2003; Thapa and Sijapati, 2003; Upreti, 2004a). The 1990's popular movement was the first attempt to dismantle this feudal system and somehow succeeded in challenging the interests of feudal elite and traditional power centre. As a result, the traditional power centres persistently attempted to weaken the newly evolved democracy (Kumar, 2004). Malpractices and irregularities observed in the 12 years of democratic rule are the sole result of the deliberate strategies and actions of these traditional power centres. They were able to penetrate the political parties and pursue undemocratic actions. Breaking up of the major political parties is one of the widely accepted examples of this kind (Thapa, 2003; Raj, 2004).

It has been well documented that social exclusion, acute inequalities, absolute poverty, lack of access to resources and failure of political structures to address these issues have inflected the Maoists' 'people's war' (Hachhethu, 2003; Upreti, 2003b, 2002a; Hogger, 2001). Deep-rooted social cleavages in terms of caste, ethnicity, gender and regional, cultural, linguistic and religious forms of discrimination provided fertile ground to escalate the conflict. The Maoists successfully capitalised on the disillusionment of people towards poor performance of the ruling and opposition parties. Democratic transition of the 1990s regarding the transformation of the state, politics and society turned out to be unsatisfactory. Dominance of certain elite groups (e.g., Brahmin, Chhetri and Newar, family dominance in politics, nepotism, etc.) in all social, political and economic sectors promoted a feeling of injustice and revenge as ethnic groups and "lower" caste people strongly believe that they have been excluded from opportunities and resources. The Maoists have tactically utilised this sentiment by organising people not only on the basis of social concerns but also in terms of ethnic and geographical identity. Now ethnic and geographical identities are becoming dominant in the political discourse.

Further, the ruling Nepali Congress Party took a very repressive approach in the early 1990s to wipe out UPF from its stronghold areas by using explicators of panchayat period[5]. The former panchas brutally suppressed the members and supporters of UPF. Because of such repressions, ordinary people did not feel secure and observe any change in their daily life situation even after the widely acknowledged political change of 1990. The excessive and unlawful act of police under Operation Romeo severely terrorised local people. The Parliamentary Investigation Committee has highlighted this situation. The following statement also clearly highlights the police repression in a more concrete way, "*Between 1990 and 1996 successive regimes in Kathmandu, starting with that of strongly anti-communist Girija Koirala, pursued a conscious policy of trying to undermine and ultimately dismantle the considerable electoral clout of the Maoists in Rukum, Rolpa, Salyan and Jajarkot - a region with strong left support since 1950s. ...Mobilising not only party cadre, but local and regional civil administration and the police force as available and necessary, the Girija government started a trend of committing and compromising state resources to undermine opposition parties to win local and national election. ...If free and fair elections are to be regarded as forming the most inviolable aspects of democracy, then the trend initiated by the Nepali Congress government under Koirala in the Maoist hinterland and beyond can be taken as the beginning of a series of egregious and systematic violence of democracy from within the state in post 1990 period* (Pahari, 2003:7). Karki and Seddon (2003) have also made similar observations in this regard. This event implanted deep frustration within UC and ultimately they organised to fight the government-sponsored aggression (Jwala, 2002).

A strong psychological factor contributing to this conflict is the deeply cemented ambition of social elites (not only political but also economic, civil society and bureaucratic elites) to grab power, perhaps learned from the northern Indian states. This is clear from the failure of leadership in major political parties, social and economic sectors, and NGO activists during the last 12 years of democratic rules and other three years of experiment of autocracy.

Centralisation and regional imbalance, skewed distribution, access and control of natural and other productive resources, dominating influences of religiously- and culturally-biased traditional Hindu cultural values, discrimination against women, ethnic minorities, so-called lower castes, and Dalits have created a feeling of injustice, frustration and have fuelled the conflict. Definitive action on radical land reform was not taken. The performance of privatisation was extremely poor. After the political change of 1990, new elites are emerging within the socially excluded groups (such as women, Dalit, ethnic minorities, etc.) at the cost of whole segment of the socially excluded groups.

1.4.2 Development failure

Unlike the naïve belief of development interventions bringing about positive impacts to the well-being of socially excluded, after more than five decades of experiences of planned development, it has became clear that such interventions often overlook or exclude the most worst-off population (Upreti, 2002a & b; Shrestha, 1997; Pandey, 1999). In this context, an important question emerges regarding the performance of programmes and projects funded by donors and the role of the National Planning Commission in Nepal. What achievements in addressing inequality and social exclusion donor-funded development projects have taken place after several decades of their engagement? Why they are not able to ensure the development supported by donors to address these issues? Why do they still want to continue the same approaches, strategies and mechanisms, if they are not able to achieve the stated goals? It is time for donors to rethink their development support strategies and practices and refine their approaches. So far, the unique characteristic of donors is to be sectoral, compete with each other on a particular development issue, provide contradictory advice to the government and impose rigidity and conditionality in their assistances (e.g., to relinquish incentive systems such as subsidies in agriculture, force to rise prices of basic goods and services like electricity and water that often lead to severe conflict). For example, the ADB imposed conditions to abolish subsidy in agricultural inputs and reduce the number of food depots from Mid- and Far- Western regions have exacerbated the food crisis and fuelled the conflict. Mohan Mainali severely questioned the contribution and effectiveness of donor-funded development intervention to address the root causes of the conflict. He writes, "...*What we say of the USAID implemented Rapti Zone Rural Area Development Project, and its second incarnation, the Rapti Development Project, aimed to fulfil the basic needs of the poor majority, the farmers of the mid hills. The Programme spent about US $ 50 millions in 'improving household food production and consumption, improve income generating opportunities for poor farmers, landless labourers, occupational castes and women'. In short, the project's overall goal was to increase the well-being of people. The Americans thought they'd need 15 years to achieve their objectives. And, going by their reports, they worked 'hard' for those 15 years. The project started in 1980 and ended in 1995, just a month and half before the Maoists began their armed movement. ...The government and donors both say development packages will help eliminate the Maoists. If that were true, why was Rapti Zone so favourable for the development of Maoist movement? If that is what you get after 15 years of American funded development, we were perhaps better without it*". (Mainali, 2003:125-126). Similar observations are made by Gersony (2003). Most of the integrated development projects in the late 1970s to early 1990s were operating in rural remote areas (e.g., Integrated Hill Development Project in Dolakha and Sindhuplackowk districts, Koshi Hill Development Project in Dhankuta, Bhojpur, Sankhuwasawa, Terathum, Mechi Hill Development Project in Ilam, Panchthar and Taplejung, Rasuwa-Nuwakot Integrated Development project in Rasuwa and Nuwakot, Rapti Integrated Development Project in Rapti zone, Mahankali Integrated Development Project in Mahakali, Gulmi-Arghakhanchi Integrated Development Project in Gulmi and Arghakhabchi districts, Bheri Integrated Development Project in Bheri zone, etc.). Similalry, Remote Area Development Committee, Special Area Development Committee and so many other remote and inaccessible areas-focused developments programmes and projects have been implemented in the last six decades. Nevertheless, poverty, inequality, discrimination exist in these areas and now the Maoists are successfully expanding their influences based on these developmental weaknesses and these remote and rural areas are in control.

If we examine the history of planned development of Nepal, the concepts and models are frequently changed according to the interests of the donors without considering local needs and specificities. For example, donors brought Integrated Rural Development (IRD) model in Nepal and started to create massive and unsustainable infrastructures (e.g. the office infrastructures of IHDP with more than 60 buildings in Dandapakhar, rural areas of Sindhupalchowk district or KHARDEP or Nasuwa-Nuwakot IRDP), and dependency syndrome (see the implementation model of Resource Conservation and Utilisation Project of USAID where people were given everything when they were involved in the project). After some time other concepts were introduced in the name of Rapid Rural Appraisal (RRA) and PRA (participatory Rural Appraisal). Nothing was done to introduce a new concept however, donors started to make conditions of using PRA/RRA in implementing programmes and projects supported by them. Then, everything had to be changed to implement these concepts. The process approach was introduced in the development sector. All these new concepts and ideas were creating confusion to development agents and ordinary people.

Every five years, donors bring new concepts, jargons and technologies that are either not suitable to rural Nepal or not familiar to the Nepalese people. Therefore, they invest huge resources and time to make these notions familiar and then they change again. The unique characteristic of a donor-focused programme is to play with concepts, forgetting every reality of rural Nepal. For example, the notion of integrated development programme was changed to poverty-focused programme, to empowerment programme to social inclusion programme without fully operating any of these to have some real impacts. Large numbers of inexperienced and extremely expensive expatriates and advisors come to these development projects and start to instruct the development without knowing the reality of people. Some of them recycle information generated from Nepalese people to justify their existence. Nepal does not need so many experts tied with the development aid conditionality. In agriculture, forestry, rural development, natural resource management and environment, rural infrastructure development Nepal has enough expert manpower. They never focus on developing local capacity. Instead, they bring their own expatriate staff. If we compare the efficiency of financial and knowledge resources, local experts are for more efficient than the expatriate staff. However, this is not an issue of consideration.

Donors' aid conditionality is one of the main obstacles in development. Many donors talk much about the transparency of Nepalese organisations but they never talk about transparency of their own organisations. If these questions are raised, they always skip them and are not ready to reveal the truth. Do any of the donors, donor-funded programmes and INGOs make their budget coming to Nepal transparent (how much money is received for Nepal, where this money is spent and how it is spent, who is getting how much for what and actually how much poor people are getting)? None of them is ready to be transparent. Some of them are transparent on the amount given to NGOs and ask transparency with them but not wholly.

Development mismatch is another fundamental cause of the conflict (Upreti, 2004m). The following conceptual matrix presents this mismatch leading to violent conflict in Nepal:

BOX 1.1 Matrix Showing Relationship Between Conflict and Development Mismatch

Conflict Prognosis	*Political development*	*Social development*	*Economic development*	*Manifestation of effects of mismatch in Nepal*
No overt conflict	High	High	High	Never observed high level of all three developments
Greatest propensity for overt conflict	High	Low	Low	The situation of current conflict
Medium propensity for overt conflict	High	High	Low	Not observed yet
Existence of latent (not overt) conflict, which may require multiple triggers to emerge	Low	Low	Low	Observed during autocratic panchyat political system before 1990
No overt conflict (mainly urban phenomenon)	Low	Low	High	Existing situation in urban areas and city centres

Source: Adapted from Upreti 2004l.

Of the three, political development is the most sensitive indicator of conflict if it mismatches with the other two. In contrast, social development sans political and economic development does not lead to overt conflict, while economic empowerment alone leads to the further pursuit of economic wealth at least in the short and medium-term. Low development on all three indices leads to latent conflict, which may not erupt in violence for a long time. However, the grave potential for such situations becoming violent remains strong, and even 'insignificant triggers may result in full-blown conflict. The 1990s' popular movement is an example of manifestation of this situation. The post-1990 empowerment phenomena show that overall political empowerment is high and social and economic empowerment is low and only elite, and neo-elite got benefit of social and political development. Nepal's planned development has the proven history of grand failure (Pandey, 1999; Upreti, 2004a) in terms of addressing root causes of the conflict, upon which the Maoist insurgency is breeding (Philipson, 2002; Raj, 2004; Upreti, 2004a). Thus, it is imperative that mismatch between social, economic and political development and empowerment is one of the major causes of conflict in Nepal.

The general public had great expectation form the 1990's political change. However, the post-1990 polity failed to govern the country based on the democratic ideals and the constitutional provisions detailed in the Constitution of Nepal 1990 (Thapa, 2003; Thapa, 2002). That made the general public very frustrated and unhappy (Dahal, 2003; Upreti, 2003a & b, Hogger, 2001). This frustration became a mighty ground for the Maoists to undertake armed rebellion. The state is not able to reduce poverty, control exploitation of the disadvantaged communities by those in power and generate employment opportunities for the large mass of unemployed people. Semi-educated, left-out and unemployed frustrated youths are becoming a risky reservoir of mass movements like the Maoist insurgency in Nepal (Hogger, 2001). Corruption and irregularities are increasing and becoming an integral part of the political process (Thapa, 2002).

It is widely recognised that the post-democracy phase of Nepali politics, dominated by the Nepali Congress Party (NCP), failed to govern democratically. Main opposition party was also not playing a constructive role to resolve the conflict. Maoist conflict was blatantly used by political parties as a bargaining chip to go to power. A detailed analysis of this failure can be found in the writings of Jwala (2002); Karki and Seddon, 2003); ICG, (2003a & b, and c); Upreti, (2005 a to c; 2004 a to f; 2003b and 2003c); Thapa, (2003); Pahari, (2003).

Civil administration was fully politicised. Even police force was abused for political gains of the ruling party. Political parties and the government did not work sincerely to restructure the malfunctioned civil administration to make it factually competent to devise and implement reform agenda and exercise inclusive democratic practices. The bureaucracy was absurdly used to fulfil vested political and party interests, which are often contradictory to the will of the general public (Upreti, 2002b). These weaknesses helped to develop distrust in the democratic process.

1.4.3 Dissatisfaction of the Palace

It is widely accepted in Nepal that the palace was not satisfied with the 1990's tripartite agreement between the king, Nepali Congress and United Leftist Front to reduce power of the palace. During the time of preparing a new constitution, the palace did everything to ensure its power[6]. The Palace wanted to restore the lost power in 1990 and therefore it was waiting for an appropriate time and context to do so. Hence, all activities of the palace were concentrated to achieve the lost power. During 12 years of democratic rule, palace worked with a game plan and became successful in utilising political parties and leaders in this endeavour.

The late king Birendra did not take a confrontational approach in gaining power. Rather, he used a more slow and peaceful but strong approach contrary to his brother's. After the assassination of King Birendra, the situation within the palace changed and the new strategies emerged. Ambition of the new king to be assertive, constructive, proactive and not only to be seen but also to be heard as a ruler of the 21st century Nepal and his subsequent action to dissolve the parliament (on 8 Jestha 2059 BS) and to sack the elected government (18 Ashoj 2059 BS) had pushed the country into a deep crisis instead of solving the Nepalese problem. Capturing the frustration of the general public towards the performance of political parties, the palace has started experiments of different models of forming government under the conceptual framework of guided democracy, keeping aside all political parties. First, the king picked up technocrats, NGO activists and sidelined political loyalists of the palace to form the government. At the beginning the frustrated society with very short memory, appreciated the move mainly because of a hope of some positive change towards governing system and security situation. While resuming the executive power and forming the experimental Chand government the King gave specific tasks (restoring peace and security, good governance, holding fair and free election, etc.). As assumed by some and not expected by many, however, the government failed to achieve any of these tasks. Consequently, the general public have lost their faith in the experimental government. Again, another experiment came in with the government of Prime Minister Surya Bahadur Thapa with some specific tasks (bringing all constitutional power together to have consensus, to restore peace and security, etc.). Though declared as the government with full executive power, it appears to be just another form of Chand government. The difference in Chand and Thapa governments was that the Thapa government was strongly backed by India. Some unique tricks of Thapa himself to cope with resistance were additional to the Chand government. The performance of Thapa government in terms of peace and security is a complete failure, as peace talks were broken and thousands of people killed. This government was not able to bring support of parliamentary parties too. Consequently, this government was also thrown out.

The King's action led to deeper conflict between the parliamentary parties and the monarch. Consequently, the parliamentary parties did not support peace process and negotiation. The Maoists successfully capitalised the contradictions between the king and the parliamentary parties to their advantage. Mobilisation of security forces (civil police force, armed police force, Royal Nepal Army, state intelligence service) as a unified command under the Royal Nepal Army did not get full support of political parties. All democratic institutions were weakened. In absence of the parliament, the country has been ruled by ordinance and royal order. This has great bearing on the expansion of Maoists. Almost 80 per cent of the country is said to be under the control of rebels at present. Next experiment of the King was to nominate Mr Surya Bahadur Thapa, an established track record of coercion and suppression. However, the demise of Thapa government on 7th May 2004 came with full confrontation and agitation with five political parties.

After the untimely demise of the Thapa government, a unique and very unusual process of finding a new prime minister was started by the king by publicly inviting applications. Vendors, farmers, cart pullers, ex-panchas submitted their applications to be nominated for the post of prime minister. Ultimately, among the applicants, Ser Bahadur Deuba, who was sacked from the prime minister with categorically labelling as 'incompetent', was picked up as next prime minister with several democratic compromises (particularly to complete unfinished work required to move from democracy to autocracy on the 1st February 2005).

The actions of the king after 4 October 2002 clearly demonstrate that he wanted to take a leading role in all political processes. The King's action indicates that he seems much committed to the South

Korean and Malaysian models of guided democracy to achieve economic progress and therefore he wants to implement this model in Nepal. This is the underlying reason why the king is not willing to be limited to be only visible and wants to be audible too. On 1st February 2005 he resumed executive power by removing the nominated multi-party government, detaining and or arresting political leaders, civil society members, journalists and human rights activists, censoring media, and imposing the State of Emergency (which was lifted on 30th of April 2005, two days before its natural expiry) and suspending civil rights. Even after nine months of the Royal takeover (until October 2005), the political and security situation did not improve. Rather, it is worsening. The USA, the UK and India suspended military aids to Nepal to an objection of the king's takeover. Similarly, Denmark, Switzerland, Norway and a few other countries suspended their development. Many other donors sued the 'wait and see' strategy. Nepal seriously lost international support.

In the first foreign-media interview[7] given by the King to Alex Perry of the US based Weekly Time Magazine (2004), he has clearly indicated that he is not satisfied with the political parties and he is intervening. But political parties did not take it seriously. In responding to the future of Nepal he said, "The future of Nepal, yes, lies in constitutional monarchy and multiparty democracy. Economically, it lies in openness and competition, and in joining the WTO [World Trade Organization]. Socially, we are in a difficult phase: some infrastructure, some of the basic things that were gelling the country together, have been trampled. There has been a lot of injury to much of rural Nepal, which needs to be addressed". Giving reason to sack the elected government he said, "I did not dismiss the government on Oct 4, 2002, out of my own free will. Are you saying I liked doing what I did, what I had to do? The compulsions of those days made me do what I had to. I was given a written request by the Prime Minister on the advice of all the parties to invoke the last clause of the constitution. So I was surprised when the parties accused us of regression. I had become regressive on their advice. Now, we can go on debating forever whether it was the correct thing to do. I thought it was my constitutional obligation, otherwise the constitution was as good as dead. Don't forget I am the constitution's custodian: as long as it is there, I am going to pull everyone within its ambit. And had I not acted as I did, I think that Nepal would be in a worse situation that it is today." The king was blaming the parties are not talking about people. He said,

"...the government of the day and the political leadership of Nepal must be pro-nation, pro-people. Everyone talks about the impasse between the "triangle" of the Maoists, the political parties and the palace. But this country is not a triangle. They are forgetting the most important component of any nation: the people. Who is going to talk for the people? If the Maoists are not, if the political parties are not, if they don't want to, then shouldn't the King? Someone must". He was pretty confident with the international support to suppress the insurgency. He said, "The government is grateful that so many countries are supporting us in this; the fact that their help could have been more expeditious is another thing, but no one wants to see a 'one-party proletariat state' in Nepal". The King was confident in obtaining same level of international support even after 1st of February takeover too. But his expectation became wrong when the international community did not buy his argument. His assessment of human rights violation by the state was different from the general understanding. He said, "But do you mean to tell me that earlier on, when other so-called governments of the day were in power, there were no human rights abuses? It's all cropping up [as an issue] now. But is it because the security agencies are becoming effective that these questions are being asked, or because they are failing? Is it success that is leading to this? In the case of the army alone, they were not deployed before 2001 and now they are. But which country does not have friendly fire, which does not have accidents? Many people have told me that the Fourth Estate is being unkind to the security agencies". The journalist asked, 'But given the unfortunate manner in which you came to throne, have you felt your acceptance by the country, your legitimacy, has been damaged?' The king replied, "My question is, 'If the Crown Prince had lived, would the kingdom have accepted him, knowing all the facts. My whole, prime and first effort when I came to the throne was for the consolidation of the monarchy. From reports that I was hearing, there was a conspiracy to get rid of the institution". The palace always believes that they are the incarnation of God. In this regard the journalist asked, 'What's it like being a living god?' His answers were, "I've been waiting for you to ask this. On the question of the living-god thing, let me interpret it this way: we were given the personification of Vishnu and Vishnu is the preserver of all things. And I'm glad that my role—the role I have to play—has been spelled out like that, just as it is in the constitution. But I'm a pragmatic and practical person. I've never said I'm God".

This interview indicates that the king prefers guided democracy, a model similar to Malaysia or South Korea, which focuses on economic growth over full-fledged democracy. This is one of the fundamental differences between the political parties and the king. The expression of the King during the civil society consultation held on 17th May 2004 at Gokarna Palace clearly shows his dismay with the performance of political parties. The *Kathamndu Post* quotes, "*If you would want me to give it to the corrupt and those who misgovern, I would do it tonight*". This was the response of the King to the request of Kanak Mani Dixit (senior journalist) to hand over the power to the parliamentary parties. Therefore, the 1st February takeover was not an abrupt decision. Rather, it was a well-planned, precisely calculated and fully orchestrated takeover. I will discuss in detail this issue in other chapters.

1.4.4 Ideological causes

There is strong ideological dimension in the Maoist conflict. Whether it is right or wrong, the Mao's ideology and people's war strategy adopted by Mao Zedung guides and shapes the Maoists insurgency (Thapa and Sijapati, 2003). Shining Path (*Sendero Luminoso*) insurgency of Peru is also an inspiring source for the Maoist insurgency in Nepal (Nickson, 2003; Raj, 2004). The CPN (Maoist) is the founding member of the RIM (Revolutionary Internationalist Movement) and CCOMPOSA (Coordination Committee of Maoists Parties and Organisations of South Asia). Perhaps CPN (M) is the most influential member of both organisations. The 'people's war' of Nepalese Maoists must have ideological influence of RIM and CCOMPOSA (see box 1.2 below).

BOX 1.2 Co-ordination Committee of Maoist Parties and Organizations of South Asia (CCOMPOSA)

1. Communist Party of Nepal (Maoist)
2. Communist Party of India (Marxist-Leninist)(People's War Group)
3. Maoist Communist Centre (MCC)
4. Revolutionary Communist Centre of India (MLM)
5. Revolutionary Communist Centre of India (Maoist)
6. Communist Party of India (ML)(Nakshalbari)
7. Purba Bangla Sarbahara Party (CC)
8. Purba Bangla Sarbahara Party (Maoist Punarghathan Kendra)
9. Bangladesh Samyabadi Party (ML)
10. Communist Party of Ceylon (Maoist)

The Maoists perceived that the deep-rooted oppression coupled with the feudalistic mode of production relations and unequal power structures, monarchy and the capitalistic democratic system are the problems and communism is the solution. They even developed their own ideological framework from 2001 February's second convention called *Prachanda Path*. The CPN (Maoist) claim that new theoretical orientation, i.e. *Prachanda Path*, is needed to address new challenges of the 21st century, which is not possible by a classical proletariat revolution. It is claimed that Prachanda path allows going beyond the classical communism and envisioned a model of revolution combining a Chinese strategy of protracted people's war (entering from villages to town and cities) and Russian strategy of armed insurrection (Sharma, 2003). On the contrary, parliamentary parties believe in capitalist type of multi-party democracy and constitutional monarchy[8]. Further, the palace seems determined to establish supremacy of monarchy (in other word autocracy). These three seemingly opposite ideologies are leading to ideological conflict between the warring parties.

1.4.5 Constitutional causes

Some scholars and activists argue that the 1990's constitution is not able to deal with some fundamental issues that have to be addressed by multiparty democracy. Some scholars even blame this constitution as sexist and racist (Lawati, 2003, 2005). They argue that the constitution is racist because it promotes one language, one culture and one religion and sexist because it does not treat men and women equally in fundamental issues like citizenship. This constitution also promotes majoritarian institutions, which discriminate against minority religious groups, women, low caste people, etc. They ague that the constitution has provided freedom of expression but has not ensured equity. This constitution has declared Nepal as a Hindu state, which betrayed many non-Hindu Nepalese people. As against the non-Hindu feeling, many influential political elites view appropriateness and rationality of the present constitution. They vehemently oppose developing a new constitution that could address some fundamental issues and help to resolve Maoist conflict. They argue that the present constitution is sufficient to resolve Maoist conflict. Some argue that the constitution-making process was not participatory, people have never endorsed this constitution and this constitution has several limitations (for example, Commission of Investigation of Abuse of

Authority (CIAA) has to get approval from prime minister to take action against minister and prime minister does not like to take political risk allowing his or her powerful and corrupt minister to take action by CIAA).

1.4.6 Paradox of conflict

Why did the Maoist insurgency start immediately after the 1990s political change that has overthrown the autocratic partyless feudalistic and suppressive political system and established democratic politics? A plausible explanation of the emergence of the Maoist conflict at the initial period of democracy is the growing awareness and empowerment of the Nepalese people during the initial years of multiparty democracy. People become more aware about poverty, inequality, discrimination, corruption and lack of employment opportunities. They are empowered to raise their voice against injustice, poverty and social exclusion. Therefore, paradoxically the current crisis is not only the syndrome of system failure but also an indicator of people's empowerment. The Constitution of Kingdom of Nepal 1990 had opened windows of opportunities to entertain rights of Nepalese citizens. From the 1990 popular movement Nepalese people moved from a closed hierarchical society to open society. This 1990 movement also raised unrealistically high expectations of the people where the political parties in early 1990s irrationally fuelled these expectations to win popular vote. At the same time, the state failed to address their concerns and meet their expectations.

The political change of 1990 gave ample opportunities to different categories of people to organise, to form organisations to fight for their rights that had tremendously helped to empower people. The NGO sector emerged strongly after 1990 and advocacy became one of the crucial components of many NGOs. Several identity-based organisations emerged to protect their rights or fight to secure the rights they deserved from the state. Likewise, several INGOs came to help Nepal and some of them were explicitly focusing on empowerment of the marginalised groups of people.

BOX 1.3 Why did Conflict Erupt in the Early Years of Democracy?

1. The Maoists entertained the freedom and openness brought about by the multiparty democratic system. They strategically used this opportunity to organise and preach to people;
2. Some people argue that ambitious and idealised people, with extremely high political ambition, came to Maoist leadership that has triggered to opt for violent conflict to change political system
3. It became easy for people to express their frustration in the democratic space ,which was not possible at the time of autocratic panchayat political system
4. Development of information and communication networks in Nepal after 1990 has also helped Maoists to initiate war.
5. Repressive approach of the government towards the United People's Front (UPF) in the mid-west forced them to take up weapons; even in Kathmandu (centre) UPF leaders did not get space to engage in.
6. There was no political influence of NCP and CPN(UML) in the hill districts of mid-west region. Therefore, they welcomed politicians of previous autocratic system, who were brutally exploiting people, to increase their political influence. These newly entered politicians unlawfully suppressed the UPF abusing local administration. NCP and its government attempted to either bring UPF in their party or to suppress them to end their political influence.
7. The civil society and human rights activists did not sufficiently criticise wrongdoings of the Maoists.
8. NCP and CPN (UML) had miscalculated the Maoists. Sometimes NCP kept quiet or even indirectly supported when the Maoists attacked the workers of CPN(UML) and vice versa. This approach of the NCP and CPN(UML) became helpful to the growth of Maoists.
9. The political parties failed to successfully manage democratic transition.

1.5 TRIGGERS AND CATALYSTS

Triggers or catalysts are time- or context-specific events that initiate or fuel conflict (Upreti, 2004a). While looking to the Maoist conflict, several triggers or catalysts have contributed to escalate conflict. Some of them are:

1.5.1 Coercive approach

Although the performance of parliamentary system was not the fundamental cause of the Maoist insurgency, failure of ruling political parties to address causes of the conflict through radical state reform and good governance practices are responsible (Upreti, 2004a; Hutt, 2004). They never tried sincerely and honestly to address the root causes and to settle the conflict politically. Rather, they used the conflict as a means of grabbing power. They interpreted the Maoist insurgency simply as a law and order problem and attempted to control by using force (e.g., cordon and search-Killo Sera II operation, unified command). A special 'Armed Police Force' was created to control the insurgency. They imposed the State of Emergency and mobilised militarily. The government also declared the Maoists as terrorist, issued red-corner notice through Interpol and fixed the bounty on the heads of the Maoist leaders. Consequently, the insurgency did spread from a few districts to all over the country, mainly because of extremely coercive approach. Home-grown insurgency based on discrimination, injustice, poverty, inequality and misgovernance cannot be controlled by the use of force and coercion.

1.5.2 Royal massacre

The Royal massacre added another complexity to the conflict as it created a power vacuum at the palace and disturbed the normalcy. Immediately after the royal massacre, the Maoists publicly declared that the conventional monarchy had come to an end and the circumstance had become favourable to initiate republican set-up in the country (Thapa and Sijapati, 2003). They concentrated their efforts to undermine the new king and weaken the monarchy. The royal massacre created for them an environment to convince their cadres and organise their military to expand the insurgency. People also lost trust in the palace and government, saying that 'if palace and government are not able to protect royal family, how they will protect people'.

1.5.3 Terrorist attack of 11 September 2001 in USA

Terrorist attack on the twin towers in New York and the Pentagon in Washington on 11 September 2001 had direct impacts on the Nepalese conflict. India, the USA and other many countries strongly supported Nepal with arms, technology and military aid as a package to control terrorism. India also declared Maoists as terrorist and formally sealed the border. Nepalese government got strong support from India to control the Maoists militarily. After 11 September 2001, Nepal government took an aggressive approach. This approach further worsened the situation and the conflict was further aggravated instead of being controlled or resolved.

1.5.4 Role of Media

For a long time, the potential of media in contributing to peace building was not realised. Therefore, this dimension did not get enough attention from the Nepalese media sector. Sensational news tied with commercial motivation was the focus of printed and electronic media in the early days of insurgency. Even the armed conflict was glorified. In the past, particularly before August 2003, the Nepalese media had disseminated sensational and escalatory news instead of peace-promoting news. This had a great impact on escalating conflict (Upreti, 2005c). There was no code of conduct while reporting the war news. However, after August 2003, the role of media is becoming more responsible and positive in promoting peace.

1.5.5 Role of the Election Commission

When conflict between the CPN (Mashal) mounted on the issue of participation in the parliamentary election of 1991, the faction led by Babu Ram Bhattarai separated to participate in the election under the banner of UPF, a political wing of Unity Centre. The Unity Centre won 9 seats in the parliament and became 3rd largest party. The UPF had also stood in the local election. Within UC a debate on 'new direction' led to its breakdown into Unity Centre (Maoist) and Unity Centre. Both the factions applied to the Election Commission for legitimacy and recognition. However, the Election Commission only recognised the minority breakaway faction led by Nirmal Lama whereas the majority faction led by Babu Ram Bhattarai (Prachanda group) was barred from participating in the election. This case gave no room for Maoists to engage in the parliamentary practices and ultimately gave way to rebellion. If this faction were also allowed to participate in the parliamentary election, the immediate scenario might have been different. There would be strong opinion within the Maoists to continue parliamentary struggle, which could delay or stop the armed rebellion. Even critiques like Prakash Jwala (ex-MP of UML) argue that assassination of central member of the CPN (Maoist) in Dhanusha in 1994 by the NCP government forced Maoists to take up arms (Jwala, 2002).

1.5.6 Erosion of trust

Distrust is pervasive in the present Nepalese politics and destroying political process and fuelling endemic conflict. Trust plays fundamental roles in the democratisation process, to promote civic engagement, public participation, mutual learning, concerted action to achieve negotiation and political stability (Azar, 1990; Bercovitch, 1996 and 1984; Harris and Reilly, 1998; Bercovitch and Rubin, 1992; 2004). When the civil war had pitted Nepalese people against each other, hostility and suspicion mounted. Restoring mutual confidence is needed on all sides to overcome distrust and to resolve conflict and restore lasting peace in Nepal. Creating and maintaining peace require an active engagement of all actors of society from ordinary citizens and security actors to politicians. Pragmatically, restoring peace is more than ending the armed rebellion and goes beyond. Peace cannot be achieved without addressing the root causes of conflict and political and social transformation process (structural change in governance, security and development, human rights policies and practice). However, restoring trust and creating a conducive environment has never been a priority of the warring parties (Upreti, 2004b; Upreti and Dhungana, 2004).

1.5.7 Social psyche: frustration, revenge and retaliation

Another important but less debated and discussed factor contributing to the escalation of conflict is the frustration of youth, unemployed mass, students failed in SLC and those who were expecting more from the political change of 1990 and getting nothing. Their expectations were unrealised, unheard, and sealed under the unfair political ambition of parties. Likewise, the brutality of the state and the Maoists towards the innocent civilians (kidnapping, torturing, killing, raping, forceful donation, blaming of spy and supporters, etc.) have developed a strong sense of injustice and forced them to engage in revenge and retaliation to those who carried out brutality. It has contributed to escalating the armed conflict.

1.6 INTERNATIONAL FACTORS

There is also important international influence in the Nepalese conflict. The role of major international and regional powers was inconsistent, contradictory and often catalytic in the escalation of conflict. In the beginning, the international community was not interested in engaging in resolving this conflict. Vested interests of some international players have direct bearing on sustaining the peace process in Nepal. A brief discussion on the role of major international players follows.

1.6.1 India factor

It is very hard to assess the exact strategy of India towards the Nepalese crisis. Its responses towards the Maoists are always contradictory and reflect double standards (for example, handing over of some Maoist leaders arrested in Indian territory to the Nepalese government at one time and taking legal action in the Indian court at others, supporting the military action and saying that the insurgency problem should be solved politically; etc.). Major routes and sources of arms and ammunitions for Maoists are Indian territories. But India is not doing enough to stop them. India does not like the involvement of international mediation of the conflict and has objected when the UN showed interest in mediation.

India is a major factor in this conflict. Escalation or resolution of the conflict depends upon India's attitude towards the Maoists, its level of support to the government, its influence on the political parties and its perceived security concerns. Maoists are using Indian territory, they have easy access to India, strong ties with Indian ultra leftist groups, obtaining weapons from there, using Indian territory for meetings, organisation and publications. Though, after 11 September 2001 India more strongly supporting the Nepalese government in military front, declared Maoists as 'terrorist', searching Indian Territory for Maoist cadres and arms caches, reinforcing border security (deploying troops), sealing the borders and providing military equipment and helicopter support to crack down on the rebels, it is only one dimension of the complex role of India in this conflict. Another dimension is that its sincerity and commitment to politically resolve the ongoing armed conflict is always questioned by many scholars and political analysts. It is also common feeling in Nepal that India is not supporting to bring UN in resolving the conflict[9]. This feeling was further strengthened when Indian foreign ministers and diplomats said, 'Nepal is capable of dealing with this conflict and (does) not need external support[10]. Some critics even say that India is not really willing to resolve the armed conflict of Nepal and wants to keep the conflict going[11].

With the change in Indian government after the wipe-out of the BJP led coalition in the May 2004 national election, newly appointed Foreign Minister of the Congress (I)-led coalition government of India, K. Natwar Singh visited Nepal on 4-5 June 2004. It was his first foreign visit after his appointment as new Foreign Minister. He pledged support to Nepal to strengthen its security capabilities to fight the Maoist insurgency. On the eve of his visit Indian police had arrested 11 Maoist leaders[12] (including 6 central leaders) in Patna, India on 3rd June 2004. On 13th June two Indian modern fighter helicopters arrived in Kathmandu to fight insurgency. They were purchased by Nepal from India on partial payment. Since the beginning of insurgency, the Indian government has provided more than four billion rupees military aid to Nepal including arms, weapons and training). Until January 2005, India was the largest military aid provider to Nepal[13]. However, after the 1st February Royal takeover, the Indian position changed.

Indian foreign policy towards Nepal is imperialist and envisioned by Jawaharal Lal Nehru in the 1950s (as reflected in the 1950's India-Nepal Friendship Treaty), which is always unfavourable to Nepal. India's big brother attitude towards Nepal has created numerous problems. One of the several glaring examples is 'Bhutanese refugee problem' where India has played a very negative role.

1.6.2 USA Factor

The USA is another main international player in the Nepal's conflict. The USA is more consistent in its approach towards dealing with the Maoists. It wants to control the Maoists militarily. Therefore, it is supporting the RNA in terms of financial and material resources as well as in knowledge base. The Maoists are also very negative toward the USA. A vast majority of Nepalese people do not agree with the US approach of dealing with the Nepalese conflict, as it is worsening the situation instead of solving the problem. The USA has a very clear and tough approach towards Maoists. After the 11 September 2001 terrorist attack on the World Trade Centre and Pentagon, its international security interests in Nepal are growing even more. The then US Secretary of State, Colin Powel visited for first time in the history of Nepal. High-level visits from the USA, its direct response to the current conflict and military aid clearly indicate the USA approach. The strong reaction of the US Ambassador to the Maoists and listing them in the category of the terrorist list by the USA are examples of hardline stance of USA towards the Maoists. The USA placed Nepal in the list of top six countries to support for the 'war against terrorism' and provided military assistance in security intelligence, training and millions of US dollars financial support to strengthen the RNA. Occasionally senior US army and intelligence officials visit Nepal to help the government. In essence, the approach of the USA seems to control the insurgency through military means, a "peace through war" approach, which is far too costly to Nepal and not sustainable.

In an interview to *Spotlight* (9-15 April, 2004:22-23), outgoing US Ambassador Michael Malinowski said, "T*errorism in Nepal is of great concern to the United States. We have been a friend of Nepal for many years. We root your democracy but the democracy is being threatened by the Maoists. We don't want to see the democracy brought down by the groups that use terrorism as tactics anywhere in the world. In this region and other, we have decided to provide considerable amount of assistance. In the last two years, we have increased our economic development budget from US $ 24 million a year to 40 million. We also have developed security relationships, which has risen from maybe a couple of hundred thousand dollars a year to package that now totals over the last two years about little over US $ 22 million. We developed programme and training including anti-terrorist training, anti-crime training and Human rights training...".* Position of new Ambassador J. F. Moriarty was also same until January 2005. However, the 1st February royal takeover pushed the USA in a very difficult position, especially when Senators and congressmen vehemently opposed the royal coup[14]. The US Congress set conditions for military aid to Nepal (they are: (a) Winding up of Royal commission for Corruption Control, b) Providing National Human Rights Commission, UN body and Judiciary free access to detainees, (c) Restoration of civil liberties and (e) ensuring Royal Nepal Army complies with Geneva Conventions[15]. After the royal coup, India, the USA and UK are working together. Nepal became an agenda of discussion between US President George Bush and Indian Prime Minister Dr Manamohan Singh[16].

After the 1st February 2005, US politicians show deep concerns. Assistant Minister of SU State Department for South Asia Donald Camp visited Nepal from 26 to 28 July 2005 and consulted the king, leaders of political parties, civil society leaders and diplomats and expressed the position of the USA. He clearly mentioned that security cannot be above democracy, the USA is in favour of democracy and freedom all over the world including Nepal, the unity of political parties is appreciated and the king must respond to the concerns of political parties, though some political detainees are freed and the state of emergency has lifted, civil and political rights are still controlled and violated. His statements in a press conference on 28 July 2005 were a serious setback to Nepal. Former US Senator Thomas Daschle visited Nepal from 21 to 27 July 2005 to asses the situation after the royal takeover. On the final day of his visit on 27 July he organised a press conference and urged the king to dissolve Royal Commission for Corruption Control, not to give space for the convicted criminals in government, place and restore democracy and civil rights. He had discussed with the king, leaders of political parties, civil society and high-ranking governmental officials[17]. However, the US government is not tough like other European countries and India.

1.6.3 UK Factor

The UK is another ambiguous player in this conflict because of its double standard, as it says one thing and does another. It says that this conflict should be settled politically and gives arms and military support[18]. However, in terms of human rights issues, the UK has shown more concern. The approach taken by Department for International Development (DFID) is more pragmatic than the Foreign and Common Wealth Office (FCO) to settle Nepalese conflict. The UK is intimately engaged in Nepal's conflict. Prime Minister Tony Blair appointed Sir Jeffrey James as especial envoy to Nepal, Jack Straw, Foreign Minister discussed Nepal's issue with India in New Delhi after the royal coup. The UK has organised international donors meeting in 2002 summer in London to discuss the Nepal's crisis, numerous studies have been conducted and lot of visits have been organised. However, how much contribution all these efforts have made to settle the conflict is not yet clear. These efforts are becoming ineffective particularly its dual position (to support militarily and seeking political solution).

1.6.4 Other bilateral countries

There are other bilateral countries such as Switzerland, Norway, Finland and Germany who want to see the conflict settled in a peaceful manner. They are also ready to help to settle the conflict. Their development support is also tied with the peaceful settlement of conflict. However, a country like Belgium has interest to sale arms[19] to Nepal. Most of the bilateral countries except the USA, UK, India and to a lesser extend China, are not much involved in military assistance. Their influence lies on the development aid and they are more committed to peaceful resolution of conflict. They are interpreting Maoist insurgency differently than these three countries. Most of them do not agree with the government approach of dealing with the ongoing armed conflict in Nepal. They always advocating for the negotiated settlement instead of military means. Norway and Switzerland are making especial efforts to resolve this conflict peacefully and they have also offered any help Nepal may need in this process. However, the government is not interested. After the 1st February 2005 Norway decided to cut the planned financial assistance for 2006 by 10 percent. On 20 July 2005, issuing a press statement Norwegian ambassador stopped 28 million dollars financial support for Melamchi Drinking water project. He said, 'the decision has been made to terminate, with immediate effect, the bilateral agreement on the financial support for the Melamchi Water Supply Project'[20]. Norway has also decided to stop any new bilateral agreements with Nepal. Switzerland also reduced its financial assistance to Nepal for 2006 by more than 15 percent.

1.6.5 Intern-governmental organisations and INGOs

United Nations, European Union, Amnesty International, Human Rights Watch, Centre for Humanitarian Dialogue, ICRC are other major international actors in favour of peaceful resolution of the armed conflict. European Union has sent its high level mission (troika) twice[21] to assess the situation and suggest Brussels for possible resolution of the conflict. It is also urging the warring parties to resolve conflict politically. ICRC is actively helping to minimise effects of civil war and mediating to release detainees and abducted people by the warring parties. Amnesty International and Human Rights Watch, are constantly monitoring human rights situation, warning warring parties for their human rights violation and globally lobbying for the protection of human rights. International Alert, Carter Centre, Centre for Humanitarian Dialogue and many other INGOs working in the field of conflict are also active in contributing to resolve this conflict peacefully.

United Nations has repeatedly expressed its concern and working hard to resolve this conflict. Secretary General Kofi Anan assigned Samuel Tamrat as special political officer looking for Nepal's conflict and he has visited six times and having meetings, discussion with different power centres to discuss possible ways of resolving conflict. General Secretary several times issued statements about the Nepal's political crisis. Kul Chandra Gautam, a senior official off UN (chief of UNICEF) and Nepali citizen is also making several efforts to resolve conflict politically. After the royal takeover, Kofi Anan met with the king in Indonesia and discussed to restore democracy. He became unhappy when the king did not fulfil the promise he made with him in Indonesia. Later he also sent Lakhdar Brahimi[22], a senior most advisor of General Secretary, who had played crucial role in Afghanistan, Iraq and other many warn-torn countries. He met and discussed with the king, Vice Chairperson of Council of Minister Tulsi Giri, leaders of political parties (Girija Prasad Koirala, Madhav Kumar Nepal and others), civil society leaders, diplomats and international community. Visit of Lakhdar Brahimi clearly indicates the seriousness of the Nepal's conflict. Now, UN has informed to its member countries about the mounting political crisis in Nepal. UN has also opened its largest Human Rights Office in Kathmandu.

On 18 March 2004, CPN (M) again requested the UN to help mediate in negotiation between them and the government. However, CPN (M) did not elaborate modus operandi of the UN involvement. After 4 days, without referring the Maoists request the UN General Secretary issued on statement through his spokesperson Fred Eckhard. He said, "*Civilian casualties and serious human rights violations are routine occurrence, and the country's economic and social development is being severely hampered. The general Secretary does not believe there is a military solution to the conflict. Government of Nepal and the CPN (M) are to take immediate steps to end the fighting and resume the peace process with the participation of all political and civil forces in the country. The secretary general is available to help search for a solution in any manner the parties consider useful*". Regrettably, the government does not see any relevance of the involvement of the UN in the peace process (Adhikari, 2004)

It is extremely hard to settle the political crisis of Nepal without the full support and confidence of India. However, India's role is not supportive enough to reach a negotiated settlement. The problem would be solved if India fully endorses UN involvement and plays a positive role in supporting the UN and mobilising international community (particularly the UK and USA) for a negotiated settlement.

1.7 REFLECTIONS

The Maoist insurgency is not the cause of the failure of the 12 years of democracy in Nepal. Rather it is the manifestation of the failure of 236 years of governance system of modern Nepal. The feudal, exclusionary, top-down and elitist ruling system is the fundamental cause of the problem.

All three major power centres are working so far in false imagination, perceived risks, false sense of supremacy and wrong course of action, which have betrayed the people and pushed the country into deep crisis. All of them are prisoners of false imagination because they are claiming that they represent interest of majority of people but they fail to realise their weaknesses and contribution to bring the country to such a crisis. The first and foremost need for ordinary Nepalese people is peace and prosperity, freedom and functional multiparty democracy, which are to be achieved through dialogue, discussion and negotiation, not from the violence, counter violence and war. The king imagines that guided and regulated democracy under his assertive leadership (as he has publicly expressed that he wants to be a constructive and proactive monarch of the 21st century, who does not want to limit himself as symbolic and unheard) is the will of the Nepalese people and they support him. Civic receptions organised by the government in different parts of the country might have further strengthened his imagination. He might have perceived that he is the best choice among three power centres, as the parliamentary parties have already failed and the world did not support the Maoists. The 4 October 2002 royal takeover and subsequent actions (nominating base-less politicians to the government, discrediting parliamentary parties, solving Maoists problems through military means, etc.) and the 1st February takeover are the clear reflection of this imagination. His reliable base for this new experiment is traditional forces like the army and hardliner royalist Panchas. However, the 3 years of direct rule of the king have demonstrated that his approach is not able to produce desired results.

The parliamentary parties imagine that they are the true representatives of the Nepalese people because they are elected from the people. However, they are not yet able to fully realise that their behaviour in the past 12 years (April 1990 to September 2002) had deeply betrayed Nepalese people. They talk a lot about democracy but there is serious democratic deficit within their political parties. Parliamentary parties alone are not fully responsible for what is happening at present in this country, which goes back to modern Nepal's history. However, they are responsible for not taking a constructive role in resolving the Maoist conflict during their tenure and demonstrating democratic characters. Their course of action during past 12 years was visibly and invisibly shaped by the force who wanted to weaken multiparty democracy, create and maintain instability in the country and strengthen the traditional position of the palace.

Similarly, the Maoists have a false imagination and false sense of supremacy. They feel that what they are doing (change through violence, killing, extortion, abduction, etc.) is acceptable to Nepalese people and they can change the state structures through violence. They are totally undermining the potential of peaceful change. They are also ignoring the reality that death of more than 13,000 people and hundreds of thousands of victim and the difficulties and insecurities faced by Nepalese people are the product of the ongoing insurgency and their actions. They are not able to internalise the role of international power centres unfavourable to their 'people's war' and the wastage of billions of rupees in arms and ammunition, which could otherwise be spent in social development. Most people will not disagree with the change agenda of the Maoists on social and economic issues; however, most people disagree on the approach they took to achieve these changes.

It is not possible to resolve this conflict militarily, whatever support the USA, India and the UK may give to strengthen military capacity (ICG, 2003a &b). The only best way of resolving this crisis is to address the structural causes, i.e., fundamental restructuring of the state. The armed rebellion brought century-old problems to the surface, empowered ethnic minorities, backward and suppressed people, women, dalit, and poor section of society to seek their rights and severely challenged the status quo of the traditional elite and power centres. This insurgency had also raised tremendously high expectations of people such as rights to self-determination and territorial division of ethnic grouping that could lead to unexpected problems like ethnic conflict or separatist movement, if not able to manage properly.

At present, the country is facing an unprecedented crisis and all executive power is concentrated on the King. Therefore, the king must take initiative to overcome the triangular conflict and settle the Maoist insurgency through a negotiated settlement. Otherwise, it would be too late for all and there will be no other option left but to regret for the past mistake. When situation gets complicated and out of hand, the prime loser will be the palace.

Rampant poverty, structural inequality, political oppression, social discrimination against certain groups like Kamaiya, women, Dalit, etc., failure of the public administration, widespread corruption and continuous failure of the successive governments to address these structural problems are the root causes of the current conflict in Nepal. The Maoist insurgency is only the manifestation. Feudal legacy, political instability, dependency syndromes, lack of transparency and social exclusion are further contributing to fuel the conflict. In addition, another plausible explanation for the emergence of the Maoist conflict in particular time is the growing awareness of the Nepalese people during the period of multiparty democracy. They are becoming more aware about poverty, inequality, discrimination, corruption and lack of employment opportunities. Destruction of indigenous social networks in Nepal has also contributed to the conflict. Therefore, paradoxically the current crisis is also an indicator of social awareness.

The current approach of conflict management cannot manage this crisis, as there are not enough efforts from the government, political parties, and international communities to address the root causes of the conflict ensuring the fundamental rights of Nepalese people. Neither the military support from the UK and US nor the Indian military assistance could solve this problem unless addressing the real causes of the conflict. Nepal needs support form India, the USA, UK or any other well-wisher countries in addressing root causes of the rebellion, not providing arms and weapons that further worsens the situation and inflicts human rights violation. A peaceful resolution of the present conflict depends upon due recognition and internalisation of political and socio-economic characteristics of the Nepalese conflict.

NOTES

1. Later the name was changed to Communist Party of Nepal-Maoist (CPN-M).
2. United Front was formed by seven communist parties of Nepal to make the MRD successful. United Front worked closely with Nepali Congress to restore multiparty democracy.
3. A large section of civil society was vehemently criticising the activities of the political parties when they were in power and that may have contributed to develop a false understanding to the king (criticising the political parties means civil society will support royal takeover).
4. See Bhattarai Baburam (2003). Maobadi Samasya ki Maobadi Samadhan (Maoist problem or Maoist solution) in Bhattarai, B: Barta ra tatkalin

rajnatik nikas ko prasanga (The question of contemporary political resolution through negotiation. Kathmandu: Pawan Prakasan.

5. A popular documentary called "Killing Terraces" (2001) vividly illustrates this situation.
6. Laxman Aryal, one of the members of 1990's Constitution Draft Committee repeatedly said that the King was not happy and frequently sent several revisions. Similar opinion was expressed by the Chairperson of the 1990's Constitution Draft Committee Vishwo Nath Upadhaya in Kantipur television interview on 9 October. He said that he had spent 12 hours with the king alone to sort out some of the differences.
7. See http://www.time.com/time/asia/2004/nepal_king/nepal_intvu.html for detail.
8. However, major political parties are separated from the position of constituently monarchy, perhaps still using it for bargaining.
9. Often politicians and former foreign ministers publicly have said that 'India is objecting to involve UN'. The prominent role of India in Nepalese conflict was clearly observed when the USA and UK publicly announced that they have accepted the lead role of India in responding to the 1st February Royal takeover.
10. Such expressions are commonly heard from the Indian ambassadors and foreign ministry officials of India.
11. This school of thinking is more strong with the 'nationalists' and pro-palace analysts.
12. Those Maoist central leaders arrested in Patna, India on 3 June 2004 were: Kul Prasad KC, Lokendra Bista, Kumar Dahal, Hit Bahadur Tamang (head of the *Tamang Swayatta Janaparisad*), Anil Sharma Chitra Bahadur Shrestha (General Secretary of the All Nepal Peasants Association) and other 5 leaders. They were in Patna for treatment.
13. See *Himal* Magazine, 27-Feb. 13 March 2005 (year 14, No 22, Vol. 142), Pp 26-27 for detail.
14. On 28 July 2005 US Senator Patrick Leahy made statement in the American Senate. The statement was very tough. He mentioned, "...the situation was made significantly worse on February first when king Gyanendra with the backing of the security forces, dissolved the multiparty government, arrested and jailed political opponents, human rights activists, and journalists, and declared a state of emergency. ... Last week, the Senate revisited the conditions on our military aid to Nepal. Since those conditions were enacted prior to February 1st, they have in large measures been eclipsed by subsequent events. The Senate determined that modifications were needed, and those changes were adopted unanimously on July 20, 2005, in an amendment to the fiscal year 2005 State Foreign Operation Appropriations bill. I ask unanimous consent that the amendment, which if agreed to by the Senate-House conference Committee will apply to the United States military aid for Nepal for the fiscal year beginning October

2006, be printed in the Record at the end of these remarks' (see *The Kathmandu Post* of 31 July 200 for the full statement.

15. See The Himalayan Times, 1st August 2005 for detail.
16. White House spokesperson said that in a meeting between Dr Singh and Mr Bush in Washington on 21 July 2005 the royal takeover was discussed and both the leaders agreed that the civil rights must be restored and power mush be handed over to politicians.
17. See Kantipur Daily July 28, 2005 (13 Shrawan, 2062BS) for the full text of his statement.
18. See Rajdhani Daily newspaper 12 December about the objection of UK's Liberal Democratic Party on UK arm selling deal to Nepal.
19. Despite the EU provision of not to sale arms to a country fell in civil war, and despite the strong opposition within Belgium, Belgium government sold 5000 arms to Nepal.
20. See *The Himalayan Times,* 21 July 2005 for detail.
21. The last visit of troika was on 5 October 2005 to Kathmandu to discuss 'future of ceremonial king, democracy, election and the Maoist agenda'. The team was led by Tom Phillips, the director for South Asia and Afghanistan in the FCO/UK. The team discussed with leaders of political parties, vice chairman and military chief. But the king cancelled the scheduled meeting them citing the reason of his Pokhara visit (as the king went to western development region at that time).
22. Lakhdar Brahimin, special advisor to Kofi Anan visited Nepal from 11 to16 July 2005 to explore the ways of resolving conflict. He was accompanied by his special assistant Asif Khan and senior political affairs officer of the UN Department of Political Affairs Samuel Tamrat.

CHAPTER 2

Concept of Conflict Transformation and Peace Building

2.1 INTRODUCTION

It is important to conceptualise conflict transformation and peace building to achieve a negotiated settlement of any violent conflict. A conceptual framework is extremely important to analyse the peace-building process in Nepal. This chapter highlights some conceptual issues, different approaches, strategies and methods related to conflict transformation and peace building[1]. These concepts and approaches are linked with the ongoing armed conflict of Nepal. The remaining chapters of the book have mainly used the conceptual or theoretical framework discussed in this chapter. Without a proper understanding of conceptual discourses of peace building, conflict transformation and resolution of crisis is difficult. Therefore, the aim of this chapter is to shed some light on the role of theoretical concepts, analytical frameworks and approaches in resolving conflict

2.2. UNDERSTANDING CONFLICT

Conflict is a fluid and ambiguous term, therefore different people in different contexts interpret conflict differently. Conflict can refer to a debate or contest; a disagreement, argument, dispute, quarrel; a struggle, battle or confrontation; or a state of unrest, turmoil, chaos and violence (Warner, 2001). Conflict occurs when two or more people oppose one another because of the difference in their needs, wants, goals or values. Conflict is usually accompanied by feelings of anger, frustration, hurt, anxiety, or fear. Conflict in this paper covers observable differences in opinion, misunderstandings, clashes of interest, disagreements, complaints in public, protests by argument and physical assault, antipathy, filing cases with local administration, police and courts, violence and bloody war (Baechler, 2002; Upreti, 2004a). Feelings of unfairness, suspicion, injustice, mistrust, ultimately lead to conflict. Conflict is inevitable and an integral part of the social process.

Generally, the term 'conflict' has been interpreted as the opposite of peace (Warner, 2001). Many people interpret conflict as undesirable and destructive to society and something to be avoided, contained or eliminated. However, this is a narrow and one-dimensional interpretation of conflict. Such interpretation does not allow distinguishing between different levels and forms of conflict (Galtung, 2000a and b; 1996; 2004a and b) and their possible contribution to positive social change. Conflicts occur in all societies. It is manifested within an individual, between individuals, within a family, between families, among community members and social groups, between community groups and external organisations, between different castes and ethnic groups, between political parties and between countries. Conflict is an indicator of a changing society. Rapid changes due to new technologies, commercialisation of common property resources, privatisation of public services, growing consumerism, and government policies all contribute to emergence of conflict (Buckles, 1999; Warner, 2001). It is merely impossible to stop these changes and associated conflict. The only way is to acknowledge, manage and transform conflict into a force for positive social change (Nyheim et al., 2001; OECD, 2001; Upreti, 2004 a&b; Varyrynen, 1991).

Conflict occurs in any society. It may or may not be managed or resolved. It transforms over time and leads to different outcomes with a multitude of short-term and long-term effects. These outcomes may be positive or negative to society (Scimecca, 1993). Conflict has two stages: (i) latent conflict - a relatively permanent condition between conflicting parties with divergent and competing interests or (ii) active conflict - actual interplay of the disputants over a specific problem. Based on manifestation, conflict is divided into: (a) peaceful (like civil disobedience) and (b) violent (like armed rebellion, war, terrorists' attack) as well as (a) silent and (b) open conflict. Conflict can be categorised into four groups, based on its solvability. They are: (i) a terminal conflict that seems unsolvable by agreement and results in a win-lose situation; (ii) a paradoxical conflict, which looks obscure and of questionable solvability having a lose-lose outcome, (iii) a litigious conflict, which seems solvable and produces a win-win or a consensus result (Martinelli and Almeida, 1998), and (iv) Illusory conflict where disputants want the same thing but fail to realise it (Upreti, 2003a & b). Conflict can be constructive as well as destructive. Constructive conflict is a type of manifestation that has a positive result.

Conflict transformation refers to a change/improvement, in the nature of a conflict, especially a de-escalation of conflict or reconciliation between people in conflict. Unlike conflict resolution (which denies long-term existence of conflict) or conflict management, which assumes that relationships can be managed), the concept of conflict transformation reflects the notion that conflicts go on for long periods of time, changing the nature of the relationships between the people involved, and themselves changing as people's response to the situation develops over time (Galtung, 200a and b; BHCT, 2003).

People in a violent social setting interpret conflict as violence or bloody war. Conflict is an active stage of disagreement between people with opposing opinions, principles and practices manifested in different forms such as grievance, conflict, dispute and war (Buckles, 1999). Grievance is an initial stage of conflict in which individuals or a group are perceived to be unjust, and provides grounds for resentment or complaints. This condition potentially erupts into conflict (Vayrynen, 1991). When clash of cultural, political, social or economic interests between individuals and groups causes antagonism that leads to conflict (Ury et al., 1989). In the final stage of conflict, people make the matter public and opt for confrontation (Bush, 1995; Caplan, 1995).

Two main schools of thought exist in conflict discourse (Rubin et al., 1994; Rubestein, 1993, Sanddelin, 1997). One school of thought views conflict as 'pathological and dysfunctional'. In this perspective, conflict generally carries a negative connotation and is interpreted as something irrational that needs to be suppressed because it is opposite to co-operation and peace. This view is mechanistic in its interpretation of conflict (Martinelli and Almeida, 1998). Another school of thought considers that conflict can also be a functional means for social change. This perspective acknowledges prevalence of conflict and it could also be a constructive social process to establish group boundaries, strengthen group consensus, develop a sense of self-identity, and contribute towards social integration and progressive economic and social change (Doughorty and Pfaltzgraff, 1990). According to this perspective, conflict is a continuous social process and has great influence in shaping and reshaping social relations and the power structure of society (Martinelli and Almeida, 1998). Unlike the mechanistic view, Galtung (2000a and b) argues that conflicts encompass adaptation by a society to a new political, economic and physical environment. New innovations, policies and procedures, laws and regulations, local power relationships and privatisation and globalisation processes determine the causes and intensity of a conflict. Destructive conflict is a type of violent confrontation and often has largely negative results. It pushes people apart, destroys relationships, and leads to a host of negative personal and social changes including an escalation of violence, fear, and distrust. It is contrasted with constructive conflict, which has more benefits than costs, which pulls people together, strengthens and/or improves their relationship, by redefining it in a more appropriate or useful way and one that leads to positive change in all of the parties involved. Some conflicts like the Maoist insurgency in Nepal and people's war in India are intractable in nature. It refers to conflicts that go on for a long time, resisting most attempts to resolve them. Typically, they involve fundamental value disagreements, high stakes distributional questions, and domination issues, and/or denied human needs -- all of which are non-negotiable problems. They often involve unavoidable win-lose situations as well.

BOX 2.1 Basic Causes of Conflict

- Opposing interests
- Competition over scarce resources, power and position
- Ambiguity over roles, responsibilities and authorities
- Poor communication and lack of information
- Differences in perceptions, work styles, attitudes among individuals
- Contradictory reward and incentive systems
- Tension between equity (reward relative to contributions) and equality (everyone receive same)
- Divergent ideologies
- Lack of basic understanding of social processes
- Development mismatch
- Resistant to social, political, cultural, technological, economic and any other changes
- International vested interests.

Sources: Folger and Jones, 1994; Bush and Folger 1994a&b; Caplan, 1995; Jandt and Pedersen, 1996.

Whether wanted or not, conflict is a part of social process and an outcome of social development and change. How to use conflict to serve a useful social function is to be the central concern. In functionalism theory, Durkheim argues that society is held together by the values that people in that society share; hence society is normally in a state of equilibrium based on moral consensus. Functionalists rule out disequilibrium or conflict. Talcot Parson's structural functionalism theory also considers conflict as dysfunctional and abnormal condition of society (Vayrynene, 1991; Upreti, 2002a). An alternate perspective was put forward by Karl Marx citing a vivid case of conflict between two basic economic classes of people (Scimecca, 1993). He emphasises that there is always constant conflict between the bourgeois who own the means of production and the proletariats who sell their labour. Dahrendorf further elaborates that social organisations typically contain two groups (those who rule and those who are ruled) with opposing interests, thus conflict is not only limited to class struggle over economic resources but also can be a power struggle between interest groups. Scimecca (1993) criticises the Marxian analysis of conflict on the ground that it emphasises only an economically determined system of social relationship and conflict than co-operation. Max Weber in his Social Action Theory suggests that societies vary between conditions of equilibrium and conflict. In this perspective conflict is endemic in social process but tends to operate in favour of powerful people of the

BOX 2.2 Characteristics of Conflict

Conflict

- Requires at least two parties
- Arises from position scarcity, resources scarcity or power scarcity
- Behaviour attempts to destroy, injure, thwart, or control another party
- Requires mutually opposed interaction actions and counteraction among parties
- Relation attempts to gain control of scarce resources and positions or to influence behaviour
- Relations constitute social-interactions with important consequences
- Process represents a temporary tendency of interaction between the parties
- Relations shift in the governing norms and expectation.

Source: Sidaway, 1996; Upreti, 2004a; Pruitt and Carnevale, 1993; Pendzich et al, 1994; Smith, 1997; Galtung, 2000.

society. Weber gives explanations of how power is legitimatised and stabilised in society. Weber's social action theory has four major components (Weber, 1948): (a) Role of power, (b) Emphasis on organised system; (c) Legitimacy and (d) Self-interests.

Essential elements of Weber's conflict theory (Upreti, 2004a) are: (a) Conflicts are endemic in social life, (b) Power is differentially distributed among groups and individuals in society, (c) Social order is achieved in any society through rules and commands issued by more powerful persons to less powerful people and enforced through sanctions, (d) Both the social structure and normative system of a society are more extensively influenced by powerful persons and come to represent the interests of these powerful people, (e) Social changes are often disruptive to powerful people than ordinary people. Hence powerful people oppose or resist change, (f) Changes in a society occur as a result of action by persons who stand to benefit from these changes.

Conflict has always both positive and negative impacts on individuals and society. Some examples of positive outcomes of conflict are discussed here. Conflict can motivate people to try harder to win. It increases commitment and enhances group loyalty. It also clarifies problems or identifies main issues of concern. It leads to innovative breakthroughs and new approaches, techniques, procedures and contents. It clarifies or brings underlying problems and facilitates change process leading to solutions. It galvanises or increases energy level and makes key values visible. It also sharpens people's capacity to bargain, influence, compete and negotiate. Finally, it contributes to agrarian reform and social change.

Similarly, conflict could have severe negative outcomes too. Conflict can lead to anger, avoidance, snapping, shouting, frustration, fear of failure, and sense of personal inadequacy. It could also withhold critical information or distort information. It reduces productivity of people engaged in it. In organisation aspect, it sidetracks careers, ruins relationships and disrupts established working patterns. It wastes brains, money and time, which leads to loss in productivity. It often promotes violence and disintegrates social harmony and contributes to breaking down of society. When peaceful/silent conflict turns to violence and war, human rights violations, human casualty and destruction increase and that ultimately turns to 'state-failure'.

TABLE 2.1 Structural Causes of Conflict in Society

Causes	*Key characteristics*	*Examples*
Social	• Unequal, unjust or unrepresentative social structures • Social exclusion • Vertical social stratification	• Difference in education, wealth and income, information, etc. • Lack of legal awareness • Insecure social system, vulnerability and deprivation • Inaccessible social benefits
Legal	• Legal systems with bias towards certain group	• Legal arrangements providing privilege to powerful, e.g., Land Act discriminative to unregistered tenants or bounded labour
Economic	• Economic arrangement and power biased towards certain group of people	• Economic power and influence of commercial companies over indigenous practices • Government policies and provisions favouring extractive industries while ignoring local interests and customary ownership
Political	• Party and ideological biases and discrimination	• Misuse of power and administrative resources by the ruling political party members and government to create problems to the supporters of opposition and minority parties
Cultural	• Ethnic minority groups hold deep-seated values that define their identity • Cultural discrimination by state/government	• Indigenous people and minority hold different values for their identity • Elites and politicians exploit racial, religious, tribal, ethnic or linguistic differences and prejudices • Groups dislike each other

Source: Upreti, 2004a; Warner 2001; BHCT, 2003.

2.3 CONFLICT TRANSFORMATION FRAMEWORK

Conceptual framework is extremely important to analyse the conflict and peace-building process in Nepal. Therefore this section highlights some conceptual issues related to conflict transformation and peace building. In understanding the discourse of peace, one needs to understand some basic approaches of conflict. These approaches are presented in Table 2.2.

TABLE 2.2 Understanding Basic Approaches of Dealing with Conflict and Peace Building

Approaches	*Conceptual focus*	*Dominant conflict behaviour*
Conflict management	Power	Contain conflict and maintain peace by constraining aggressions and violence by using different deterrence mechanisms like alliances, balance of power, coercive conflict behaviours, collective security, border sealing,
	Values	Encourage and promote execution of ethical and legal norms and provisions such as Geneva convention and other international human rights laws and conventions, economic and social justices, principled or moral conflict behaviour, etc.
Dispute settlement	Interests	Focus on win-win solution by encouraging parties in dispute, Disconnect interests from positions, problem solving approach from co-operative behaviour
Conflict resolution	Needs	Encourage to respect other party's needs, seek to identify and acknowledge the legitimacy and relevance of needs, explore alternatives
Conflict transformation	Relationships	Develop empathy for other party's needs by transforming stereotypes and perceptions about self and other party. Empathetic and transformative conflict behaviour
Conflict transmutation	Toxic memories	Transforming stereotypically based memories of responses to conflict build upon negative memories, emotions, fear, anger, resentment, and agony, etc. Conflict behaviour is transformative in character.
Conflict prevention	Human dimension	Looks at phenomenon of conflict and its human dimensions Not merely the conditions that create an environment of conflict and the structural changes required for removing it, but more importantly, the promotion of conditions that create *cooperative* relationships.

Source: Adapted from Salla, 2000; Burton and Dukes 1990; BHCT, 2003.

Conflict transformation and peace building are two parts of a coin. Lederach (1997) views the peace building as a long-term transformation of conflict dynamics into a peace dynamics based on the values of peace and justice, truth and reconciliation. Conflict transformation is a process of change in the personal, structural, relational and cultural aspects of conflict in short-, mid- and long-term time scale. Peace building is a continuous process with appropriate strategy to build a peace constituency encompassing a vision of the desired future and an awareness of the current crisis. Lederach visualises a pyramid with elite leaders and decision-makers at the top, leaders of social organisations, churches, and top journalists at mid-level and grass-roots community leaders at the base. A comprehensive peace process should address complementary changes at all these levels (BHCT, 2003). Lederach goes beyond the conflict resolution and suggests the scope for drawing peace-building resources from the wider society.

2.3.1 Conflict transformation and peace building

Conflict transformation refers to outcome-, process- and structure-orientated long-term peace building efforts, which aim to truly overcome revealed forms of direct, cultural and structural violence (Lederach, 1997; Curle, 1971; Galtung, 1996). Conflict transformation moves beyond the aims of conflict resolution and conflict management. Conflict transformation refers to a change/improvement, in the nature of a conflict, especially a de-escalation of conflict or reconciliation between people in conflict. Unlike conflict resolution (which denies long-term existence of conflict) or conflict management, which assumes that relationships can be managed), the concept of conflict transformation reflects the notion that conflicts go on for long periods of time, changing the nature of the relationships between the people involved, and themselves changing as people's response to the situation develops over time.

Protracted violent conflicts are often the result of unequal and suppressive social and political structures and power relations. Effective transformation of conflict therefore needs empowerment and recognition of marginalized groups of society to ensure social justice. Dealing with immediate needs and concerns of marginalized people at the local level and exerting pressure on conflict actors is one of the important conflict transformation strategies that contributes to end the violence and enter into meaningful negotiations. In Somalia during the early

1990s (Lederach 1997), the bottom-up approaches were commenced with a series of discussions and agreements on how to end the war. These consultations were conducted in the form of local peace conferences that brought the various sub-clans together. These conferences took care to invite legitimated representatives who could properly advocate each clan's fears and concerns, and, thus, put centre-stage issues of immediate concern at local levels. As these local conferences approached agreements, a similar decision-making process was then repeated at higher levels involving an ever-wider range of clans (BHCT, 2003).

Practitioners and scholars working on conflict resolution focus on a problem-solving approach with specific analytical frameworks than the conflict settlement practitioners and scholars, who focus on interests and rational behaviour (Clements, 1998). A common reason for the use of different theoretical approaches by different scholars and practitioners is the theoretical orientation and built-in perspective based on certain assumptions. When scholars and practitioners consider conflict transformation as a conceptual model, a combination of rational choice theory, human needs theory and non-violence action theory give a strong analytical framework (BHCT, 2003). For example, the non-violent action theory of Mahatma Gandhi (1938 and 1950) and Martin Luther King (1963) stresses the need for respect for the adversary and search for mutually beneficial outcomes (Mitchell, 1981). People working with a game theoretical approach use 'mutually beneficial outcomes' in conflict studies.

A combination of game theory, human needs theory and non-violent action theory provides a strong conceptual basis for conflict transformation and peace building. While analysing conflict from perspectives of conflict theory, human needs and non-violent action theories, a conflict transformation strategy should begin with a three-fold understanding of the nature of conflict, i.e., (a) conflict as an element of political control, (b) a catalyst for social change, and (c) a usual expression of non-violent struggle for social justice. Hence, conflict transformation provides dual understanding of conflict as an agent of both social control and change (Clements, 1998). Conflict transformation focuses beyond conflict resolution, conflict settlement and conflict management. Its primary emphasis is on social justice and social change.

Literally, peace is a stable situation or period of time in which there is no tension, violence, and there is harmony, cooperation and respect for each other among and between the members of society. If there is a stable peace, there is less chance of tension and violence, as observed in the Scandinavian countries. Stable peace is the situation in which two parties or countries do not even consider war to be an acceptable or possible option for dispute resolution between them. It is contrasted with unstable peace (in which parties or countries are at peace but think that war is possible at a future time).

Peace building is the process of restoring normal relations between not only the warring parties but also communities that are severely disturbed by armed conflict. It requires the reconciliation of differences, apology and forgiveness of past harm, and the establishment of a cooperative relationship between groups, replacing the adversarial or competitive relationship that used to exist. Peace dialogue is extremely important in the peace process. Galtung argues that peace dialogues explore diagnosis, prognosis and therapy together, avoiding linearity and maintaining back and forth discussion focusing on what went wrong in the past and what could have been done (Galtung, 2000a and b, 2004a and b).

Pragmatically, peace making and keeping is more than just ending armed rebellion. It goes beyond it to address the root causes of conflict and promotes peace transformation. Therefore, it is a political and social transformation process as it has to focus on structural change in governance, security and development, human rights policies and practice and regaining eroded trust (Ury et al., 1989; Upreti, 2004 c & d). In this respect, democratising peace process is extremely essential in Nepal (Upreti, 2003b).

At the conceptual level, peacekeeping is a process of putting neutral intermediaries between fighting factions to physically keep them apart. This can cool down a conflict enough to allow for successful peace making (the development of a settlement agreement) and long-term peace building (the re-establishment of normal relations). A commonly observed neutral intermediary in many peacekeeping efforts is the United Nations. There are also some other credible institutions to declare peace zones. Peacemaking is essentially negotiation of an agreement formally ending a particular dispute. This is then followed by peace building, which implements the agreement and brings the parties back together in some sort of 'normal' relationship. Peace scholars like Kenneth Boulding introduced the concept of 'stable peace', which is the situation when two parties do not even consider war to be an option, no matter what conflict occurs between them

(BHCT, 2003). Examples would be the relationship between the Scandinavian countries.

Transforming different forms of 'negative peace' into just and democratic peace require work far beyond terminating diverse forms of structural and cultural violence. This requires transformation of social relationships and social structures. Some people argue that democratic exercises (such as peaceful protest, rallies, public protests, etc.) disturb or hamper peace and therefore such activities should not be practised at the cost of peace. Post-1st February 2005 arguments of the establishment are based on this principle (peace first and only then democracy). However, democracy and peace are not mutually exclusive and they are an integral part of the stable democratic society. In Nepalese discourse, peace without democracy is termed as *Murda Santi*. Democracy is a precondition of durable and just peace and peace is the fundamental basis of democracy.

The armed conflict results on direct violence and the obvious outcome is negative and destructive consequences. All strategies that aim to end violent conflict start with cease-fire and cessation of deep-rooted hostilities. In the conflict settlement strategies, success is defined as a sustained win-win solution and immediate peace instead of having the objective of longer-term 'positive peace' or social justice. Building peace has to start with conflict resolution. 'Conflict resolution refers to all process-orientated activities that aim to address the underlying causes of direct, cultural and structural violence.

Structural violence is defined as social, political and economic structure of a conflict situation when unequal power, domination and dependency are perpetuated. Cultural violence refers to the social and cultural legitimisation of direct and structural violence' (BHCT, 2003). Burton, Kelman, Fisher and Kriesberg-like scholar-practitioners use the game theory in order to overcome the self-defeating dynamics of the zero-sum conflict management approaches to reframe the conflict as a shared problem with mutually acceptable solutions (ibid). In contrast to the conflict settlement approach, conflict resolution begins by defining protracted conflict as a natural result of unmet human needs. Consequently, the origin of protracted conflict can be found in the underlying needs (for identity, security and distributive justice) of its participants (ibid). Hence, conflict resolution has to focus on the 'human need theory' of Burton, which emphasises the universal drive to satisfy basic and ontological needs, such as security, identity, recognition, food, shelter, safety, identity, participation, recognition, distributive justice and development (Burton, 1990).

Addressing human needs and security requires conflict expressed in a non-violent manner and an element of essential catalyst for social change. Therefore, the aim is to eliminate the violent and destructive manifestations of conflict arises from the unmet needs and fears of the parties in conflict. In this approach, the important task is to make the parties aware of these underlying needs for identity, security, and participation, and then to use them to redefine both interests and positions.

A thorough conflict analysis provides an understanding of the conditions under which the basic needs of people can be satisfied and which needs are more important than others. A proper analysis of the conflict focusing on need of people brings strategies that go beyond the outcome-orientated conflict settlement strategies with their focus on negotiable interests. It requires process-orientated and relationship-orientated strategies and approaches that are non-coercive and unofficial activities such as facilitation or consultation in the form of controlled communication, problem-solving workshops or round-tables (BHCT, 2003).

A proper conflict analysis identifies key actors in addressing human needs. A greater number of actors needs to involve in the process. These actors are from civil society groups, academic institutions, 'civil mediation' or 'citizen diplomacy' groups, including local and international conflict resolution NGOs), government, rebels, security forces, business communities, donors, etc. (Upreti, 2004b). A deeper common interest and shared needs through increased cooperation and improved communication between parties may constitute a form of 'successful outcome' of conflict management (Upreti, 2004c).

2.3.2 Use of conceptual framework in conflict analysis

Conflict transformation and peace building are relatively new areas of research and study. Therefore, they are only gradually emerging as separate disciplines in term of scientific research and theory building (BHCT, 2003). There are still many ontological, epistemological and methodological issues to be elaborated, debated, discussed and applied in terms of scientific inquiry for justifying knowledge generated from the field to the theory building process. Theorising different approaches of conflict transformation need to be based on some specific conflict theories as well as empirical evidences (Bottomore, 1969). Then the obvious difficulty is to choose whether to apply deductive or inductive methods of inquiry. Conflict transformation being a relatively new discipline, the use of grounded theory can be worth using as it builds on the empirical evidences and grounded reality based on the inductive method of inquiry. Conceptualising armed conflict management starts with a theoretical basis of proper understanding of violent conflict (Jandt and Pedersen, 1996). However, such an understanding is not simply theoretical; rather it is more practical and based on the reality observation (Moscovici and Doise, 1994). Only then does it contribute to the process of conflict transformation.

Conflict management and transformation literature reveal that most approaches dealing with conflict are not based on such a broad or explicit theoretical concept of conflict[2]. Therefore, Scimecca writes, *"there is ...no real theoretical justification for when and why to use conflict intervention techniques"* (Scimecca, 1993:217). Often, so far most research on conflict is less theory-driven and more comparative case studies (Stedman, 1991; Princen, 1992).

Theoretical frameworks for conflict transformation and peace studies have been drawn from sociology, anthropology, political science and international relations. The works of Max Weber, Karl Marx, Talcott Parson and other sociologists and political scientists have widely been used in the contemporary conflict studies. Scimecca argues that 'Weber's conflict theory' lends itself well for use as a single overarching framework within which to situate both the practice and the theory of different approaches to conflict management. While many scholars might challenge his exclusive reliance on Weber's sociology, Scimecca raises important questions concerning the theoretical shortcomings of the field of conflict management and its lack of any explicit theory of conflict (BHCT, 2003).

The use of theory in conflict studies depends upon the degree of its usefulness, practical applicability and relevance in guiding and orienting researchers and practitioners towards finding ways to transform violent conflicts into durable and democratic peace. The question can be raised, that if the focus of conflict discipline is to transform conflict (which is a pragmatic work instead of complex conceptual discourse), then why do conflict researchers-practitioners need theory? This is a narrow argument and limited understanding of the role of contribution of theory in the process of conflict management, conflict transformation and peace building. Theory offers a conceptual framework to enable researchers and practitioners to accurately analyse, describe and predict trends of the conflict situation. In reality, conflict transformation consists of characteristics, strategies, and the behaviour of the conflict parties and intervening variables, such as third-party resources (coercion, expertise, reward)[3].

The theory of conflict transformation draws concepts from conflict management and conflict resolution. Conflict transformation is not an entirely new invention. Instead it is a re-conceptualisation of the field in order to make it more relevant to address contemporary conflicts. Different theoretical approaches used in conflict transformation practices, which offer different paradigms and mode of interventions from state and non-state, and internal and external actors.

Contemporary violent conflicts around the world are often asymmetric and marked by inequalities of power and status. Many of them are protracted, politically and economically backed by international powers. Protracted conflicts warp the societies, economies and regions in which they are situated, creating complex emergencies, fuelled on the one hand by local struggles and on the other by global factors such as the arms trade and support for regimes or rebels by outside states (BHCT, 2003).

Berghof's Handbook *for Conflict Transformation* (2003) highlights that conflict management theorists see violent conflicts as an ineradicable consequence of differences of values and interests between conflicting parties. The propensity for violence arises from existing power distribution patterns and historical relationships. The conflict management theory highlights that complete resolution of violent conflicts may not be immediately feasible and therefore the best way is to manage and contain them, and work to reach a compromise in which violence may cease and start to rebuild normal relations.

Conflict management is an art of appropriate intervention into a conflict situation to achieve acceptable settlements by those actors who have power and resources to exert pressure on the conflicting parties in order to settle the conflict. It is also the art of designing appropriate institutions to guide the inevitable conflict into appropriate channels (BHCM, 2003). Bloomfield and Reilly state, "*Conflict management is the positive and constructive handling of difference and divergence. Rather than advocating methods for removing conflict, [it] addresses the more realistic question of managing conflict: how to deal with it in a constructive way, how to bring opposing sides together in a cooperative process, how to design a practical, achievable, cooperative system for the constructive management of difference*"

(Bloomfield and Reilly, 1998:18). However, conflict resolution scholars do not emphasise the power aspect of conflict. They argue that in communal and identity conflicts people often do not compromise on their fundamental identity and needs. In such a situation, it is only possible to transcend conflicts through proper facilitation.

Therefore, emphasis of conflict resolution is on mediation by skilful and neutral third parties to facilitate new thinking and improved relationships between conflicting parties. Hence the role of facilitators and mediators is crucial. They explore root causes of the conflict and identify creative and acceptable solutions that the parties in conflict may have missed in their commitment to entrenched positions. Therefore, conflict resolution is a way of intervention that helps to move from lose-lose and destructive outcomes to win-win and constructive outcomes. The aim of the conflict resolution is to develop processes and generate options that are acceptable to parties in conflict.

As discussed elsewhere in this book, conflict transformation is far wider than conflict resolution and conflict management. Conflict transformation fundamentally constitutes peace building. Conflict transformation theories highlight that contemporary conflicts require more than reframing of positions and the identification of win-win outcomes. Conflict transformation scholars lay emphasis on the process of engaging conflicting parties and transforming the relationships, interests, discourses and structure of society that supports the continuation of violence. Conflict transformation endorses the role of constructive conflict, which is a catalyst for social change. In the conflict transformation perspective, conflicting parties, people affected by the conflict and outsiders engage to play complementary roles for achieving long-term peace building.

Conflict transformation uses a comprehensive and holistic approach that emphasises collective efforts of all stakeholders to transform conflict into peace through continuous efforts. In this context, Lederach writes, 'Conflict transformation must actively envision, include, respect, and promote human and cultural resources from within a given setting. This involves new perspective, which does not see the people as the problem and the outsider as the solution. Rather, we understand the long-term goal of transformation as validating and building on people and resources within the setting' (Lederach, 1995).

As mentioned earlier, conflict transformation theories have been built upon different conceptual building blocks borrowed from many other disciplines. The notion of conflict formation is one of the conceptual building blocks drawn from the work of the European structural theorists like Senghaas (1973) and Krippendorf (1973), who had analysed conflict formation process and conditions. Later Galtung (1996) did substantial work on building conflict transformation bringing economy, religion, politics and sociology together.

Galtung (1996) argues that once emerged, conflicts pass through a series of transformational processes, i.e., articulation or dis-articulation, conscientisation or de-conscientisation, complexificaticn or simplification, polarisation or depolarisation, escalation or de-escalation. Incompatibilities arise between conflicting parties can be overcome by transcending the contradiction, or by compromise, or by deepening or widening the conflict structure, and by associating or dissociating the actors (ibid: 116). Galtung (1996), Krippendorf (1973) and Curle (1971) emphasise the ever-growing global asymmetric relationships as the structural source of conflict around the world. Asymmetric relationships can be transformed through a shift from unbalanced to balanced relationships, through a process of conscientisation, confrontation, negotiation and development (BHCT, 2003).

The non-violence theory is another building block of conflict transformation (Sharp 1973; Wehr, Burgess and Burgess 1994; Clark 2000). A non-violent campaign transforms conflict by detaching from violence and harnessing conciliation, co-operation and exploring peaceful alternatives. The conflict transformation theory enforces practitioners to address root causes of the violent conflict such as basic needs, governance, identity, security and economic development (Azar, 1990; Azar and John, 1986).

Vayrynen vividly highlights the importance of conflict transformation theory in handling conflict in society. He writes, 'The bulk of conflict theory regards the issues, actors and interests as given and on that basis makes efforts to find a solution to militate or eliminate contradictions between them. Yet the issues, actors and interests change over time as a consequence of the social, economic and political dynamics of societies' (Vayrynen 1991:4).

Table 2.3 gives an overview of his perspective in conflict transformation and peace building:

TABLE 2.3: Vayrynen's Approach to Conflict Transformations

Areas of transformation	*Illustration*	*Details*
Context transformation	Change in the international or regional environment	
Actor transformations	Internal changes in parties, or the appearance of new parties	Changes of leadership changes of goals intra-party change change in party's constituencies changing actors
Issue transformations	Altering the agenda of conflict issues	Transcendence of contested issues constructive compromise changing issues de-linking or re-linking issues
Rule transformations	Changes in the norms or rules governing a conflict	
Structure transformations	The entire structure of relationships and power distribution in the conflict is transformed.	Change from asymmetric to symmetric conflict change in power structures changes of markets of violence
Elite transformation	Alter elite structures to more equal social structures	Change in perspective, change of mind and heart, change in will and gesture of conciliation

Source: Adapted from Vayrynen 1991, BHCT, 2003.

Context transformations refer to changes in the context of conflict that may radically alter each party's perception of the conflict situation, as well as their motives. For example, end of the Cold War and the establishment of the World Diamond Council have changed the rules of the diamond trade to outlaw 'conflict diamonds', that could well have a significant impact on the conflicts in Sierra Leone and Angola.

Structural transformations refer to changes in the basic structure of the conflict that is to the set of actors, issues and incompatible goals, conflicting beliefs or relationships, or to the society economy or state within which the conflict is embedded. Asymmetric conflicts cannot be transformed without changing the unbalanced and contested relationships that lie at their roots. For example, the Anti-Apartheid

Movement in South Africa helped to press the case for dis-investment by foreign-owned businesses well before the end of the apartheid regime. Many recent conflicts in West Africa have demonstrated the futility in attempting conflict transformation without addressing the economic interests that fuel wars.

Actor transformations include decisions on the part of actors to change their goals or alter their general approach to conflict. This would include decisions to seek peace or to initiate a peace process. They also include changes on leadership, often crucial to the securing of transformation in conflicts. Finally, they include changes in the situation of the public constituencies and supporters of the respective political leaders.

Issue transformations focus on the positions that parties take on key issues at the heart of the conflict as well as the way in which parties redefine or reframe those positions in order to reach compromises or resolutions. A good example of issue transformation was the decision by the Unionist Party in Northern Ireland to accept a de-linking of the decommissioning issue from the question of the convocation of the Northern Ireland Assembly. Another recent example is the Israeli decision to contemplate a degree of Palestinian autonomy within areas of Jerusalem.

Rupesinghe (1995, 1998), based on his work, also prefers a comprehensive, eclectic approach to conflict transformation that embraces multi-track interventions. Rupesinghe (1998) focuses on building peace constituencies at the grass-roots level across the civil society level, and also creating peace alliances with business communities, professional groups, the media, and the security forces, political parties, etc. He sees conflict transformation as a broad approach incorporating conflict resolution training and Track I interventions including diplomatic interventions and peacekeeping.

Fishers and Keashly (1991) argue that the nature of intervention should be matched to the stage of the conflict. In the early stages of conflict, facilitation may be appropriate; but when a conflict has reached a high stage of polarisation power-based mediation (or even coercion) is required.

2.4 DIFFERENT APPROACHES OF DEALING WITH CONFLICT

Peace and conflict transformation theories are complex and multidisciplinary in nature and generated from different disciplines such as anthropology, international law, psychology, philosophy, sociology, international relations, political science, economics, etc. There is no one predominant discipline in peace studies. Peace studies focus on conflict and its management as a generic social phenomenon (BHCT, 2003).

Contemporary conflict transformation and peace research largely devotes to the analysis of causes and consequences of armed or violent conflicts (Bercovitch and Rubin, 1992). Ontologically, peace studies are based on the subjectivist and the objectivist approaches. The subjectivist approach mainly focuses on minimising the perceived incompatibility of goals of the conflicting parties. The objectivist approach basically focuses on searching compatibility of goals of the conflicting parties to have peace and minimise misinformation, misunderstanding, or misperceptions such as stereotypes, mistrust and emotional stress, structurally unfair or unjust relationships and structure of society (ibid). However, in practice the distinction between subjectivity and objectivity is difficult to demarcate in conflict transformation and peace study, as the 'objective' researcher could understood a social structure is violent as against to the perception of the conflicting parties, based on subjective values and criteria of the researcher.

Similarly, the objectivist approach cannot be value-free, as it only reflects subjective assessment by someone (Woodhouse, 1991). Exclusive reliance on either a subjectivist or objectivist framework alone cannot capture the essence of peace studies. Hence, it is more pragmatic to combine subjectivist and objectivist approaches. The following three methods are commonly used in analysing conflict (Bell et al., 1989):

1. **Interpretative analysis**: It is empirical in nature and describes how people behave: how they perceive uncertainties, accumulate evidence, and update perceptions; how they learn and adapt their behaviour; why they think the way they do. Interpretative analysis is mainly used by social scientists to analyse conflict without influencing the behaviour of people.
2. **Abstractive analysis:** It deals with how idealised, rational persons act. This analysis is more common in behavioural analysis of individuals involved in conflict. Psychologists often use this method.
3. **Prescriptive analysis**: It is more advisory in nature and focuses on what people should do to make better choices, what thoughts,

decision aids, conceptual schemes and methodology are useful, not for idealised, mythical people, but for normal people (Bell et al., 1989; Kremenyuk, 1991). It is evaluated by its pragmatic value (i.e. ability to help people to make better decisions).

In peace study, different activity tracks are commonly used. Activities in Track I approach range from official and non-coercive measures, such as good offices, fact-finding missions, facilitation, negotiation/mediation and peacekeeping, to more coercive measures, such as power-mediation, sanctions, peace-enforcement and arbitration (BHCT, 2003). In contrast to Track I, Track II approach refers to all non-official and non-coercive activities such as 'facilitation' or 'consultation'.

The difference between Tracks I and II is the use of strategies. However, some features of both Tracks complement each other and sometimes even overlap in practice. For example, in Northern Ireland during the early 1990s Track I approach adopted by the former British Secretary of State of Northern Ireland had overlapped with the Track II activities of the Community Relations Council (CRC) (Bloomfield, 1997). Track III approach is a new discourse in conflict transformation and peace study. This approach refers to all process- and structure-orientated initiatives undertaken by civil society actors involved in grass-roots capacity building, trauma work, human rights and development work, and humanitarian assistance (ibid).

In these days, some scholars-practitioners have introduced the 'multi-track approach' to adequately capture the richness of peace

BOX 2.3 Multi-Track Diplomacy

A pioneer of this concept, the Institute for Multi-Track Diplomacy identified 9 separate tracks that must work together in creating a peaceful society. They are:

- Track 1: government
- Track 2: conflict resolution professionals
- Track 3: business
- Track 4: private citizens
- Track 5: research, training and education
- Track 6: activism
- Track 7: religious
- Track 8: funding
- Track 9: public opinion/communication (media)

Source: Diamond and McDonald (1996: 4-5).

building activities and efforts at different levels (Track 1, II and Track III). The concept of multi-track diplomacy was developed in the early 1990s in recognition that establishing sustainable peace requires the involvement of many different parts of society, and not just governments ("Track One") (Diamond and McDonald, 1996).

Since the early 1990s, an appropriate analytical focus on inter-relatedness and interdependence has emerged in conflict and peace study. It stresses on an integrative and complementary approach (Prein, 1994).

In the context of different track approaches, Berghof's *Handbook for Conflict Transformation* (BHCT) highlights that 'these complementary and integrative approaches not only shed a different light on the dichotomy of Track I and Track II strategies, but also provide orientation and new insights into the various complexities of contemporary violent conflict situations and peace building activities. It is crucial to make a more conscious combination of different actors with conflict management activities and strategies. These must be properly matched with the political and social priorities, which will arise at the different stages of conflict and de-escalation'.

A 'contingency model' of Fisher and Keashley (1991) highlights that the greater the level of conflict escalation, the intervention must be more direct and strong in order to be effective. The contingency model has two implications; first, that some peace-building activities will be more critical at some stages rather than at others; and second, that practitioners may need to return to an earlier stage of conflict management strategies as they gauge the progress of their peace building activities (Bercovitch, 1996).

Lederach (1997), Curle (1971), Burton and Dukes (1990) and Galtung (1996) are some of the pioneer scholar-practitioners working in the field of conflict transformation and peace building research and analysis (BHCT, 2003). The work of Burton and Dukes (1990) had focused on 'horizontal' relationships, i.e. the dialogue and cooperation between conflicting parties of relatively equal status. However, building dialogue and cooperation between actors of unequal status, i.e., vertical relationships are more important and difficult in armed conflicts like the Maoist rebellion in Nepal. Conflict transformation approach addresses to improve vertical as well as horizontal relations (Lederach, 1997).

TABLE 2.4 Different Approaches, Actors and Strategies in Conflict Transformation and Peace Building

Approaches	*Main actors*	*Main strategies*
Track I	Political and military leaders as mediators and or representatives of conflict parties	Outcome-orientated, From official and coercive measures like sanctions, arbitration, 'power mediation' to non-coercive measures like facilitation, negotiation / mediation, fact-finding missions and 'good offices'
Track II	From private individuals, academics, professionals, 'civil mediation', 'citizens diplomacy' to international and local non-governmental organisations involved in conflict resolution	Process-orientated, Non-official and non-coercive measures mainly facilitation / consultation in form of problem-solving workshops and round tables
Track III	From local grass-roots organisations to local and international development agencies, human rights organisations and humanitarian assistance	Process- and or structure-orientated, Capacity building, trauma work, grass-roots training, development and human rights work
Multi-Track	All stakeholders of the conflict act to building peace by complementing each others	Process as well as outcome oriented-combination of efforts of all stakeholders to achieve durable peace

Source: Adapted from BHCT, 2003.

A successful conflict transformation strategy must include Multi-Track approach in the peace building process that focuses on those most affected by the effects of violent conflict (Lederach, 1997). Lederach argues that potential for peace building always exists in any conflict situation. Such potentials depend upon the particular region or community and existing culture of society in conflict (Lederach, 1999; 1995). Existing traditional conflict resolution approaches could also contribute to solve the bloody conflict. For example, clan members in Somalia exert their traditional authority over the conflicting parties to settle conflict and accept an agreement.

Conflict transformation through Track III approach is mainly based on the conceptual framework of non-violent action, which was put forward by Sharp (1973), Ghandi (1938 and 1950), King (1967) and other peace theorists and leaders. Non-violent theories are based on different religious convictions and ideologies, values and commitments. In this theory, conflict is a *non-violent struggle for social justice and change, as Gandhi did in India. The notion of n*on-violent actions for social change brings tensions and contradictions to the surface that already exists in society but are denied and covered up (McCarthy and Sharp, 1997).

Both Track I and Track II approaches of conflict resolution do not emphasise civic engagement and therefore third party intervention does not result in proper conflict transformation. Neither Track I nor Track II approaches alone are sufficient to transform complex nature and dynamics of armed conflict like the Maoist insurgency in Nepal. Conflict transformation and peace-building activities in the context of the Maoist insurgency in Nepal need a multi-track approach, linking with domestic peace constituencies in an integrative and complementary way.

Peace-building activities and strategies must be focused on long-term reconciliation and social justice that can be facilitated through a multi-track approach. Exclusive reliance on one approach of conflict management often fails to effectively deal with complex and protracted conflicts like the one in Nepal. Hence, integrating and synthesising Track I, II and III activities at practical and theoretical levels are essential to transform conflict into peace. Integrating these approaches to conflict transformation is getting less attention. Similarly, different theoretical approaches such as empowerment theory, human needs theory and non-violent theory are not fully applied in peace building.

Different approaches such as conflict settlement, conflict management, and conflict transformation are common in conflict study. The conflict settlement approach focuses on logic of management, and it is strongly associated with paradigm of power politics. Especially in the early work conducted in the field of conflict management, scholars tended to focus on identifying differences than discovering similarities between schools of thought, as the discussion about the conflict settlement vs. conflict resolution approaches (BHCT, 2003). Dichotomies such as objectivist vs. subjectivist interpretations of conflict, conflict settlement vs. conflict resolution are still dominating the field of conflict studies. However, it is too simplistic to use such a framework in transforming conflict into peace.

As discussed above, conflict transformation is a long-term, multi-track and dynamic process, which effectively combines Track I, II and III approaches and short-, middle-, and long-term goals. Hence, it brings a wide variety of actors, including official, military and political leaders (Track I); informal conflict resolution experts and (I)NGOs working in conflict resolution (Track II); grass-roots, indigenous NGOs providing development cooperation and humanitarian assistance (Track III) (BHCT, 2003). It focuses on peace building in terms of outcome, process and content of social justices. On the outcome level, conflict transformation aims to achieve a settlement on substantive issues related to needs and fears raised by the conflicting parties. Obtaining this outcome requires appropriate process. Hence a process-oriented approach has to be used to change mutually negative conflict attitudes and values among parties in order to increase cooperation and communication between them. The conflict transformation approach is a change-orientated approach, it emphasises on creating a new political and social infrastructure for empowerment and recognition of underprivileged groups, dalits, ethnic minorities, etc. to foster enabling social justice. Satisfaction of basic needs on the personal and relational levels will not be sufficient. Rather, efforts have to be made to achieve equal access to resources and assemble the infrastructure that will make it possible to address structural inequalities with the aim of longer-term social reconstruction and reconciliation. Hence conflict transformation needs to ensure human security (physical, mental, psychological, social, economic security).

2.4.1 Political approach

The political approach is one of the most appropriate and commonly used in the high intensity conflict and civil wars. To effectively resolve the conflict, all other approaches need to be guided, commanded and decided within the framework of political approach. The decision of use of force, ceasefires, negotiation, state restructuring and addressing root causes of the conflict has to come from within this framework. Other activities include political party building and democratisation of political parties; promotion of civic organisations, establishing independent oversight bodies, strengthening political institutions, establishing, promoting and reforming anti-corruption commission, election commission and human rights commission; promoting roles of parliamentary committees and parliament; power sharing mechanism (e.g., all party government, fair allocation of power and resource); promoting decentralisation and strengthening democratic governance, peace talks, etc. (Dahal, 2004; Bercovitch, and Rubin, 1992; Upreti, 1004b; Lund, 1996; Fisher et al., 2000; Bercovitch, 1996; Bercovitch and Wells, 1993).

2.4.2 Diplomatic approaches

Another important approach of conflict resolution is diplomacy. At the time of war, generally diplomatic efforts concentrate on two fronts. They are:

1. War diplomacy: concentrating diplomatic efforts to obtain arms and weapons, military assistances, building coercive alliances, accepting use of external forces and military interferences, etc.); and
2. Peace diplomacy (diplomatic efforts devoted to peace enforcement, creating international peace support groups, stopping arm supply, exerting pressure for ceasefires and negotiations, inviting peace experts, activists and scholars to promote peace agenda in country, etc. (BHCT, 2003; Fisher et al., 2000; Lund, 1996; Fisher and Ury, 1981; Fisher and Keashly, 1991).

2.4.3 Economic Approach

The economic approach is one of the main interventions in conflict transformation. It includes economic development assistance in the conflict-affected areas, economic policy reforms, trade promotions (export and import), market creation, high investment in basic services (such as education, health, drinking water, etc.), rural infrastructures development and rural investment, inter-community trade promotion, promotion of private investment, aid conditionality and economic sanctions, modernisation of agriculture, land reform (land consolidation, assuring land entitlement to tenants and land less, defining land ceiling, land-use classification), rural entrepreneurship development, commercialisation of prospects of bio-diversity, rural people's access to and benefit sharing in natural resources (such as land, forest, water, mines, etc.) and public resources, etc. (Fisher *et al.*, *2000*; Lund, 1996; Fisher and Keashly, 1991; Fisher 1997)

2.4.4 Judicial or legal approach

Judicial approach of conflict transformation is not much in debate in Nepal. Global experiences have demonstrated that judicial or legal approach plays crucial role in resolving conflict and sustaining peace (Lederach, 1999). Common areas involved in this approach are commissions of inquiry, war crime tribunals, strengthening and promotion of indigenous and customary legal institutions and practices, court reform, judicial and legal oversight of security sector, easy access to justice, punishment to wrong doers, constitutional commission, arbitration, adjudication, and legal aid to poor, etc (Lund, 1996; Fisher *et al.*, 2000; Fisher, 1997).

2.4.5 Combination of informal and formal methods

The experiences of other war-torn countries of Africa, Asia, Eastern Europe and South America ((Armon and Carl, 1996; Armon and Philipson, 1998; Barnes, 2002; Crandall, 2004; Lucima, 2002; Galtung, 2000 a and b; Galtung, 2004a and b; Crandall, 2004; Hendrikson, 1998; Misra, 2002; Armon, *et al.,* 1997; McCartney, 1999; Stankovitch, 1999 and Bloomfield and Reilly 1998) have demonstrated that successful conflict management requires combining formal and informal approaches to make them more effective and result oriented. No single approach is enough in the context of complicated violent conflict.

Interest based mediation and strengthening indigenous conflict resolution; supporting and strengthening legal institutions; establishment and expansion of conflict research and prevention centres and peace commissions; promoting human rights and peace monitors; creating and mobilising peace support groups; inviting eminent personalities peace activists and (such as Nelson Mandela, Nobel peace laureates, etc.); organisation of massive peace rallies and non-violent campaigns and round table conferences; exchange visits and learning; civil fact finding meetings are some of the common informal and unofficial methods of conflict transformation (Lederach, 1999; BHCT, 2003; Fisher et al., 2000; Lund, 1996) that Nepal needs to promote to restore democratic peace in this country.

2.4.6 Media, communication and awareness approach

Media plays a crucial role in both escalation and resolution of conflict. Lack of communication or misinformation, or distorted communication often contributes to escalate conflict. Over exaggerating the fights, killings, brutalities and underplaying the peace initiatives, reconciliatory activities contribute to worsening conflict. A general tendency of the media is to catch audiences with negative sides, sensational news and views. Instead, if the media adopts a code of conduct to discourage sensational news that promotes escalation it would contribute to resolving conflict. The media, communication and awareness approach includes expansion of peace programme in radio and televisions, code of conduct for sensational news, professionalisation of media, mass scale peace training to journalists, civic education, incorporation of peace education on curriculum, peace campaign, exchange visits and creation of peace network, declaring certain areas as zone of peace (e.g., schools, religious areas, public areas, roads, etc), massive training and awareness campaign to train politicians, civil society leaders, journalists, teachers, bureaucrats, business people, in conflict transformation, peace building, etc.

2.4.7 Human rights approach

Human rights violence is one of the major impacts of armed conflict. Human rights violence and intensity of armed conflicts are positively correlated because human rights violation is high at the time of escalation of armed conflict and it human rights are protected the arrogance of the armed conflict is less. Therefore, prevention of human rights and civil liberties at the time of escalated armed conflict is a global priority. The international community, human rights activists and bilateral land multilateral donors show deep concern on the violation of human rights. They appeal to respect human rights covenants, principles, and standards (collectively known as human rights laws). The main reason of such appeals is to prevent human rights violation that ultimately helps to create a favourable environment for the negotiated settlement of the conflict. The international community had learnt the lessons form Rwandan genocide in 1994 that if it does not intervene in time, massacre and crime against humanity in a full-fledged civil war running country is highly probable. In this respect, the human rights approach is extremely important.

2.4.8 Military approach

In civil war and high intensity conflict, this is one of the most common approaches in dealing with conflict. It is characterised as a coercive approach because use of force is the core of this approach. However, this approach is not limited only to use of force. Common activities include use of preventive peacekeeping forces; military interventions in peace enforcement; control of arms and weapons proliferation; disarmament and demobilisation; early warning; training and professionalisation of armed forces; security sector reform and civilian oversights; contingency and alternate defence strategies; strengthening defence intelligence; creation of homeland security and expansion of network of security force (military, Para military and police forces); confidence building of security forces; military to military exchanges and visits; non-aggregation agreement; declaration of non-military and military zones; deterrence; armed embargoes and blockade; crisis management and response mechanisms; etc. (Fisher, 1993, 1997, Fisher et al., 2000; Lund, 1996; Fisher and Keashly, 1991).

2.5 NEGOTIATION AND MEDIATION IN CONFLICT RESOLUTION

Negotiation and mediation are two common methods widely used in conflict resolution practices. These two methods are discussed in the following section:

2.5.1 Negotiation

Negotiation is a voluntary process that deals with a conflict situation between the negotiating parties. Negotiation includes any instance in which two or more people meet face to face and communicate with each other for the purpose of influencing each other's decision, to reach a mutually acceptable solution of the conflict issue. Negotiation takes place between parties (maybe individuals, groups or organisations) to resolve incompatible goals. Hence, negotiation deals with diverse interests in conflicts (Pruitt and Carnevale, 1993). Negotiation clarifies conflict situations. People have different and often conflicting interests and objectives. Therefore, negotiation is part of the problem-solving processes (Gulliver, 1979). Some recent authors (Upreti, 2002a; Buckles 1999) argue that the role of negotiation is increasingly widening and is not only limited to CM but it is also becoming a wider methodological principle and basis of organising broader participatory development efforts. The purpose of negotiation is to discover mutually acceptable outcomes in disputes through the means of persuasion or inducement. Gulliver (1979) explains that patterns of interactive behaviour in negotiation are essential despite marked differences in interests, ideas, values, rules and assumptions among negotiators of different societies. He argues that a fuller understanding of the negotiation process will be achieved when it is considered in its full socio-cultural context. Therefore, he focuses his attention on the process of negotiation, recognising that a conflict and its negotiation occur in broad cultural contexts and in social institutions. He compares joint decision-making (negotiation) by seeking common patterns that characterise interactive behaviour with adjudication or unilateral decision-making (using third party judges to adjudicate disputes).

Negotiation can be categorised into two distinct forms i.e. distributive and integrative. Characteristics of distributive negotiation are to focus more on resource distribution (win-lose). The attitude of negotiating parties is firm with attention given to their own interests and a far-reaching consequence may be a lose-lose situation. Characteristics of integrative negotiation are to create resources (win-win situation) where negotiating parties are open to alternatives and also give attention to the interests of others, through participatory problem solving. It leads to a collective decision and commitments by the negotiating parties to achieve an optimally collective solution (Moscovici and Doise, 1994). This type of negotiation is more important. Integrative negotiation is a voluntary process in which conflicting parties meet face to face to reach a mutually acceptable solution.

Negotiations generally focus on the best alternative for a negotiated agreement, interest (issue, position and criteria), and process (they create a condition for effective problem solving). Existing power relationships play an important role in the negotiation process. Actor specific characteristics such as position, function and personality determine power relations in negotiation. The actual use of the power depends on the context.

Pruitt and Carnevale (1993) have distinguished five broad strategies useful in negotiation. They are:

1. Concession making (reducing goals/demands).
2. Contending (trying to persuade the other party to concede or trying to resist similar efforts by the other party).
3. Problem solving (trying to develop other alternatives).
4. Inaction (doing as little as possible by putting off meetings and talking around the issues).
5. Withdrawal (dropping out of the negotiation).

BATNA (best alternative to a negotiated agreement) is a term invented by Roger Fisher and William Ury (1981), which is popular in negotiation. Any negotiator should determine his or her BATNA before agreeing to any negotiated settlement. If the settlement is as good as or better than one's BATNA, the agreement should be accepted. If the alternative is better, it should be pursued instead of the negotiated settlement. When one party's BATNA is good, it is unlikely to be willing to enter into negotiations, preferring instead to pursue the alternative option. As a negotiation proceeds, constituent involvement strategies help negotiators involve their constituents in the process. This is critical, since constituents are less likely to accept an agreement that is obtained if they have not been involved in the process enough to understand why the agreement was designed and why it is the best alternative available.

2.5.2 Mediation

Mediation is a process of intervention in a conflict by an acceptable, impartial and neutral third party to assist contending parties in reaching an acceptable settlement of the conflict. Mediators have no decision-making authority. The mediator's neutral role as facilitator involves assisting parties, privately or collectively, to identify the issues in dispute and develop proposals to resolve them. Mediators may meet privately and hold confidential and separate discussions with the parties to a dispute. In some cases mediation may be compulsory under the terms of laws or court rules. In other cases it may be voluntary, by agreement of the parties. Some jurisdictions have rules requiring mediation of disputes at some point in the litigation process. Mediation helps parties seek to resolve their disputes in a manner, which avoids hostility and preserves an ongoing relationship.

Mediation holds an important place in CM because it is a problem-solving approach and creates opportunities for mutually benefiting resolution. According to Bush and Folger (1994a), mediation has the potential to change the people themselves who are in the very midst of conflict, giving them both a greater sense of their own efficacy and greater openness to others. Mediation has transformative potential for recognition and empowerment (Bush and Folger, 1994b). It makes agreement possible, which the disputants find satisfactory and improves their relationships. Mediation focuses on reframing the process of changing how a person or party to a conflict conceptualises his, hers or another's attitude, behaviour, issues and interests and how a situation is defined (ibid.). In the procedural context, mediation involves a third party who makes it possible for conflicting parties to reach an agreement. The role of mediators is important in discerning interests from positions, reframing issues, and questions, giving fair consideration to different opinions, assisting in finding mutual gain and solutions and writing up an agreement in a contractual language for its effective implementation (Pendzich et al., 1994).

Mediation is a method of conflict resolution that is carried out by an intermediary who works with the disputing parties to help them improve their communication and their analysis of the conflict situation, so that the parties can themselves identify and choose an option for resolving the conflict that meets the interests or needs of all of the disputants. Unlike arbitration, where the intermediary listens to the arguments of both sides and makes a decision for the disputants, a mediator will help the disputants design a solution themselves. In some cases, mediators play a problem-solving role focused upon negotiating an agreement to the immediate dispute. In other cases mediation focuses more upon improving relationships, with the assumption that the improved relationship will lead to conflict resolution or constructive confrontation. Historically, mediation is one of the most common indigenous methods of conflict resolution. The following are some important principles of mediations:

- Mediation is an art and a science
- Conflict is not inherently destructive
- Mediators are neutral
- Mediation requires the consent from the parties in the conflict
- Mediators do not impose or prescribe solutions
- Separate mediation from advocacy and enforcement.

2.6. STRATEGIC OPTIONS IN DEALING WITH CONFLICT

Resolution of conflict is a complex and dynamic process and a blueprint method may not be applicable to all conflict. It requires wide ranges of strategies, tactics, procedures and options. Global experiences of conflict resolution show that there are several strategies used in different armed conflicts in different parts of the world. Some of them are:

2.6.1 Strategy of accommodation

If the conflicting parties give priority to relationships and keep goal as secondary, they prefer accommodation strategy. Accommodation is basically a relation-centred strategy and the party does not resist or oppose the saying or demand of other party at the cost of relation. Generally parties in the conflict show characteristics such as agree, appease, smoothing over, give up disagreement, positive to other's information and controlling behaviour. Hence, in the high intensity conflict situation, this strategy may not realistically be the best one.

2.6.2 Strategy of avoiding

If conflicting parties are not much concerned either with relations or goals, they adopt this strategy. They want to avoid, flee, deny, delay, ignore or even withdraw the issues of contentions. Parties in conflict avoid interring into dialogue and settling the conflict (Fisher, 1993, 1997; Fisher and Keashly, 1991). This is not applicable in most of the high intensity conflicts.

2.6.3 Strategy of compromise

This is the most pragmatic and widely used strategy in settling any type of conflict (ranging form family conflict to organisational conflict, to civil war to international conflict). In this strategy, the very basic principle is "I will give some if you do the same". The dynamics involved in this strategy involves reducing own expectations; use soft and continuous bargaining; explore the differences and alternative options; ready to give up some, engage continuously in dialogue. In this strategy, the parties in conflict become very calculative, cautious and open. They give equal importance to maintaining relations and achieving goals.

2.6.4 Strategy of confrontation

This is a coercive strategy and one party does not bother at all about the relations with other party. The aim is to confront to achieve goal. Use of force, pressure, sanctions, detentions, etc. are often common. The conflicting parties do not show any accommodative behaviour and are not ready to recognise the other party as credible to initiate dialogue.

2.6.5 Strategy of controlling

This strategy is slightly softer than confrontation, but it also aims to focus only on goals and does not give consideration to relationships. The guiding principle in this strategy is: 'I do it in my own way, and don't bother about the interests of other party'. Hence, the courses of action are competition, use of force, fight, distortion and manipulation of information, etc. and they are not patient with dialogue, discussion and negotiation (Fisher, 1993, 1997; Fisher and Keashly, 1991).

2.6.6 Strategy of problem solving

In the conflict management efforts, problem solving is said to be the most desired strategy because of its conceptual basis of 'collective action to solve the problem'. Hence, both parties have high commitment in solving the problem with a win-win result. It seeks to bring all conflicting parties together to settle the problem. The main foci in this strategy are exploring alternative options, engage in continuous dialogue, gather required information and analyse properly. Parties in conflict seek concerted efforts form all stakeholders of the conflict.

2.6.7 Strategy of inaction

In some cases one of the conflicting parties does not bother about the conflict or they deliberate distance from proactive response. The main aim of the 'strategy of inaction' is to make another party passive or avoid getting entangled into conflict so it may turn into a passive form of conflict. This strategy is commonly used in family or low intensity social conflict.

2.7 CONCLUSION

This chapter has briefly presented some theoretical and conceptual bases of conflict transformation and peace building, different approaches, strategies and methods of conflict transformation and peace building. Finally, this chapter discussed the social characteristics of armed conflict with especial reference to Nepal. An informed debate in conceptualising conflict transformation and peace building is badly needed in Nepal. Without proper understanding of the theoretical dimensions and formulating conceptual framework, it is extremely difficult to properly operationalise conflict transformation and peace building, as theories and concepts inform actions. In this chapter, some efforts have been made to provide conceptual understanding that will enhances capabilities of the actors and stakeholders to implement conflict transformation and peace-building efforts.

NOTES

1. A detail elaboration of theories, concepts, approaches and methods of conflict transformation and peace building are presented by the author in a separate book entitled 'Dunda Byabasthan ka Sidanta ra Bidhi haru: Eka Parichaya (Theories and Practices of Conflict Management: An Introduction), Kathmandu: Bhrikuti Academic Publishers.
2. For details, see Scimecca (1993), *Theory and Alternative Dispute Resolution. A Contradiction in Terms?* In: Sandole and van der Merwe 1993, pp. 211-221.
3. For further details, see Bercovitch, "The Structure and Diversity of Mediation in International Relations" in Bercovitch and Rubin 1992, pp. 10-21.

CHAPTER 3

Local Approaches of Conflict Management

3.1. INTRODUCTION

This chapter deals with some of the approaches and practices used by local people to resolve social conflict. Nepal had a rich tradition of resolving family conflicts, social conflict and religious conflict locally with its own strategies and methods (Upreti, 2001; Oli, 1998; New Era, 1988). However, these practices are not getting enough attention. The Maoist armed conflict that started in February 1996 further contributed to the disappearance of local methods and practices of conflict resolution mainly because they introduced their own legal system that replaced the traditional ones.

Conflict experts and scholars argue that traditional approaches can contribute in resolving conflict and crisis (Galtung, 1996, 2000b; 1950, 1938; King, 1963). In Nepal the formal approaches of conflict resolution failed to reach a negotiated settlement of the ongoing armed conflict even after six rounds of talks between the government and the insurgents in 2001 and 2003 peace talks. In this context, there are arguments that Nepal has not yet fully exhausted all traditional approaches of conflict mediation and it is essential to assess the potential of existing traditional approaches before entering into a debate on the need of third party mediation. Therefore, this chapter attempts to examine the practices and capabilities of traditional approaches of conflict management in Nepal.

The aim of this chapter is to discuss strategies and practices of local people dealing with conflict they face in their daily life and draws some lessons based on those observations. This chapter is based on the primary information collected from Surkhet, Ramechhap, Dolakha, Saptari, Sankhuwasawa, Dhankuta, Sunsari, Kaski, Doti, Accham and Chitwan districts of Nepal. The analysis is also supported by secondary information.

3.2. TRADITIONAL APPROACHES OF CONFLICT RESOLUTION

Traditional approaches are widely used for conflict resolution in Nepal since historical time (Oli, 1998; Upreti, 2001; Bhandari and Pun, 2002). From the observation and documentation of local conflicts in the study areas, it is found that local conflicts are either related to appropriation, use, and control of locally available natural resources such as land, forest, water, minerals, or family matters (issues related to polygamy, alimony, partition of parental property, etc.) or social issues (related to lending and borrowing, religious discrimination, etc.). In addition, increasing numbers of local conflicts are related to political prejudices and revenges. Therefore, traditional approaches are mainly used to resolve these conflicts. Traditional practices are mainly informal but sometimes endorsed by formal system. Formal practices involve official procedures, government's rules, regulations and laws and lead by government employees, for example, courts, police officers, administrators, etc. (Upreti, 2001). On the contrary, informal practices are locally developed and enforced by communities, may or may not follow the government's rules and regulations and procedures and are led by local people. The author has extensively documented that in traditional approaches two or more parties working together to examine their interests and needs, and working out a solution that will give the best possible outcome to both sides (Upreti, 2002a, 2004a, 2004j, 2004i).

My earlier research (Upreti, 2004i, 2004d, 2004e, 2001, 1998) revealed that the possibility of successfully negotiating an agreement can be greatly increased when the local mediators understand the appropriate time and process for negotiation. In traditional approach, a trusted intermediary (often male members of community) plays an important role in helping the parties to communicate more effectively when the parties are unable to discuss or even communicate effectively with one another. Even when conflicts are being confronted, not resolved, local mediators help both parties deal with the issues more effectively than formal authority engaged in conflict.

Local mediators (in fact they are not only mediators but also leaders, negotiators, facilitators, initiators and sometimes decision makers) help the parties to reach an agreement. In some cases, mediators play a problem-solving role focused upon negotiating an agreement to the immediate conflict. In other cases, mediators focus more upon improving relationships, with the assumption that the improved relationship will lead to conflict resolution and harmony in community.

Indigenous organisations were instrumental in resolving social conflict in earlier centuries and decades. Nepalese history reveals that many social and family conflicts were resolved through indigenous organisations and locally granted positions (either by the rulers or by community members) such as *Gram, Panchali, Kulari, Yug, Arya Sangh, Birtawal, Mapchowk, Lingual, Bichari, Pancha-Bhaladmi, Praman, Dandadhish, Pancha-Kachhahari, Amal, Dware, Thari,,Mukhiya, Kachari, Jhankri emerged at different period of time.* "*Gram*" (a community organisation responsible for managing local issues and concerns) and *Kulari, Yug* were active in settling all local disputes, and performed other judicial functions, etc. (Bhandari and Pun, 2002; Upreti, 2004c). Traditional institutions at the time the *Lichhvi* period responsible for settling local issues and disputes were *Panchali* (a local mediator looking after social issues such as marriage), *Arya Sangh* (a religious committee to settle social and religious disputes), *Birtawal* (local elite having land entitlement from the rulers as recognition of services and established as socially recognised power at local level), *Lingual* (practices of settling disputes related to land and irrigation), "*Mapchowk*" (dealing with disputes between male and female), *Mukhiya* (village chiefs, generally male members) *Bichari* (local legal administrators, often mail members), *Pancha-Bhaladmi* (selected village elders to take decisions on local social issues and disputes), etc. to resolve disputes and perform other judicial and social functions (Upreti, 2004c; Sharma, 2004). During the *Malla* Period, indigenous dispute resolution institutions such as *Praman* (officials appointed by palace responsible for implementing decisions of the king) and *Dware* (officials appointed by palace responsible for screening and submitting cases to the king if they are not resolved locally) were responsible for settling local disputes. *Dandadhish* was an administrator appointed by the palace responsible for regulating the social system in a defined territory. During the Shah period, various traditional arrangements such as *Pancha-Kachhahari* (at the ruling period of Ram Shah), *Pancha* (five local elites designated from the community responsible for dealing with local disputes), *Dware*, *Thari*, *Birtawal* and *Mukhiya* (at the time of Prithivi Narayan Shah) and *Amal* (local revenue collector appointed by the rulers) in Terai and *Kachari* (local arbitration meeting attended by state's representatives and community) in hills (at the time of Rana regime) were active in dealing with dispute at community level (Upreti, 2001; Bhandari and Pun, 2002). In community, *Jhankri Pratha* (a type of faith healer practice to deal with some disputes) was another important institution in traditional dispute resolution (Upreti, 2002a). In this way, traditional conflict settlement practices are developing over time. Often these local organisations perform both state assigned tasks as well as community- related tasks. The indigenous conflict resolution exercises were widely accepted and respected in the community.

BOX 3.1 Example of Traditional Approach

In the process of documenting local mechanisms dealing with conflicts, I found a unique local provision in Surkhet (7-10 Nov. 2004). In an in-depth interview, recalling his memory of the past 7 decades, Mr Naina Singh Vishwokarma[1] said that local people were practising a special conflict resolution system called "Ghatu". "Ghatu" was a responsibility assigned to an individual (almost always to a man) by the community who has the trust of community and who specialises in dealing with social conflicts and the "Ghatu" was responsible for settling all local conflicts in his assigned territories. Local people engaged in conflicts go to "Ghatu" to complain. He invites other villagers, mainly neighbours, as 'witness' in the meeting and interrogates disputants to find the actual cause of the conflicts, inviting opinions of people gathered in the meeting. Local people arrange 'truth revealing materials' (having spiritual values) consisting of water-filled copper vessel, lightened oil-lamp, and flowers and invite disputants one by one to touch 'truth revealing materials' to ensure that the disputants are not giving rise to false causes of the conflict. Sometimes even witnesses are asked to touch the truth-revealing materials. Based on the expressions of the disputants in the public meeting and hearing the opinions of the people gathered, "Ghatu" gives his verdict. Most often, the disputants accept the decision to maintain their social relations (as all neighbours attending meeting ask to abide by the decision that often disputants cannot ignore), and fear of sin (as the disputants have to touch the spiritual truth revealing materials in the "Ghatu" gathering) if they do not abide by the decision. If one of the disputing parties disagreed with the decision of "Ghatu" or felt victim of the verdict, he or she was referred to '*Sarkari Adda*' (government office in Dailekh where *Badahakim* (an administrator appointed by the Kathmandu to administer the reason) resides. This arrangement was prevalent (in modified form) until the Panchayat regime.

Source: Upreti, 2004i; Upreti, et al., 2005.

Majhi, an indigenous community residing in the river belts of Tamakosi River, expanded from Dolakha district in the north to Ramechhap and Sindhuli districts in the south has a system of electing *Mijhar* as their leader to take care of his community, to settle conflicts and to guide youth and younger people. All members of the community respect his decision and instruction. This is one of the most organised societies in terms of leadership and resolving conflicts (Upreti, 2004i). Similar ethnic practices of conflict resolution can be found in other indigenous communities such as Jirel, Thami, Surel and Sunar in Sindhupalchowk, Dolakha, Ramechhap and Okhaldhunga. A study conducted in Sunsari and Saptari district of Eastern Terai by this author (2004n) revels that several ethnic groups mainly depended on natural resources such as *Sunaha*, *Khanwas*, *Mallahs*, *Bote*, *Mushahars*, *Bantar*, *Gongi*, *Mukhia*, *Dushad*, *Sahani*, *Kewat*, *Danuwars*, *Darai*, *Kumal*, *Barhamus*, *Dhangar*, *Pode*, *Kushars*, *Majhi* have their own ways and procedures of dealing with conflict. Often they do not inter into formal conflict resolution mechanism. The main reasons they expressed were their lack of trust in the formal system, which was administratively complicated and expensive.

Many severe conflict cases related to collecting grasses, firewood, driftwood, fishing, hunting and gathering were observed in Sunsairi and Saptari districts where indigenous communities[2] reside. All these conflicts were created by the Koshi Tappu wildlife reserve when it stopped the traditional ways of using local resources which is the main basis of livelihood of poorest people and indigenous communities. When the government park authority restricted and obstructed access to natural resources they were using since time immemorial, the conflict became inevitable. The same park authority, which has conflict with local indigenous people, has the legal mandate to punish local people and therefore it was abused. The park authority collaborates with a few rich landlords to manipulate the situation and exploit poor people.

The following are some of the main problems created by the park authority for poor people in the study areas, which is a constant source of conflict between the park authority[3] and local people and means of manipulation by park staff:

a. Destruction by wild animals:

Wild water buffaloes, wild boars and sometimes elephants have been regularly destroying the crops of the people. Women and men both have to guard their plantations, keeping awake at night. In case of attacks women have to rush around gathering children and household goods to save them while men attempt to defend themselves against the animals. But the park authority is not concerned with this issue, which is a cause of conflict.

b. Fishing Restrictions:

The occupational castes e.g. *Mallah, Godi, Sada, Bochi,* depending on fishing for their livelihood have no choice but to go to the reserve for fishing but the park authority prevents it. This is considered as a major livelihood threat by the community.

c. Restriction on collecting *patters (a type of grass)*:

Batar/Sardar women collect patter and make mattresses. Batar/Sardar men sell goods produced by their women. The problem is the restriction by the park authority to collect patter that ultimately ruins their basis of livelihood.

BOX 3.2 Common Wage Rate in the Study Area of Sunsairi and Saptari Districts

- Agricultural work is not available for more than 2 months for landless people. The daily labour wage rate in kind is 4 kg rice with one time lunch and snack for women and 8 kg rice with lunch and snacks for men. The wage is Rs 60 per day without lunch and snacks. The daily wage of skilled labour is generally Rs 100-150.
- Due to unavailability of work, majority of the young people leave for India (Delhi, Punjab and other areas) for six months. On an average, they earn Rs 1500-2000 per month. Adults from Muslim and hill communities also go to Arabian countries for the same purpose.
- Landless people occupy the public lands and lands owned by big landlords (usually lands of rich Rana family). However, they have no tenure rights over these lands.

Box 3.2 shows the situation of the poor people. When their livelihood bases are restricted without other alternatives, conflict is inevitable. However, the park authority is not taking this situation seriously. Though there is a much government-highlighted project called ‘Park People Programme’, which was renamed as ‘Participatory Conservation Programme’, its impact on poor people and indigenous community, according to local potential beneficiaries, is almost insignificant.

Traditional conflict-resolution approaches in Nepal are localised, cast- and ethnicity-specific, and shaped and guided by traditional norms, values, customs and religions. For example, in Kaski district, *Tamudhin* (*Gurung-ghar* earlier led by *Jimmual/mukhiya*), *Magar-samaj* and *Thakali-samaj* were active in settling community level conflicts (Bhandari and Pun, 2002). Likewise, *Mukhiya System* in Lower Mustang and *Raja system* in Upper Mustang are common arrangements of local conflict resolution. In Manag district, there was a *Dhapa system* (four village leaders elected by all the villagers for a year to deal with all village-level conflicts[4]) to effectively deal with conflict. In the traditional conflict- resolution systems, enforcement of the decision made by local mediators/negotiators is not the government regulations and state laws but social sanctions, religious faiths, morale and ethics (Khadka, 1997; Upreti, 2001).

3.3 PERFORMANCE OF FORMAL CONFLICT-RESOLUTION APPROACHES IN NEPAL

The performance of government-instituted bodies responsible for conflict resolution has been severely questioned by media, rights activists, advocacy organisations and individual scholars (Bhandari and Pun, 2002; Upreti, 2004i). Erosion of trust of these organisations is a major challenge. Several studies (Upreti, 2001; 2002; 2004b; 2004n; Khadka, 1997; Oli, 1998; New Era, 1988) show that different indigenous approaches have been in use at the community level to resolve social, family and transaction-related conflicts. In many cases, they were more effective, less expensive, administratively less complicated and easily accessible compared to the formal conflict-resolution provisions (Upreti, 2001).

A comparative study on the performance of formal and informal arrangements of conflict resolution conducted by this author in Dolakha district revels that 66 per cent respondents view the traditional arrangements as effective to resolve local conflict and 84 per cent respondents suggest reforming the existing state-sponsored formal conflict-resolution arrangements (Upreti, 2004b; 2001).

TABLE 3.1 Performance of Formal and Informal Systems Assessed by the Disputants

S.No.	*Performance*	*Formal system*		*Informal system*	
		Number	*%*	*Number*	*%*
1.	Good	10	5	50	25
2.	Satisfactory	30	15	100	50
3.	Poor	130	65	30	15
4.	I don't know/no comments	30	15	20	10
	Total	200	100	200	100

Source: Primary Data, 1998-2001, Upreti, 2004b.

From the observation of the data presented in Table 3.1 it is observed that only 5 per cent of 200 respondents assessing the performance of the formal conflict resolution system as 'good' compared to 25 per cent of the informal system. In fact, a vast majority (65 per cent) of the respondents concludes that the performance of formal conflict resolution system is poor and only 15 per cent respondents are satisfied. The remaining 15 per cent did not know or was not willing to comment on the performance of the government agencies. The reasons for 'no comment' expressed by some of the respondents were 'feeling risks' to talk against powerful District Administrative Office, courts, police and other semi-judicial offices such as district forest office, irrigation offices, etc. as government offices and officers do not want to listen their criticism. Sometimes they take it personally and revenge may be the ultimate result of such expressions.

In the other side, 50 per cent respondents are happy with the performance of informal system, 15 per cent are not satisfied and the remaining 10 per cent did not know or was not eager to comment. Table 3.1 indicates that the formal system does not win public trust and its credibility is questionable. The main reasons for loss of trust and credibility of government conflict-resolution institutions and mechanisms reported by the respondents were 'manipulations' by powerful elites and nexus of professional trouble makers, and corruption[5]. The informal system is believed to be more effective than the formal one. These 130 respondents who were not satisfied with the performance of formal system were asked to identify the major causes of under performance. This research confirms the findings of earlier research (Khadka, 1997, Kaplan, 1995; Oli, 1998; New Era, 1988).

TABLE 3.2 Factors Affecting Performance of Formal Practices

S.N.	*Reasons for poor performance*	*Response*					
		Yes		*No*		*Total*	*Remark*
		Number	*%*	*Number*	*%*		
1	Political interfere	120	92.3	10	7.7	130	Respondents gave up to five reasons. So the total number of responses is more than total respondents
2	Legal complications	100	76.9	30	23.1	130	
3	Inaccessible/ expensive	110	84.6	20	15.4	130	
4	Influence of money	100	76.9	30	23.1	130	
6	Elite bias decisions	115	88.5	15	11.5	130	
7	Lack of transparency	120	92.3	10	7.7	130	
8	Need for reform	130	100	-	-	130	

Source: Primary Data, 1998-2001, Upreti, 2004b.

Table 3.2 shows the result of the assessment by the respondents of factors affecting poor performance of formal conflict resolution mechanisms constituted by the government. This table indicates that 92 per cent respondents perceive 'political interference' and 'lack of transparency' as the two major causes of poor performance of the formal conflict resolution systems in Nepal. 'Legal complications' and 'influence of money (bribe)' are other main causes of poor performance of formal systems of conflict resolution for almost 77 per cent respondents. Similarly, 88 per cent believes that 'elite biased-decisions' as the main causes of under performance of formal system. Among the 130 respondents 85% feels that the formal process of conflict resolution is expensive and inaccessible to poor and powerless people. A unanimous agreement among all the respondents is urgent need of reform of the existing formal systems (Table 3.2). Other researchers (Pandey, 2001; Regmi, 2001; Oli, 1998) have also made similar observations on the issues of political interference, abuse of power, lack of transparency, etc.

TABLE 3.3 Forms of Corruption in Formal Conflict Resolution

Means used to win cases	*No*	*%*
Bribe[6]	70	35
Influence from political parties	80	40
Mobilisation of *afnomanchhe*[7]	*32*	*16*
Fair, without any illegal means	18	9
Total	200	100

Source: Primary Data, 1998-2000; Upreti, 2004b.

Table 3.3 presents intensity of corruption in conflict resolution. A total of 200 conflict case winners were asked to indicate the means they used to win their cases. Among them, 127 cases were related to lending and borrowing, use of fake documents, physical violence, damage of property, sexual abuse, polygamy, property partition. The remaining 73 cases were related to natural resources such as ownership, sharing of benefits from forest, use of water source, access to land, forest and water, ambiguous roles of users committees, etc. Only 9 per cent respondents won the cases without using any illegal means. The remaining 91 per cent used bribes, power or mobilised their *afnomanchhe*[8] to win conflict cases. Among the different means used, the most common was influence of political party of their affiliation (40 per cent) followed by bribes (35 per cent) and use of *afnomanchhe* (16 per cent). Bribes, political influence and mobilisation of network of relative were collectively used in more complicated cases such as land conflict, polygamy and sexual abuse. Local politicians illegally influence to resolve conflict related to water source, lending and borrowing, etc. in their favour. This confirms that fair judgement and real justice is in serious question in the existing formal conflict-resolution system.

It was observed that the relationships between professional troublemakers, power brokers, and government officials shape the course of conflict resolution in formal practices. Often, professional troublemakers negotiate between disputants and officials. The patterns of corruption such as abuse of authority, illegal pressure, lack of transparency, arbitrary exercise of power, etc. are often reported in Nepal (Pandey, 2001). The types of corruption discussed in this article have been long prevalent in the South Asia (Wade, 1981).

While conducting in-depth case study in the Koshi Tappu Wild Life Reserve (KTWR) area[9] from July 2003 to February 2004 for documenting local conflicts, I found that there is a strong relationship between indigenous communities and natural resources in terms of livelihood, culture, tradition and religion and spirituality. However, most often these relations have been ruined by external development interventions and formal interventions of conflict resolution. This study shows that traditional or customary rights of indigenous communities over local natural resources upon which their livelihood largely dependents are curtailed or overridden by the park authority. This intervention has created numerous local conflicts between the park authority and local communities that were later linked with the bigger

BOX 3.2 Mr Luton Chaudhari, 76, Dholbajaya Tole, Ward No 5, Prakashpur VDC

Earlier, we had full access to natural resources available in the present Koshi Tappu Wildlife Reserve (KTWR) area. At that time communities were taking care of managing these resources. When the KTWR was established in 1976, restrictions were imposed in collecting fire-wood, grasses, fishing, harvesting of Khar-Khadi, hunting, cultivating, even the local trails used for several decades were closed. After the KTWR, wild animals are damaging crops and property but there is no compensation. Our rights to manage and use these resources have been replaced by the Sarkari kanun (government's law = National Parks and Wildlife Conservation Act) and we are suffering. Many poor people are therefore against the abusive and manipulative act of park authority.

Shyam Prasad Dulal, 68 years, ward no 8, Odraha VDC

Many people whose lands were taken by the Reserve are not yet getting compensation. Even people are not allowed to cremate dead bodies in the riverbed of the Saptakoshi River inside the Reserve area where people were using it for centuries. Such activities of Reserve authorities have given rise to severe frustrations, and disputes.

Parbati Devi Mukhiya, 24 years, Mallah Tole, Ward no 3, Haripur VDC

We have very bad experiences in this area with the Reserve authority. Recently they manhandled Jangali Devi Mukhiya and forcibly took 23 kg of fishes from here. We are facing these types of problems with the Reserve frequently. It would be better for us to die from a single shut than to face such inhumane events repeatedly.

Source: Upreti, 2004i.

armed conflict. Box 3.2 demonstrates this tension.

The interventionist approach of the government is one of the perennial sources of conflict between the Reserve authority and local people. Since the national parks and other forms of protected areas came into existence, conflicts between park and people are mounting. Collecting grasses, firewood, driftwood, fishing, hunting and gathering, etc. were the main basis of livelihood of poorest people and indigenous communities but the restrictions imposed on and manipulation of these resources by the Reserve authorities have accelerated conflicts between local people and park authority. The respondents highlighted that after the Reserve authority has imposed several restrictions and prohibitions over their traditional pattern of use of natural resources, livelihood of local people is jeopardised and vulnerability is increased. The government removed several ethnic settlements from the present Reserve to establish the Reserve in B.S. 2031-32 (1975-76) but many of the displaced households did not even get compensation irrespective of formation of more than 12 Commissions by the government to settle the compensation issue. Such delay not only provided room for manoeuvre by the bureaucrats and local elite but also created enormous conflicts in the study areas. The key informants explained that those who had a strong network with influencing power centres and ruling elites received compensation of land in Sunsari district. However, many displaced people from Sunsari district are still without any compensation. These conflicts are now directly linked with the Maoist insurgency, as they use government's manipulation convincing victims to support their 'people's war'.

3.4 INFORMAL APPROACHES IN RESOLVING VIOLENT CONFLICT

The strengths and experiences of traditional approaches in Nepal mainly lie in the resolution of non-violent family, social and resources conflicts. Though they are engaged in small-scale low intensity violent conflict at local level, their potential to resolve national level armed conflict remains questionable.

As discussed elsewhere in this chapter, some of the common traditional approaches adopted in Nepal include the activities of *Dhami-Jhankri, Purohit*[10], *Mukhiya, Jimuwal,Bichari, Amal, Dware,Ghatu,* local leaders, and elderly people. In Nepal many local social conflicts (except complicated conflict cases such as rape, suspected or attempted murder, etc.) were resolved locally in informal ways (Upreti, 2002). Local elderly people often work as mediators to deal with conflict, though they have no legal status. Villagers commonly accept their settlements. Such informal conflict management practices are a blend of local customs, a sense of justice and religious feeling rather than official procedures. Elderly and socially respected people, traditional landlords, teachers, *Jhakri* (faith healers), *Purohit,* and *Mukhiya* are principal actors in resolving a wide range of local conflicts. These people do not only mediate in conflict as neutral third parties but also generally decide terms and conditions for the negotiation process. The criteria to resolve conflicts were not legal evidence and documents, but religious faith[11] (*Dharma Bhakaune, Tamo-Tulsi, Geeta and Saligram samaune*), historical considerations and practical realities. Disputants from ethnic groups such as Gurung, Mangar, Tamang, etc. strongly prefer negotiators from their own ethnic group with special reconciliation methods[12]. They only approach others if it is not possible for their ethnic leaders to resolve the conflict.

Local people in informal conflict-resolution methods use special relation of friendship such as Mit laune[13] in dealing with social conflict and practise public apology as a light punishment to improve characters[14].

People learn negotiation skills through practice while being involved in local conflict management practices. Those who had the time, credibility, temperament, willingness, articulation and vested interests were more involved in community-level CM. Generally, they carefully listen to the conflict story of both conflicting parties. They also inspect the place of conflict, if relevant, assess the past conflict track records of the conflicting parties and consult neighbours as eyewitnesses, if applicable. If necessary they call meetings in public places (or sometimes in their own homes or even in the house of one of the conflicting parties, if the parties agree), to get the opinion of neighbours. Then on the basis of their assessment and judgement, they make their decisions. Conflicting parties in most of the cases accept such decisions. They use many cultural, religious and political proverbs (which highlight the importance of resolving conflict locally rather than going through a formal process) to convince the conflicting parties. According to the context and situation, they also threaten, harass and sometimes even beat offenders to reveal the truth and/or to force them to accept the prescribed settlement. Occasionally, they also integrate their resolution measures with formal process (Upreti, 2001; 2002; 2003).

The main reasons expressed by people in preferring informal mechanisms are, trust in mediators, comparative ease in settlement, maintenance of social harmony and lack of resources (money, knowledge and time) to use a formal conflict-resolution process. Nevertheless, particularly after 1990, the credibility of such informal practices is eroding fast, due to social and political changes (Upreti, 2003, 2004a,b,c,d).

The importance of informal conflict-resolution practices is reflected by this local saying: *"Deskalagi rajako niti chahinchha tara gaonko kam ma prajako riti thiti ko badi mahatto chha"* (King's policy is needed for the whole country, whereas local values and customs are more important for managing village resources). Several conflict management activities carried out at local level are traditionally based on their values and customs (*riti-thiti*), which play a powerful role in binding people together for collective actions. The following paragraph presents a local custom-based method of resolution of conflict called *Sagun Garne* (reconciliation). *Sagun garne* (reconciliation) is a method based on cultural tradition. In this method, a gift is exchanged between disputants, in the presence of villagers, as a form of reconciliation. This exchange is performed after discussing the matter in meetings where villagers, negotiators and conflicting parties are present. When they reach a settlement, they start '*sagun garne*'. The conflict is declared as settled when both parties accept the gift. Then there is small celebration where all people take some *Jaad* (a type of fermented liquor). However, there are no written documents of such settlement. The villagers, who are present at the *sagun garne* ceremony, are witnesses to the settlement. This practice is most common in Matwalis and Tibeto-Burman ethnic groups. The gifts are usually in kind such as liquor, eggs, meat, etc. (Khadka, 1997). Some occasions are particularly important for informal conflict-resolution and reconciliation. For example, *Dashain*[15] is traditionally used as an occasion to reconcile and strengthen relations by visiting each other's houses, exchanging gifts and good wishes. Likewise, *Tihar* (another important Hindu festival) is also used as an important occasion to promote harmony and reconcile conflict. *Ghewa* is another occasion to reconcile conflict. Many of the conflicts resolved in villages are verbal, based on faith[16] and not supported by written documents. When powerful people reactivate these cases, the weaker party usually loses when the case goes to the formal process of conflict resolution. The efficiency of the local procedure is context-specific and mixed, sometimes effective and sometimes exploitative and ineffective.

As discussed elsewhere in this book and shown by various studies (Buckels, 1999; Bauchler, 2002; Upreti, 2001 and 2002a; Oli, 1998), violent conflicts at local levels often emerge from or are related to resource conflict. Therefore, resolving resource and social conflicts is a fundamental step in addressing wider violent and armed conflict. Therefore, potential of traditional approaches of conflict resolution lies in their strengths of resolving local conflict rather than having ability to directly address the armed conflicts.

3.5 RELIGIOUS APPROACHES IN RESOLVING VIOLENT CONFLICT

Religion is a means of reconciliation as well as source of conflict.

When the religious extremists use religion to spread hatred against other or fulfil vested interests, it implants conflict. But when religious leaders use religion as a means of reconciliation, it greatly contributes to resolving conflict. For example, Bin Laden abused Islamic religion to create conflict and Desmond Tutu used Christian religion to reconcile divided South African people.

Another potential approach is the use of religious and ethnic leaders in resolving conflict. This approach is effectively working in some part of the world, particularly when the conflict in question is religious or ethnic. Religious and ethnic leaders of South Africa, Northern Ireland and the Philippines had greatly contributed in resolving conflict. However, in this country religious leaders are yet not able to demonstrate their relevance in resolving this conflict because of different reasons.

The Hindu religion and Hindu clerics have neither properly recognised nor promoted other religions. Sanskritisation and Hindu orthodoxy dominate whole religious leadership in the past and even now in Nepal. They are too negative towards the Maoists and their attitude does not allow them to constructively engage in negotiated settlement. Most Hindu leaders of Nepal are politically supporting the king incarnation of god Vishnu. This feeling blocks possibility of their active engagement because of the credibility and acceptance by the Maoists seems virtually negligible.

Hindu religious leaders have not so far demonstrated reconciliatory ability. Rather they are deeply engaged in religious politics around the periphery of the palace (e.g., Vishwo Hindu Mahasangh). One Hindu pundit[17] emerged as a successful social reformer and extraordinary orator. He was intimately engaged in social reform, but Hindu orthodox clerics were extremely unhappy with his approach. He was assassinated in April 2005 but the cause of assassination and killer is still unknown. Some blame Maoist insurgents and some suspect the Hindu religious community itself as he had serious contradictions with extremist Hindu religious leaders. Hindu religious leaders in Nepal are biased and contribute to escalate conflict rather than resolving it.

Buddhist religious leaders, by Buddhist principle, could be more reconciliatory and compromising in dealing with conflict. However, experiences of Sri Lanka do not give successful examples of this kind. Nepal has a similar observation of the contribution of Buddhist leaders to resolve conflict. Their efforts are limited only within their religious groups with minimal impacts to the warring parties of Nepal. Experiences also show that they are not open to have concerted efforts with non-Buddhist and non-religious groups to reach negotiated settlement of the armed conflict in Nepal.

Christian religious leaders seem more active in resolving conflict but they are in minority and mainly suppressed by other religions. Christian religion is not yet easily accepted in Nepal and Hindu extremists feel threatened by the expansion of Christian religion, therefore they attempt to undermine Christian conflict-resolution efforts. Christian religious leaders are engaged in expanding their religious base in Nepal and therefore their priority is not conflict resolution but strengthening and expansion of religious base. Few Christian leaders are committed to resolving this crisis and working to contribute in this effort. For example, SEFJAR (United Efforts of the Christian Community in Nepal for Peace, Justice and Reconciliation) is a novel effort of the Christian community to contribute to peace and reconciliation.

Some energetic multi-religious leaders with the facilitation of Friends of Peace have created an Inter-faith Religious Committee to work for peace and reconciliation. Hindu, Christian, Buddhist and Muslim religious leaders formed this Committee and it is working in an integrated manner. However, many religious leaders are not supporting this novel effort.

Many religious leaders are biased; their status quo is threatened and therefore may not be able to substantially contribute alone in resolving this complex conflict. Due to these reasons, religious leaders, an important traditional force, may not be able to resolve this conflict acting as facilitators or mediators. However, they can greatly contribute to convince their supporters in resolving conflict. They can be an active part of the greater civil society efforts and create enabling environment through positive pressure.

Traditional approaches were effective in managing community level social and resource conflict. Their merits were based on accessibility, credibility and cost effectiveness.

Findings of previous studies have clearly demonstrated that failure in properly managing local-level social and resource conflict have tremendously contributed to escalation of the Maoist's armed rebellion (Oli, 1998; New Era, 1988; Upreti, 2002a and 2004b).

However, these approaches may not be effective in mediating national level, extremely complex, ideologically guided and militarily orchestrated political conflict because of the following reasons:

1. These methods do not have experience in dealing with extremely complex political conflicts like the Maoist insurgency.
2. Almost all traditional approaches are based on certain traditions, which Maoists want to change or dismantle.
3. Many of them maintain status quo, traditional hierarchy based on the feudal social system and often favour the elite and powerful. Hence, their theoretical orientation and practical operation are not suitable to address such a complex conflict, which has to settle the state restricting and social transformation issues.

However, many positive elements and experiences of these methods can be very useful to learn and incorporate in resolving the bigger national conflict.

3.6 CIVIL SOCIETY EFFORTS IN RESOLVING ARMED CONFLICT

Strong civil society is a characteristic of democratic state. Civil society plays important roles in strengthening civil state. It performs different functions such as facilitator, mediator, negotiator, watch dog in conflict-ridden societies (Barnes, 2002; Upreti, 2004b).

Not the traditional, but emerging modern force contributing to resolve this conflict is 'civil society'. Civil society is using a multi-track approach. Considering the past deep engagement and good contribution of the facilitators to peace talks, initiatives taken by the civil society organizations and leaders in exploring options, creating pressure over warring parties, shuttle diplomacy and established dialogue and communications, etc. civil society has demonstrated that it can be one of the best options within the country to mediate this conflict. However, the government, the Maoists and the King are not yet ready to fully accept their mediation, and sometimes they are hesitant to acknowledge the efforts of civil society in settling this conflict. There is still a strong perception within the government and military that civil society (human right activists, media, intellectuals) is not supporting government or supporting the Maoists (periodic press briefings of RNA and press conferences of the government have clearly indicated that perception). There is also another perception or blame that some civil society organizations or leaders are working on behalf of the King/government to resist change or knowingly or unknowingly supporting the Maoists to dismantle the monarchy. These perceptions and feelings of partition are also hindering the civil society from taking lead. These observations have some basis, as intellectuals, media, and civil society did not give impartial views or influenced by partitioned thinking and biases. However, civil society immensely contributes to create enabling environment and it is continuously engaged in this task.

3.7 BUSINESS COMMUNITY IN RESOLVING ARMED CONFLICT

The business community is one of the most powerful domestic actors with relatively high potential to facilitate negotiated settlement of the armed conflict. Federation of Nepalese Chamber of Commerce and Industries (FNCCI), Chamber of Commerce, Chambers of Nepalese Industries like interest-based business organisations are influential in Nepal. Their members have financially supported all political parties of Nepal and consequently they could strongly influence political parties. Many of them have also personal relations with and easy access to the King. However, their interests, efforts and relations are so far concentrated on economic issues rather than political settlement of the armed conflict. Revisiting their peace efforts reveals that in the recent past, they have made some efforts in restoring peace and resolving the ongoing armed conflict in Nepal. The notable one is the National Business Initiative, which a consortium of major private sector business groups such as organisation of private boarding schools, association of private nursing homes, Nepal Chamber of Commerce, Federation of Nepalese Chambers of Commerce and Industries, travel associations, etc. The business sector has the potential to mediate conflict but the efforts made so far in this line are not enough to achieve the negotiated settlement.

Though the business sector is one of the major victims of the ongoing armed conflict, industrialists and business men did not engage for a long time to contribute in resolving armed conflict. Even they had celebrated the royal takeover of 1st February 2005 assuming that the political change will protect them. However, their assumption was proved false and the direct rule with no international and domestic support was able to protect industries and business form the effects of armed conflict. Within seven months the new leader of FNCCI[18] publicly announced to support democratic movement of Nepal that was fighting to restore the democratic system taken away on 1st February. Now, business community seems to have realised that they cannot stay alone without responding to the changing political situation and ongoing armed conflict.

3.8 CONFLICT RESOLUTION PRACTICES IN 'NEW REGIME'

The Maoists have labelled themselves as a 'new regime' and the state as 'old regime'. The meaning of 'new regime' is to denote the areas where they have control and formed their local government (called *janasarkar).* In several parties of the counties they have formed local governments

The Maoists have their own conflict resolution system in the areas where they have formed *janasarkar*s (people's government). Conflict settlement practices of the Maoist are operating under the 18th point of the Minimum Policy and Programme of Revolutionary Peoples' Council[19] and implemented by local people's government (Janasarkar). The 18th point states, "people's courts at various levels shall be constituted in order to dispense justice to the people. House of People's Representatives of the concerned levels shall appoint its office bearers and they shall be responsible to them".

Maoists administer conflict-resolution practices through their own court system. They constitute village, district and regional courts (Panti, 2004). If the conflict is not settled at lower level, the lower court refers it to a higher court. Joint Revolutionary Peoples Council at all levels is their supreme legal authority. According to Mr Kishwor Panthi (an investigative journalist), *Janapratinidhisawa* (Peoples Representative Council) elects lawyers and judges for the people's courts. They have *Sarbajanik Kanuni Sangraha 2060* (Public Legal Code 2003/4) to guide the conflict settlement processes and practices. In Gulmi district, basic qualification for judge and lawyers is intermediate degree and high school-level certificate respectively. Quoting Ghana Shyam Parajuli, Chief of Village Janasarkar, Kishwor Panthi writes, 'in Arje VDC of Gulmi District 150 conflicts were registered within 2 months (October-November 2004) and 50 per cent cases were already settled' (Panthi, 2004). The number of conflicts reaching the government offices in the Maoist areas has drastically reduced mainly because of the prevailing Maoist conflict settlement practices at the local level and fear. In their areas, they have settled almost 90 per cent of the cases locally (Panti 2004).

Reputed Nepalese printed media (dailies, weeklies, fortnightly and monthly)[20] have also frequently reported that the number of cases in district courts and government offices are drastically reduced. The information collected from the recent field visit in Doti, Achham and Dadeldhura district (15-20 September 2005) also confirms that ordinary people generally do not go to the district headquarters to settle the conflict cases, as number of exploitation related conflict cases are drastically reduced in the village because of Maoists. Many local conflict cases were related to the exploitation and suppression of poor and marginalised people by the local powerbrokers and elite by abusing or manipulating laws, rules and regulations or mobilising networks and special relations with state power centres. But this situation has been completely stopped by the Maoist fear and action. Most of exploitative elites from the rural areas are displaced from the fear of Maoists, consequently the bare exploitation in rural areas has been decreased.

How do Maoists decide cases? In an interview with Mr Panthi, Gulmi District Judge of the Maoists, Mr Khum Raj Acharya said, We decide cases based on the provision of *Sarbajanik Kanuni Sangraha 2060* (Public Legal Code, 2003/4) in a creative way focusing to class interests. Our judicial system is not based on the volumes of book; it is pragmatic to give real justice. We use *samajik* and *prakritk naya* (social and natural justice) system, international standards/ provisions and theories of conflict in judgement. Punishment under our judicial system is to reform guilty parties, not to control them'. He further says, 'peoples are attracted to people's court because justice is right and appropriate, quick, inexpensive, no risk of winning by wrong doers by using bribe, and verdicts are based on social realities. We do look at evidences, record statements (*bayan linchhau)* and give verdicts. The claims should be proved; we do not decide showing guns and creating fear. We have some similarities with the court of old regime in using principle of natural justice and social justice system and standards of international laws. But in reality, the intention of old regime is not to give justice but to decide for economic benefits, they also take long time to decide, and therefore people do not like them. We can change the *karar* (contract) with the old regime, which are based on the manipulation by lawyers. Our judgement system is favourable to the people with low level of awareness and income. But we do not take biased decision on the basis of the economic status (poor or rich). Disputing parties can use their lawyers to plead for their case, which is their right'. In responding to the question on torture to the disputing parties as a part of interrogation in the peoples court, the Maoist judge says, 'It is wrong, we ideologically convince them to realise their wrong-doing and we have reformed them. But we don't claim we do not touch them during interrogation.' He further talks, 'The judicial system should be independent and neutral. However, we are in the class struggle, until we capture *kendrya satta* (central political power) and therefore our judicial decisions focus more on *bargiya pakchhedharta (*class preference) rather than *nirpekchhya* (absolute impartiality). At present our judicial system cannot be independent from the party'.

The above interview brings important, interesting and contradictory issues in the Maoist judicial system. The bias towards one class and the lack of possibility to work independently seriously undermines independence of judicial system. It also contradicts international legal standards. Another aspect of this legal system is the general practices among the Maoist insurgents at local level, which are not in line with the expression of Mr Acharya. The following case reveals this contradiction:

A case of settling conflict by Maoists in Parwanipur VDC of Sarlahi district is described here[21]. The local Maoists suspected Mr Surya Bahadur Khadka to have murdered his daughter-in-law and arrested him. They interrogated him and found him guilty. Then, they ordered him to be kept in jail. They had no protected jail building and therefore they ordered him to be confined within certain areas under their control, which belong to *Sthaniya janasatta* (local people's government) where Mr Khadka's house was situated. During the interrogation process, they used torture and physical violence. They even punished former VDC chairperson Mr Jatan Budhathoki for hiding the murdered case. But he was released on the condition that he would appear whenever they needed him. They have also kept a few other relatives of Mr Khadka under watch list. Sometimes, the Maoist pressurise villagers to punish wrong doers instead of doing it by themselves. The Maoists' people's court also use bail system. However, there are cases that the Maoists are not refunding the bail even after getting clearance from the charges.

So far, it is difficult to find a standard Maoist conflict settlement pattern and procedure. It is mainly based on the judgement of the local judges. Even though they claim to use the principles of *samajik* and *prakritk naya* (social and natural justice) in their conflict settlement practices, it is not generalised. *Bargiya pakchhedharta (*class preference) is their main guiding principle in local conflict settlement practices, which ultimately ignores the principles of *samajik* and *prakritk naya.* However, they use some elements of both informal and formal conflict resolution practices such as use of eyewitnesses, recording of the statements, etc.

3.9 CONCLUSIONS

Fairness, ethics, rules of law and judgement so far play a minor role in resolving social, resource and family conflicts in Nepal and existing socio-political system, more than anything else, determine the outcome. There is no assurance whatsoever from the belief to legal systems for fair resolution of conflict. All in all, there appears to be a little supportive evidence of effectiveness of existing legally engineered top-down system to address conflict. Only powerful people and elite are benefiting from the current systems.

Conflict is the product of human relation. Conflict prevention and resolution strategies and practices require learning processes and processes for integration of external knowledge and local experiences, accountable bureaucracy, transparent procedure and accessible judicial system. The people dealing with conflict needs appropriate knowledge and skill on negotiation, facilitation, communication and mediation skills. In essence, responding constructively to social conflicts requires more ingenuity, creativity, commitment and alternative methodology, which is seriously lacking in Nepal. Therefore, the existing conflict resolution systems in Nepal need fundamental reform.

Existing religious, traditional and community approaches so far demonstrate no firm ability to go beyond small-scale social conflicts. However, traditional and informal conflict-settlement approaches are still effective in resolving social, family and transaction-related conflicts. In many cases, they are more effective, less expensive, administratively less complicated and easily accessible compared to the provisions of formal conflict resolution.

A pragmatic framework of resolving conflict at local level is compromise with collective commitment. Local conflicts are also becoming a means of adjusting the existing pattern of relationships to changing conditions. Government laws, rules and regulations, policies and development interventions and bureaucratic manipulations are major sources of local conflicts in society. However, these conflicts are not straightforward and static. They are dynamic, organic and shaped and reshaped by local social relations and changing power structures in society. State-imposed laws and regulations are therefore not able to address the changing nature and dynamics of local conflicts. State ambition to regulate society through legal engineering is too simplistic and often they are not able to envision multi-dimensionalities of local conflicts. Implementation of legal provisions and their manipulations in actual practices however, have tremendously contributed to develop capacity of local people as they have to engage in negotiation and renegotiation with different powerful actors and thereby strengthening grass-roots democracy. Wherever the indigenous conflict settlement practices are combined with the legal practices, they are becoming effective. Therefore, it is essential to adopt a complementary approach by combining strengths of both systems in conflict settlement practices.

Indigenous and traditional conflict-resolution approaches are not strong enough to deal with the very complex armed conflict of Nepal. They have some serious drawbacks and weaknesses as well. Emerging civil society approach is by far the strongest with great potential in dealing with the armed conflict. Nevertheless, it alone cannot produce the desired result. Traditional approaches of conflict resolution can complement to resolve the ongoing Maoist insurgency too if they are integrated into the formal system.

NOTES

1. Interview with Mr Vishwokarma on 8th November 2004 at Lati Koili VDC ward No 6, Surkhet district.
2. They are often landless or having very minimal landholding. They base their livelihood mainly on wage labour and forest- based resources. Therefore, locally available natural resources are other important sources of their livelihoods.
3. Since national parks and other forms of protected areas became a major conservation strategy in Nepal, conflict between park authorities and people are mounting. Budathoki (2003:22) states, "*...the success of conservation is not always beneficial to the people of Nepal. The strict protection measures, which deny traditional resources rights have come to direct conflict with the local communities as their livelihood is threatened*". This is not uncommon when there are scarce natural resources upon which people are based their livelihoods and state wants to regulate (often prevent access) these resources (Upreti, 2004a).
4. Interview with Kabi Ghale (71 years) on 9 May 2004.
5. Most of them said it is almost impossible to do any work in government office without giving bribe. If people do not officer bribe (often in the form of cash or some times in kind) to the government officials, they create numerous difficulties to the clients (e.g., they do not move forward files, they linger every thing, they cite various confusing reasons of delay of the

work, etc. that cause ordinary people to stay some days in expensive district headquarters) to harass them or to give some money and finish work immediately (they do not create any problem and even they do work immediately which usually takes long time from the normal procedure if the clients offer bribe). Therefore, it is almost impossible to escape from this 'corruption trap'. If the client is relatively smart and makes complaints to the seniors, they either escape citing very unfamiliar reasons or simply ignore complaints or supporting their subordinate. Realizing this rampant corruption in all government office, His Majesty's Government of Nepal made compulsory provision to have 'citizen's charter' in all government offices. However, this provision is limited to hoarding boards and papers but no any real impacts, as almost all senior government officers and even ministers are engaged in corruption. See Anatomy of Corruption (Thapa, 2002) to get real severity of corruption (which deals on the corruption at high level, ranging from ministers and parliamentarians to senior government officials)

6. Bribe includes both cash and kind. In kind, items included were: rice, fruit, vegetables, animals, animal products (hides, ghee, milk, fur, etc.), fish, honey, and furniture, forest products (wood, herbal medicines), clothes, gold and even occasionally land. Often the clients fetch kinds in their home and handover to family members as present and cash is either provided directly or deposited in the bank account and submit the 'bank deposit slip'.
7. *Afnomanchhe network of relatives, friends, political allies, etc.*
8. *See Fatalism and Development (1991) by Dor Bahadur Bist to know more about how network of powerful people abuses state resource and power in their personal gain. He has termed this strong network as afnomanchhe.*
9. KTWR area covers parts of three districts namely Sunsari, Saptari and Udayapur.
10. *The Purohit* is a culturally and socially recognised person who performs religious ceremonies and also acts as a bridge between villagers for information and communication. He (there is no provision of a female *purohit*) has frequent house-to-house contact and good relations. Generally, his clients did not prefer to go against his arguments.
11. *Dharma Bhakaune (sacred test)* method is based on the principle of an 'oath of innocence'. In this method negotiators invite contending parties to the local temples and ask them to take an oath of innocence touching sacred materials like *saligram* (a sacred stone), copper, sacred plants such as *Ficus religiosa* (peepal), *Ocimum sanctum*, (basil), *Cynodon dyctolen* (dub grass) or sacred books. Sometimes conflicting parties are asked to hold their children while performing such vows. These tests are undergone in the presence of villagers, negotiators and the conflicting parties. A sense that it would be sinful if the matter were falsified plays a strong role in this method.
12. *Sagun garne (reconciliation)* is a very common method where a gift is

exchanged between disputants in the presence of villagers. The conflict matter is discussed in a meeting attended by villagers, negotiators and the conflicting parties. When a settlement is reached they start *sagun garne*. The conflict is declared as 'settled' when both parties accept a gift, and this is followed by a small celebration where all people drink *jaad* (a type of fermented liquor). However, there are no written documents of such settlements: the evidence is the witness of villagers present at the *sagun garne* ceremony. This practice is most common among Matwalis and Tibeto-Burman ethnic groups. The gifts are usually liquor, eggs, meat, etc.

13. *Mit laune* is a unique mode of development of a special relationship. It is a form of negotiation if and when two individuals or groups are in low intensity conflict. In this process, the two individuals exchange money, flowers, clothes or some other special gift in the presence of an audience, with or without a simple religious ceremony. *Mit laune* symbolises an accommodative way of negotiation, and results in a win-win situation.
14. *Mafi magne (public apology): In this practice* negotiators invite villagers and disputants to discuss the conflict issue and decide the case and ask for a public apology by a guilty party. The guilty party, in the presence of villagers and the local elite, begs for pardon and swears not to repeat such offences. This is sometimes also combined with an additional fine or other punishment. This method some times also combines sacred test.
15. A major Hindu festival where all community members gather in public places and resolve pending conflicts, unsettled issues and decide collective community works.
16. *Dharma Bhakaune* (sacred test) is a common informal method of determining the truth in managing conflict. This method is based on the principle of 'oath of innocence'. It is common when there is lack of other evidence. Common methods observed in this test are: taking contending parties to the local temples and asking them to undergo a test, asking conflicting parties to touch sacred materials such as *saligram* (a sacred stone), copper, sacred plants such as *Ficus religiosa* (peepal), *Ocimum sanctum*, (basil), *Cynodon dyctolen* (dog grass) sacred books and take an oath of innocence. Some times, conflicting parties are asked to hold their children while performing such vows (Khadka, 1997). These tests take place in the presence of villagers, negotiators and conflicting parties. A feeling of sin, if the matter is falsified, plays a strong role in this method to find the wrongdoing. This method is also used occasionally in formal CM practices.
17. Mr. Narayan Prasad Pokharel was very popular in Nepal for his contribution to social change and religious reform but he was assassinated.
18. Chandi Raj Dhakal, newly elected chairperson of FNCCI publicly announced in Reporters Club programme that FNCCI will support democratic movement to restore democracy in Nepal.
19. On 25 Feb 2001 the Maoists approved *Prachandapath* as their new

ideological base from the Second National Convention, where they had also formulated different ethnic and political policies. The Minimum Policy and Programme of Revolutionary Peoples' Council of the Maoists was an outcome of these political policies.

20. Kantipur Daily, Samacharpatra Daily, Rajdhani Daily, Annapurnapost Daily, Nepal Magazine (weekly), Samaya (weekly), Himal Magazine (fortnightly) and Mulyankan.
21. A detail description of the case is reported by Bishwo Mani Pokharel and Chudamani Wagle in "Samaya Saptahik" Year 1, No 35, pp 2-8

CHAPTER 4

Failed Negotiations and Peace Talks Revisited

> *Peace is not merely the absence of war but the presence of justice, of law, of order-in short of government,*
>
> ***—Albert Einstein.***

4.1 INTRODUCTION

Nepal, previously recognised as a peaceful country, is now facing severe violent conflict, which has already taken more than thirteen thousand lives, as well as billions of rupees worth of damage to property and infrastructure. It is creating fear, mistrust, insecurity, civil strife, and social, political and development instability. The current Nepalese polity appears incapable and ineffective to maintain security and peace in the country, which is forcing Nepal into chaos and anarchy. The 1st February Royal takeover has further damaged the democracy, pushing Nepal from a fragile state to a failed state. Now the most important challenge is how to build confidence to create an acceptable democratic space that could force the restart of the negotiation process to restore lasting peace in Nepal. Previous efforts to reach a negotiated settlement between the state and the insurgents have failed. This chapter attempts to critically examine the past peace talks and negotiation process, causes of failure and lessons to be learnt from the mistakes.

4.2. THE CONTEXT

It is well documented that social exclusion, acute inequalities, absolute poverty, lack of access to resources and failure of political structures to address these issues have made the Nepali society extremely vulnerable to conflict and mass movements like the Maoists' 'people's war' (Hachhethu, 2003; Upreti, 2003b, 2002a; Karki and Seddon, 2003). Deep-rooted social cleavages in terms of caste, ethnicity, gender and regional, cultural, linguistic, and religious forms of discrimination provided fertile ground for escalation of the conflict. Corruption, politicisation of the bureaucracy, police force and intelligence, etc. were other hidden causes of the conflict. Maoists successfully capitalised on the largely unsatisfactory democratic transition of the 1990s. Centralisation and regional imbalance, skewed distribution, access and control of natural and other productive resources, dominating influences of religiously- and culturally-biased traditional Hindu cultural values, discrimination against women, ethnic minorities, so-called lower castes, and Dalits have created a feeling of injustice, frustration and have fuelled the conflict. Though the 1990 Constitution was democratic, it contained contradiction in its preamble, i.e., sovereignty rested in the people and four fundamentals provisions cannot be changed. If people are sovereign, they should have rights to change anything in the Constitution. Hence, the Constitution became one of the sources of conflict. It has also declared Nepal as a Hindu state ignoring its multi-religious nature. It is also a perennial source of conflict.

There is also overwhelming agreement that the protracted conflict in Nepal cannot be addressed without resolving these structural causes (Thapa, 2003; Upreti, 2003a&b, 2002a&b, Pahari, 2003; Hutt, 2004; Karki and Seddon, 2003; Onesto, 2005). Since the inception of the Maoist conflict, different approaches have been used to resolve it (e.g., police operation, military mobilisation, integrated security and development, cordon and search operation, state of emergency, use of special terrorist control act, ceasefire and peace talks, etc.). The state, the rebels, parliamentary political parties, civil society, human right organisations, and business communities are active to settle the ongoing conflict and to restore peace in Nepal. However, these efforts have not resulted in any significant achievement so far. Though the need for peace is even more urgent than ever, the current political situation does not show any hope. In this chapter, I am examining past efforts of the two negotiations to resolve the bloody conflict in Nepal. This chapter extracts heavily from a peace process review paper prepared by the author and Daman Nath Dhungana (former Speaker of the House of Representatives and one of the facilitators of the past two negotiations).

4.3 EFFORTS OF THE STATE TO UNDERSTAND THE MAOIST INSURGENCY

For a long time, the government and political parties were totally confused in interpreting the Maoist insurgency and contradictory in their expression, behaviour and actions. Sometimes they say it is a political movement and sometime an act of terrorism. Even if they said it is a political movement they were not dealing with it politically. And when they say it is a terrorist act, they were not clear about relationships between terrorism and characteristics of an exclusionary state (feudal, centralistic and undemocratic in nature and elite-centric power base). Because of such confusions, they were not able to devise and implement proper strategies and mechanisms to respond to the armed conflict. The international community did the same and their views on Maoists were fully divided. It is true of the civil society as well. Hence, whatever responses were made to resolve the conflict were haphazard, confused, inconsistent and therefore unproductive (Upreti and Dhungana, 2004). Realising this confusion and contradiction the governments made some efforts by forming task forces to understand the insurgency[1].

The first time under the premiership of Lokendra Bahadur Chand, the government formed a task force[2] to suggest possible ways of resolution of Maoist armed conflict. This task force suggested considering the Maoist insurgency as a political problem and can only be solved through reform in the governing system and socio-economic sphere. Though the report did not recommend many radical reforms, it was quite clear about interpreting Maoist insurgency and ways to address it. If the government had implemented the recommendations of this report, Nepal would not have to face this crisis now.

On 6 January 2000 the K.P. Bhattarai government formed a 'High Level Committee to Provide Suggestions to solve the Maoist problems' under the convenorship of former Prime Minister Ser Bahadur Deuba. This was formed as a result of intense intra party power struggle within the Nepali Congress Party, as the Prime Minister wanted to show something good to his rival Girija Koirala.

BOX 4.1 Deuba Committee members

Mr Ser Bahadur Deuba - Convenor
Mr Ram Chandra Poudel - Member
Mr Sushil Koirala - Member
Mr Chirinjibr Wagle, - Member
Mr Khum Bahadur Khadka - Member
Mr Purna Bahadur Khadka -- Member
Mr Govinda Raj Joshi - Member
Mr Chakra Bastola - Member
Dr Prakash Sharan Mahat - Member Secretary

The Deuba committee submitted the final report to the government on 7 November 2000. This was one of the most comprehensive reports prepared by the state-instituted body to resolve the armed conflict in Nepal. The main conclusions of the report are as follows:

- The Maoist problem is not because of the failure of democracy. It is because of the weaknesses in the state governance system, frequent changes in the government, poverty, discrimination, injustice and exclusion.
- This problem has to be solved through peace talks with the Maoists but this is only an immediate political solution.
- Root causes of the insurgency are the social and economic structures of Nepal. Proper solution of the armed conflict is possible only by restructuring social and economic structures.

4.4 A BRIEF REVIEW OF THE PAST NEGOTIATIONS TO RESTORE PEACE IN NEPAL

In this section, I am briefly reviewing the negotiation and peace talks related to the Maoist conflict. Peace is a state of wellbeing that is characterised by trust, compassion, and justice (Ury, 1999 and 1991; Wall and Lynn, 1993). In a peaceful state people can be encouraged to explore as well as celebrate diversity and search for good in each other without concern for personal pain and sacrifice (Uyangoda, 2002 and 2000; Zartman and Berman, 1982; Zartman, 1985, 1995 and 1987). Hence, peace is defined as the absence of reduction of violence of all kinds and non-violent and create means of conflict transformation (Galtung, 2000).

Peace-building is a process of rebuilding normal relations between warring parties and people in conflict with each other (Ackerman, 2000; Barnes, 2002; Bailey, 1993). It involves rebuilding trust, re-establishing cooperative relationships, apologizing for past violent deeds and forgiving those deeds so that the former enemies can become friends and neighbours, who can successfully live and work together in the future (BHCT, 2003; Burton,1987, Carndall, 20004; Duffield, 1997; Galtung and Jacobsen, 2000; Hill, 1982).

4.4.1 Analysis of 2001 (first) negotiation and failure of peace talks

After 6 years of the insurgency, a ceasefire was declared for the first time on 25 July 2001, immediately 2 days after Sher Bahadur Deuba became Prime Minister (23 July 2001).

The ceasefire was declared in the following situation:

> **BOX 4.2 Dialogue Teams 2001**
>
> **Government:**
> Mr. Chirinjibr Wagle, Convenor
> Mr. Mahesh Acharya, Member
> Mr. Narahari Acharya, Member
> Mr. Bijaya Gachhedar, Member
> Mr. Chakra Bastola, Member
>
> Maoists:
> Mr. Krishna Bahadur Mahara, Convenor
> Mr. Agni Sapkota, Member
> Mr. Top Bahadur Rayamajhi, Member

- When country was just mourning the royal massacre of 1 June 2001.
- Pressure from the Nepalese people was mounting for peace, as they witnessed the unimaginable royal massacre.
- The new king was struggling to establish legitimacy and a ceasefire could pave some ground to strengthen the image of the monarch as a peace-loving person.
- The Maoists were aggressive towards the new King, saying that traditional monarchy in Nepal had finished with the royal massacre and that it was time to institutionalise the republican system.
- Powerful anti-communist Prime Minister Girija Prasad Koirala unexpectedly stepped down with the allegation that Royal Nepal Army did not cooperate him when the Maoist abducted 69 police officers from the Holleri-Rolpa and he wanted to mobilise RNA.
- Sher Bahadur Deuba, officially a democrat but noted royalist came to power with the sole agenda of settling the Maoist conflict. He had to demonstrate his capability and better performance when the Girija Prasad Koirala was not supportive of him. Sher Bahadur Deuba was Chairperson of the High Level Committee instituted by the then Prime Minister Krishan Prasad Bhattarai, a fierce competitor of Girija Koirala, to recommend to the government how to resolve the Maoist conflict. The Deuba Committee concluded that the Maoist insurgency is of a political nature and could be settled only through political means and democratic process. Deuba wanted to give the impression that he was fully committed to settle this conflict at a political level. Therefore, he declared a

ceasefire even before he took 'oath of office'. He wanted to demonstrate that he was able to politically settle the complex Maoist problem, in which his rival Girija Koirala had failed. Hence, he came with a peace agenda with two ambitions:

1. First, wanted to show that he was more able than other political leaders to solve the country's problem.
2. Second, he wanted to politically sideline anti-communist Girija Koirala by improving relations with communists and Maoists. His unusual loyalty towards Maoists got unusual appreciation from them as "*Hiloma fuleko kamalko ful*" (lotus flower of the mud). Deuba also wanted to clear the negative public image of abuser of the state resources and destroyer of the democratic values, as he had introduced Pajero (very expensive Japanese vehicle) and pension culture, buying and purchasing of members of parliament instead of solving a national problem.

- When Girija Prasad Koirala formally blamed RNA for their non-cooperation to the elected government and the RNA denied the allegation, RNA wanted to demonstrate that they are not against the elected government and therefore the relations between the new Prime Minister Deuba and RNA were better. Perhaps other un-revealed reasons might be the loyalty of Deuba to the palace and his family relations with the Rana elite family (the source of most of the RNA leaders and their family relations with the palace).
- All these socio-political and socio-psychological factors contributed to declare the ceasefire and start peace talks for negotiated settlement of the conflict (Upreti and Dhungana, 2004).

The first round of talks started on 30 August 2001 at Godavari Resort, on the outskirts of the Kathmandu city. The talks ended with introduction and familiarity, without discussing any specific agenda. This was the first experience of formal peace talk for both the warring parties. It was realised that in comparison to the state, Maoists were more prepared and systematic in negotiation at that time.

The second round of peace talks was held at Thakurdwar in Bardiya district on 13 and 14 September 2001. The core of the political issues put raised by the Maoists at that talk were:

(a) To start a 'process of institutionalising republican system;

(b) Withdraw the present constitution; and
(c) To authorise Nepalese people to make a new constitution'.

The Maoist negotiators had also submitted a written agenda for the talks. The negotiators from the rebel side were reiterating that the 'exercise towards establishing republican state have already begun'. At the same talk, they also tabled the proposal of releasing the imprisoned Maoists. The government released some Maoist prisoners including central leader Matrika Yadav. The Maoists had also tabled the following demands to the government:

- To clarify the condition of those prisoners who had disappeared from police custody;
- To withdraw the security regulations and the Armed Police Force[3];
- To withdraw the Integrated Security and Development Programme[4];
- To return the army to the barracks (who were mobilised for the Integrated Security and Development).

In the third round of talks, the Maoists were putting pressure on the government negotiators to pull out the army and armed police force from their controlled areas (Kattel, 2003). The Maoist supremo Prachanda, just before the third round of the talks issued a statement setting 'constituent assembly' as the political demand. Then the rebel side demanded an interim government and the new constitution through the constituent assembly whereas the government side was rigid that multiparty democracy, constitutional monarchy and fundamental rights are non-negotiable. The government negotiation team was not able to talk on constituent assembly as both main political parties CPN (UML) and Nepali Congress Party were not ready even to listen about the constituent assembly.

When the Deuba government was busy in peace talks, the establishment within the Nepali Congress Party was busy to make the Deuba government a grand failure. Even within the government and the negotiation committee, there was difference of opinion in dealing with the conflict. Consequently, these were instances where some members of the government Talk Committee were even non-cooperative with the government. Sincere commitment to the negotiated settlement was not there in some of the government negotiators. On the other hand, though there was parliament, the government was not able to take it into confidence and support. Hence, role of the parliament was minimal in the whole negotiation process. Political parties were also not fully co-operative to make the negotiation a success.

The Maoists wanted to demonstrate their public strength. Hence they had planned to organise a massive 'national rally' in Kathmandu (on 5 Aswin 2057BS) gathering more than two hundred thousand people. The Deuba government was very fearful of the possible confrontation if they organised this rally. Therefore the government wanted to ban or cancel it and ultimately this became source of deep mistrust and means of fierce rivalry. The government made it the sole condition for the further continuation of the negotiation. Ultimately, the organisers cancelled it but they became highly suspicious of the intention of the government. It ruined the environment for the negotiation.

Unfortunately, the Maoists withdrew from the negotiation table on 21 November 2001 saying that 'the significance of ceasefire was over as the government locked up all possibilities of reaching the solutions of the present political crisis through the peace dialogue'. The main cause of the break down of the ceasefire was the stalemate on the issues of constitutional assembly. Though the Maoist leaders had already withdrawn the issue of republican state, the constituent assembly became the cause of the failure of the negotiation. It was also noticed that the rebel leaders were deeply suspicious of the government for potential encirclement and action against them. The cited basis of their fear and suspicion were:

1. Formulation and implementation of the integrated security and development programme in 8 districts during the periods of ceasefire.
2. Arrest and killing of some of the Maoist cadres.
3. Establishment of the Armed Police Force.
4. They also claimed that they had information about the transfer of a large number of weapons to Ghorahi of the Dang district to start strategic attack on the Maoists in the mid-western region.

Immediately after the breakdown of the ceasefire, the Maoists proclaimed National People's Government and started major violent attacks in different parts of the country (e.g., Dang, Syanga, and Solukhumbu). In response, on 26th of November, the King declared a State of Emergency (SoE) exercising Article 115 of the constitution. Consequently, constitutional rights[5] of Nepalese people were suspended except the right to file habeas corpus. The Terrorist and Destructive Activities Control and Punishment Ordinance were also executed. The government declared Nepal Communist Party (Maoist), its sister organisations and supporters as 'terrorists'. Royal Nepal Army came to the battlefield and intense fighting continued. Human rights violations, censorship on media and suspension of civil rights has mounted during the SoE. Many national and international human rights organisations and international community had asked warring parties to respect the Universal Declaration of Human Rights. The parliament had approved the SoE for the second term with the support of the CPN-UML. The Terrorist and Destructive Activities Control and Punishment Ordinance became an act for another two years by the approval of the parliament.

In the 2001 peace talk, observing the process and the dynamics of the negotiation, both sides (the government and the Maoists) were not fully committed to peace. The period of ceasefire and negotiation was used as a strategic pause for tactical purpose to strengthen and consolidate political and military power. The Maoists used it:

- To weaken the monarchy: They were strongly arguing that the conventional monarchy in the country was finished after the royal massacre. Therefore, their entire efforts were concentrated for this purpose through public expression, training and orientating their cadres and taking debate into general public during the period of ceasefire
- To strengthen their political and military position: The Maoists formed the United Revolutionary People's Council (URPC) in September 2001 at the time of the first ceasefire. At the same time, they also established and expanded the "People's Liberation Army (PLA)". In the first week of September 2001, the Maoist negotiators were busy in talking with government negotiators in Kathmandu; the Maoist leaders were organising conferences of "URPC" and "PLA" in Kureli village of Eastern Rolpa (Sharma, 2002). Three days after the Maoists broke ceasefire on 23 November 2001, Baburam Bhattarai was appointed as the convenor of the 37-member URPC, Krishna Bahadur Mahara (who led the Maoist team during the first peace talks) was appointed as Co-convenor and Dev Gurung (Chief of Ethnic Department) was appointed as

BOX 4.3 Facilitators of 2001

Mr. Daman Nath Dhungana
Mr. Padma Ratna Tuladhar

secretary of URPC. The principal aim of URPC is to institutionalise the New Democratic Republic under the leadership of CPN (Maoist). Its constitution describes a four-layered organization viz. central, regional, district, and village/ town. They have also proposed nine autonomous regions (Upreti, 2004a; Sharma, 2002). These autonomous regions were:

- Seti-Mahakali Autonomous Region--- Hill area of Seti and Mahakali Zone;
- Bheri- Karnali Autonomous Region--- Hill area of Bheri and Karnali Zone;
- Tharuwan Autonomous Region --- Western Terai area of Rapti to Mahakali Zone;
- Magarant Autonomous Region --- From Kali Gandaki region to the hill area of Dhaulagiri, Rapti and Lumbini Zone;
- Tamuwan Autonomous Region -- Gandak Region;
- Tamang Saling Autonomous Region -- Hill area of Bagmati, Narayani and Janakpur Zone except Kathmandu valley;
- Newar Autonomous Region -- Kathmandu valley;
- Kirant Autonomous Region -- Hill area of Mechi, Koshi and Sagarmatha Zone;
- Madhesh Autonomous Region -- Awadh area of mid Terai and Bhojpuri and Mithila Pradesh of Eastern Terai.

Sharma (2002) highlights that 'out of these nine autonomous regions under URPC, six have been formed based on ethnicity and the remaining three (Seti-Mahakali, Bheri-Karnali and Madhesh) are based on regional classifications. They have started to constitute the leadership of these autonomous regions. The Regional or Ethnic Fronts have been given the authority to take up that responsibility until the "People's Republic" is fully established'.

All these actions of the Maoists clearly demonstrate that they were using ceasefire more for the strategic strengthening of their political, ethnic, military and ideological basis than to make the peace talk successful. During the period of ceasefire:

- They have extraordinarily strengthened their military base, which has been proved by their big offensive attack in Dang military base where they captured a huge amount of weapons just after 3 days of breaking the ceasefire.
- They were able to release their workers from the prisons.

- They formally introduced their agenda to the government, established them as legitimate political force by having official negotiation with the government.
- The have revived all public contacts, strengthened and renewed political linkages with wider sections of society.

The Maoists also used this ceasefire as a tool to test public response towards them. They wanted to test their agenda with people, parliamentary parties, and the king. The ceasefire was a litmus test to learn the attitude of people, the new king, and the parliamentary parties, whether they are really committed to peace. This was also an opportunity for the Nepalese people to test the intrinsic motive of the Maoists towards monarchy.

Even after breaking the 2001 ceasefire from the Maoist side, in March 2002 Maoist Chief Prachanda offered the possibility of another ceasefire if the state wanted to resume peace talks. However, the then Prime Minister Sher Bahadur Deuba flatly rejected the offer and said that he would not talk with the Maoists unless they surrendered their arms (Upreti and Dhungana, 2004). So for the period from late November 2001 to early January 2003 the country faced continuous attacks and counter attacks between the warring parties, gross violation of human rights and abuse of authority.

4.4.2 Analysis of 2003 (second) negotiation and failure of peace talks

The second ceasefire was announced on 29 January 2003. It is said that Narayan Singh Pun from the government side sent a letter with the cabinet decision to one of the underground Maoist leaders stating that the government was ready to discuss the three-point demand[6] (round table conference, interim government and the election

Box 4.4 Negotiators of 2003

A. Government:

1. From Chand government

Mr. Badri Prasad Mandal - Convenor
Mr. Narayan Singh Pun - Member
Mr. Upendra Devkota - Member
Mr. Ramesh Nath Pandey - Member
Mrs. Anuradha Koirala - Member

2. From Thapa government

Dr. Prakash Chandra Lohani, Convenor
Mr. Kamal Thapa - Member

B. From Maoists:

Dr. Baburam Bhattarai, Convener
Mr. Ram Bahadur Thapa-Badal, Member
Mr. Krishna Bahadur Mahara - Member
Mr. Dev Gurung - Member
Mr. Matrika Yadav - Member

for the constituent assembly). This paved the ground for the ceasefire. There was a unique background to this ceasefire. On the 4th of October 2004, the King resumed executive power, overthrowing the Deuba government, blaming it as incapable. After a few days, a new cabinet was formed under the leadership of noted pancha and loyalist of the king Lokehdra Bahadur Chand. The cabinet ministers were selected either from non-political background or from small political parties or people from politically sidelined status with the 'clean' label. All major political parties were sidelined and consequently they vehemently opposed the Chand government. Restoring ceasefire and bringing rebels to the negotiation table would be a visible and great success for the government to undermine the political parties and legitimise the direct rule of the king. Therefore, the government made utmost efforts to have a ceasefire and negotiation talks. Minister Narayan Singh Pun, with the help of Birendra Jhapali and Dhani Ram Lamichhine played a crucial role in negotiating for declaring a ceasefire and initiating negotiation[7].

In the 2003 peace talks, the Maoists came with strong preparation and a high-level negotiating team led by Dr Babu Ram Bhattarai. In their agenda, the Maoists strongly raised the internal contradictions that existed between castes, linguistic groups, regions, and categorically proposed to restructure of the state. The document submitted to the government states, "*Although the political movements in 1950 and 1990 tried to address this problem, the experience shows that these revolutions could not deliver desired results. Therefore, the oppressed groups, classes, communities raised arms in 1996 with an aim of establishing a new progressive regime in order to catalyse social, political, economic, cultural and other changes. It is also a clear fact that the strategic balance between the old regime and the newly emerging regime coupled with the geo-political situation of the country prompted a progressive political solution through dialogue. So, both sides announced a ceasefire on 29 January 2003. Accordingly, the CPN Maoist negotiation team has put forward this list of proposals, which can be further elaborated as the dialogue proceeds*".

In the 2003 peace talks, the Maoists were reasonably soft, well prepared and came with the motive of achieving negotiated settlement of the ongoing armed conflict. However, the government did not work hard to achieve the negotiated settlement by not being sufficiently prepared, not bringing mainstream political parties on board and ignoring the voices of civil society and international community. The 29 January 2003 ceasefire and the subsequent three rounds of 'peace-talks' on 27 April, 9 May and 17-19 August 2003 ended with no tangible result on 27 August 2005.

BOX 4.5 Unofficial English Text of Code of Conduct

Dr. Baburam Bhattarai, Convenor of the Negotiating Team of Nepal Communist Party (Maoist) and Narayan Singh Pun, Convenor, Negotiating Team of the Government signed the Code of Conduct on 29 Falgun 2059. The CoC contains:

1. Both parties should be committed and make efforts to find a peaceful solution through dialogue.
2. Both sides are committed and make efforts to find mutual agreement on matters of national importance.
3. Both parties will stop violent activities and will not deploy security forces that could ignite fear amongst general public.
4. Both parties will refrain from aggressive activities around high security areas.
5. Both sides will gradually release prisoners.
6. Both sides will work for the interest of the general public peacefully and without hindrance.
7. Ideas of both sides to get fair and impartial treatment in the state media.
8. Both sides to refrain from publishing comments that could mar the talks and peace process. Both sides to be civil while making comments.
9. Both sides to refrain from forcibly taking money or goods as donations.
10. Both sides to organize peaceful meetings and protests; there will be no strikes, bandhs or transport strikes during the ceasefire.
11. Both sides to refrain from searches, arrests and kidnappings.
12. Both sides to help each other in maintaining peace during the ceasefire.
13. No obstacles to be created in the transportation of food, medicine and essential goods.
14. Both sides will not obstruct the free movement of people.
15. No obstructions to be placed by both sides while exercising fundamental rights.
16. Both sides to allow movement of negotiators without impediment.
17. Both sides will help in the return home of displaced persons and their assimilation.
18. A monitoring team will be formed with an understanding of both.
19. Changes to the code of conduct can be made with mutual understanding.
20. Both sides will amicably settle differences in the interpretation of the code.
21. The code of conduct can be terminated through mutual understanding.
22. This code of conduct will come into effect immediately and should be fully implemented within 3 weeks from the date of signature.

The third round of negotiation efforts of 15-17 August 2003 between the government and the Maoists were by far the most acknowledged, as the talks were based on the written agenda forwarded by both parties (see Box 7 for the main agenda of the government and Box 8 for the main agenda of rebels). However, hopes of attaining lasting peace in Nepal have been shattered due to the rigidity of both parties, as they did not demonstrate enough flexibility in talks and stuck to their own agenda, they did not follow the internationally established negotiation procedures and principles. Though Nepalese people were enthusiastically optimistic and ambitious after the declaration of ceasefire, this enthusiasm has been eroded and fear, worry and frustration widened after the 27 August ceasefire break. The stalemate on the issue of constitutional assembly on the third round of the peace talks in the Hapure village of Purandhara VDC, Dang district could have been managed if both sides had shown flexibility and if the army had not undertaken the Doramba killing. There could be several routes to resolve this stalemate through non-violent means[8]. Lack of trust, fear, and feeling of insecurity on both sides had severely constrained the progress in the negotiation.

Delay in formation of the government's negotiation team, issue of representation of individual members on the Code of Conduct Monitoring Committee (selected to fulfil interests of nominators rather than performing proper monitoring), controversy in execution of the agreed issues from the second round of the peace talks (the negotiators agreed to limit the movement of RNA to 5 km radius of their base but this was not documented and the army opposed this agreement and government did not take a stand and said there was no such agreement[9]) , non-compliance in the agreed code of conduct[10], controversial expression by the members of negotiating team, ministers and the rebel leaders, non-cooperative attitude of the parliamentary political parties indicated that not one of the major players genuinely wanted a negotiated settlement of the armed conflict and lasting peace in this country, except ordinary Nepalese people. Foreign interests had added another complication in the negotiation process. It is astonishing that the foreign diplomats give their definitive (right or wrong, good or bad) judgement and dictate in the issues of Nepalese concern before Nepalese people, political parties, and the government. The interfering statements made by foreign diplomats also contributed to the breakdown of the ceasefire.

The January 29 ceasefire was non-transparent and came as a surprise

Box 4.6 Facilitators 2003

Mr. Daman Nath Dhungana
Mr. Padma Ratna Tuladhar
Mr Sailendra Kumar Upadhaya
Mr Karna Dhoj Adhikari

and therefore many analysts suspected that the rebels and the government (representative of the Monarchy) could have already agreed on the main contested issues. The five parliamentary parties, who were in power struggle with the King, had also suspected that the ceasefire might be an unholy grand design between the two gun powers to cease democracy. However, they were proved wrong when the Maoists broke the ceasefire.

It took a long time to start the peace talks after declaration of the ceasefire. The 7-month duration of the ceasefire was said to be undemocratic peace because:

- Important democratic institutions such as parliament were dissolved.
- Major parliamentary political parties were forced to remain out of the mainstream.
- The government was formed from the nominated people loyal to the king instead of full commitment to peace and therefore losing credibility and trust of the people.
- Weak international support for the peace process and negotiation.
- Resistance from the army on crucial issues (e.g., restriction of movement of army in 5 km).

There was a huge pressure from civil society, human rights activists, and international community to formulate and sign the CoC and institute CoC Monitoring Committee and start the peace talks. The worry of the civil society organisations was the possibility of resumption of war and human rights violation. There were continued complaints from the human rights activists that the Nepalese government was not sufficiently respecting the international human rights treaties and accords, where the state is signatory (Adhikari, 2004; AI, 2004; Upreti and Dhungana, 2004).

Only on 13th March 2003, the Code of Conduct (CoC) was signed between the representatives of the government and the rebels (see Box 4.5 for the details of CoC). They also agreed to institute the CoC Monitoring Committee (CoCMC) under the convenorship of the National Human Rights Commission (NHRC). However, the CoCMC was not functional because the government and the Maoists did not formally issue a letter to NHRC to initiate the monitoring and both the parties did not respect the CoC.

After 3 months of ceasefire, the first official peace talks started in Shankar Hotel at Kathmandu on 27 April 2003 where the Maoists handed over their agenda for negotiation to the government team. The talks concentrated on procedural issues and ended after 4 hours. The Maoists' demand was concentrated on the constituent assembly. In the beginning, the press was not allowed and the journalists present there made a strong protest.

The second round of peace talks started on 9 May 2003. This meeting was also limited to the procedural issues. Limiting the movement of the Royal Nepal Army within the radius of five kilometres was the key issue in this meeting. Another important issue agreed upon was the release of three central leaders of the Maoists from the jail. This controversial topic of limiting RNA mobility became one of the main causes of the collapse of the Chand government and consequently the peace talks fell into limbo.

Prime Minister Chand resigned on 30 May 2003 after massive protests of students and a controversy created by the second round of peace talks on the issue of constraining the movement of the army. At different programmes and rallies, five parliamentary parties spoke aggressively against the monarchy that could have also some implications on the resignation of Chand. His government was also not supported by the royalists and some powerful members of Rastraya Prajatantra Party.

On June 5, His Majesty the King appointed Mr Surya Bahadur Thapa, a veteran strategist and noted pancha, as the new Prime Minister. After the resignation of the Chand government, the peace process was in an extremely fragile situation and any time Maoists could go back if the government did not take any steps to continue the peace talk. The new Prime Minister appointed two ministers (Mr Kamal Thapa and Dr Prakash Chandra Lohani) as members of the government negotiation team. The government, with constant efforts of the facilitators, released three central leaders of the Maoists. In comparison to the work of the negotiators of previous government, this government did more homework, clarified procedure, established peace secretariat, organised informal consultative meetings and produced the government's agenda. However, the Maoists were already suspicious of the government and repeatedly asked to implement the agreement on restriction of army movement made in the second round of peace talks, which this government flatly denied on technical grounds, arguing that there was no evidence of such agreement.

BOX 4.7 Highlights of the Government's Agenda

1. Roadmap for the forward-looking reforms:
   Step 1. Creating consensus through negotiations between the government and the rebel side on the objectives, contents, and process of the reforms.
   Step 2. Organizing a Round-Table Conference with the participation including that of the political parties in order to establish the consensus reached as the document of national consensus.
   Step 3. Formation of an interim electoral government including the rebel side as well.
   Step 4. Holding of the election to the House of Representatives.
   Step 5. Amending the Constitution in accordance with the document of national consensus.
2. Bottom Line of the proposed reforms:
   Sovereignty vested in the people, constitutional monarchy, and multiparty democracy.
3. Objectives of the reforms:
4. 1. Building a political system that can accommodate and ensure participation of all Nepalese people.
   2. Creating equal opportunities for self-development of all the Nepalese people.
   3. Developing a political system on the basis of contemporary balance among the political forces.
4. Creating an egalitarian society by ending all kinds of inequalities, discrimination, and exploitation.
5. Proposed New subjects in the Reforms:
   1. Neutral electoral government to be formed three months before the general elections.
   2. System of proportional representation in elections.
   3. Upper house structure to include representation of ethnic groups, indigenous people, and Dalits in proportion to their population.
   4. At least 25% of seats in all representative institutions, including the parliament, to be reserved for women.
   5. Complete revamping in the local bodies with constitutionally guaranteed local self-governance with additional authority to local bodies.
   6. New structures to be created at the regional levels in accordance with spirit of local self-governance.
   7. Provision of national referendum on issues of national importance.
   8. Local bodies to be allowed to choose to use second working language from among the national languages.

9. Special provision for reservation of women, indigenous people, ethnic groups, and Dalits for a certain period of time in education, health, representative institutions, and employment sector.
10. Open and liberal market-oriented economic policies to be adopted by the state.
11. Parliament to be given a role in the appointments to the constitutional bodies.

6. There is agreement on several economic and social proposals put forward by the Maoists.
7. The concept of reforms may be reviewed on the basis of mutual understanding.
8. Government for including the issue of handing over of the arms and ammunition held by the Maoists in the agenda.
9. Government for including rehabilitation and reconstruction aspects in the agenda of the talks.
10. Suggestion for developing agenda on the basis of the proposals of both sides.
11. Emphasis on not creating obstacles in the government activities and the activities of the political parties.

Proposal for expression of commitment from both sides not to break the ceasefire under any circumstances.

The third round of peace talks started in the Maoist stronghold area (Hapure Village of Dang district) but ended with no results. The negotiators directly entered into the political agenda, which was most unusual and contrary to the general principle of negotiation. Consequently, the negotiation talk was withdrawn without exhausting all avenues of agreement (see Box 4.9 for the reasons given by the Maoists to discontinue ceasefire and negotiation). As has been discussed in the preceding section, the stalemate on the issue of 'unconditional constitutional assembly' and 'Doramba massacre' became the prime cause of the ceasefire breakdown. The following four fundamental provisions existing in the 1990's constitution were the bottom line of the government to negotiate with the Maoist negotiators:

- Sovereignty inherent in the people,
- Constitutional monarchy,
- Democracy, and
- Safeguarding and strengthening of the national territorial integrity and unity.

However, both sides used 'sovereignty of people' only to justify their own arguments rather than to really give people a chance to exercise their sovereign rights. Its real meaning was misinterpreted. The government denied the sovereignty of Nepalese people to elect representatives to write the constitution. If Nepalese people were granted the right to write their constitution by the people elected by them, there would be sovereignty of Nepalese people. There was a real fear in the government to agree on constitutional assembly before clearly spelling out the guarantee of existence of institution of monarchy.

The Maoists had accepted the King as one of the three powers (the Maoists, the King, and the parliamentary parties). In this respect, there should not be any problem to proceed further through negotiation. There was a very powerful invisible force mobilised by weapons traders to ruin the negotiation process. Unfortunately, the ceasefire ended from the Maoists side and they resumed the war. Both sides did not explore different possibilities and modalities of making a constitution where the concerns of all could be accommodated. Using 'hit-and-run' methods Maoist cadres attacked Royal Nepal Army Colonels in their resident areas of Kathmandu. Then the government promptly started retaliatory responses, declaring them as 'terrorists' and attacking the insurgents.

After the cessation of the negotiation and breakdown of ceasefire, the ongoing civil war severely threatened the already weakened nation. Looking at the aggressive war strategy of both sides, it can be easily predicted that this country is facing an unprecedented crisis. If the parliamentary political parties, the government, and international community do not act urgently to ease the situation civil state failure is unavoidable.

BOX 4.8 Highlights of the Maoists agenda for the talk

1. Main political agenda

   As the issue of regime is the key issue of the conflict, the political agenda should be the priority. The key issue should be formation of a new progressive regime and a new progressive constitution. Although there are some strong points in the 1990 constitution (such as multiparty competition, timely election, rule of law, press freedom, freedom of speech, etc) there are some grave faults and imperfections (such as so-called unchangeable points, contradiction between the royal regime and sovereignty, dissolution of the true democracy of the poor and the oppressed groups, regions, castes under the British "formal democracy", etc). Therefore, it is essential that the method of formation of a new constitution and the contents of the constitution have to be more progressive than that of the 1990 constitution.

a. The process or method of formulating a new constitution:

1. The leadership of the revolutionary party. With the consent of the revolutionary force and all the other parties, a broad round-table conference should be organised.
2. That conference should formulate an interim constitution without curtailing the democratic rights. enshrined in the 1990 constitution and reflecting a new political power balance and an interim government should be formed under the leadership of the revolutionary party.
3. The interim government should conduct an election to a constituent assembly within six months. The CA will be inclusive of different groups, castes, regions and communities. CA will form a new constitution.

b. Minimum contents of the new constitution:

1. The people should be fully sovereign and the regime should fall entirely upon the hands of the people.
2. As a supreme representative of the people, an elected people's house of representatives will be formed which will include representatives from all sectors and groups, such as women, dalit, janajatis, ethnic minorities, linguistic groups, different religions, regions, etc. All the organs of the regime will be accountable to this house of representative. Accordingly, there will be representation of different groups in the government as well.
3. The provisions will be such that with a two-third majority in the people's house of representatives or with a national referendum, any point in the constitution can be changed.
4. The Royal Nepal Army (RNA) and the People's Liberation Army should be unified by making certain structural changes and the unified national army should be brought under the control of the elected people's representatives.
5. The widely supported civil and democratic rights, such as multiparty competition, timely election, right to franchise, rule of law, freedom of press and speech, personal and human rights and civil rights should be guaranteed.
6. A regional and ethnic self-governance system should be implemented to give people the right to self-determination.
7. The country should be made a fully secular state.
8. Education, health and employment should be established as personal rights. All citizens should get free and readily available basic education and health services.
9. A new "land relation" should be formed on the basis of "one who works for the land owns the land". A just land distribution law should be enforced. The industrial development should be geared towards the nation's self-sufficiency. A protection policy should be formulated in

order to protect the national capital and resources.

10. An independent foreign policy should be implemented by abrogating the 1950 Treaty with India and all the other asymmetrical treaties and based on the principle of non-alignment and *Panchasheel* (literal meaning 5 traditional disciplines) A two thirds majority in the people's House of Representatives should ratify all the treaties with foreign countries.

c. We believe that the parties who believe in the progressive political outlet can come to an agreement on these progressive outlets. However, it is impractical to forecast all the contents of the new constitution, as the Constituent Assembly will be convened without any pre-conditions. We want to clarify that the political forces can go to the people with their views before the election to a constituent assembly.

2. National and socio-economic questions:

1. All the treaties, agreements, military assistance, presence of foreign military personnel, and their activities in the name of controlling terrorism should be stopped immediately.
2. The open Indo-Nepal border should be controlled and managed properly. All the cross-border encroachments should be stopped. There should be a system of work permit while employing a foreigner.
3. Gurkha recruitment, a national black mark, should be stopped. And the Nepalese should be given an honourable job within the country.
4. The foreign monopoly on the national industries should be stopped. The national industries and the inland industrialists should be promoted. The foreign debt should be wiped out within a certain time period.
5. The foreign encroachment and internal destruction created in the name of NGOs and INGOs should be stopped. The policies imposed by the international financial institutions should be declared null and void.
6. A united and concerted water resources policy should be implemented. The entire nation should be electrified by giving priority to the smaller and medium scale power plants.
7. The debt of all the landless and the poor should be cancelled and they should be provided with an employment.
8. All the landless people should be rehabilitated and provided with land and employment. Kamaiya, Haruwa, Charuwa and such other discriminatory practices should be dismantled.
9. The farmers should be provided with good quality seeds, irrigation and potential market.
10. The abrupt and continual price hike of the petroleum and other basic needs should be controlled. The wage labour and the salaries of the employees should be increased.
11. An effective instrument should be formulated to quickly punish the corrupted, smugglers and those who receive graft.
12. A national and scientific education system should be implemented. A job oriented education system is to be formed. The commercialization and

privatization of the education should be immediately stopped.

13. Free health service should be made available to specially the rural areas.
14. Special services to the disabled and the elderly.
15. All discriminations against women should be stopped.
16. Equal rights to dalit by eradicating the problem of untouchability.
17. The minimum wage and fixed hour work (40 hours per week) should be implemented effectively. The employees also should be included in management of the factories.
18. A concrete programme should be implemented for the welfare of the youth.
19. Ensure intellectual independence and occupational protection to the professionals, such as litterateur, doctors, engineers, etc so that they can best deliver their services to the people.
20. The production and distribution of documents that spread open western cultural pollution should be stopped.
21. Infrastructure development in the villages should be carried out rapidly.
22. The rights and privileges of Nepalese working in the foreign lands should be ensured.
23. Those killed in the different revolutions of the country should be declared martyrs and the murderers should be punished.
24. All the pro-people demands put forward by the pro-people organisations should be addressed immediately.

3. The issues of human rights and compensation and rehabilitation:

1. A high-level human rights commission should be formed with the involvement of the representatives of the human rights organisations to carry out an independent investigation of the human rights abuses and to punish the perpetrators.
2. The families of the martyrs should be immediately supplied with relief supports and compensation.
3. Those injured in the civil war should be treated freely.
4. Those displaced in the civil war should be rehabilitated in their original locality or somewhere else.

Examining the role of international communities in the Nepalese peace process, Thania Paffenholz (203:9) writes, *"Here we can see different points of views of international players. The US, India, and the UK favour an approach to peace through war, most of the EU countries and smaller neutral states support dialogue and political options. The latter position is also supported by international and local civil society peace and human rights groups"*.

BOX 4.9 Ceasefire off: An Unofficial Summary of Prachanda's Statement

Issuing a statement posted on the Maoists' website on Wednesday afternoon on 27 August 2003, Maoist chief Prachanda said, *"The rationale for ceasefire, code of conduct and talks process is now over for the time being. We decided to sit for talks giving supreme priority to people's will to find a peaceful political outlet. While making the ceasefire announcement, we took it seriously hoping the old regime will also be serious. But the royal army of old regime started to violate the code of conduct from the very beginning of the announcement despite the fact that our people's salvation army was totally devoted to the ceasefire. The royal army not only unnecessarily increased arrest and checking incidents but also continued to seize our people's army and to murder non-armed cadres brutally. Such acts were severe blows to our party and people's expectation and enthusiasm for a peaceful political outlet. Despite these facts, our party feeling the optimum responsibility towards nation and people, did not let the talks atmosphere spoil. Finally the first round of formal talks began and our party presented a minimum political agenda. In second round of talks, we agreed to limit royal army within five kilometres. But the royal army not only rejected the agreement but the government also changed with their pressure. With this, the talks process itself became orphan and questions arose over the possibility of a peaceful political outlet. After a long gap, through exchange of letters with the new talks team of the old regime and with their commitments to keep the royal army in discipline and as they released some of our central leaders, the party directed its talks team to sit for the third round of peace talks. The political agenda presented by the government during the third round of peace talks could not even address the basic problems of the country, but conspired to strengthen the feudal regression which came into being after October 4, 2002. The concept paper could not address even the demands of parliamentary parties who believe on multiparty democracy and constitutional monarchy. Their political agenda ended the rationale of peace talks on the very moment when they asked us to surrender our weapons. We rejected the proposal totally and made it clear the fourth round of talks will be held only if the establishment brings a new proposal of going for constituent assembly. At the same time, the royal army massacred 17 un-armed cadres and two civilians in Ramechhap. In particular, the concept paper presented in the third round of peace talks by the old regime and massacre of 19 people by the royal army in Ramechhap are the main reasons for the ceasefire break. It is the immoral and paradoxical attitude of the old regime to say that they are still committed for talks. Everybody knows our party is fighting for a people's republic state. We 'adjourned' the republic state demand for the time being and came to talks table to fulfil the people's desire for peace, with the demand of constituent assembly. But unfortunately, the old regime is not*

> *ready to go for a constituent assembly. Hence the government's double standard has ended the possibility for a forward-looking political outlet. With this, we want to make it clear that the rationale for ceasefire, code of conduct and talks process is now over for the time being. But we still express our commitment for regular interaction with all well-wishers to make our relations strong. We will not close the door for talks from our side. We can again sit for talks if people's sovereign right and their basic welfare are guaranteed. We urge all to help create such conducive environment for talks".*
>
> *Source:* nepalnews.com 27 Aug 2003.

Observing the Nepalese negotiation process, one of the leading conflict resolution and peace-building scholars ,John Galtung wrote, "*In Nepal we have negotiation process, although I am not quite convinced that it has started touching the real problems. ... What would be constructive for a peace process in Nepal would be a part of the Maoists disarming and part of the RNA disarming*" (Galtung, 2004:122). Pulling from his wide experiences around the world, he puts much weight to the role of king to make negotiation successful. Galtung states, "*In Nepal's case two aspects of the king - His Majesty's Government and Royal Nepal Army. An Ambassador to Latin America talked about frequent military coup in the region. A famous Argentinean friend said it could be explained in two ways. It could be explained by saying that the military is strong and hence it is always projecting its power through coup d' etats. It could also be saying that civil society is weak. And the latter is the most important explanation because we can do some thing about this. To touch the military is very difficult but we can make the other force much stronger. Now the first issue deals with the condition that the Maoists give up some of their demands, but the question is whether king will give up some of his demands. My reading of it is that the Maoists have been more forthcoming. The King might go to his friends in USA and UK and the king may come to the idea that there are two parties in this conflict. If the king could apologize for the 4 October 2002 and the mainstream political parties could apologize for the events before 4 October for failing in tasks- if that could happen, in my view the prospects for peace would be very real* (Galtung, 2004:115-116).

International Crisis Group, in its assessment of the causes of ceasefire break highlights "*the proximate cause of the breakdown in the ceasefire was the Maoists unwillingness to discuss issues other than the constituent assembly in the third round of the peace talk. By most considerations, however, the return to war must be seen as the culmination of steady erosion in confidence between the Maoists, the royalist government and the largely marginalised political parties* (ICG, 2003c:2).

4.4.3 Summary of the basic causes of failure of the negotiation and breaking of the ceasefire:

Three fundamental reasons are the fatal causes of the breaking of the ceasefire as:

1. Rigidity on the Maoist side.
2. Uncompromising conditions (sovereignty vested in the people, constitutional monarchy, multiparty democracy, and preservation of and promotion of the national integrity and unity) put forward by the government.
3. The Doramba massacre (the Maoists became seriously suspicious about the intention of the military, as unarmed 17 Maoists and 2 civilians were killed by the security force). This case was further signalling the helplessness of the government and its negotiation team. The independent inquiry team set up by the National Human Rights Commission confirmed that the security forces had unlawfully killed the unarmed Maoists and local people[11].

The other reasons the ceasefire collapsed were:

- Non-transparent ceasefire.
- The preparation, especially from the government side until second round of the talks was very poor.
- Basic principles of negotiation process were ignored. There was severe mistrust, lack of confidence and a deep sense of suspicion on both sides. The main basis of mistrust were: increase in weapons and army in both sides, mobilisation of the army by the government to perform health camps in rural areas, active US support to RNA during the ceasefire period too, controversy in implementing the agreement of the second round of the talk (5 km controversy) and violation of CoC by both sides. Harris and Reilly (1998) highlight the importance of procedural aspects in negotiation to restore peace in conflict situation. According to them commonly perceived deadlocks should break first that requires flexibility, building trust, promoting clarity and understanding, building coalition, use

of unofficial channels and third- party assistance. However, these issues were not considered in both the negotiations.

- Negotiating parties were reluctant to develop and agree on a Code of Conduct. With severe pressure from the international community and civil society, they agreed to have a Code of Conduct but they did not respect it.
- Nomination of the individual members of the CoC Monitoring Committee raised serious questions of neutrality. Sometimes they were publicly arguing on behalf of or against one or another party.
- CoC Monitoring Committee was not functional because both the parties did not support the Committee.
- The role of facilitators was severely constrained and used only as witness, if needed. They were committed to peace but not well equipped with the negotiation skills.
- Political parties were not supportive and did not constructively engage in the peace process.
- Both the government and the Maoists used period of ceasefire as a strategic pause to strengthen their military capabilities. The military thinking on both sides dominated the political side and therefore civilian solution got less attention.
- International community (mainly the USA, UK and India) played an ambiguous role. Some international powers were not interested in bringing international help of UN, EU or other relevant actors. Some international actors were using a strategy of 'wait-and-see', avoiding the proactive roles. Perhaps they wanted to distance from contradicting with the interests of the USA, UK, and India.
- The National Human Rights Commission had developed a human rights accord and sent to both parties to sign. However, they were not ready to sign it. If they had signed this accord, it could have prevented the collapse of peace talks and breaking down of ceasefire.
- Hardliners in both parties were in favour of military solution of the conflict. Conflict scholars (Zartman, 1989; Kleiboer, 1994; Paffenholz, 2002) say that a conflict should be 'ripe for resolution' i.e., parties involved in conflict should realise that they can achieve the goal through negotiations, instead of war.
- There was a distinct lack of involvement of relevant representative groups of actors in the negotiation process and

consequently they lacked broad-based support. Palestine peace process was in jeopardy when Oslo Peace Agreement excluded radical Palestinian groups. The same problem was observed in Congo when local militia groups were excluded (Paffenholz, 2003).

- Inconsistent and controversial role of international powers active in Nepal.
- Procedural weaknesses and poor handling of the negotiation process.

The response of the Maoist spokesperson Mr Krisahna Bahadur Mahara (23 January 2004, Kantipur) indicates that they are ready to accept the constitutional monarchy if the king is ready to give up the commandership of the army and a few hundred senior army officers loyal to the palace are terminated. However, he himself suspects that the government is not creating a conducive environment and therefore it is less likely to resume the talk.

BOX 4.10 Maoist Position on the Royal Nepal Army

Spokesperson and politburo member of the Communist Party of Nepal (Maoist), Krishna Bahadur Mahara talking to reporters at Badakanda Village in Junga Thapachaur VDC said, "The king must not lead the army and around 200 military officials should resign from their respective posts. But it is very difficult for him (king) to do so. We still accept multiparty democracy. But there is no constitutional monarchy as the king has a control over the army. But we are still committed to peace."

Source: In the http://www.kantipuronline.com/php/kolnews.php?&nid=6547, 22 January 2004

The government is also repeatedly saying that if the Maoists genuinely want peace the government is ready to hold talks. However, it is very difficult for ordinary people to believe them, as they have not yet shown any positive attitude towards resuming talks. Both sides are more aggressive in these days. Even the government rejected the proposals from UN and EU to get their help in resolving conflict in Nepal.

Though the Maoists broke the ceasefire and peace talk, the government had failed to create a conducive environment to continue negotiation[12] particularly due to the Doramba incidence. If the warring parties had discussed to make a new constitution in the House of Representative there would be strong pressure on the Maoists from the general public and international communities to accept this arrangement that could prevent the ceasefire break. From this ceasefire and the talks during the 7 months, the Maoist and the government tried to maximise political and military gain. The government maximised its political and military gains by doing the following:

- Strengthened its military capabilities, brought weapons from the USA and other countries, trained its military on intelligence and countering guerrilla warfare tactics, recruited new forces
- Massively collected intelligence information about the insurgents activities, bases, military strengths, supporters and their networks that make the security force easy to devise their military strategy
- Exchanged information with other security agencies abroad, sent staff for the training and exchange
- Physically identified many Maoists when they came out in the public.

The Maoist maximised its political and military gains by doing the following:

- Released their workers from the prisons and succeeded in removing red corner notice, withdrawing cases filed against them.
- Able to implant confusion to security forces about the government role and actions. When the government withdrew filed cases and court released the prisoners a strong voice from the security sector heard that what the government is doing is confusing and how security force can work if the government releases them.
- Far longer consequence is their public relations with general people, openly organising political rallies, meetings, discussions, debate in their favour. They use the open environment to strengthen the relations with the business community, media, and political parties and largely they succeeded. Business community was eager to welcome them.
- Another political achievement they gained from this ceasefire and peace talk is the public open debate on the need of constituent assembly. Constituent assembly election no longer limited to the agenda of the Maoist. It became a national democratic agenda and one of the best alternatives to resolve this violent conflict. Business community, democratic leaders,

professors, political scientists, lawyers, doctors, professionals all have started to think of the constituent assembly as one of the pragmatic ways out of the problem. Even within the main parliamentary political parties, the issue of the constituent assembly started to be openly discussed and many members have debated in support of constituent assembly. That gave ample moral boost and political backing to the Maoists.

- They also strengthened their military power during the period of ceasefire, they have recruited new fighters, trained them, and massively mobilised them to different parts of the country.
- Working for international relations was another important achievement of the Maoists as they were able to establish contact with many international strategists, specialists, and international relations officials within the country and abroad.
- Tried achieving from the negotiation table if possible what they wanted to achieve

4.5 MAOISTS STRATEGIC TACTICS

The sayings of the Maoists have created confusion in parliamentary parties, the king, the government, and ordinary people as well. They say the nominated governments (both the Chand government and the Thapa government) are *abidhanik* (illegal). However, they were ready to talk with these governments. They say that they are participating in the negotiation talk with the representative of the king, but still they recognised the government.

They have proposed three procedural steps to resolve the conflict, i.e., *golmech samelan* (round table conference), interim government, and the election for the constituent assembly. However, they never give the details, a clear model, or the framework of the roundtable conference and the constitutional assembly, which has ultimately created confusion.

The writings of the left leaders (such as Shankar Pokharel, Mohan Bikram Singh) reveal that the Maoists are either confused themselves or they want to create confusion in others and get benefits of confusion.

The Maoists reiterate that they want peaceful solution of the conflict but their current approach has not confirmed that interest. Before the fifth ceasefire from the Maoists unilaterally on 3 September 2005, they were inhumanly killing people, collecting donation forcefully, not allowing political activities of other political parties in their controlled areas, and recruiting young people to their military forcefully[13]. Not all these activities are conducive to the peaceful negotiation of the conflict.

Before the 1st February 2005 royal takeover, their position towards existence of constitutional monarchy was confusing to public[14]. However, this situation has now been changing. Now, constituent assembly election, a top priority of the Maoists is becoming a national agenda because of the action and behaviour of the king. Parliamentary political parties were working as a buffer between the king and the Maoists before 1st February but this has changed and political parties became fierce opponent of the king and the constituent assembly election become their agenda too.

As the Maoists frequently said, the nation is at the stage of strategic stalemate where no one could win war and therefore they want peaceful resolution. If they really want a peaceful settlement of the armed conflict through negotiation, they need to change their present mindset. Thania Paffenholz (2003:8) argues that the Maoists, as part of their people's war philosophy, are prepared to fight for very long time. Hence, they may continue protracted war if the state is not prepared for negotiated settlement. On a political level, the longer the insurgency continues, complicates the political situation. For example, the king took over the executive power citing the cause of insurgency. Hence the Maoists insurgency became a cause strengthening autocracy and militarization of the nation.

4.6 CONCLUSION

While assessing the peace process in Nepal, the negotiation process was not accomplished correctly[15]. The six rounds of talks for the negotiation during the period of two ceasefires were not accomplished according to the internationally accepted principles of negotiation. Proven negotiation procedures and steps were not followed. Both sides (the state and the Maoists) used the ceasefire as a 'strategic pause' to strengthen their military capabilities instead to make genuine efforts to make the talks successful. The Maoists made the mistake unilaterally breaking the ceasefire this August 2005. They must know peace talks and negotiation is the only viable and lasting solution.

One of the main reasons of the failure of negotiation and the ceasefire break is the perceived risk. All major political players of this country are severely suffering from the perceived risk of cessation of their existence. The supporters of the 4 October 2002 royal takeover perceived that a successful negotiation with the rebels agreeing on the constituent assembly might end the existence of the constitutional monarchy. They perceive that constituent assembly could result in a republican system. Therefore, they vehemently oppose negotiation with constituent assembly.

Before the 1st February royal takeover, Nepali Congress Party, CPN (UML), and Rastray Prajatantra Party were not ready to compromise with constituent assembly election and therefore they were vehemently opposing it for la ong time. Furthermore, corrupt leaders of the all political parties were very worried about potential actions against them as they were heavily involved in corruption and irregularities during their rule that could ultimately jeopardise their political future, if reached political settlement. Hence, they were trying their best to make the negotiation unsuccessful. Some of non corrupt leaders of political parties were genuinely worried about the risk for multiparty democracy, as the Maoists were fighting for a communist state. Hence, they were not willing to go for constituent assembly to settle conflict. The Maoists are fearful of the possibility of wiping them out from political scenario (like in Peru) by the collective efforts of the palace and the parliamentary political parties, even using external military support. Therefore, they were always trying to widen the gap between the parliamentary parties and the palace, and urging international community to stop external military intervention. Many bureaucrats might have perceived that they could face punishment for their wrongdoings and corruption in the past decades after the negotiated political settlement. Therefore, they are giving wrong advice to the government, parliamentary parties, and the king. However, the entire political scenario has changed from the 1st of February. The distance between the political parties and the Maoists is decreasing and the distance between the political parties and the king is widening.

The current approach of resolving the Maoist conflict of Nepal is wrong and it needs to change. The state should opt for multi-track approach that includes negotiation efforts from all actors at different levels with different scales and mandate. The political parties, civil society, the Maoists, palace and the government must start dialogue at different levels as an inclusive approach. The political crisis between the palace and the parliamentary parties is adding whole complication in negotiated settlement. The only way to overcome this problem is to completely handover power by the king and be ready to accept the decision of Nepalese. Further, the Maoists have to stop violence against ordinary people, allow internally displace persons to return their home, allow political parties to organise their activities in the Maoist control areas. Political parties must promote internal democracy, issue a white paper for their past misdeeds and failure and apologise to the Nepalese people and come together for concerted action to establish functional democracy and peaceful settlement of the armed conflict. The major problem for political parties so far is to work out the differences and come to a common understanding on how to restructure the state to address the root causes of the conflict that ensure durable and democratic peace in Nepal.

After 1st February, the government lost credibility and legitimacy because there is no provision in the constitution to lead the government by the king. Further, the state must start the state reform process and should not wait until the negotiation with rebels. The government, in consultation and full agreement with the political parties, must invite UN to help Nepal in resolving the Maoist conflict. The good intension of multi-lateral international community (especially UN and EU) must be acknowledged and Nepal must utilise their experiences, their image of acceptability and the resources they have. If we fail to involve the UN, we may be indirectly (knowingly or unknowingly) inviting bilateral powers in the Nepalese conflict, which could be far more costly later.

Nepal must learn lessons from other conflict-ridden countries. The Maoists should realise that violent actions produce cycle of counter violence and retaliation that is counter productive to the whole negotiation and peace process. The king must realise that slavery cannot be accepted in the 21st century. Democracy cannot be promoted by detaining political leaders, journalists, civil society members and human rights activists, censoring media and creating terror. Therefore, the first condition for king is to return power to political parties. Both the government and the Maoists should realise that military solution of the conflict pushes the nation to militarization that cannot flourish in a democracy.

The rapid militarization process in Nepal is weakening the King, the parliamentary parties, the Maoists and civil society. It is also pulling massive resource from the social development budget to spend in unproductive areas. Killing people, expelling them from village, creating terror cannot win genuine support of Nepalese people. If the Maoists and the government continue the current approach, their actions will soon lead to state failure, military rule, and foreign intervention. In this situation, warring parties cannot achieve what now they are claiming to achieve. Therefore, they need to rethink their military actions, stop terror, declare ceasefire, start dialogue, and reach a negotiated agreement.

The state has so far completely failed in dealing with the insurgency. The government approach is based on the military thinking and action, which has proved to be wrong in insurgency like the one of Nepal, developed on the state failure in tackling poverty, injustice, discrimination and unequal resource and power distribution.

The Maoist conflict is not difficult to resolve, if concerned actors are willing. This is not an ethnic violence, this is not a separatist movement to break the nation and it is not a religious conflict, which are far more difficult to resolve. The Maoist insurgency is a political conflict. If the main aims of the government, the political parties, the king and the Maoists are to alleviate poverty, injustice, discrimination, to establish democratic governance procedures and practices, to make Nepalese people happy, prosperous and to develop equal and just Nepalese society, they must be ready to achieve them collectively. If they are genuine to these problems and changes there are no fundamental differences. The differences are just on procedural issues' how to do that, which could be easily worked out if the above objectives are real for all forces and if they are willing to find the appropriate procedures.

If all key stakeholders do not sincerely commit for peaceful solution of the problems, repeated ceasefires and negotiations will not work. First, there should be a common understanding and commitment to resolve this crisis before proceeding to any negotiation and peace talks. That needs appropriate mechanisms, instruments and procedures to bring all key actors together, to develop a consensus on dealing with negotiation and to facilitate future course of actions.

Future negotiation should proceed with clear mandate, elaborated framework and well illustrated procedure on dealing with the crucial issues and state reform agenda. We have learnt lessons from the previous two negotiations that without clear visions, full commitments, and appropriate framework for negotiated settlement the problem cannot be solved. It is also not possible to solve the crisis without involving the Maoist in the government and therefore future course of actions must explore possible ways to bring them in the interim government and to settle the constitutional issue and post conflict transformation.

NOTES

1. See Upreti, B. R. (2060), Maobadi Dwonda Samadhan: Bigatka kamjori ra Bhavisyako bato, Mulyankan Monthly, Issue 113 kattik- Mangshir, pp. 41-43, 2060 and Upreti, B.R. (2061) Nepal ma Maobadi Sashastra Dunda: karan, ashar ra samadhan ka prayash haru. Kathmandu: Bhrikuti Academic Publications (Nepali) for detail.
2. In April 1997 the government formed a Task Force on the Study of Maoists Problem and Solution under the leadership of Prem Singh Dhami, Member of the Parliament. Other members of the Task Force were Yogesh Bhattarai, Praddep Samser Rana (Inspector General of Police), Devi Ram Sharma (National Investigation Department), and Krishna Murari Sharma (Ministry of Home) as Member Secretary.
3. The government created a special Armed Police Force to deal with Maoists. However, Royal Nepal Army was not happy to bring another security apparatus instead of strengthening them. Until that time the military was not formally mobilised to fight insurgency and police force alone was not enough. That might be the reason the special force was created.
4. The government had introduced a special package of development programme where security forces were mobilised to deliver development package and combined security operation with development. It was initiated in Gorkha district on a trial basis and expanded t o another 7 districts. However, it did not work and later it had to stop.
5. Freedom of opinion and expression, freedom to assemble peacefully, freedom to move throughout the Kingdom and reside in any part thereof, freedom of any profession, or occupation; freedom of press and publication rights; rights against preventive detention; right to information; right to property; right to privacy and right to constitutional remedy.
6. So far there is no systematic documentation of the peace process and there is no public access of any information related to the negotiation and peace talks. Only one document i.e., the forward-looking agenda of the government submitted to the government in third round of 2003 negotiation is publicly available. All other correspondences and decisions are not publicly available and therefore it is very hard to get the official version of the government on critical issues. Often the issues come in public and the government ministers either oppose or say ‘no idea’.
7. It is said that Narayan Singh Pun worked to achieve the ceasefire process with direct instructions of the King. He was quite active and sometimes unbelievably assertive, which does not seem possible without the consent of the king.
8. Referendum is the most suitable means to resolve contentious issues but it is more useful only if issue is single (like whether to go to Constituent Assembly election or whether to rewrite the existing constitution, etc. However, it is too complicated if there are several issues coming together like in the current conflict. Similarly, in the problems or issues, demanding

consensus for the full settlement referendum divides people into majority and minority and consequently the conflict or problem remains unsettled.

9. Three of four facilitators have publicly said that there was agreement between the negotiators on limiting the movement of army. According to them the negotiators from the Maoists side demanded to limit the military in barracks and in response the government negotiators proposed to limit RNA movement on a 5 km radius. However, there were no written documents and when the government said this was not agreed and the Maoists and the facilitators (Daman Nath Dhungana, Padma Ratna Tuladhar and Sailendra Kumar Upadhaya) said it was verbally agreed upon, there was a controversy that ultimately implanted severe suspicion and mistrust in Maoists on the ability of the negotiators and the government in fulfilling the commitment.
10. Human rights activists frequently complained about the violation of the Code of Conduct by both sides (e.g., continuing aggressive activities, searching, arrests and kidnapping, not amicably settling difference, violation human rights, etc.).
11. See Amnesty International press release at www.amnesty.org/library/index/engasa310 8 3 2003.
12. After the third round of the talk at Hapure, the Maoists took 7 days to assess the Doramba event and progress in the negotiation. The press release related to the ceasefire break came in only after 7 days. Considering this duration, we can argue that they might be debating within their party on whether to continue the negotiation talk and at the end the hardliners' decision might have prevailed.
13. Numerous reports of INSEC, CWIN, Amnesty International, Human Rights Watch and other national and international human rights organisations and journalists have revealed such activities.
14. Padma Ratna Tuldahar frequently shared his experiences of facilitation. He has cited that in one of the discussion with Government negotiators (Dr Prakash Chandra Lohani and Kamal Thapa) in Hapure where Dr Babu Ram Bhattarai said that CPN (Maoist) is ready to carry over 'constitutional monarchy' if a tacit understanding is made between the state and the Maoists. This means that they were ready to accept existence of Monarchy if other things were settled. Though they were consistent on the Constituent Monarchy, they said that Nepalese people are the ones to decide the fate of Monarchy and it must be tested through the election of Constituent Assembly.
15. See the author's expanded article entitled 'Maobadi Dyunda Samadhan: Bigat ka Kamjori ra Bhabisya ko Bato (Resolution of Maoist Conflict: Weaknesses of the past and direction for future), Mulyankan Monthly, Issue 113, Kartik, Mungsheer, pp. 41-43. (Nepali)

CHAPTER 5

Civil Society, Political Parties and Media in Peace Process

5.1 INTRODUCTION

This chapter briefly assesses the efforts made by civil society, political parties and media in conflict transformation and peace building. Conflict transformation and peace building is a relatively new area for Nepal, therefore civil society, political parties and media sectors are also inexperienced in dealing with these issues and gradually gaining experiences. However, the pace of gaining experiences and of learning is quite slow. Political parties particularly are too slow and even resistant to learn and change their approaches.

The first part of this chapter deals with civil society, its initiatives and activities in conflict transformation and peace building. The second part discusses the brief efforts of political parties in resolving the ongoing armed conflict. The third part deals with the role of media in conflict transformation.

5.2 CIVIL SOCIETY IN PEACE PROCESS

5.2.1 People's participation in negotiation and peace process

Civil society (CS) is a fuzzy term with no precise definition. Defining civil society, Bhattachan (2003:34) writes, "Civil society comprises different types of groups such as economic, social, cultural, religious, educational, informational, interests and lobby groups; civil organisations, non-governmental organisations, and public trusts. In

Nepal minorities themselves are part of the civil society...". Civil society for the purpose of this book covers a wide range of actors (other than military and security forces, government, political parties and international communities) such as professional organisations, business community, media, human rights activists, scholars and researchers, teachers, writers, lawyers, engineers, doctors, professional experts, NGO staff, religious groups, etc.

The history of war and peace has shown that civil society has tremendous potential and firm ability, far more than anyone else, to enhance peace process. The unquestionable reality is that creating and maintaining peace requires active engagement of all actors of society, from ordinary citizens, security actors to politicians. However, civic engagement in peace making and peacekeeping in Nepal is not getting enough attention. It is very hard to realise any genuine efforts from the state to promote public participation in peace process in our country. Pragmatically, peace making and keeping is more than ending armed rebellion. It goes beyond addressing root causes of conflict and it promotes peace transformation. Therefore, it is a political and social transformation process as it has to focus on structural change in governance, security and development, human rights policies and practice and regaining eroded trust (Carl and Garasu, 2002; Clements and Ward, 1994; Cohen, 1999; Crocker et al., 1994). In this respect democratising peace process is extremely essential but severely lacking in Nepal (Gurung, 2003).

If and when public engagement in peace process is ignored, the success is rare or even if, by any chance, success is achieved, it is temporary (Barnes, 2002). The general public may not own elite-guided peace negotiation, if people are not active participants. If the peace talk is brought into public sphere it promotes transparency and accountability, enhances constructive dialogue and gets public support and ownership. African examples in war and peace sufficiently tell us that peace in a war-torn society is seldom permanent when real civic engagement is not promoted (Armond et al., 1998; Armond and Carl, 1996; Barnes, 2002; Hume, 1994; Lord, 2000; EPCP, 1999; Kona, 1999). Achievement of viable and lasting peace is only possible when capacity of local people is utilised and complemented with the efforts of government, human rights organisations, media and other peace actors.

In South Africa, conflict transformation and peace building was the outcome of genuine collaboration between religious people (churches), businessmen, politicians, and civil society (Barnes, 2002). The resolution of conflict in Guatemala was the outcome of sincere efforts of 'Citizen Assembly' composed of several civic organisations, churches, indigenous unions, women's groups, and business people. The Citizen Assembly was able to offer an agenda for negotiation between the parties in conflict (Armon et al., 1997; Crandall, 2004). In Northern Ireland, women from different communities formed a strong 'Northern Ireland Women's Coalition', which had greatly contributed to achieve the 1998 Belfast Agreement (popularly known as Good Friday Agreement) (McCartney, 1999). The UK, one of the power centres of the world, was not able to solve the Northern Ireland conflict without engaging local people. One of the elements of John Major's Triple Lock' programme was people's approval of the agreement through referendum (Bloomfield, 1997; Coogan, 1995; Fitzduff, 1999). This indicates that even 'western', 'democratic' governments cannot resolve conflict and maintain peace if they ignore civic engagement. In the Philippines indigenous people, churches and local community made marvellous efforts to build peace (Armon and Philipson, 1998). They have declared some territories as peace zone where citizen rights were respected. Local communities made similar efforts in Columbia (Garcia-Duran, 2004). Similar observations can be found in the Middle East (Corbin 1994a and b), Croatia (Fetherston, 2000) and Afghanistan (Misra, 2002; Maley, 1994).

Peace cannot be built and maintained without creating and promoting social infrastructures of peace, developing people's ownership in peace process and abolishing obstacles. A widely held misperception in Nepal is that peace will be achieved when the Maoists and the government negotiate and sign a peace agreement. But this will not be the case. There will be numerous obstacles to implement the agreement, if (and when) there is an agreement. So the successful negotiation between the government and the rebels will be only a minimum condition for peace. Restoring political tolerance and coexistence, indispensable elements of peace (Barnes, 2002; Lucima, 2002), will be a major unsolved challenge in the Nepalese peace process. Unless people own the peace process and are ready to develop a feeling of tolerance and coexistence, it will be a meaningless optimism to restore lasting peace. The Nepalese state has not yet realised the people's participation in peace process.

People's participation brings interests, aspirations and values of peace constituencies to peace negotiation and makes the negotiated settlement sustainable. At a theoretical level, three approaches of civic engagement or people's participation in peace process exist (Barnes, 2002). They are:

- Representative participation of people in peace process,
- Consultative participation of people in peace process, and
- Direct participation of people in peace process.

Representative Participation:

In representative participation, political parties represent their constituencies in peace process and negotiation. In representative participation, there is always the risk of elite domination. The National Unification Commission and Civil Society Assembly of Guatemala and Philippines were also part of representative participation (Armon et al., 1997; Stancovitch, 1999).

Consultative Participation:

In consultative participation, civil society raises views and formulates recommendations for negotiation. In Mali, community decision process has contributed to peace making. In civic participation, churches, religious leaders, business community, media and local leaders played a crucial role in war-torn countries to build peace. However, these modes of peace-building efforts are not prominently seen in Nepal.

Direct participation:

In direct participation, all stakeholders are involved in peace making. They participate in developing and implementing negotiation. South Africa and Northern Ireland are examples of direct participation of people in peace process (Barnes, 2002; McCartney, 1999). Another direct mode of participation can be referendum where the general public is directly involved in decision process. In Columbia, Regional Peace Committees were directly involved in localised peace making (Garcia-Duran, 2004). The same thing happened in South Africa. In these countries local leaders had facilitated process of involving all interested community members in peace process.

It is hard to find any of the above forms of participation in the Nepalese peace process and negotiation. Exception was the failed negotiation of 2001, where elected representatives were involved (Upreti and Dhungana, 2004). However, they were not able to represent the aspirations of the people for the peace on the negotiation table mainly because of their vested interests. All the subsequent governments failed to recognise importance of multi-track approach and contribution of citizens in peace process.

The important question is how to promote people's participation in Nepalese peace process. One of the potential answers would be to promote peace advocacy/lobbying and massive campaigns at local level in a non-partisan way. Creating a mechanism of local participation is essential to achieve that objective. The important question is how to engage larger civil society and promote people's participation in peace process. The state and international community needs to realise that more resource flow to community for peace campaign is essential.

Though not recognised by the state, some good initiatives by citizens have been started in Nepal. The huge peace marches of more than 50,000 people (most of them women and children) on 29th of August and 1st June 2003, 21 September (in the occasion of UN Peace Day), a series of peace rallies organised at Chitwan, Pokhara, Biratnagar and other parts of the country were some of the noble initiatives. However, these local initiatives are not getting recognition and appreciation from the state.

Further, there were no efforts from the government to form expert panels; establishment of formal mechanisms of engaging people in peace process and even not established any contact point where people can give feedback on the negotiation and peace process. Though the government, with intense pressure from civil society and international community had established a Peace Secretariat, it is totally inaccessible to general public as it is heavily guarded compound by circles of police and army. Therefore, only people having formal invitation from the government can enter the Secretariat with tiresome security checks. After the 1st of February, even this Secretariat is also almost dysfunctional as the government has no priority on negotiation with the rebels. The avenue for giving individual inputs and expert opinions and feedbacks has also been completely closed after the 1st February royal takeover because of the media censorship and other restrictions. Those who advocate for political dialogue between the government ands rebels, speak in favour of negotiated settlement and criticise the wrong course of actions of the government that are ruining the environment for the peaceful resolution of the armed conflict are treated as the enemy of the government. The government is attempting to develop a culture of silence suppressing individual opinion makers and civil society at large.

5.2.2 Women in peace process and conflict transformation

Experiences of Nepal on the previous peace talks, and conflict history of the world have shown that peace process is complex, sensitive, delicate and very fragile (Upreti and Dhungana, 2004; Upreti, 2003b; Barnes, 2002). The global experiences of conflict settlement have proved that women play a crucial role in resolving conflict and restoring stable peace by involving in peace making, peace building and peace keeping. Peacemaking is essentially a negotiation of an agreement to formally end a particular dispute. In this process civil society around the world has played an extremely important role in the background (Barnes, 2002; Galtung 2000a and b). The peacemaking is then followed by peace-building, which implements the agreement and brings the parties back together in some sort of normal relationship. In this process, women as a major section of civil society, using their accommodative behaviour and inherent quality of forgiveness, help to reintegrate the conflicting parties into society. African and Latin American experiences show that the roles of women in peace-building process; rebuilding normal relations between people in conflict were extremely important. Women were involved in rebuilding trust, re-establishing cooperative relationships, apologizing for past violent deeds and forgiving those deeds to make former enemies friends and neighbours. Peace building to achieve stable peace is a process that must involve all citizens: women, children, men, poor, and rich, not just the elite. Stable peace is a situation when two parties do not even consider war to be an option, no matter what conflict occurs between them (BHCT, 2003). However, civic engagement and role of women in peace making and peacekeeping in Nepal is not getting enough attention. Some efforts to promote women's participation in peace process in Nepal have been initiated, especially by women peace activists.

Despite the total ignorance of the state and marginalisation by political parties, Nepalese women have greatly contributed to promote and sustain peace process. Various initiatives taken by Nepalese women at national and local levels are constantly pressurising the warring parties and other political forces to restore peace[1].

5.3 AREAS OF ENGAGEMENT OF NEPALESE CIVIL SOCIETY IN PEACE PROCESS

Civil society organisations, individual professional experts, opinion makers, activists, business community, writers, lawyers and many others are engaged in activities related to conflict transformation and peace building in Nepal. A brief discussion about the main areas of their engagement has been discussed in the following sections:

5.3.1 Awareness rising on peace and small arms

Proliferation and misuse of small arms and light weapons (SALW) is fuelling the armed conflict and severely undermining the peace process in Nepal. Lack of awareness in the detrimental effect of SALW is a challenge in Nepalese peace process. However, awareness of illegal trading, proliferation and effects of SALW is an entirely new area and a very small segment of civil society actors has engaged in this debate. Peace awareness is a fundamental step to mobilise people for conflict transformation. Armed conflict is new and therefore the peace awareness is also a new area of engagement for Nepalese civil society actors. Awareness raising on SALW related issues such as the international provisions and arrangements in addressing SALW issues; security implications and policy concerns in terns of national security, on society and on economy, need of establishment of Independent Watchdog Organisation (Commission on SALW Control, Identification of Focal Point, etc.), regulatory, institutional and policy arrangements, commitment of the state in international provisions, making regulatory and legislative provisions, need of concerted efforts and cooperation between government and civil society in developing guidelines and criteria, assessing implications (research and analysis), awareness, lobbying and advocacy and import control and dealing with existing stocks (stockpile management, disarmament and destruction) (Upreti, 2005a). However, not much work has been going on in these important areas. Recently, South Asian Network on Small Arms Nepal has started some work in these areas, particularly studies, exchange of information and advocacy. So far these initiatives are too small to have influence at national and international levels.

Global experiences reveal that illegal trading of small arms and light weapons is increasing (IANSA, 2003). Landmines are becoming severe problems in successfully transforming violent conflict.

Proliferation of SALW always triggers conflict to escalate and poses severe challenge to peaceful settlement. Since the beginning of the armed rebellion, transaction and flow of SALW are tremendously increasing[2]. Nepalese civil society needs to further expand awareness raising on effects of illegal SALW and prevention and clearing of landmines.

5.3.2 Protection of human rights

Civil society efforts in this area are relatively consolidated. Many professional organisations have been developed in the field of human rights and greatly contributing to protect human rights. Nepalese human rights defenders have played an important role in the time of severe human rights violation by the state and the rebels. However, their actions so far are more concentrated in curative measures rather than protective measures. National Human Rights Commission though attempted to be used by the state in favour of its interests and suffered from its own internal conflict, is gradually developing its competency in defending human rights. International human rights organisations like Amnesty International, Human Rights Watch, the United Nations Office of High Commissioner for UN Human Rights (OHCHR), International Committee of Jurists are raising their concerns over human rights violation in Nepal by warring parties and putting pressure on them to respect basic human rights of people, provision of Geneva Conventions and other UN conventions and protocols.

Informal Sector Service Centre (INSEC), Child Workers in Nepal (CWIN), Women Rehabilitation Centre (WOREC), Centre for Victim of Torture (CVICT), Advocacy Forum, Beyond Beijing Committee (BBC), Legal Aid and Consultancy Centre (LACC), Himalayan Human Rights Monitors (HimRights), Maiti Nepal, Jagaran Nepal, Nepal Tamang Women Association, Women Welfare Society, Women Awareness Centre, Centre for Human Rights and Democratic Studies, Human Rights and People Service Centre, Alliance for Human Rights and Social Justices, Prisoners Assistance Mission, Constitutional Lawyers Forum, Collective Campaign for Peace, Public Health Concern Trust, Physicians for Social Responsibilities Nepal, Concern for Children and Environment Nepal, Children Women in Social Service and Human Rights, Children at Risk Network Group, Children Welfare Society, Nepal Tamang Ghedung, Dalit Womens Organisation, Jagaran Media Centre, Feminist Dalit Organisation, Janautthan Prastisthan, have formed Human Rights Treaty

Monitoring Coordination Committee. Shanti Samaj, Human Rights Organisation, etc. and human rights activists have been actively engaged in protecting human rights violation and raising awareness on the human rights situation within the country and around the world. Other organisations like Federation of Nepalese Journalists, National Dalit Commission, National Women Commission, and many others are raising awareness on human rights issues.

Realising the high degree and intensity of human rights violation in Nepal, OHCHR opened its largest office in Nepal in April 2005. Since then OHCHR Nepal office is monitoring human rights violations by the warring parties.

Advancing human security through human rights in a situation of conflict is very challenging. Rampant poverty and internal displacement of people due to violence makes the situation more complicated at the time of armed conflict. However, success of conflict transformation and peace building mainly depends on the extent of protection of human rights during the wartime. Therefore, human rights approach of conflict transformation and peace building is becoming crucial (Galtung, 2004b, Adhikari, 2004). In this ground, UN concludes that 'the best conflict prevention strategy, at the end of the day, is a strategy of respecting human rights'.

Civil society has played an important role creating violence - limiting mechanisms. These mechanisms are different advocacy forums, regular communication campaigns, periodic sharing (e.g., Martin Chautari, Social Science Baha, etc.). However, such mechanisms need to be expanded.

5.3.3 Rebuilding the lost trust

Trust building is one of the important areas where civil society is slowly engaged, contacting warring parties, creating platforms for debate and discussion, and working as a channel between the warring parties. Civil society played a crucial role in negotiation between the trade union close to the Maoists and industrialists in late 2004 when there was long industrial action by the trade union. Similarly, civil society leaders played an important role in reaching negotiation between the student union close to Maoists and boarding schools' associations to open the schools closed by the students[3]. These are some of the trust-building efforts. Role of trust is becoming very effective in conflict transformation and peace building. Winning mind and heart of people is crucial for successful conflict transformation to which women greatly contribute. For example, mothers' club in Sri Lanka had started massive reconciliation efforts by organising meetings with conflict victims. Public relations are crucial in conflict transformation. It is almost impossible to build peace engaging public where women could play a great role. Hence, women could bridge the gap between civil society, political forces, government and media to build trust.

5.3.4 Disarming and demobilisation, reconstruction, rehabilitation, reintegration and reconciliation

Herculean tasks in conflict transformation are post-conflict activities such as disarming and demobilisation, reconstruction, rehabilitation, reintegration and reconciliation. Disarming and demobilisation of ex-rebels and their management (both temporary and long term either by integrating part of rebel army into national security force or engaging them in other tasks) is an extremely complicated task and if not handled properly factions of rebels continue violence. Nepal needs to learn lessons from Guatemala and Angola where they have faced this type of problem already. Civil society in collaboration with the government, the Maoists and international community needs to work together to achieve disarming and demobilisation of the rebels, reconstruction of the damaged infrastructure and new infrastructure required to meet the requirements laid in the negotiated settlement, rehabilitation of the conflict victims and internally displaced people in community and new areas, etc. So far even awareness raising is not enough in these areas. Massive civil society efforts are essential but only very few professionals have started to work in some of these areas[4].

Conciliation is a process where civil society works to improve the relationships between two or more people affected by the armed conflict. In escalated conflicts like ours in Nepal, distrust is inevitable. The pervasive distrust is severely hampering the ability of the conflicting parties to negotiate. Initiatives for promoting trust-building measures are extremely essential where Nepalese civil society actors are still far behind. Civil society needs work with the disputants to correct misunderstandings, reduce fear and distrust, and generally improve communication between the parties in conflict. Women have made successful reconciliation in many countries like Sri Lanka, Northern Ireland, etc. especially in community reconciliation. One strategy for dealing with the combatants is to focus on the admission of guilt, the paying of reparations, the asking of forgiveness, and the granting of amnesty, where role of women is crucial to facilitate the reconciliatory actions. Further expansion of similar efforts is needed in Nepal too.

5.3.5 Peace empowerment

Peace education and awareness is an important step for peace empowerment. Without empowerment of local people, it is very hard to achieve durable peace. Hence, civil society organisations are engaged in empowerment activities to help disempowered groups, strengthen their power so that they can advocate for peace, and participate strongly in exploring options for resolution of conflict. Interest-based organisations (e.g. Dalit, women, ethnic minorities, etc.) have played an important role in local empowerment. NGOs are other important actors engaged in the peace empowerment process. Even warring parties need empowerment in the understanding of importance of peace and power of peaceful means to negotiate armed conflict. So far they are extremely weak to realise the power of peace in state reform and social transformation.

5.3.6 Creation of peace zones

Another important work of civil society in conflict transformation process is to create peace zones. These are proposed geographical areas where warring parties are prohibited to enter for the purpose of war. Civil society leaders urge the warring parties to create peace zones, where peace talks could be organised, or other peace related activities could be accomplished. For example, the United Nations had administered such peace zones in Jerusalem for the benefit of all ordinary people who live there. In Nepal, peace activists, human rights and child rights organisations, teachers, organisations of private schools are pressuring warring parties to declare 'school as zone of peace'.

5.3.7 Working as coalition for peace

Civil society organisations have built coalitions for peace. Civil Solidarity for Peace is a coalition of more than 200 national level organisations. Similarly, Professionals Alliance for Peace and Democracy (PAPAD), Collective Campaign for Peace, Shanti Mallika, National

Development Network, Himalayan Human Rights Monitors, National Alliance for Human Rights and Social Justice, Nepal, etc. are some of the examples of the coalition for peace initiative in Nepal. Similar networks have been created at the district levels too. However, their efforts are not yet enough to bring warring parties in the negotiation table. Nepalese peace activists have to further strengthen their power base and ability to pressurise the government and the Maoists.

5.3.8 Engage in humanitarian assistance

In addition to being engaged in human rights and people's empowerment for peace building, a few civil society organisations have also started to work in some humanitarian areas such as financially supporting conflict victims, psychological treatment and trauma healing, educating orphans of conflict, engaging conflict victims in income generation activities, reconciliation, rehabilitation of some conflict victims, physical support to some conflict-affected schools, etc.. Though this issue is not taken seriously in Nepal by the state, larger civil society as a whole and international community, it is a fundamental part of conflict transformation and peace-building process, as it provides human needs to conflict victim and helps to engage in peace building process. Management and rehabilitation of internally displaced persons is becoming one of the major challenges in the Nepal's conflict. However, this issue is not taken seriously by the state and international community.

5.3.9 Citizen diplomacy for dialogue

Citizen diplomacy is yet a new concept in Nepal. However, in addition to conventional style of official diplomacy from government, Nepalese citizens (intellectuals, civil society leaders, professionals, etc.) are gradually engaging in citizen diplomacy. They started discussions about how to solve the armed rebellion in Nepal. They are focusing on improving interpersonal understanding and confidence between groups. For example, Civic Solidarity for Peace is working under the framework of citizen diplomacy. Even civil society has explored different options for negotiated settlement; suggested ideas to initiate innovative approaches such as having Citizens Peace Commission (Upreti, 2003b). Many roadmaps and frameworks have been prepared by civil society organizations, conflict experts and peace activists. These activities have contributed to facilitate dialogues at national levels. Dialogue is a process in which parties engage in deep and meaningful conversations with their opponents for the purpose of developing a better understanding of the concerns and interests of warring parties, to break down negative stereotypes, deep-rooted feelings, values, and needs, and come to a common understanding. Though not enough, contribution of Nepal's civil society in peace process is positive.

5.3.10 Media monitoring

The risk in all war-ridden countries like Nepal is that the media often tends to sensationalize conflict events and covers only newsworthy issues, which is triggering conflict (Upreti, 2004a). Similarly, sometimes media covers up or down-plays important information based on the influence and interests of some actors, which people need to know to lobby and advocate for peace. Civil society needs to constantly monitor the role of media and the information they disseminate to ensure such coverage do not unfairly damage peace efforts or help to escalate violence. Some civil society organisations have started to function as media watchdogs, monitoring news, reports and their contribution in escalating or deescalating the ongoing armed conflict. However, some big civil society organisations/NGOs are engaged in several activities and therefore there is not yet professionalism and speciality is developed.

5.3.11 Overseeing and fact-finding

As a part of the expert team, civil society leaders are involved in joint-fact finding. Joint fact-finding helps the government and the Maoists to resolve factual disagreements (human right violations, for example). Similarly, civil society leaders, particularly the human rights activists are also involved in overseeing the process of fact-finding. Overseeing is a type of alternative to joint fact-finding, which is applicable in situations where one of the parties is conducting the fact-finding and another party has to decide whether or not to believe the fact-finding results. These are a crucial part of conflict transformation where neutral civil society leaders greatly contribute.

Civil society also acts as an observer if there are hostile confrontations between the Maoists and the government. In this situation, both the government and the Maoists attempt to harm or terrorize other party, which will widely affect larger society and nation as a whole. In these situations, role of civil society organisations is to observe, document and lobby to minimise effects on community and vulnerable individuals. The observer's role of civil society leaders is to report aggressive behaviour and human rights violations.

Civil society organisations and leaders have been engaged in investigating contentious issues such as Doramba massacre, Pili attack by Maoists in the army camp operating for the construction of road, etc. Particularly, human rights organisations have been very active in investigating human rights abuses committed by warring parties.

5.3.12 Emergence of peace-focused civil society organisations

Since 2002 various civil society organisations (CSOs) have been actively engaged in exploring potential paths to resolve conflict. Many organisations have been created and are active in finding ways. Compared with other countries, evolution and contribution of civil society in peace process in Nepal is fast and effective. Though it is not possible to include all CSOs involvement in such initiatives, in the following section initiatives of some of the CSOs deliberately emerged for working in peace have been discussed:

Civic Solidarity for Peace (CSP):

It is an umbrella organisation composed of more than 200 CSOs ranging from business community, religious groups, professional groups, NGO federation, etc. It is very active in peace-building process. In the history of Nepalese armed conflict, CSP had organised a Round Table Conference, actively engaged in consulting international community, the Maoists, the government and prepared a roadmap. The proposal of this organisation was by far the most progressive and addressing most of the contending issues. However, political parties and the government did not take it seriously. This alliance is also organising a series of peace marches and rallies, talk programmes, think tank discussions, and consultation with different key stakeholders of the conflict. This is the biggest initiative and if it works more proactively, it will have wider effects because of being an alliance of all powerful organisations such as journalists, lawyers, professors and teachers, doctors, NGOs, etc.

Volunteer Mediators Group:

It is a deliberate effort of some peace activists to assist conflict resolution in Nepal. By its nature this is a very small structure. It has prepared a roadmap to settle the armed conflict. It has suggested resolution within the framework of multiparty democracy, nationalism and national unity. It has suggested having the monarchy fully transparent, and the government to be fully responsible for the security, management and expenses of the Royal Palace. However, this roadmap was not clear enough to address the aspiration and needs of Nepalese people mainly because it has not elaborated upon the state restructuring process. It also does not elaborate on control of army issue, a major source of power struggle between the palace and people. Main weakness of this proposal is lack of focus on issues.

Civil Society for Peace and Development (CiSoPD):

It is another initiative taken by some members of civil society to contribute to resolving the bloody conflict in Nepal. CiSoPD is composed of personalities from various sectors such as business, university, politics, civil services, research, journalism, etc. This loose network has not publicly presented a specific roadmap but is actively engaged in transforming violent conflict into durable peace.

Friends for Peace (FFP):

It is a research and resource organisation created by well-known personalities of Nepal to expand knowledge base through conducting research on conflict transformation and peace research, sharing global experiences and documenting local initiatives that contribute to the negotiation and peace process. It has also developed a resource library specialised in conflict transformation and peace building, first of its kind in Nepal.

Nepal Nagarick Manch:

This is another initiative started by some people devoted to peace. This organisation is also hosting different peace related activities, exploring options and creating pressure on the warring parties to reach a negotiated settlement. Being lead by a well-known economist and banker from Rana family and having family links with the palace, many people expected to have better access with palace and easy to get perspective, opinion and position of the monarch to resolve the problem. However, so far civil society did not get benefit of such links to end this bloody conflict.

Professional Alliance for Peace and Development (PAPAD):

It is an alliance of professional organisations such as journalists, lawyers, university teachers, medical doctors and others. It is also actively engaged in contributing to restore peace in Nepal. Because of influence of its members, it has good potential to influence conflict dynamics but it is not much active in that scale.

Citizen's Peace Commission:

There is also a voluntary and informal organisation formed by peace activists and civil society leaders to contribute to the peace process. Its main aim is to facilitate negotiation process from the citizen's level by creating conducive environment and trust building, by exploring options and exerting pressure over the conflicting parties for peaceful resolution of the armed conflict. This Commission is engaging in some peace related activities at a very slow and narrow pace. The author was one of the first of peoples' peace commission and advocated for its establishment, prepared concept proposals and presented in media and series of discussion groups. Based on the experiences of other countries, the expectations of Nepalese people, the original proposal was made with wider mandate, scope and nature of the commission. However, its scope, mandate and nature were constrained. Therefore, this much-expected Commission has a big challenge to establish its credibility and prove its relevance.

Nagarik Awaz:

This is an initiative of some women peace activists to restore peace and justice in Nepal. It is focusing on restoring confidence of youth victims of conflict, to develop their skills and capabilities to live as a dignified citizen. Further, this organisation is training youth victims of conflict in reconciliation and harmony and using them as the peace ambassador for their villages. It is also organising regular sharing programmes on peace and conflict transformation related issues.

Santi Malika:

This is the newest initiative of several feminist organisations and individuals to restore peace in Nepal. Basically this is a network organisation dedicated to 'women and peace' theme. Its strength is grassroots-national linkage. It has brought more than a hundred women from different parts of the country to discuss role of women in process and to formulate future strategy.

Collective Campaign for Peace:

This is a network institution of more than 40 organisations, most of them from out of Kathmandu. It is an advocacy organisation for peace and mobilising its members' rural remote areas. COCAP has some special features compared to other NGOs in Nepal such as total transparency in its budget, expenditure and programme activities, devoted to capacity building of its member organisations, engaged in proactive advocacy.

In addition to these initiatives, there are several organisations engaged in peace and conflict transformation. A unique tendency is developing in Nepal. Most of the development NGOs are now engaging in conflict transformation and peace building mainly because their donors asked them to do so and there are financial resources available in the field of conflict transformation and peace building.

5.3.13 Relation between civil society and post-1st February political change

There is a very bitter relationship between the proponents and supporters of the 1st February royal takeover and the mainstream civil society leaders and human rights and peace activists. The high-handed control of the civil society activities by the post-February government made civil society annoyed and alienated from the state that virtually turned into bitter relations of mainstream civil society with the government and palace. The government attempted to develop parallel civil society efforts in support of the royal takeover and allowed to have rallies, mass meetings and street gathering to the supporters at the time of the State of Emergency where all such activities were banned for other people. The government also started to develop code of conduct from the Social Welfare Council to regulate and control activities of civil society organisations working in the field of civil rights, peace and democracy and those who do not support the royal takeover. That act of the government not only chilled relations between the government and the mainstream civil society but also raised concerns internationally (as Secretary General of the United nations and other leaders from different countries had expressed there deep concerns on the intention of the government to bring a code of conduct which is the responsibility of the civil society itself).

5.4 INITIATIVE OF POLITICAL PARTIES

Though in the strict sense political parties are different from civil society, their initiatives in restoring peace in Nepal are also discussed in this section. Political parties earlier were not able to realise the complexity of the armed conflict and did not take it seriously. Later when it went beyond their grip, they started to rethink and explore ways to solve it. As a result, different political parties have prepared different political agenda to settle this armed conflict. Among them, CPN (UML) was more engaged in preparing and publicising the options. The following are some of their initiatives of the political parties:

5.4.1 Initiative of CPN (UML)[5]

While searching the documents of different political parties, I found that CPN (UML) is more active in documentation and dissemination of issues related to the ongoing armed conflicts and different approaches to resolve it. It has constituted two committees to specifically look into the Maoist armed conflict and suggest ways to resolve them. CP Mainali (1997) led one task force and Jhala Nath Khanal (2002) led another.

Proposal of National Consensus for a Progressive Way Out

Further, CPN (UML) has prepared a document entitled 'Proposal of National Consensus for a Progressive Way Out' which was endorsed by Central Committee of the CPN (UML) held from April 21 to 27, 2003. Main texts of this agenda have been discussed here.

Their text wrote, "*Our Party the CPN (UML) has been putting forward proposals for progressive reforms and change for the solution of political, economic and social problems that have emerged in the country. We continuously raised our voice in the parliament and tried to forge national consensus. The 27 point consensus issued by us at the time of the promulgation of this constitution was also related to the goal of gearing the country to the path of progress. We had put forward the proposals for progressive amendments in the constitution with the realisation that the country's problems could not be solved in the status quo*". The CPN (UML) has put forward the following programmes to end the ongoing conflict.

(a) To acquire additional achievements while safeguarding the gains made by the 1990 People's Movement, the past experiences shall be reviewed, people's rights shall be expanded, shortcomings shall be removed and democracy shall be safeguarded, consolidated and developed.

(b) The achievements scored by the 1990 people's movement shall be extended to the people, people shall be further empowered, the people's sovereignty shall be clearly established by consolidating the inherent supremacy of the people. It shall be extended to social, economic and cultural fields to ensure that the benefit of democracy percolates down to the people. Accordingly transformation shall be brought in the field of politics, society, economy and culture.

(c) Democracy shall be transformed into real and participatory democracy without limiting it to formal and procedural matters. Good governance shall be established by pursuing responsible and transparent policy by fully democratising the state and society.

(d) The vicious cycle of murder, violence and anarchy shall be put to an end and the dialogue going on between the Maoists and the government shall be made successful and result oriented.

This agenda proposed by CPN (UML) is more generic and general. In achieving these it has also illustrated some points as:

1. The sovereignty and state authority inherent in the people shall be made clearer, effective and consolidated. Provision may be made for holding referendum on issues of national importance.
2. A national anthem shall be decided upon incorporating

nationalism and patriotism.

3. Monarchy shall be made transparent and democratic.
4. The army shall be put under people's elected government. It will be loyal to country and the people. It will be made more professional by freeing it from political interference.
5. Correcting its present shortcomings shall evolve an effective electoral system.
6. National Assembly shall be restructured to include the renowned personages from among the ethnic groups, downtrodden (Dalit), women and other distinguished people.
7. The state shall be declared secular. In doing so national peculiarity, original culture, civilisation, national identity and good traditions shall be preserved. The discrimination existing in the field of religion, language and culture shall be removed.
8. A long-term peace shall be established by solving the ongoing Maoist conflict in conformity with national consensus and on the basis programme for progressive reforms.
9. The local bodies shall be given the right of autonomy in line with decentralisation by restructuring their administrative set up. In doing so attention shall be given to ethnic-lingual specialities and diversities. They shall be developed as the local government bodies by providing them with resource and authority. The women's representation shall be made 33% progressively increasing their representation in local bodies.
10. The existing political and administrative structure shall be readjusted making it reflect the social and cultural diversity and geographical reality.
11. Provision shall be made for allowing every political party to field female candidates with an objective of progressively increase the women's participation to 33 per cent.
12. Women shall be given equal rights to property. Provision for harsh punishment shall be implemented for domestic violence and human trafficking by eliminating all the discrimination against women.
13. Untouchability shall be considered as an unpardonable and heinous offence and the people at the political, administrative and representative levels shall be forthwith removed from their post if they are found to have committed such offence.
14. A special policy shall be pursued for the development of languages, religions and cultures of all nationalities. Policy

shall be adopted to provide equal opportunity and access to the people of all walks of life without discrimination.

15. Discrimination against the people of Terai shall be done away with. Highest priority shall be given to the east-west railway and trunk roads for the speedy development of the Terai region.
16. A special programme shall be formulated for the development of remote areas by adopting the concept of proportional development.
17. People under the poverty line shall be identified. A planned special programme shall be implemented for their upliftment.
18. A special programme shall be formulated and implemented for the solution of the problem of unemployment. Employment in foreign countries shall be regulated and systematised.
19. The backward classes, communities and areas shall be identified and a special programme shall be formulated and implemented for their development.
20. A special programme shall be formulated for the education, skill and employment of the downtrodden (Dalit), backward, orphan, disabled, ethnic and impoverished people.
21. A clean and efficient administrative mechanism shall be developed. Bureaucracy shall be democratised and professionalized by keeping it away from political interference.
22. A provision shall be made for easy and accessible justice. A system of alternative mechanism for conflict resolution shall also be developed.
23. The problem of citizenship especially in Terai shall be solved by deciding upon the threshold year on the basis of national consensus.
24. All kinds of feudal exploitation shall be eliminated. Land shall be distributed to the landless, Kamaiyas and squatters by implementing a revolutionary land reform. Short-term, medium-term and long-term development program should be adopted according a high priority to the development of agriculture.
25. Corruption shall be effectively controlled. Nobody shall be immune to it. The constitutional and legal mechanism against corruption shall be made strong and active.
26. The operation of the political parties and their accounts shall be made more transparent.
27. The existing impunity shall be done away with and the rule of law shall be effectively implemented.

28. A programme for industrialisation shall be implemented with a clear thought about it. Foreign investment shall be attracted in the interest of the nation. Economic policy shall be adopted suiting the requirement of the country. Special emphasis shall be given to the development of private and cooperative sectors.
29. Priority shall be set for the economic development of the country. High priority shall be accorded to the development of physical infrastructure such as agriculture, hydro-electricity and human resource. The general expenditure of the government shall be controlled and development expenditures shall be increased.
30. A special programme for social security shall be implemented for the people who are backward, neglected and impoverished.
31. A special attention shall be given to vocational, technical and non-formal education. Provision shall be made to make education conform to the national interest and requirement by making it accessible to the common people. A special national campaign shall be launched for the elimination of illiteracy.
32. Health service shall be made easy and accessible to the general people and a policy of community health shall be pursued for that purpose.
33. A special programme shall be implemented for the resettlement of the people displaced during the course of ongoing murder, violence and anarchy and for the reconstruction of physical infrastructures that have been destroyed during the conflict.
34. A foreign policy based on non-alignment and Panchasheel shall be pursued suiting the national interest.
35. All the unequal treaties and agreements including the 1950 treaty with India shall be reviewed, amended or repealed and new treaties and agreements made on the basis of equality and mutual interest.

This was a good initiative. However, implementing it requires common understanding from all political parties. Furthermore, it is still a narrow framework to holistically address the current conflict, as this framework is a political agenda of one political party coming without national consensus. It also does not address the core issue of making constitution by the representative elected by people through the constituent election process. Basically this is a compromise document.

The Proposal for Resolution of National Problem

Based on the above programme, again CPN (UML) prepared another proposal called 'The Proposal for Resolution of National Problem' on 10 January 2004 to resolve the armed conflict. It is popularly known as the Nine Point Roadmap of CPN (UML). These nine points are:

1. The present nominated government should be dismissed and an all-party government should be formed with the Prime Minister appointed on the basis of understanding and recommendation of all political parties represented in the dissolved parliament and should move towards maintaining the House of Representatives.
2. The environment for dialogue should be created declaring a cease-fire both by the government and the Maoists. Both the government and the Maoists should agree on the human rights accord and code of conduct and they should express their commitment for full implementation of those codes during cease-fire.
3. All political parties represented in the all-party government should develop a comprehensive forward-looking package in order to bring about changes in the current situation of the country. On the basis of the package, the all-party government should hold dialogue with the Maoists.
4. The forward-looking common program should address the issues and concerns of dalits, women, ethnic groups, and marginalized people of Terai region. It should address problems facing the unemployed and those below the poverty line. It should build on the principles of national independence, pro-people democracy, decentralization, good governance, corruption control, and end of impunity and wider democratization of the society and the State.
5. After conciliation with the Maoists, the all-party government should convene a roundtable conference. Delegates of political parties represented in the dissolved House of Representatives, the CPN (Maoist) and other individuals, invited as per the agreement of the political parties participating in the conference should participate in the roundtable conference. The conference should decide upon the forward-looking program and procedures. And this should be the basis for national consensus.
6. For the implementation of the program agreed upon in the

roundtable conference, there should be an agreement in relation to the issue of constitution as to whether to go for the amendment of the Constitution or to opt for a new constitution. Whatever the agreement, the process should move ahead to get fresh people's mandate organizing the election for the House of Representatives. Following the agreement on holding the election for the House of Representatives, an interim government should be formed in the participation of Maoists and all other parties concerned.

7. The United Nations should be invited to help undertake elections for the House of Representatives. This is to ensure that elections are held fairly in an atmosphere of peace, where the people caste their votes free of any kind of fear, terror and coercion. During the election period, the security arrangements should be made as per the established principles, norms and process of the United Nations.
8. The elected House of Representatives should either amend the constitution or frame a new one as agreed upon in the roundtable conference. In case of the requirement to frame a new constitution the present Constitution should be amended to facilitate the process. Accordingly, a constitution commission should be formed to draft a new constitution and the constitution commission should submit the draft-constitution before the House of Representatives within a specified time frame. The draft constitution should be adopted unanimously or by a two-thirds majority. After the promulgation of this new constitution, the Constitution of the Kingdom of Nepal, 1990 should be repealed.
9. The government formed as per the new constitution should address the concerns and problems of the Maoist armed combatants. Similarly, the government should undertake a rehabilitation program for the displaced people and reconstruction scheme for destroyed infrastructures.

Though not enough, this was another good initiative of CPN (UML) to resolve the crisis. But the question is how to honestly translate it into practice. CPN (UML) is publicly known for its glaring differences on saying and doing. CPN (UML) is also often charged for its power-centric approach. General Secretary of this party has initiated dialogue with Maoist leaders (meetings were held, first at Siliguri, second at Lakhnao and third at Delhi of India). These were very good initiatives to engage in dialogue with Maoists. However, such initiatives have yet to produce results.

5.4.2 Nepali Congress

Nepali Congress party was ruling the country for more than 75 per cent of the democratic period (1990 to 2003). It has allowed the Bhattarai government to constitute high-level committee to study the insurgency under the leadership of former Prime Minister Ser Bahadur Deuba. It also asked its government to have ceasefire and arrange peace talk first time in 2001. However, it is difficult to publicly assess any roadmaps or agenda of conflict resolution at party level. Most of its activities and agenda of restoring peace in Nepal were concentrated in party decisions or individual opinions of its members. Later, Narahari Acharya, its Central Committee Member published proposal for state restructuring but the party has not endorsed it. By far, works of Narahari Acharya[6] at the individual level, several political leaders of Nepali Congress Party proposed opinions, roadmaps or perspectives but there is no formal document publicly available except their discussion on the Maoist issues in the regular meetings of central committee. I made several attempts to get any official documents of Nepali Congress Party on the conflict transformation and peace building in Nepal and requested its senior members but was not able to get any and therefore am not able to elaborate here.

5.4.3 Rastrya Prajatantra Party[7]

Rastraya Prajatantra Party was formed by all leaders of the partyless political system overthrown by 1990's popular movement. Therefore, their philosophy, principles and strategies are dominated by the legacy of Panchayat. At the party level, discussion in central committee meetings about the Maoist insurgency and ways of resolving it were reported in the media but not publicly available any formal documents. However, the government of this party (led by Surya Bahadur Thapa) prepared the position of the government to negotiate with the insurgent for the first time. The State Restructuring Proposal submitted to Maoists at the time of Hapure Peace talk at the time of Surya Bahadur Thapa's government was the first document on the government position. Recently, with intense power struggle this party has again broken down and Surya Bahadur Thapa has formed Nepal party called Rasstrya

Janasakti Party. I have not discussed this party as separate as it is too new to have much initiative.

5.4.4 Samukta Janamorcha

In case of conceptual understanding and political position, this party is by far the most clear, less controversial and straightforward. It has initiated a campaign against the Maoist brutality in different parts of the country at a time where all political parties were passive in their political activities. This party has also put forward a clear approach of resolving the ongoing-armed conflict. Because of its most clear position, quite different and radical, other major political parties were not ready to acknowledge the proposals of this party for a long time. Perhaps, being together in the same party with Maoist leaders for several years, many of its agenda points are similar with CPN (Maoists) including constituent assembly election. If all political parties had agreed to hold the constituent assembly election proposed by this party and Nepal Sadbhawana Party earlier, the conflict could have been resolved earlier. Perhaps, cleanliness, clarity and straightforwardness of this party might be coming form opportunity non-existed for this party to involve in the government and exercise power.

5.4.5 Nepali Congress (Democratic)

This is a new party, splintered from the Nepali Congress, with only 3 years of history. However, it has worst performance in terms of peace building and conflict transformation. Its leader Ser Bahadur Deuba is one of the leading spoilers of whole peace process in the entire history of the armed conflict in Nepal. When he got power, he forgot what he had recommended when he was heading a Commission. Every worst activities from the peace building perspective such as imposing state of emergency, imposing Terrorist and Destructive Activities Control Ordinance, declaring Maoists as terrorist and fixing bounty of heads of Maoist leaders, mobilising military in domestic conflict and expanding military size and budget, proliferation of arms, excessive use of arms and weapons, etc. have been initiated, promoted and advocated by him, mainly to satisfy regressive force and interests of palace with the hope to holding power contumeliously. The only one good step in peace building this party done is the establishment of Peace Secretariat but it is not fair to credit this party alone for the initiative taken by four-party coalition government.

Leader of this party Ser Bahadur Deuba was also a major actor for all regressive activities such as dissolving parliament, preventing to extend the tenure of local elected representatives, and preparing ground for 4 October 2002 and 1st February 2005 events. Though some of its leaders seem committed to peaceful resolution of the armed conflict they were not able to influence party as a whole, as it was entirely dictated by its failed leader. Formal document of this party on how to resolve ongoing armed conflict is not available publicly.

5.4.6 Nepal Sadbhawana Party

Nepal Sadbahwana Party (Anandidevi) is a regional party concentrated in the Terai region of Nepal. It has many confusing and controversial political issues with regional focus. It is said to be close to India. However, this party is very clear from the beginning in one fundamental step in resolving conflict, i.e., constituent assembly election. It has not much influence in changing conflict dynamics but its leaders are more clear on how the Maoist conflict can be settled. Recently, a small faction dominated by royalists separated from the Sadbhawana Party. However, there is no published document of the breakaway group on conflict transformation and therefore not discussed here.

5.4.7 Communist Party of Nepal-Marxist-Leninist (CPN-ML)

CPN (ML) is the breakaway part of CPN (UML) with relatively less influence in Nepalese politics. CPN (ML) is relatively more clear on how to resolve the ongoing conflict. It has proposed very important ideas and documents for state restructuring and advocating for national convention, interim government and constituent assembly election as the way out of conflict, which are in many aspects similar to the proposal of Maoists. However, because of lack of political influence these important ideas and roadmaps are not coming into national debate and discussion.

5.4.8 Initiative of other parties

There are other small initiatives from different small political parties but they are not able to generate national debate because of their size and influence. Nepal Peasants and Workers Party, Nepal Samata Party are few of them directly engaged in conflict transformation debate to a lesser extent.

5.4.9 Agenda of Alliance of Five Parliamentary Parties

After the 4 October 2002 takeover of the executive power by the king, five major political parties - the CPN (UML), Nepali Congress, National People's Forum, Nepal Peasant Worker's Party and Nepal Sadvawana Party (Anandidevi) - came out on the streets to protest it. In the course of their protest, with extensive discussions and dialogues, the parties have come out with an *18-point agenda*, which was termed as *'Forward Looking Reform Agenda'* to address the current problems of the country. These 18 points were endorsed by a special session of the dissolved House of Representative last July. According to the parties, the present impasses of the country can only be resolved through their implementation. This became weak when the UML decided to join the Deuba government nominated by the King.

18-point Agenda of the Alliance of five parties for political solution:

1. People's sovereignty and executive power shall be made unambiguous, effective and consolidated. A provision of referendum shall be introduced in the constitution to take decisions on major issues of national importance including constitutional and political issues.
2. Monarchy shall be made transparent by bringing the king under complete constitutional framework.
   - 2.1 The existing practice of allowing King to draft laws as he wishes shall be abolished.
   - 2.2 All the administration of Royal Palace and the management of Royal Palace services shall be brought under the Ministry of Royal Palace.
   - 2.3 Existing provision in the constitution-allowing king to use his discretion on any issues shall be eliminated.
   - 2.4 A system shall be developed where the king will have to make his property public on a regular basis.
   - 2.5 The royal title shall be limited only to the king, the queen and the crown prince. The Prime Minister's position shall be placed 4th in protocol order.
   - 2.6 The provision of Royal Council (privy council) shall be

abrogated.

3. The Royal Nepal Army shall be granted national status and mobilized as per the democratic norms and values at the same time making them responsible towards the country and people. A system shall be introduced to place the RNA under the elected parliament.
4. The present national anthem shall be replaced by an anthem, which is nationalistic, dignified and is able to reflect the sentiment of national unity and patriotism.
5. Parliament shall be made stronger and more effective to completely establish the sovereignty of the people. A provision of restoration of parliament and its continuity shall be included in the constitution if the election declared by the Prime Minister could not be held at a fixed time. An effective system shall be introduced in order to make elections freer and fairer and impartial and to increase the representation of women, dalits and people of other marginalized and socially oppressed communities in the parliament. Political parties shall be made organizationally democratic and economically transparent. With regard to constitutional appointment, a system of parliamentary hearing shall be introduced.
6. A forward looking national agenda shall be prepared on the basis of consensus to resolve the Maoists problem politically and to establish a lasting peace through a successful and result oriented dialogue. The families of the victims of the conflict will receive compensation, relief and rehabilitation from the government.
7. The National Assembly will be restructured and changed into an assembly of minority, oppressed people, women, *dalits* and other prominent figures of the country.
8. Foreign relations shall be conducted on the basis of UN Charter, policy of non-alignment and in the interest of the people and the county.
9. To resolve the problem of centralization, the governing system shall be gradually reformed as per the needs and constitutional arrangements shall be made to make the local governing bodies resourceful, decisive and powerful.
10. The country is in the grip of the problem of citizenship. Especially in Terai, a large number of people are kept without the citizenship certificates. This problem shall be solved on the basis of national consensus by deciding on a threshold

year adopting constitutional and other possible measures.

11. All the economic, social, political and law related discrimination against women shall be eliminated. Special laws and programs shall be formulated and implemented in order to create equal opportunity for women. Women's representation in parliament and local elections shall be d gradually increased to make 33 per cent.
12. The state shall not give special treatment to any religion. The discriminatory practices on religion, language and culture shall be eliminated. Special policy shall be formulated to protect, preserve and develop all castes, race, people's religions, languages and cultures. Through the introduction of special laws and programs, the economic, social and cultural status of marginalized and oppressed people shall be uplifted and equal opportunity and equal access given to them. For this, the most marginalized and oppressed section of the society shall receive special treatment.
13. Special system shall be introduced to uplift the *dalits* and oppressed communities. Practice of untouchability shall be regarded as a crime and effective laws shall be introduced to punish those who practice it.
14. All forms of discriminations based on caste, creed, community, geography, language, culture and religion shall be eliminated.
15. Special programs shall be formulated in order to accelerate the development programs in backward and remote areas including Karnali area.
16. Special programs shall be introduced in a planned way to improve the situation of those people who are living under the poverty line. Special and concrete programs shall also be introduced to end unemployment; problems of landless people and to uplift the economic, social and cultural situation of Kamaiyas, agricultural and industrial labourers and other economically marginalized people.
17. Administration system shall be made clean, fair, transparent and accountable. In order to guarantee good governance, administration shall be made democratic and professional by keeping it out of political influence and intervention.
18. Corruption shall be effectively controlled. No one shall enjoy immunity from it. Corruption control laws and mechanisms shall be made more effective and active.

However, this proposal is based on the assumption that the king will share power with them. And the agenda is not fully able to address the intensity of the problems. For example, the agenda point nine highlights the gradual reform of the governing system according to the existing constitutional framework, which is not able to resolve the state restructuring.

5.4.10 Political parties and the post-First February government

The relationship between the political parties and the post-First February government is extremely bitter since the government arrested or detained most of the senior leaders of political parties; seriously undermined their existence and negatively pictured them as responsible for the crisis of the country. Their party workers and district-level leaders were arrested or detained. Their party offices were patrolled by security forces. Many ordinances were issued to limit their activities. Very hardlined people with a partyless panchayat and anti-political party background were appointed as regional and zonal administrators to restrict the activities of political parties. Leaders of the political parties were also targeted by the Royal Commission for Corruption Control (two senior leaders, Ser Bahadur Deuba and Prakash Man Singh were arrested and jailed). Nevertheless, the track record of most of the political leaders of this country in terms of corruption is very bad and no one would have any sympathy for the corrupt leaders if the corruption action is fair and without political revenge. Ultimately, political parties, which were the buffer between the Maoists and the king, turned opponents of the king and some of them decided to go in for a republican political set-up. The relationship between the political parties and the king has been almost irreparably damaged and extremely difficult to restore to the original state.

After the first February takeover, seven political parties strongly opposing each other earlier came to form an alliance. The Alliance produced a collective action agenda to restore the democratic political system derailed from the royal takeover.

5.5 ARMED CONFLICT, POLITICAL CRISIS AND MEDIA[8]

Media includes newspapers, magazines, radio, television, World Wide Web, locally produced films, music, and videos[9]. Media in any nation is said to be the brain of the state, where knowledge and information are processed, produced, transmitted and utilised for the betterment of the nation and people. Therefore, free media is the indicator of democracy and rule of law. The right to information is increasingly becoming a global human right concern where media plays a fundamental role to provide information. Free and fair media shapes the course of action of any responsible nation.

Since the Maoist insurgency started in February 1996, Nepalese media faced unique experiences, tremendous challenges and difficulties. The media sector has also greatly influenced the conflict dynamics. From the beginning, the Maoists tactically used the media in their favour. However, the state media strategy and Nepalese media responses were conflict-blind in their approaches and actions for earlier 5 years (1996-2001). The media were largely ignorant of the social reform initiative started by Maoists in the rural areas. Maoists might have felt that positive social change initiated by them did not catch the attention of media. They changed their approach towards more violence and retaliation. Then the media became attentive and started to glorify the war: killings, fights, brutality, horrors and all negative aspects of the armed conflict.

Before the first State of Emergency (November 2001), the media did not fully realise its social responsibility in the situation of conflict and contributed directly or indirectly to escalate it. After the SoE, the media sector became more conflict sensitive to its role in contributing to peace or escalation of war. Media became particularly sensitive after the breaking of the second ceasefire in August 2003. Several journalists were killed, tortured, detained and interrogated by the state and the Maoists during this period. Till the last of January 2005 the role of media in promoting peace and denouncing war was increasing. According to the Nepalese Federation of Journalists, 18 journalists were killed; hundred others were arrested, tortured, detained, harassed or threatened since the initiation of the armed conflict. Furthermore, the media sector faced an unprecedented crisis and obstructions from the state when the king took over the executive power on 1st February 2005.

5.5.1 Changing political context and the media

The Maoist insurgency, failure of the parliamentary parties and the unrealistic ambitions of the king to rule the country under his leadership created a total political crisis in Nepal. Hence, the conflict dynamics changed very rapidly. The dissolution of the parliament was a result of an intense power struggle between political parties. Consequently, capitalising on the parliamentary vacuum, the King removed the elected Prime Minister on 4 October 2002 and started to rule the country by nominated governments. Furthermore, the Nepalese politics turned into a total crisis from the political change of 1st February 2005. The political change includes the resumption of executive power by the King, removal of the nominated multi-party government, detention and/or arrest of political leaders, civil society members, journalists and human rights activists, censorship on media, and imposition of the State of Emergency (which was lifted on 30th of April 2005, two days before its natural expiry) and suspension of civil rights. Even after ten months of the Royal takeover (until November 2005), the political situation was deteriorating. As an objection to the king's takeover, the USA, UK and India suspended their military aids, some donors stopped their development projects (e.g. Denmark stopped NARMSAP Project, Switzerland stopped education- and employment-related projects, Norway withdrew from the Melamchi Drinking Water Project) and many donors reduced their total volume of aid to Nepal (e.g., Switzerland, EU, Denmark, etc.). Many other donors are using a 'wait and see' strategy. Nepal seriously lost international support.

At present, the deep political vacuum in the absence of elected government accountable to the people, is filled by loyalist royal nominees, whose single priority is to satisfy the king. The current approach of the king is more confrontational with the parliamentary political parties. Hence, the 1st February Royal takeover has further worsened the overall political situation, ruined international relations, and posed a serious threat to the infant democracy in Nepal. The royal takeover has severely constrained political space and is pushing the country from a 'fragile state' to a 'failed state'. The king lost opportunity to restore peace, which was announced as a high agenda of the takeover. If there were a ceasefire, peace talks and negotiated settlement of the armed conflict immediately after the royal takeover, Nepalese people would greatly appreciate the king because peace is their prime desire[10].

The media faced severe problems after the royal takeover. The role of free media is crucial in the situation of political crisis and armed conflict to protect violation of human rights and contribute to resolve conflict. Though Nepalese media has some weaknesses in reference to the ongoing conflict, it has greatly contributed to transforming Nepalese society. If the government has no ill intention and is willing to resolve the crisis, why should it be afraid of the free media?

5.5.3 Media and human rights

The INSEC record shows that all total 12577 people including 2027 farmers, 141 teachers, 5653 political workers, 1280 police, 411 ordinary people, 324 students, 566 staff of different organisations, 13 social workers, 146 business people, 210 wage workers 6 health workers, 595 security forces (excluding police) 5 photographers, 14 journalists, 2 lawyers, 4 prisoners, 10 dacoits, 1 engineer and 1169 unidentified people between 13 February 1996 and 10 July 2005. Other human rights abuses include forced displacement detention, rape, eviction form homes, police interference in displaced people, etc. In the past, media has played an immensely crucial role in exploring human rights abuses by the warring parties. Media became successful in attracting international attention on human rights abuses. Reporters working in the core-conflict areas performed excellent roles even at high personal security risks.

5.5.4 Media in conflict situation

The history of the armed conflict around the world (Abdullaev, and Barnes, 2001; Armon, and Carl, 1996; Armon, and Philipson, 1998; Armon et al., 1998; Armon et al., 1997; Barnes, 2002; Carl, A. and Garasu, 2002; Conen, 1999; Crandall, 2004; Garcia-Duran, 2004; Hendrickson, 1998; Lord, 2000; Lucima, 2002; McCartney, 1999; Stankovitch, 1999; Lode, 2002; Macrae, 2002; Misra, 2002; Senghaas, 2001; Susskind & Cruikshank 1987 and Upreti, 2004a) has proved that the media is both accelerator of conflict and the promoter of the peace. Scale, quality and volume of conflict reporting greatly influence dynamics of conflict. In the situation of conflict, states often attempt to use media in their favour or to negate or damage the opponents. This is one of the major problems in conflict reporting. Revealing truth by investigating reality and minimising vested interest-based propaganda requires ethics and honesty, which is very hard to maintain. Revealing truth at the time of conflict is often risky, particularly when the revelations are related to misbehaviours of the fighting forces of warring parties. Several journalists and reporters are deliberately killed in such situations. Warring parties fear journalists and reporters more than their enemies mainly because of the possibility of exposure of the crime they have committed. If they have not committed any crimes and respect the provisions of Geneva Conventions, they should not be afraid of journalists and reporters. Journalism and media could function properly only if the following conditions are met: They are:

5.5.4.1 Freedom from interference and biases

One of the conditions for the successful operations of media in conflict situation is non-interference in the journalists (editors, producers, reporters, etc.) by the conflicting parties. However, generally warring parties always fear journalists and therefore they want to prevent journalists from investigating their crimes. This situation has been distinctly observed in Zaire (Democratic Republic of Congo), Angola, Mozambique, Guatemala, and Chechnya. Even we can observe this situation in Nepal. Warring parties do not entertain journalists investigating the truth. Every day, daily newspapers report that there are threats from Maoists and security forces to the reporters working in the remote areas. Journalists and reporters were taking severe risks and potential threats when they reported the arms shipment of UNITA. They were transiting through Zambia en route to conflict-ridden neighbours and consequently Zambia refused UNITA airlifting their arms in 1976. Similarly, getting information from the journalists, Benin seized arms going to Nigerian conflict that posed a risk to journalists.

The Constitution of the Kingdom of Nepal has protected freedom of media and it is the responsibility of the state to execute the constitutional provisions. However, at present the government is blatantly ignoring the constitutional provisions and controlling media in Nepal. The ordinance promulgated to control media is a glaring example of such control. Tanzanian Judge James L. Mwalusanya once said: '*In a democratic system the actions or omissions of the government must be subject to close scrutiny, not only by the legislature and juridical authorities, but also by the free press and public opinion. The principal roles of the media are to expose shortcomings of the government, educate the public, popularise peace initiatives, and promote dialogue*'[11]. Any government claimed to be democratic should not be fearful of the media. Rather, the states have to promote free media by applying principles of non-interference and freedom from biases.

5.5.4.2 Capacity building of journalists in conflict situations

Only capable, competent and knowledgeable journalists and reporters can better investigate truth. Working in a situation of armed conflict is entirely different in terms of risks, source of information and triangulation/ verifications, maintaining confidentiality and transparency than in normal situations. As expressed by Christina Amnpohre, a senior correspondent of CNN reporting on war, fear, insecurity and uncertainty are always part of life in conflict reporting. The subject matter, discourses and semantics, and issues of conflict reporting are different. Therefore, the reporters and journalists require proper training in these subjects. At the end, journalists are human beings and they have emotions, fear and anxiety. When they continuously stay and report at the situation of intense armed conflict, their reports may be affected by these psychophysical factors. Proper training and capacity building help considerably to improve the scale, quality and quantity of conflict reporting.

Misreporting at the situation of armed conflict escalates. This was observed in Rwanda. Training provides knowledge, commitment and technical and organizational skills to media practitioners to improve reporting and analysis of conflict situation. Training facilities for local and national journalists on issues relating to peace, reconciliation and rehabilitation can facilitate national campaigns on these issues and influence policy makers and practitioners.

There are some organisations supporting to develop capacity of media in reporting conflict such as Institute of War and Peace, Search for Common Ground and African Centre for the Constructive Resolution of Disputes (ACCORD). Similarly, there is a number of organizations who protect journalists working in conflict situations such as Reporters sans Frontiers, the Committee to Protect Journalists; Amnesty International, Human Rights Watch, etc.

Often rural media organisations severely lack the resources required to properly and effectively report conflict cases. Reporters working in conflict situations in remote areas often lack required equipment such as tape recorders, cameras, facsimile machines, word processing and graphic design and layout equipment that reduce performance both in quality, quantity and timeliness of the news. Therefore, this is one of the important areas of capacity development of journalists working in remote areas.

4.5.4.3 Ethics in conflict reporting

Conflict history around the world has demonstrated that at the time of the conflict, it is extremely difficult to get factual information, opinion and analysis, which help ordinary people to understand the situation of conflict and influence its dynamics ((Abdullaev, and Barnes, 2001; Armon, and Carl, 1996; Armon, and Philipson, 1998; Armon et al., 1998; Armon et al., 1997; Barnes, 2002; Carl, A. and Garasu, 2002;

Conen, 1999; Crandall, 2004; Garcia-Duran, 2004; Hendrickson, 1998; Lord, 2000; Lucima, 2002; McCartney, 1999; Putnam, 1993; Stankovitch, 1999; Lode, 2002; Macrae, 2002; Misra, 2002; Senghaas, 2001; Susskind, .& Cruikshank 1987 and Upreti, 2004b and d). The mass media heavily shapes popular perceptions of people and opinions and decisions of key players. In such a situation, ethics of the journalists determines the course of action on authenticity, neutrality, confidentiality, transparency and source of information as well as nature of conflict (escalation or resolution). Observing the situation of African conflict (Rwanda, Burundi, Liberia, Somalia, Sudan, Sierra Leone and Zaire), David Keen once wrote, *"The need for good information on political process is underlined by the fact that interest groups who are manipulating crisis may also be manipulating the information surrounding the crisis."* Therefore, bringing fair and authentic information is a serious challenge in the conflict situation. Therefore, only journalists with full ethics can bring un-manipulated information.

It has been observed in African conflict situation that "*brown envelop syndrome*" (compromising professional integrity with bribes, or indulge in other illegal practices, such as blackmailing, bargening, etc.) has been developed in many reporters. Blackmailing, character assassination, petty politics, insisting on undue advantages and favours, ignoring or distorting expert opinions, breaking confidentiality are often common weaknesses of journalists observed in conflict-affected society. Nepal is also not free from some of these malpractices. This is one of the major challenges of Nepalese media sectors to maintain credibility and trustworthiness.

5.5.4.4 Maintaining credibility and neutrality:

Media requires to maintain credibility and neutrality to protect civil liberty (CIJ, 2004). Sometime reporting of media might be favourable to one party and unfavourable to another, which ultimately poses the risk of being opposed by the affected party. Occasionally, some journalists work in line with the interests of a particular group that creates suspicions. Maintaining professional integrity, social credibility and impartiality is a major challenge for media sector in Nepal.

5.6 RESPONSIBILITIES OF THE MEDIA

Media has great responsibility to provide information at the time of conflict especially when the regime is repressive and freedom of expression of general people is curtailed. Media has played a crucial role in Liberia, Sierra Leone, Kenya, and Nigeria to mobilize individuals and groups to lobby against violence, human rights abuses and torture that had a big effect on mediation. Nepalese media could learn a lot of useful lessons from the media sector working in African conflict.

In the Sudan conflict between 1970 and 1972, media has collaborated with the World Council of Churches and the All African Council of Churches to accomplish fact-finding mission. They identified the crucial actors of conflict so that the Sudanese government and the Southern Sudanese Liberation Movement could adopt the findings as a starting point for negotiation. Later the National Council of Churches in Kenya continued with the findings to push forward the negotiation between the two southern Sudan factions in 1991. Similarly, media has contributed in Liberia's civic involvement of peace building. It was led by the Inter-Faith Mediation Committee in collaboration with the Liberian Council of Churches and the National Muslim Council of Liberia. Nepalese media could learn from these experiences on how media and religious groups can work together in restoring peace and discouraging violence.

Essentially, conflict resolution is a change in mentality, attitudes, perceptions and behaviour of the conflicting parties, especially their leaders. Media greatly contributes to change the attitude and behaviour of warring parties by providing new knowledge and information, facilitating a process of creative problem-solving process by reshaping perception or reframing the conflict context and using effective communication.

5.6.1 Informing society and revealing the truth

The experience of the conflict-ridden countries (Abdullaev, and Barnes, 2001; Armon, and Carl, 1996; Armon, and Philipson, 1998; Armon et al., 1998; Armon et al., 1997; Barnes, 2002; Carl, A. and Garasu, 2002; Conen, 1999; Crandall, 2004; Garcia-Duran, 2004; Hendrickson, 1998; Lord, 2000; Lucima, 2002; McCartney, 1999; Putnam, 1993; Stankovitch, 1999; Lode, 2002; Macrae, 2002; Misra, 2002; Senghaas, 2001; Susskind, .& Cruikshank 1987; Mackinlay and Upreti, 2003; Raune and Todd, 1996 and Upreti, 2005b and c) has shown that journalists, reporters and media persons are the first source of information on conflict issues. Journalists often reveal the truth about conflict situations, as other people do not generally have access. They analyse conflict; provide means for the exchange of opinions and options to resolve conflict. Reporters and journalists keep general public informed of the course of conflict, they monitor behaviour of the fighting forces and leaders of the conflict and report to public.

It is demonstrated in many conflict-ridden contraries that journalists can substantially influence conflict resolution processes. In other countries, in addition to reporting the facts, journalists have played a proactive role in peace process. They provide a forum for conflict parties to express their views and alternatives. For example, people are aware about the Maoists through the articles or opinions of Baburam Bhattarai and other Maoist leaders published in *Samaya Weekly*, *Nepal Weekly*, *Himal Fortnightly*, *Kantipur* and *Kathmandu Post Dailies*, *Mulyankan Monthly* and other daily and weekly newspapers, and World Wide Web and Nepali Service of the British Broadcasting Corporation. Otherwise, it may not be possible for the general public to understand the actual opinions and perspectives of the Maoist leaders. In some cases, the journalists have succeeded in bringing the parties into face-to-face discussions. For instance, in Sierra Leone, the local radio station tried to move away from just reporting the conflict and tried to make things better by introducing a forum for discussion to help modify the perceptions of the disputants in its listening area (Busby, 1996)[12].

On the gloomy side, often the media has a tendency to dramatise conflict-events, offer sensational conflict news or broadcast extreme or incendiary statements. Reporting negative dimension is often a preferred strategy in media, particularly for the economic reason (to sell more and to earn more). On the contrary, media in Nepal has a tendency to ignore local peace initiative, voices of community, and opinions and perspectives of ordinary people. In this context, Botes argues that media ignores important story - how local institutions can prevent destructive conflict from occurring -- remains untold[13]. He further emphasises that better informed and trained media people can do a lot to increase the amount of factual information and analysis available to negotiators and decision makers. They also help the general public to understand conflict and probably influence the conflict resolution by offering their options.

So far there is lack of analysis in media about different dimensions of conflict: power relations in conflict, sociological interpretation of insurgency, internal political, financial and military dynamics of insurgency, weapons trading and associated commissions, truth and reconciliation, disarming and demobilisation, actual situation of internally displaced persons, international provisions of war crime, etc. Media could develop a wider consensus on focusing analysis of these issues, if they accommodate the perspectives of experts, independent analysts and observers. However, there is a great tendency in many of the Nepalese print media to limit analysis to a very narrow circle having special relations with journalists and senior editors.

5.6.2 Protecting human rights

Human rights abuses are often the immediate effects of armed conflict. Abusers often hide their crimes. Constant monitoring of their abuses is essential. Independent media can monitor and assess the situation and report to the public. The experiences of human rights protection in the high-intensity conflict countries show that collaborative work between media and human rights community is more effective in protecting human rights of ordinary citizens. One approach of capacitating journalists and media persons in protecting human rights is to incorporate human rights protection issues into journalist training programme.

5.6.3 Contribute to negotiating conflict

Media and journalists can greatly contribute to reach a negotiated settlement of conflict. If journalists want to contribute in a negotiated settlement of the conflict, they need to engage in empirical and analytical examination of the armed conflict and its consequences, coping mechanisms of conflict-affected communities, the humanitarian situation, indigenous methods of resolving conflicts and social, cultural, political, international dimensions. Exerting positive pressures over warring parties to reach negotiated settlement of the conflict is another important area where media could contribute greatly.

Constant vigilance on the proliferation of illegal trading of small arms and light weapons, rising awareness on effects of landmines, advocating for certain areas as 'no military zone', 'zone of peace', revealing the hidden interests and attitude of warring parties are some examples of other important elements that journalists could focus on to support negotiated settlement.

In summary, the potential contribution of media in peace building and resolution of the armed conflict, the following major works can be envisioned. However, this is not a complete list.

- Supporting peace networks, and alliances,

- Exploring options and roadmaps,
- Raising awareness on effects of Small Arms and light Weapons (SALW) and landmines,
- Facilitating trust building, citizen diplomacy and dialogue,
- Helping for reconciliation and harmony building,
- Contribution in disarming and demobilisation, reconstruction, rehabilitation, reintegration and reconciliation,
- Promoting violence-limiting mechanisms,
- Peace sensitive awareness of conflict-affected societies,
- Support in humanitarian activities,
- Fact-finding and overseeing.

5.7 Conclusions

All actors of peace have contributed something in conflict transformation and peace-building efforts in Nepal. However, their efforts and initiatives were not able to achieve the ultimate objective, i.e. negotiated settlement of the conflict. The performance of political parties and the government extremely was poor compared to civil society and media. Main reasons for not being able to reach negotiated are the lack of sincerity and commitment of political parties and the king, as they always used Maoist conflict as a stepping stone and bargaining chip to grab power.

History of war has shown that media, civil society and religious groups have tremendous potentiality and firm ability to human rights protection, conflict transformation and peace building (Armond and Carl, 1996; Hendrickson, 1998; Abdullaev, 2001; Stankovitch, 1999; Upreti, 2004; Conen, 1999; Armon et al., 1997 and 1998; Barnes, 2002; Armon and Philipaon, 2002; Lord, 2000; Gracia-Durna, 2004; Lucima, 2002; McCartney, 1999; Carl, 2002). Protection of human rights at the situation of intense armed conflict requires an active engagement of media, strong reporting team and backup support. However, the role of these sectors in resolving conflict and restoring peace in Nepal is weak.

NOTES

1. Detailed information about the contribution of women in peace process and negotiated settlement of armed conflict can be found in the keynote speech of the author on the inaugural session of national conference (29-31 August 2005) of Shantimalika, A network organisation of Nepalese women represented by 57 districts of Nepal.

2. See a recent study report on SALW conducted by Friends for Peace, Kathmandu.
3. Padma Ratna Tuladhar, Malla K. Sundar, Sudip Pathak were among few leaders to reach negotiation between the trade union and industrialists and students and the boarding schools.
4. For example, Friends for Peace has initiated research work on D2R4, CVICT is engaged in trauma healing and reconciliation. Nagirak Awaj is engaged in rehabilitation and reconciliation of the conflict victims, etc..
5. With the permission of CPN (UML) leader Jhala Nath Khanal I have included a part of the text of CPN (UML) agenda in this section.
6. He wrote four books related to state structuring, king, Nepali Congress and inclusion, basically to convince voters general convention of Nepali Congress where he had contested in the chairperson with Girija Prasad Koirala, who is head of the party since 3 terms. Though he lost in the election, the general convention accepted his opinions and thinking.
7. Though Rastrya prajatantra Party is officially divided in late 2004 and large numbers of RPP members follow the path of RPP leader Surya Bahadur Thapa, who had reorganised RPP members in a different group called Nepal Janasakti Party. Most of the activities, principles and value system of these tow parties are entirely the same as almost all member of RJP are RPP members. And it is very difficult to find conceptual and procedural differences in these two parties. Therefore, no separate analysis has been made.
8. This section is based on the paper I presented at 'Media, Conflict Reporting and Human Rights' Conference organised by South Asian Free Media Association (SAFMA), Nepal in Hotel Annapurna, Kathmandu on 27-28 July 2005.
9. Media also include traditional means of communications such as storytellers, dancers, street entertainers, musicians, and poets, which are an important part of information source in Nepal.
10. Even if there is a negotiated settlement between the king and the Maoists excluding parliamentary parties, it would not last longer and therefore it is not an appropriate and viable solution. However, at present general public may not bother about the long-term consequences of exclusion of parliamentary parties form the negotiation process if the king and Maoists restore peace. Because peace is their absolute need.
11. See African conflict and the media (Part One by Abiodun Onadipe and David Lord).
12. See Anne Busby, 1996 "Report on Election Coverage Workshop", mimeo for Conciliation Resources and the Sierra Leone Association of Journalists, 1996 for detail on the role of media.
13. See Botes, Johannes "Journalism and Conflict Resolution" *Media Development* 4/1996 for details.

CHAPTER 6

Third-Party Negotiation of the Ongoing Armed Conflict

6.1 INTRODUCTION

Today, Nepal is facing an unprecedented crisis, because of the ongoing armed conflict and the autocratic rule of the palace. The king took over the power, undermining democratic principles and misinterpreting the specific provisions of the constitution. Since then, the nation is divided; the democratic system, which has theoretically proved to be the best system for managing economic, social and political process of any state, is derailed; democratic institutions envisioned by the constitution are almost non-functional or paralysed, and the country is ruled under ordinance. Mutual respect, coexistence and tolerance are severely eroded. The role of free media and basic rights of Nepalese people granted by the constitution of the Kingdom of Nepal 1990 such as freedom of speech and freedom of movement have been restricted. Conflict triggers such as blame and counter blame, threatening the other side, (ab)use of power and resources, and self-defensiveness have rapidly increased. The post-first February political forces with different perceptions, schools of thought, governing style and political ambitions are sidelining the existing democratic forces and shaping new courses of action. As a result, concerted efforts of all constitutional forces to achieve a politically negotiated settlement of the ongoing armed conflict offer only a distant hope.

The fundamental causes of the crisis at present are the failure of the democratic leadership; and fundamental differences of the post-February political actors in perception and understanding of 'democracy' and 'peace'. They have unrealistic ambitions founded in the miscalculation of governing the country. The regressive political force, which supports the 1st February political change, perceives that democracy is different from peace and wants to restore peace by imposing a state of emergency, intensifying counter-insurgency military operation, arresting and detaining political leaders and regulating media. For them democracy comes after peace. Against this school of thought, democratic forces view that democracy and peace are integral parts of the democratic system and one cannot be achieved without the other. This school of thought acknowledges the prime role of free media, freedom of speech and movement, and freedom of organisation. These fundamental differences are the prime obstacle to politically address the armed insurgency. The post-first February government publicly denounced the political negotiation with the Maoists and asked the insurgents to surrender their arms and get amnesty.

Obviously, in the past 10-12 years the political parties have missed the opportunity to vividly demonstrate that democracy works in Nepal. However, the 10-12 years of young democracy had opened the windows of opportunity for Nepalese people to experience democratic rights, freedom and interdependence of open society (Mahat, 2005). They are connected to a wider world of democratic system. This is a fundament step in refining, strengthening and expanding democracy in the country. Blaming democracy for all ill practices the governing elite did in the past does not reflect a proper understanding of democracy. Democracy is a self-correcting system of governance and the wrong-doers get punishment by periodic election. Those who are utterly blaming democracy as a source of all misdeeds need to realise the philosophical and practical dimensions of the king's recent remark that 'democracy is the only alternative of democracy'. If this statement is conceptually internalised and practically translated into behaviour and action, half of the crisis would be solved. However, this situation is becoming further complicated.

The post-February 2005 government is categorically denouncing the political dialogue with the insurgents. However, this chapter discusses the importance of dialogue on settling the ongoing armed conflict and political crisis of Nepal. It further examines the prospects and problems of third-party engagement in the negotiation of the Maoist conflict. Denying reality cannot solve the problem and asking the rebels to surrender their arms is an ideal but unrealistic expectation. Some analysts argue that demanding the surrender of arms could be a deliberate strategy to delay the negotiated settlement of the conflict.

6.2 PEACE EFFORTS OF THE FOUR-PARTY COALITION GOVERNMENT: CONFUSIONS AND CONTRADICTIONS

After the collapse of ceasefire on 27 August 2003, the then government intensified militarisation and so did the insurgents. Despite the severe criticism of the international community; the government continued its violent approach to eliminate the Maoists. However, failure to properly handle the crisis, the then government collapsed in the midst of serious power struggle within the ruling party that virtually divided the party. Then, Ser Bahadur Deuba was nominated as Prime Minister and formed a collation government. This government was a coalition of four major parties; it also had good international support. This government started some peace initiatives. It had created a Peace Secretariat and instituted a High-Level Peace Committee but it did not produce any results. From the beginning, the government was not clear on how the peace process and negotiation should proceed. Coalition partners had publicly demonstrated that they had severe differences on how to start peace talks. A glaring example was the contradictory position of coalition partners in declaring ceasefire (for example, UML was advocating and other three coalition partners were resisting declaring a ceasefire). The priority agenda of the coalition on restoring peace of the coalition partners was different, which they publicly expressed on different occasions. Against the public commitment of UML (one of the main coalition partners with the responsibility of ministry of finance), the government raised security expenditure in its annual budget. Despite the vehement opposition of civil society, human rights organisations, and political parties, the coalition government again issued Terrorist and Destructive Activities Control and Punishment Ordinance. It has also extended red corner notice through INTERPOL to three Maoist leaders.

The government was not ready to opt for ceasefire even if the CPN (UML) asked it to do so. The government was desperately making all-out diplomatic efforts to get military-related support from international community to deal with the armed conflict. All these activities were further enhancing the distrust and ruining the environment for the peace talks. On one side, members of the government and coalition parties were tirelessly reiterating peace talks. On the other side, their decisions and actions (e.g., TADO, resistance to ceasefire, etc.) were contributing to obstruct possible peace talks. The decision of the government to give extra benefits and facilities from the state fund to the members of the Peace Committee (representatives of coalition parties in the government) equal to the government ministers got serious criticism from media, civil society and public. It is alleged that the intention of the government to create a Peace Committee was to give jobs to their party workers, as this committee had not demonstrated any visible result for peace talks but opposed removing the terrorist tag and red corner notice to Maoists' potential negotiators and declare a ceasefire that could create a conducive environment.

Instead of seriously working to settle the crisis, the government was busy in distributing taxpayers' money from the state fund as 'assistance' ('Dashain bonus') to party workers of coalition parties in the government. Consequently, the government faced a humiliating situation when the Supreme Court asked it to furnish complete distribution of 'assistance' from the Prime Minister's Assistance Fund to political leaders and cadres on the eve of the festival (*The Kathmandu Post,* 3 November 2004). Hence, the Deuba-led coalition government was in total confusion and full of contradictions in relation to peace talks and negotiated settlement of the conflict.

Because of the military focus of the government, and the past experiences on the ability and authority of the governments in negotiation, the Maoists did not trust them and wanted to talk directly with the King or his true representative. Although the Maoists had not ruled out the peace talks they were continuing extortions, killings and destruction of public infrastructure. Considering the changed position of India and its tough stand towards the Maoists[1], coming under heavy pressure from civil society, political parties, international community and more importantly due to their internal organisational and managerial complications (as sharp differences between leaders to go or not to go in for negotiated settlement, constraints to generate enough resources to sustain a large mobile military operation, obstruction in Indian hiding places, etc.) The Maoists seemed more prepared than government to go in for a negotiated settlement if there were a real and meaningful negotiation. Their concerns were about process of making a new constitution and role of military i.e., constituent assembly election and control of military by civilian government.

Before the first of February 2005, power struggle within the constitutional forces and reluctance or even direct or indirect resistance to work together to address the present crisis and to settle the armed conflict through negotiated settlement was the fundamental obstruction to peace during the time of the nominated governments. This situation is further continuously deepening. Observing their actions and reactions, it was very hard to believe that the present equation of constitutional forces works to settle the crisis and therefore they themselves are disqualifying and making irrelevant the argument of 'constitutional force working together'. However, this situation has drastically changed after the royal takeover on 1st February 2005.

6.3 DIALOGUE AS A FUNDAMENTAL BASIS FOR ADDRESSING ONGOING CONFLICT OF NEPAL

If we believe in democracy, we should not be afraid of conflict, as it can be addressed democratically. 'In a democratic society, conflict is the basis of social change. If there is to be just relationship, if change is to occur, latent conflict must be made visible to all parties', once said Franklin Dukes (a noted conflict scholar). This means that even the present conflict between the establishment and the political parties can be a source of internal reform of party structures and leadership development; wider political reform; means of establishing new and just relations; flourishing multiparty democracy and resolving the on-going insurgency; if it is used as an opportunity. Dialogue is one of the best means to achieve these outcomes using the opportunities offered by the 1st February takeover.

Putnam (1993) highlights the importance of dialogue and constructive engagement and participation of concerned stakeholders in making democracy work. In Nepal too, as claimed, if all power centres want to make Nepalese infant democracy work, the very first step is to inter into constructive dialogue (with all major political forces).

In the modern history of the world, several options have been used to change or transform the state into a modern, democratic and inclusive nation. Some are coercive options such as use of force, violent actions, wars and external interventions. And others are peaceful options such as dialogue and negotiated settlement. Dialogue is the first step in reaching a negotiated settlement. If the political powers of the country want to end the bloodshed, as frequently reiterated by them, then the usual procedure is to initiate dialogue and reach a negotiated settlement.

Research findings of Berghof Research Centre of Constructive Conflict Management demonstrate that dialogue is one of the best options to transform conflict of the fragile states and therefore the conflicting parties need to acknowledge the need of dialogue in reaching a negotiated settlement. Dialogue brings comprehensive and mutual understanding through constant communication, personal contacts and constructive interactions that ultimately overcome existing grievances and differences and assist in searching a common ground.

Dialogue process undergoes the following steps:

1. Contact and face-to-face communication→
2. Realising the importance →
3. Mutual understanding →
4. Analysing problem →
5. Exploring options →
6. Joint actions in mutually beneficial options →
7. Pre-negotiations →
8. Negotiated settlement.

In this process, assistance of the third party (international or domestic) may be needed if the conflict is severe. Hence, dialogue is a method of interactive problem solving. In many conflict situations, dialogue is combined with other practical approaches such as peace rallies, mass mobilisations, non-coercive diplomacy, action research, confidential meetings and visits, etc. (Upreti, 2004b).

One of the political theories of conflict highlights that a state is a collection of individuals with their inalienable rights and they come together to set up common structure in pursuit of their own interests (Devetak, 1996). Hence, conflicts arise for the legitimating power to defend their own rights and search own interests. When legitimising power, conflicting parties even engage in strategic and operational manipulations, distorting communication, amplifying own strengths and exaggerating the weaknesses of the other side or even blaming and charging to destroying other side. We can clearly observe this situation in Nepal.

Dialogue also develops capacity (socialisation of leaders or persons engaged in the dialogue, changes in attitude, new and constructive patterns of behaviour, positive thinking, etc.) of people engaged in the dialogue process, brings differences (in terns of perceptions, issues, methodologies, proposals, practical measures, resources, etc.) on to the discussion table, provides opportunities to clarify the intentions, interests and limitations, compulsions, fears in a calm and quiet manner. If we recall the South African dialogue process, F. W. de Clark made persistent efforts to have dialogue with Nelson Mandela who was in jail. He met secretly with Mandela several times. To facilitate dialogue he even fulfilled some conditions put forward by the leaders of African National Congress. Such positive initiatives taken by President de Clark and the strong commitment of Nelson Mandela to reach a negotiated settlement resulted in a democratic and prosperous South Africa. The entry point for the resolution of the South African conflict was the initiation of dialogue.

Only dialogue is the way if major actors of the conflict want to achieve real peace. However, dialogue is a continuous and learning process and the conflicting parties need full commitment (to accept co-existence, respect differences, and diversity), ethical responsibility. Denying existence of other side cannot initiate constructive dialogue. The limitation of the dialogue approach is that it is compromising in nature and if one party wants to negate the other through use of force or violence, this approach does not work.

The Ugandan experiences demonstrate the successful application of dialogue approach to conflict transformation even in civil and military relations. The inclusive dialogue process was started in 2002 to enhance coexistence between the military (Uganda People's Defence Force) and civil society. This process led to the appreciation of the public that soldiers are also part of their society and vice versa. Consequently, they agreed to open a Civil Military Relations Office in Kampala. Coexistence Centre Uganda played an important role in this initiative[2].

Organisation of the American State (OAS) has successfully tested, implemented and expanded the dialogue process to achieve conflict transformation; build strong government-civil society collaboration in restoring peace through dialogue[3]. The Latin American experiences in dialogue and consensus building and OAS experiences of peace building and conflict resolution (Peru, Nicaragua, Mali and Caribbean) have proved that dialogue can achieve what coercive approaches cannot. UNDP Latin American Section's Political Dialogue Programme had facilitated peace building, conflict prevention and hemisphere security with very positive results and lessons (e.g., the peace-building initiative undertaken from 1990 to 2003 in Nicaragua).

Several examples and theories demonstrate that dialogue is a very basic democratic principle of confidence building, managing and transforming conflict and addressing national political crisis like the one Nepal is currently facing. It has been proved throughout history that strengthening democratic practices and delivering tangible solutions to the multiple social, economic and political problems faced by any nation requires inclusive processes that ensure engagement of every group of stakeholders. Conflict and crisis management requires, among other things, developing a positive attitude, trust and conducive environment and consensus building process. Dialogue provides these requirements.

6.4 NEPAL'S INVOLVEMENT AS A THIRD-PARTY MEDIATOR: HISTORICAL PERSPECTIVE

Nepalese history shows that Nepal was a successful international mediator in resolving conflict of British-India with China and Russia[4]. Mr. Jit Bahadur K.C., a resident representative of Nepalese government (who was at that time commonly known as Okeel and equivalent to present ambassador) had played a crucial role to mediate conflict between China and Tibet in 1912-14. China and British-India had a severe conflict and they were not able to resolve it themselves. So Mr. KC worked as mediator and was able to negotiate and return Chinese troops from Tibet and to reinstall the then exiled Dalai Lama (who was in India). Similarly, he had mediated between British India and Russia. When Russians came to construct roads and infrastructure in China close to Indian borders, British India objected and a severe conflict emerged. Mr. K.C. negotiated between these two powers and Russians returned. The then representative of Britain in India had highly appreciated the ability of Mr. Jit Bahadur KC.

6.5 PROSPECTS OF THIRD-PARTY MEDIATION IN ONGOING ARMED CONFLICT

Regarding the third-party mediation, the obvious question is: has Nepal exhausted all domestic efforts before going to external options? Experiences of the past ten years reveal that political forces constantly failed to reach a negotiated settlement internally and therefore Nepal needs external support to resolve the ongoing conflict.

Analysing the documents and expressions of warring parties and monitoring of the media, it can safely be said that the Maoists are looking for external guarantors if there is a meaningful future negotiation. Repeated expressions of the Maoists to engage UN in negotiated settlement is a clear reflection of their desire to have guarantee from neutral international force. Their willingness to invite

UN should not be understood only as their attempt to get international recognition. Even if they get international recognition while involving the UN to solve the problem, there is no harm. The important issue is to solve the problems, not whether Maoists get recognition. Further, when the Maoists get international recognition, this may force them to comply with international provisions and to settle the armed conflict politically. Regarding their recognition, they have already got it from the government of Nepal and international community at the time of the second round of peace talks.

Who can be the guarantor in a negotiated settlement is a major concern. Several potential guarantors and facilitators are available such as India, China, Scandinavian countries, Switzerland, the UN, EU, ICRC, Centre for Humanitarian Dialogue, Carter Centre, Crisis Management Institute of Finland, etc. if the state is willing to invite them for help. However, obvious questions are: Are warring parties (particularly the government as the Maoists have already demanded) ready to accept a third-party guarantor? What are the models and level of third-party engagement? Is there any possibility of combined engagement of more than one guarantor (for example, UN and India, or UN and EU or EU and India or any other combinations)? Is there any possibility of joint effort of India and China to be guarantor? Will India be interested to work with the UN in resolving conflict? Answers to these questions are needed while talking about third- party negotiation.

Nepal is a country supported by many bilateral nations, inter-governmental and international non-governmental organisations with good intentions. They want to help Nepal at the time of crisis. The 2004 NDF meeting (5-6 May) had clearly demonstrated their commitment and concerns toward Nepal. In this meeting, they had emphasised restoring peace and institute a democratically elected government as basis of their support. In this context, Praful Patel, Vice President of World Bank South Asia Region said, "*We are committed to support PRSP, but had the peace process and democratic process prevailed in the country, Nepal could have secured more assistance*[5]"This situation has further deteriorated and bilateral and multilateral donors of Nepal are very worried after the post-February political change in Nepal.

There are mainly three types of external involvements in resolving domestic conflict around the world, depending upon the nature and intensity of the conflict. First is soft approach, i.e., political and diplomatic involvement of external actors with the warring parties of the host country to settle the ongoing conflict. Second approach is through international courts and other binding legal arrangements, which are not so common in a domestic conflict. The third approach is more hardcore intervention of military force, which often goes through UN Security Council's resolution or forceful intervention by powerful nations (Upreti, 2005b). But, in the context of Nepal, the debate on need of external mediation is absolutely related to the first approach, i.e., political and diplomatic involvement. However, if the political situation continuously deteriorates, other two approaches (especially military intervention) could also occur.

Whether external or internal, mediation is effective at a time when the fighting parties are willing to reassess their policies. They do so when they:

- Fall in to stalemate, which is mutually hurting, i.e., when each party realises that it is un-winnable and stalemate is costly, not bearable. In other words, situation of strategic stalemate.
- Realise the catastrophic escalation leading to impending crisis, which they cannot afford to suffer (Zartman and Touvel, 1996).
- Tremendous external pressure and risk of external physical disruption if policy is not reassessed.

Hence, ripeness of conflict (in other words, timing) is extremely important in mediating conflict. Repeated expressions of the government ministers and RNA about their confidence to disarm the Maoists are important underlying reasons of their resistance to external mediation.

We have past experiences of external mediation. In the past India had mediated in our domestic conflict several times (e.g., 1950's Tripartite Delhi Agreement, Indian army intervention in K. I. Singh revolt, etc), and negotiated over water resource conflict related to Koshi, Gandak and Mahakali treaties and understanding on Upper Karnali, but the stakes were very high in all mediations and Nepal had to always lose in these negotiation and mediations.

6.6 WHY DO MAOISTS WANT THIRD-PARTY MEDIATION?

The Maoists are repeatedly saying[6] that they want neutral third-party mediation and the UN is their obvious choice. There could be several reasons for the Maoists' preference for external mediation:

1. They do not trust the government and Royal Nepal Army. Their expressions indicate that they are very suspicious of RNA after the 5-km controversy in last negotiation in 2003 and the Doramba killing. Hence, they want guarantee from a legitimate and neutral international power.
2. International involvement also gives legitimacy and recognition to their rebellion. This might be another motivating factor for the Maoists to advocate for the involvement of the UN. Some Nepalese scholars resist UN's political mediation, mainly based on the argument that it legitimises Maoists proposition of 'new regime v/s old regime'. But this is unfounded fear. Even if they get legitimacy, at the end there should be negotiated settlement. Therefore, the issue of legitimacy seems irrelevant.
3. Perhaps another and most important reason is to give message to the international community and general public that they are committed to negotiated agreement.
4. They might be looking to rule the country and therefore want to demonstrate their openness and to establish international relations for future political and diplomatic course of actions and financial support. Dr Babu Ram Bhattarai met several diplomats[7] when he was heading the Maoist negotiation team in 2003 peace talks. This also indicates that the motive of Maoists was to develop relations with the international community.

The following box indicates the Maoist ways of dealing with international community and UN. Prachnda in his letter to Kofi Anan immediately after the breakdown of August 2003 Ceasefire wrote highlighting the justification of 'people's war'. He has stated that progressive democratic force is fighting with feudal monarchy. He has strongly reiterated his commitment to find a political solution through dialogue and peaceful means at appropriate time. He was requesting the UN and the international community to stop possible foreign armed and other interventions in Nepal and let the Nepalese people decide their own future themselves. Since then CPN (Maoist) issued several press statements and its leaders gave several interviews to national and international media reiterating the need of third-party facilitation. They asked the international community to help in reaching a fair political negotiation. However, the government has so far categorically refusing to involve a third party in the negotiation process.

BOX 6.1 Maoist's letter to the UN Secretary General Kofi Annan

September 1, 2003
H.E. Kofi Annan
Secretary General,
UNO.

Your Excellency,

We highly appreciate the deep concern expressed by you on behalf of the august international body, the UNO, about the break down of peace talks between the old monarchical regime and the revolutionary democratic forces led by our Party in Nepal. We have also noted with high sense of responsibility your call for the solution of all outstanding problems through dialogue and peaceful means in future.

As the entire international community knows, the fratricidal and regicidal 'King' Gyanendra has systematically usurped all democratic and civic rights of the Nepalese people, including the fragile parliamentary institutions since October 4 last, and imposed a royal military dictatorship through his traditional hold over the mercenary Royal Nepal Army (RNA). Our Party, along with other parliamentary and non-parliamentary democratic forces, has been leading a powerful resistance movement in the country against this royal dictatorship, and the autocratic monarchy totally isolated from the people has been surviving merely on brutal military force increasingly backed by some foreign powers.

However, taking into consideration the state of strategic equilibrium between the two armed forces and the sensitive geo-strategic positioning of the country, our Party opted for a ceasefire on January 29 last and entered into a negotiation process with the monarchical regime to find a forward-looking political solution to the problem. In the very first round of the peace talks on April 27 we proposed a three-point compromise formula of a round-table conference, an interim government and election to a Constituent Assembly to end the half century old contention between monarchy and democracy in a peaceful manner. But after much dilly-dallying the monarchical regime rejected the said proposal enjoying overwhelming support of every section of the people in the country and instead produced a very regressive political agenda to consolidate and continue with the hated monarchy and its R NA dictatorship in the third round of talks on August 17-19. A cursory glance at the so-called 'Concept Paper' produced by the monarchical regime during the talks would suffice to expose its arch reactionary and antidemocratic essence to perpetuate the autocratic monarchy, which has been rightly rejected even by the parliamentary political parties agitating for minor reforms within the present set-up.

This obstinate stand of monarchy and its principal support base, the RNA, against a forward -looking political solution through democratic means in the form of an elected Constituent Assembly objectively sealed the fate of peace talks, which were formally broken on August.

Apart from this, whereas our Party and the People's Liberation Army (PLA) strictly observed the ceasefire throughout, the RNA provocatively flouted it all along killing dozens, the most blatant case being the brutal gunning down of 19 unarmed cadres and general masses on the eve of third round of talks on August 17 in Dorambha (Ramechhap), eastern Nepal. To comouflage its essential anti-democratic and militarist character and objective termination of peace talks through denial of progressive political solutions, the monarchical regime has now unabashedly launched Goebbel-style disinformation campaign against the revolutionary democratic forces, which deserves to be exposed by one and all.

We hope the international community would appreciate the complexities of life-and-death struggle between feudal monarchical forces and progressive democratic forces currently going on in Nepal. In this context we would once again reiterate our commitment to find a forward-looking political solution through dialogue and peaceful means at an appropriate moment, but would feel duty-bound to resist armed onslaughts of the monarchical regime against the people fighting for their genuine democratic rights. Finally, we would appeal to the international community in general, and the UNO in particular, to do everything in their might to stop all foreign armed and otherwise interventions in Nepal and let the Nepalese people decide their own future themselves.

Looking forward to cordial and mutually beneficial relations,
(Prachanda)
Chairman,
Communist Party of Nepal (Maoist)

[*Source*: cpnm.org/documents/english/information_bulletin-4.htm]

6.7 WHY IS THE GOVERNMENT RELUCTANT FOR THIRD-PARTY MEDIATION?

The unique geo-political situation of Nepal has direct consequence of involving international mediators. Whoever may be at the helm, the influence of the Indian interests is overtly or covertly reflected in the actions and behaviour of the government and even the governing political parties. The only exceptions were:

1. The 1989 Trade and Transit Treaty, and
2. The strong stand of the UML government under the leadership of Manmohan Adhikari about the 1950 Tripartite Treaty.

Whether it is openly acknowledged or not, Indian influence is expanding even in changing government, selecting the prime minister, ministers and filling other powerful positions. The fundamental reason for the repeated denial of the Nepalese governments to involve the UN or other neutral third party for mediation was clearly revealed the first time by the then Foreign Minister Bhesh Bahadur Thapa. He publicly declared that Nepal could not bypass the powerful neighbouring countries to invite the UN or other third parties for mediation of the armed conflict. Pragmatically, India does not want to see any outsider being active in Nepalese armed conflict. Considering itself as a regional power, it wants to handle all the issues arising in South Asia itself. Another worry for India is the growing expansion of Maoist insurgencies in different states of India. Indian Maoists may have developed their confidence from the growth and expansion of the Nepalese Maoists. If a third party mediates in the Nepalese conflict, this factor may not get enough attention, which is an important security concern for India. Some analysts even say that India wants a 'weak Nepal', which will always depends upon India and give it leverage for bargaining on the water resource of Nepal.

Comparatively, China is less active in the debate of negotiation of armed conflict. However, it has occasionally expressed that the armed conflict is an internal problem of Nepal and it can handle it itself. This indicates the reluctance of China to accept international mediators. There are some strong underlying reasons for Indian and Chinese interests in Nepalese politics. China is very concerned about the Tibetan issue and it does not want to see any force engaged in discussion and debate about the independence of Tibet. Therefore, Chinese scrutiny in the international involvement in mediating armed conflict in Nepal concentrates on the Tibetan issue. Another concern of China in relation to international mediation of Nepalese conflict is its security concern, particularly in a situation when bilateral or multilateral security forces enter Nepal on a peacekeeping mission or for helping the failed nation. Evidence of so-called failed nations shows that external powers make all domestic policies based on their interests. This is another possible reason why China is not supporting the international involvement. Another reason is that China wants a stable and powerful palace in Kathmandu, therefore it does not want to weaken the position of the king by involving international mediators[8] (as in the mediation process the king may need to compromise many powers and privileges).

There are always invisible forces involved in trading of small arms and light weapons to maintain or escalate war for commercial benefits.

Their strategy is to influence the government decision makers in favour of continuing war and ensure commission from the arms trade. This hidden but powerful force is said to have a strong influence over the key players within the government who deny the involvement of third-party mediation because it hampers ill intention and minimises manoeuvring and manipulation during the negotiation process if the experienced professional and independent mediators are involved.

6.8 POTENTIAL FOR THIRD-PARTY MEDIATION IN NEPALESE ARMED CONFLICT

Many potential external actors want to support negotiation and peace process of the Nepalese conflict. Bilateral, non-governmental and inter-governmental organisations have shown interest in assisting Nepal in negotiation, if the warring parties (the government and the Maoists) so desire. Padma Ratna Tuladhar, one of the facilitators of previous 6 rounds of negotiations and who has been actively engaged in creating an enabling environment for future negotiation, says that delegates from different countries and organisations have met him and offered their support in mediation if both parties accept. Some of the potential third parties likely to assist in the mediation process are:

6.8.1 Bilateral mediators

Norway, Finland and Switzerland could help in the negotiation process if they are asked. Their direct or indirect expressions in the past indicate this possibility and they have even played a proactive role in the past. There is great potential to engage them in the conflict, as they have experience, they have maintained neutrality and theoretically their acceptance should be higher from both parties compared to other nations. Austria and Denmark could be other options if the Nepalese government and the rebels request their help. They have vast understanding and experience in dealing with conflict around the world; they have also proven their commitment to post- conflict reconstruction and peace. However, their political influence is relatively weak.

Strategically, the USA and India are more visible and effective mediators if both parties trust them and seek their help. However, at the current level of their relations with the Maoists, it is very unlikely that the Maoists will accept them[9]. So far, the approach of the US to conflict resolution in Nepal is more coercive. The US wants to defeat the Maoists through the use of military force. Though the US said that the Nepalese conflict cannot be solved militarily, it is strengthening the coercive military approach by providing military aid which is exacerbating the conflict. I think there are a few reasons for the US coercive approach. They are:

1. Ideological - the USA does not want to see the expansion of communists (rather radical communists).
2. The perceived fear of terrorism - The USA is hypersensitive to terrorist activities and the US administration has wrongly equated the Maoists with Al Qaeda, Abu Sayyaf, and Lebanon's Hezbollah. The US has concluded that the civil war in Nepal threatens to make it a "failed state" and a haven for international terrorists. Therefore, it has placed the Maoists on the State Department's "terrorist list," like Al Qaeda.
3. It wants to maintain/expand its influence in Nepalese government and military providing military assistance.
4. Geo-strategic interest of US in Nepal, as this country is situated between India and China and close to Pakistan where tremendous strategic interests of the US lie.

6.8.2 Inter-governmental mediators

The United Nations is one of the most widely engaged organisations in mediating conflict, peace making and peace keeping around the world. Involvement of the UN in Nepal is widely discussed in this country and it appreciated its contribution in establishing peace in different parts of the world. In this context, it is relevant to quote the UN General Secretary Kofi Anan. He said, "*The World cannot stand aside when gross and systematic violation of human rights are taking place with grave humanitarian consequences*[10]. However, consent of both parties is required to involve the UN in the negotiation process. In Asia, the UN has been involved in Cambodia, Myanmar, East Timor, etc. In any mediation, the UN involvement is based on a set of shared values and principles, and commitment to the peace process. The intention of the UN to assist Nepal is based on these principles[11].

The UN is one of the best feasible options, when Nepal seeks external mediation. The General Secretary of the UN is deeply concerned about the deteriorating situation of Nepal and offered his willingness to assist Nepal. Civil society, Nepalese diplomats and intelligentsia, major political parties (UML, NCP and others) have largely agreed to involve the UN in mediating conflict and so have the Maoists. Therefore, this is the best choice. The UN is also constantly assessing the situation and studying feasibility. Several visits of Samuel Tamrat from the Political Division of the UN and the visit of Senior Advisor of the Secretary General Mr Lakdar Brahimi is evidence of this interest.

The European Union is another potential mediator in the Nepalese conflict. In the past, the EU had also offered support, if and when Nepal needed it. It was also heard that even the European Parliament had passed a resolution on these lines to support Nepal. Member states of the EU are heavily engaged in resolution of conflict and post-conflict reconstruction in different parts of the world and gained huge amount of experience and expertise that can be very useful for Nepal .Therefore, another better option can be the EU.

6.8.3 International non-Governmental mediators

INGOs could play an important role in creating an enabling environment and meeting pre-negotiation requirements in conflict ridden countries (Khanna, and Kueck, 2003). Some of the INGOs like ICRC, Amnesty International, Centre for Humanitarian Dialogue, Carter Centre, etc. have a great wealth of knowledge and experience in mediating and negotiating international and domestic conflict (Clements and Ward, 1994). They can assist Nepal in resolving armed conflict if the warring parties request them to do so. Carter Centre has experience in conducting elections in conflict-ridden countries (such as Dominican Republic, Panama, Nicaragua, Ethiopia, etc). In Ethiopia, this Centre created an enabling environment by which the government and two revolutionary groups (Tigerean and Eritrean) agreed to meet for peace talks. Getting help from the Carter Centre in mediating Nepalese armed conflict could perhaps minimise or neutralise the confrontational approach adopted by the US in relation to Maoists. But it works in the interests of US.

Similarly, ICRC has tremendous experience in dealing with humanitarian issues in negotiation and Amnesty International does the same in human rights (Khanna and Kueck, 2003). According to Padma Ratna Tuladhar, Centre for Humanitarian Dialogue has expressed its interest to help in negotiation if the government and the Maoists so wish. So, specialised expertise of these INGOs can be used in mediation process together with inter-governmental organisations. However, the sole responsibility of mediation on INGOs may not be suitable for them or for Nepal, as it requires commitment for large financial resources to accomplish post-conflict transformation i.e., disarming, demobilisation, reconstruction, rehabilitation, reintegration and reconciliation (Upreti and Dhungana, 2004).

There are some advantages and disadvantages of involvement of INGOs in conflict resolution. First, they have huge experience in dealing with conflict. Second, they are more easily accessible. Third, some of the renowned and experienced INGOs have already expressed their interest in helping in facilitation/negotiation. However, their main weaknesses are: less political influence to exert pressure and to implement the agreed upon agenda, less availability of resources for the post-conflict rehabilitation and reconstruction in comparison to the bilateral countries.

6.9 SOME EXPERIENCES OF THIRD-PARTY MEDIATION IN OTHER COUNTRIES

There are both positive and negative experiences and supportive and opposing arguments around the world on external mediation of domestic conflict (Zartman and Touval, 1996). The opponents argue that internal conflicts are too complicated to mediate in and external involvement violates a nation's sovereignty, legitimises actions of the rebels, outsiders lack not only knowledge and skills about the conflict circumstance but also lack a legitimate mandate to mediate. Arguments of supporters of the external involvement to mediate in domestic conflicts are mainly based on human rights and humanitarian ground, as human rights issue became universal concern beyond the boundary of a particular nation state. External involvement with the consent of warring parties and endorsed by international communities make it legitimate and increase the possibility of success. Even if external mediators involve in negotiation, this process should ensure involvement of national experts and experience to bridge the gap between external expert knowledge and local experiences.

In dealing with conflict, preventive diplomacy is used as one of the major strategies adopted by the international community. However, the result of preventive diplomacy is not satisfactory to prevent conflict (e.g., Middle East, South Asia, and Africa) (Crocker, 1996).

Generally, two types of international involvement have been observed in contemporary conflict resolution. They are: a) in agreement with conflicting parties as mediators, and b) forceful intervention like in Iraq or Afghanistan. However, both modes of involvement base their arguments on human rights and humanitarian grounds. As observed in Bosnia, contemporary conflict history also faced ethical dilemmas in international mediation, i.e., short-term goal of ending bloodshed and long-term goal of properly settling the conflict.

Preventive and curative approaches are common forms of external involvement in a conflict-ridden country. Irrespective of the desire of the countries in conflict, external involvement in any conflict-ridden countries is unavoidable due to spillover effects of local conflicts into international boundaries. Total isolation from the international engagement is impossible. The only concerns are the degree (limited to create an enabling environment for negotiation process or impose decision as the key player in the negotiation) and the duration (on-off support or continuous engagement) of involvement and more importantly, the consequences thereon. A human rights violation is the basic driving force of international involvement. International communities often do not tolerate crime against humanity and genocide. However, this issue depends upon which international actor is involved. If the conflicting parties do not want forceful external interventions, they have to respect basic human rights of people and democratic norms (Crocker, 1996).

Even in external engagement, track I, track II and track III approaches are needed. Track I approach is more formal and limited to official procedures whereas other tracks seek to help all people involved in peace process, attempting to change their way of thinking (Maley, 1994). Therefore, transformational process facilitated by track II and II approaches enhances empowerment instead of promoting power politics. Its agenda comprises basic human needs instead of strategic interests, collaborative and inclusive process instead of exclusivity and competition and therefore it is an elaborative approach of peace making (Crocker *et al.,* 1994). In Somalia, Life and Peace Institute of Sweden had initiated "Boroma Process", comprehensive efforts to organise local leaders and clans in peace process and it was scaled up to national level. That had tremendous impacts on resolving Somali conflict. This model was replicated in Somaliland later to facilitate the democratic transition.

Zartman and Touval (1996), citing the example of the US in mediating internal conflict in different countries argue that powerful countries are often motivated to mediate mainly because of their defensive and offensive self-interests, to expand their influence. Less powerful countries involve in mediation because they want to establish effective foreign relation tools. Hence, there are always some overt or covert interests when bilateral countries involve themselves in mediation of domestic conflict. Nevertheless, involvement of neutral and less power-centric nation is relatively better but obtaining results may take a longer time compared to the engagement of powerful nations.

While discussing external involvement in mediating domestic conflict, five categories of involvement are commonly observed around the world. They are:

- Inter-governmental organisations (e.g., UN, EU, etc.),
- Powerful nations (mainly USA and former USSR-earlier)
- Neutral small countries with a reputed track record of mediation (e.g., Norway, Switzerland, Finland, etc.)
- Powerful neighbouring countries (e.g., India's involvement in Sri Lanka, South Africa's engagement in many neighbouring countries)
- Independent non-state organisations (e.g., ICRC, Centre for Humanitarian Dialogue, etc.).

Whatever types of organisations among these five categories engage in mediating conflict, they need to closely work with local organisations.

Because of its nature, scope, experiences and credibility, the UN is one of the major organisations involved in mediating conflict around the world. Historically, the UN was created to resolve conflict and restore peace in the world. However, it has achieved mixed results. For example, in Afghanistan the use of the good offices of the UN succeeded in withdrawing Soviet forces but did not succeed in settling the internal conflict between warring Afghani factions[12] (Maley, 1994).

Notable examples of significant success of the UN involvement in mediation are decolonisation in Namibia and election in Cambodia. The UN mediation in Cambodia succeeded in ending armed conflict and driving the country on the democratic track. On 23 October 1991, the 'Paris Conference in Cambodia' produced the 'Comprehensive Political Settlement of the Cambodian Conflict' called "Paris Accord", which paved the way for the formation of Cambodian Supreme National Council, bringing four parties together. Cambodia's administration came partly under the control and supervision of the UN until the government was installed. Nineteen signatory nations and 12 members from four Cambodian factions signed the agreement. Election was accomplished under the UN Transitional Authority of Cambodia (UNTAC). The UNTAC also demobilised and disarmed the rebel factions to create a conducive environment for free and fair election (Mehrotra, 2003). Participants of the Paris Conference including all permanent five members of the UN Security Council agreed not to supply arms and weapons to any of the Cambodian factions. The UNTAC was to perform the following tasks (Mehrotra, 2003):

- Free and fair constituent assembly elections for 120 members
- Preparation of the constitution within 3 months by the constituent assembly
- Repatriation of refugees.
- A programme of economic and financial support for Cambodia's reconstruction and reconciliation.
- Establishing administrative structures necessary to maintain peace.
- Withdrawal of foreign forces and foreign military assistance.
- Demobilisation of 70 per cent of all armed forces.
- Creation of environment of peace and stability ensuring human rights to Cambodian people.

The UN in this way put Cambodia back on the road to democracy and re-established the exiled prince Norodom Sihanouk as the Head of the State (Ibid).

Since the Kashmir conflict began in 1974, the UN has twice brokered a ceasefire but they were violated by India and Pakistan. The UN has also put forth several resolutions aimed to end the armed conflict. However, the peace process did not succeed mainly because of the tougher attitude of the warring nations.

Chester Crocker (1996) argues that military intervention in nationalist revolutions, and civil wars often forces whole groups and classes against one another and that must be avoided. In such cases, the best way of dealing with violent internal conflict is pre-emptive action, preventing the process that leads to politicised conflict into militarised conflict. Hence, diplomatic intervention is often more suitable than military intervention. Military intervention is often effective to contain violence; it does not tend to produce resolution of the conflict (Croceker *et al.*, 1994).

Another main actor involved in mediating conflict across the world is the US owning to its continued long-term strategic interests (for example the Middle East) and willingness to involve in mediation. However, it did not succeed in mediating the Middle East conflict mainly because of its own interest rather than settling conflict. The Arab world has always suspected the attitude of the USA and its commitment to peace (Croceker *et al.*, 1994). Everywhere, the USA is judgemental and biased towards one party with some visible vested interests, which severely undermines the mediation process. The USA has established its global track record of use of force as a main means of resolving conflict. Afghanistan and Iraq are the latest examples.

Whether it is appropriate or inappropriate to involve external mediators depends on the context and circumstances rather than the wealth and power of the nation. For example, in the Northern Ireland conflict, the UK was not able to negotiate alone and it had requested military assistance from Canada and professional help from the USA and Sweden. In terms of power and resources, the UK may not need external help. However, the Northern Ireland conflict case proved that resource and power alone are not enough to reach negotiated settlement and external help is needed.

As in Nepal, the US support for peace in Columbia has been ambivalent and always subject to the pressure of the official policy priorities. For example, the USA in Columbia first focused on a 'counter-narcotics programme' and is now focusing on the 'war on terror' through funding to Columbian military (Tate, 2004). However, the US counter-narcotics programme has been an obstacle to peace efforts (e.g., fumigation campaigns have exacerbated existing social tensions and eroded public trust in government). Growing US support for the Columbian army for counter-narcotic programme (sharply raised from US $ 18 millions in 1989 to 750 million in 2003, by 1999 Columbia became third largest US military assistance in the world) has been persistently viewed by Columbian people as US endorsement of military solution (ibid:71). The US named National Liberation Army (ELN) and Revolutionary Armed Force of Columbia (FARC) as 'narcoguerrillas', portraying them simply as drug trafficking bandits. The USA did almost similar things in Nepal, listing Maoists simply as a terrorist organisation. Such response of the US has created difficulties in negotiation. Commenting on the US approach in Columbia, Winifred Tate (2004:72) writes, "*...Since the late 1990s, the US has appeared to be adopting a 'Salvadoran' style of strategic approach. Civilian and military policy-makers alike invoke the US policy towards El*

Salvador in the 1980s as the model, in which direct military intervention is eschewed in favour of escalating assistance in terms of equipments, training and intelligence technology. As in El Salvador, US officials also emphasise the need to strengthen the military to force the guerrillas to the table". If we compare the US approaches between Columbia and Nepal, many similarities are evident.

The Columbian peace process contributes to the debate on international involvement in mediating Maoist conflict. A few years back, Andrees Pastrana came to power with the commitment of political settlement of the conflict through peace diplomacy. Columbian government opted for an internationalisation of peace and invited international community to help. ICRC played an important role in humanitarian aspects. The UN General Secretary appointed his special advisor to Columbia. In agreement with the government and FARC, the 'Groups of Friends for Peace in Columbia" was comprised of 26 friendly nations and special representation of the UN and EU. This group designated small 'Facilitating Commission' of ten nations (Canada, Cuba, Spain, France, Italy, Mexico, Norway, Sweden, Venezuela and Switzerland) to facilitate peace process and even take up the functions of facilitator and mediator at key moments (e.g., extension of demilitarised zones). Similarly, another facilitating group (composed of Cuba, Spain, Norway, France, and Switzerland) was created in agreement with the government and the ELN. This group has also continuously engaged itself in facilitating the peace process and assisting the UN. The UN negotiated with both the FARC and ELN and engaged in a semi-formal role of facilitation and mediation. The Andean Community through the Lima Declaration 2001[13] has been assisting Columbia to restore peace and end violence. The Columbian peace process clearly indicates a need for engagement of wider level of international actors in a situation of complex conflict, which is seriously lacking in Nepal. So external involvement in Nepal is needed and only concerted efforts of international community can make this happen.

As the armed conflict and civil wars and inter-state wars grow, different conflict prevention methods have been developed and used to effectively prevent conflict. They are: Risk Assessments Method, Conflict Indicators Method, Early Warning Method, Peace Keeping Method, Multi-functional Observer Missions, United Nations Military Observer (UNMO) Mission, Fact-finding and Observation missions (this needs to include political, social, economic, and psychological dimensions of the conflict too), Early Warning Analysis and Policy

Planning in UN Preventive Action, etc. However, their effectiveness depends upon the conflict situation of host countries, willingness of the parties in conflict and commitment of international community.

6.10 CONCERNS OVER THIRD-PARTY MEDIATION

Neutrality and impartiality always raise the question of external involvement, as external actors often want to engage in mediation with hidden vested interests. This is more true if and when powerful or strong neighbouring countries want to involve in mediation (Upreti, 2005b). Similarly, if external mediation fails, it is even more counterproductive. Often that happens when military interventions are a package of mediation. External intervention could be effective mainly when diplomatic interventions are linked with political process (Crocker, 1996).

During the cold war period, NATO and Warsaw Pact counties competed to mediate conflicts around the world through military interventions or threat of use of force. Threat of use of force or actual use (e.g., in Afghanistan, Iraq, etc.) is still a major strategy of international community in settling domestic conflict of poor or developing nations. However, both the examples of Iraq and Afghanistan proved that use of force or threat to use force alone are not successful approaches in resolving conflict and maintaining peace. In Iraq, violence and instability has further accelerated even after the overthrown of the dictator Sadam Hussein. Afghanistan is still suffering from the same situation. Some critiques like Robin Crew, Executive Director of Peace Study Association and American citizen severely questioned the effectiveness of even UN in settling conflict and the role of US within the UN. He says that if membership criteria require that member states do not conduct warfare on one another, then nobody is living up to their membership obligation to the UN, and they should be kicked out. The US should be the first to be kicked out, and we should go from there. The UN can be re-created to function as it was supposed to do. ...The UN has to be changed fundamentally and we have to play a role on that[14] (Crews, 1994:4).

External mediation faces a hard choice between 'some degree of settlement' (could be unjust settlement) or no settlement when stake of internal power is high in the conflict. Some people argue that some settlement is better than no settlement and others argue that unjust settlement undermines the principle of justice and therefore if full settlement is unlikely then it is better to wait for the ripeness of the conflict to achieve full settlement (Burgess and Burgess, 1996).

Parties in conflict always consider EATNA (estimated alternative to a negotiated settlement) before deciding to negotiate (Burgess and Burgess, 1996). If warring parties estimate other alternatives (though not necessarily BATNA - best alternative to the negotiated settlement), they will not negotiate, even if it is based on misjudgement, as the present situation in Nepal. Only when parties in conflict see a likely outcome from negotiation as an incentive, will they negotiate. They will identify their minimum acceptable negotiated outcomes before reaching a negotiation. For example, the formation of constitution through a constituent assembly and the guarantee of constitutional monarchy could be the minimum acceptable outcome to the Maoists and the king respectively for a negotiated settlement of the ongoing armed conflict of Nepal.

So far, there is a tendency of international mediation or intervention when conflict has erupted and need to be contained or when it was time for post-conflict peace building or peacekeeping (Croceker *et al.*, 1994). The Statement of Kofi Anan immediately after the Beni attack by the Maoists is a clear reflection of his commitment to peace in the member nations in accordance with the Article 33 of the UN Charter on Peaceful Settlement of Conflict. However, Nepalese government is persistently ignoring the concerns of the Secretary General of the UN.

6.10.1 Assumptions

Without creating a supportive attitude from India, it is extremely difficult to make the negotiation successful even by involving international mediators. The assumption is that Nepalese politicians, civil society and the government will be able to convince Indian politicians to help Nepal and international community to put positive pressure on India to support to resolve the Nepalese crisis. One of the best ways to create positive pressure is to request the international community by the Maoists, the government and political parties to form a Nepal Peace Support Group, which could exert pressure more effectively.

Another assumption is that international community makes genuine efforts instead of creating an unfavourable environment and working for its vested strategic interests.

6.10.2 Risks

As discussed in the preceding sections, there are always some risks involved in external mediation of domestic conflict. Some of these risks are:

1. Vested interest of the external actors, particularly if they are bilateral powerful countries. The neutral small countries may not have vested interests and other powerful nations may attempt to influence their actions during the course of mediation.
2. If they fail to negotiate once, it is difficult for them to accomplish future negotiations.
3. It is a lengthy process and requires long-term engagement and commitment. If they drop their engagement before accomplishment of the negotiated settlement due to their domestic reasons (e.g., policy change, change in government, etc.), the whole negotiation efforts could be jeopardised and it will be very hard and costly to rebuild.
4. The UN involvement is complicated. When Security Council needs to be involved in the decision-making process, there is always a fairly good chance of exerting influence by powerful nations to get decisions of their desire (e.g., China and India could influence the Security Council according to their interests if the Security Council decides UN mediation in Nepal. Even some of the permanent members of the Security Council may use veto if they feel their interests can be affected).
5. Important internal security-related issues may be exposed and could be risky for future.

6.11 UN IS BEST AMONG EXTERNAL MEDIATORS

Failure of previous negotiations, weakness of the warring parties and international concerns have created a basis for the debate on relevance and appropriateness of involvement of external actors in mediating the ongoing armed conflict. Earlier, this debate was limited to intelligential and civil society has now been quickly widened to the political parties and donor community. UN General Secretary Kofi Anan repeatedly highlighted the worsening security situation of Nepal. He also appointed especial political officer (Mr Samual Tamrat) to work on Nepal issues and he has been frequently visiting Nepal. After the Beni attack by the Maoists, UN General Secretary Kofi Anan again expressed his deep concern on the deteriorated situation in Nepal and offered any help from UN if the warring parties want. CPN (Maoists) immediately welcomed the offer. The CPN-UML also formally accepted the need of UN involvement and NCP Chairperson expressed his openness to involve the UN. The Nepalese people positively accepted the offer of Kofi Anan. CPN (UML) has also accepted and even demanded involvement of UN in mediating Nepalese conflict. However, the governments have repeatedly rejected these offers on the ground of possible problem from big neighbours India and China if Nepal invites the UN to help in a negotiated settlement. Now the seven-party alliance is also positive towards the involvement of UN in mediating Nepal's armed change and political crisis.

After the 1st February royal takeover, the UN is becoming more worried.The General Secretary sent his senior political advisor Mr Lakder Brahimi to assess the situation of Nepal. Mr L. Brahimi is one of the most experienced senior negotiators who was also involved in Afghanistan and Iraq conflict from UN. After his intensive meeting with political parties, civil society, military officers, the government officials and the king, he came to the conclusion that though the conflict is serious, it is manageable if the major political forces want to resolve it. He also repeated the same offer and the government reiterate the same, that there is no need of UN mediation in Nepalese conflict.

If Nepalese politicians are able to solve this crisis themselves, we do not need external mediation. However, they failed to solve it. Both the king and the political parties are not capable enough to settle this crisis alone and therefore Nepal needs an external mediator. When the issue of involvement of external mediators comes in the debate, the role and resistance of India is always dominant. The government and political parties are very hesitant to talk about this. Once, the then foreign minister clearly indicated in 2004 that our big neighbours India and China would not agree to accept UN as mediator. But now the situation has changed and the earlier resistance from the USA and India has also softened. However, whoever will be the third-party mediator for Nepal's conflict will need to take India into confidence. After the 1st February 2005, the UK, USA and India have a common understanding in the crisis (though the USA is softer than India and the UK on the issue of royal coup). This is a big advantage for Nepal to mobilise this triad force to involve the UN. The following are some of the reasons for engaging the UN in Nepal's conflict transformation and peace building:

1. The UN is an independent and neutral organisation with vast experience in mediating conflict around the world (However, it was not able to prevent the US military intervention in Iraq but later all powerful nations realised the need of involvement of the UN in managing the Iraq crisis).
2. Nepal is a member of the UN and it has legitimate concern if crisis occurs in its member state. If the crisis in any member country mounts, it has to be discussed in the UN (General Assembly/Security Council). So, sooner or later, if the situation of Nepal worsens, this issue will be discussed there and it will come up with necessary measures, which may be a Peace-Keeping Force or other interventions. Hence, before reaching this stage, it is wiser to involve the UN.
3. UN's experiences of holding/monitoring elections, disarming and demobilisation, arms and weapons management at the time of constituent assembly election or referendum and forming a UN-led government can be used in negotiating our conflict. It is sure that the issue of managing weapons at the time of elections, election monitoring, etc. are key contentious issues where we need the UN's experience and engagement.
4. It is easier to generate the huge amount of financial resources required for post-conflict reconstruction and rehabilitation and involvement of UN makes it easy for generating such resources.
5. Dealing with India, the USA and other countries is also easy when the UN is engaged.

As India has indicated its flexible attitude, Nepal has a chance to start peace diplomacy to bring UN as mediator with the consent of India, which is possible.

6.12 CONCLUSION

Dialogue is one of the most appropriate and pragmatic approaches of managing the current crisis of Nepal. However, it requires mutual trust, commitment and internalisation of the potentials of dialogue approach in achieving durable and democratic peace in the country (Harris and Reilly, 1998). If dialogue is to be acknowledged by the actors of the conflict who have a deep mistrust and serious grievances as a suitable means of resolving conflict, they need to demonstrate mutual respect, develop confidence and come up with democratic solutions. Political problems need political solution that begins with constructive engagement and demonstrated commitment. Constructive dialogue can be facilitated by ensuring freedom of expression and freedom of movement, respecting human rights and promoting free media. Therefore, political forces must engage in a constructive and continuous dialogue that provides a fundamental step in the 'roadmap to democracy', restoring just peace and achieving negotiated settlement of the armed conflict. The ongoing armed conflict is a national problem and it should be tackled by national consensual efforts. Dialogue provides this opportunity too.

It is not easy to successfully negotiate the complex conflict like the Maoist insurgency and it requires huge efforts from all the concerned actors. The fundamental pre-condition for mediation for the negotiated settlement is the readiness of the conflicting parties. Negotiation through external mediation will not succeed if the parties in conflict are not ready to settle this conflict politically. The external mediators alone, irrespective of how powerful, skilful and experienced they are, cannot reach a negotiated settlement if the Maoists, the government, political parties and the king are not willing.

Negotiation is a long-term process and requires huge efforts and an enabling environment to make it successful. In this process, there is a great prospect for external involvement in pre-negotiation and negotiation stages. Pre-negotiation is a set of tasks to begin prior to negotiation, sustain, and nourish peace process through changing relationships and paving ways for negotiation (Upreti, 2005b). Essentially, pre-negotiation is a start of the political process that helps change relationship and leads to ending the conflict and to peace and reconciliation.

Nepal needs help from the international community. Who is appropriate for mediation and why, what model and approach of mediation, to what degree and duration needs further debate and discussion before any decision is taken. It has to be decided not by a single party or the government but by the whole nation unitedly. Considering the context, willingness, experiences and practicalities, Nepal should seek the UN's mediation with full support of other well-wishers of Nepal. It needs to request all well-wisher countries and intern-governmental organisations to form a Nepal Peace Support Group. This Group will back the UN, settle differences of the neighbouring countries and take them in confidence and help the UN in mediating the armed conflict to reach a negotiated settlement and durable peace in the country.

NOTES

1. Addressing the Indian intelligence, security experts and police top brass, Indian Prime Minister on 5th November in New Delhi said, *"dealing with left wing extremism is ... not merely a law and order issue, though containing violence must be a major aspect. This is more so now that Maoists in Nepal have become a major force and are trying to link up with left wing extremist groups across the border*" (The Kathmandu Post, 6 November, 2004).
2. See the Dialogue Report of The Centre for Conflict Resolution and The Coexistence Initiative, October 2004 for details.
3. See the Special Programme for the Promotion of Dialogue and Conflict Resolution Report 2004 for detail.
4. Interviewed with a historian Mr. Prem Raman Upreti on 11 May 2004
5. *The Kathmandu Post Friday, 7th May 2004.*
6. The latest proposal of Maoist supremo Prachanda issuing press release on 16th May 04 urges to have a joint dialogue between the King, all political forces, the Maoists and the representatives of the civil society with the help of UN. Even the press release requests five parliamentary parties, all political forces and civil society to take initiative to hold such a joint talk (*Nepal Samachar Patra*, 17 May 04). However, the political context is changed and the Maoists are the absolute gainer from the current confrontation between the king and the parliamentary parties. Now the strategy of the Maoists is changing and they want to isolate the palace. Hence, they are repeatedly asking political parties to have dialogue and collaboration to fight with the king.
7. US Embassy, however, refused the meeting between the US Ambassador and Dr Bhattarai, which might have also helped to increase the tension between USA and Maoists.
8. If international mediators are involved in the negotiation process, they generally follow international norms, practices and standards and consequently the government may have to accept some of the conditions that could be unfavourable for the strong position of the palace.
9. Commenting on the US involvement in Nepal Published by Foreign Policy In Focus (FPIF), a joint project of the Interhemispheric Resource Centre (IRC, www.irc-online.org) and the Institute for Policy Studies (IPS, www.ips-dc.org) quotes "*Nepal borders both India and China (Tibet). Both generally support the royalist forces, but neither is too happy about the growing U.S. involvement*" (http://www.fpif.org/commentary/2004/0402nepal.html)
10. *Kofi Anan "The Concept off Sovereignty" ,The Economist, 10 September*

1999 p.49.

11. See Upreti, B. R. (2060BS), Kina Chahinchha Nepalma Samyukta Rastra Sangh ko Samlagnata (Why UN needs to involve in the Nepal's Conflict). *Nepal fortnightly*, Kantipur Publications,1-15 Kattik, issue 5, for detail.
12. When communist groups seized control of Afghanistan in 1978 through military coup, rural population sharply opposed it. Then Soviet Union intervened in Afghanistan in 1979 and installed president of their choice. Mujahideen seriously opposed this intervention and the civil war started.
13. Lima Declaration 2001 declared to end arm trafficking, reduce defence budget, increase intelligence sharing and mutual actions, boarder regulation to promote peace and stability in the Andean nations.
14. See home page of Peace Study Association to know more on the perspective of Robin Crew.

CHAPTER 7

Human Rights Approach in Dealing with Armed Conflict

7.1. INTRODUCTION

Needless to say that Nepal is facing an armed insurgency for the last ten years and the power struggle between the constitutional forces is further deepening the crisis. Democratic institutions are becoming dysfunctional because of the absence of the parliament and the elected local bodies. The country is running on ordinances. The armed conflict and the king's directive have seriously undermined the very notion of democracy, a system of managing differences without recourse to violence. Attacks and counter-attacks between the warring parties are regular and increasing. Realistic possibility for peace talks and negotiated settlement seems distant particularly after the royal takeover, though principally both sides have not ruledout peace talks. Other approaches to handle conflict such as recognizing the needs and interests of other sides, mutually exploring the possible options for resolution, constructively engaging to hammer out the core differences, working in the commonly agreed areas (e.g., restructuring the state), respecting the different opinions and readiness to listen to them are not internalised by the warring parties. The sole strategy of both seems to weaken the other side with the use of force and distorted information. Therefore, in the present situation, it is unrealistic to expect any genuine commitment and efforts from the warring parties to achieve durable peace through negotiated settlement. Hence, only the human rights approach remains operational at the time of the escalated conflict because of its very focus on safeguarding basic rights of human beings.

In this chapter I argue that, compared to a human rights approach, other approaches of conflict management are less effective and less operational in the situation of escalated conflict. It is a pragmatic and realistic means to create a conducive environment because of its constant monitoring of the human rights violation, which is a major characteristic of the escalated armed conflict. This chapter briefly highlights factors affecting the human rights violations and escalation of the conflict where special emphasis is given to the psychological aspect. It lists relevant instruments on human rights and humanitarian laws. Further, the paper brings some international concerns and their impacts on Nepal's armed conflict. Finally, it highlights roles and responsibilities of major actors to ensure respecting and fulfilling human rights that will help to achieve peaceful settlement of the armed conflict in Nepal.

7.2 THE ARMED CONFLICT AND HUMAN RIGHTS CRISIS IN NEPAL

As the duration of the armed conflict is prolonging, human rights violations are mounting (INSEC, 2003; 2004 and 2005) and new phenomena are developing and new social characters are emerging (Upreti, 2004a). The severity of human rights violations can be realised from the press release of Human Rights Watch, Amnesty International and International Commission of Jurists at various times about the deteriorating human rights situation in Nepal. While examining the course of expansion of the Maoist insurgency during the ten years of its existence and expansion, many unanticipated and unexpected events are customized and socialized by Nepalese society (Upreti, 2004a). Though such phenomena are new to Nepal, they are frequently observed in other war-torn countries of Africa, Asia, Eastern Europe and Central and South America ((Armon and Carl, 1996; Armon and Philipson, 1998; Barnes, 2002; Crandall, 2004; Lucima, 2002; Galtung, 2000). Frequent and persistent human rights violation provides a basis for socialisation and customisation of unwanted social characters.

After the agreement in Geneva (11 April 2005) between High Commissioner for Human Rights Louise Arbour and Ramesh Nath Pandey, Minister for Foreign Affairs on behalf of Government of Nepal, the Office of the United Nations High Commissioner for Human Rights (OHCHR) has set up a monitoring operation in Nepal to help in establishing accountability for human rights abuses and prevent further violations by the warring parties. The OHCHR Office in Nepal monitors the observance of human rights and international humanitarian law,

TABLE 7.1 International Human Rights Instrument Ratified by Nepal

S.N.	*International Instruments*	*Ratification Accession Date*
1.	Slavery Convention, 1926	7 January, 1963 (A)
2.	Protocol Amending the Slavery Convention, 1953	7 January, 1993 (A)
3.	Supplementary Convention on the Abolition of Slavery, the Slave Trade and Institution and Practices Similar to Slavery, 7 September 1956	7 January, 1963(A)
4.	Convention on the Political Rights of Women, 1952	26 April 1967 (A)
5.	Convention on the Prevention and the Punishment of Genocide, 1948	17 January 1969(A)
6.	International Covenant on the Elimination of All Forms of Racial Discrimination, 1965	30 January 1971 (A)
7.	International Convention on the Suppression and Punishment of the Crime of Apartheid, 1973	12 July 1977 (A)
8.	International Convention Against Apartheid in Sports, 1985	1 March 1989 (R)
9.	Convention on the Rights of the child, 1989	14 September, 1990 (R)
10.	Convention on the Elimination of All Forms of Discrimination Against Women, 1979	22 April 1991(R)
11.	International Covenant on Economic, Social and Cultural Rights, 1966	14 May 1991 (A)
12.	International Covenant on Civil and Political Rights, 1966	14 May 1991 (A)
13.	Optional Protocol to the International Covenant on Civil and Political Rights, 1966	14 May 1991 (A)
14.	Convention Against Torture and other Cruel, Inhuman or Degrading Treatment or Punishment, 1984	14 May 1991 (A)
15.	Convention on the Suppression of Immoral Trafficking and Protocol, 1949	27 December, 1995 (A)
16.	Second Optional Protocol to the International Convention on Civil and Political Rights/Aiming at the abolition of Death Penalty, 1989	26 September, 1997 (A)

bearing in mind the climate of violence and the internal armed conflict in the country. The OHCHR field offices have started to operate at a regional level in order to monitor and respond rapidly to reports of human rights violations. At the time of signing agreement Louise Arbor said, "Breaking the cycle of serious and systematic abuses will be the first essential step toward achieving peace and reconciliation in Nepal".

BOX 7.1 Main Involvement of OHCHR

- Based on the information collected by the Nepal office, the High Commissioner for Human Rights will submit periodic analytic reports on any human rights violations committed by either side of the conflict to the Commission on Human Rights, the General Assembly, and the Secretary-General.
- The OHCHR Nepal office will also advise His Majesty's Government on matters related to the promotion and protection of human rights in Nepal and will provide advisory services and human rights support to representatives of civil society, human rights non-governmental organizations and individuals.
- The human rights monitors employed by OHCHR investigate and report all human rights violations from both the security forces and the CPN-Maoists.
- OHCHR Office maintains "impartiality, independence, objectivity and transparency" in all its work.
- OHCHR Nepal office works closely with local human rights defenders, including the press, in carrying out its investigations.

7.3 HUMAN RIGHTS APPROACH TO CONFLICT TRANSFORMATION

Human rights and violent conflict are negatively interrelated, as violence undermines human rights and protection of human rights minimises violence. Violation of human rights at the time of escalated conflict is frequent, which raises global concerns. Violations can be minimised by respecting human rights covenants, principles, and standards (collectively known as human rights laws). The International Helsinki Federation for Human Rights (IHF) issued three reports about the human rights and humanitarian law situation in Chechnya and Ingushetia, documenting severe human rights violations by Russian and Chechen security forces and the rebels that have contributed to the escalation of conflict. The experiences around the world (Rwanda, Guatemala, Burundi, Algeria, Chechnya, etc.) demonstrate that international community becomes more serious when human rights violations increase in any war-torn country. If there is high international pressure on them at the time when they do not listen domestic pleas, the warring parties become more alert because of either fear of threat or isolation and loss of support.

Conflict transformation involves a qualitative change in the conflict itself and the socio-political system in which that conflict occurs. Conflict is a dynamic phenomenon. The term conflict transformation refers to change in the conflict dynamics, the context or issue, change in actors' response, nature of the relationships between the people involved, over time. Raimo Vayrynen (1991: 4-7) argues that conflict transformation can take place in at least four different ways:

1. Actor transformation: involves either major internal change within the parties to the conflict.
2. Issue transformation: involves an alteration of the political agenda of the conflict through a transformation of what the conflict is about.
3. Rule transformation: involves a change in the norms involved in the conflict and the limits within which the parties conduct their relations.
4. Structural transformation: involves changes in the whole structure of inter-party relations.

7.3.1 Factors affecting the violation of human rights at the time of armed conflict

Experiences of the 36 years (19960-1996) of Guatemalan armed conflict as well as Columbian conflict show that without respecting the basic human rights of people, violent conflict cannot be transformed (Garcia-Duran, 2004; Crandall, 2004 and Barnes, 2002). Even Nepalese cases clearly demonstrate that coercive measures further complicate the situation. Several visible and invisible factors affect the violation of human rights at the time of the escalated conflict. They are as follows:

7.3.1.1 Psychological factors

Any armed conflict induces deep division in society. It creates severe negative psychological impacts such as fear, agony, frustration, hopelessness; feeling of revenge, etc. to individuals. Many people become direct victims. The question concerns on defining the victim. In this context, United Nations Declaration of Basic Principles of Justice for Victim of Crime and Abuse of Power and UN General Assembly Resolution 40/34 of 29 November 1985 defines victim as " *persons who, individually or collectively, has suffered harm, including physical or mental injury, emotional suffering, economic loses or substantial impairment of their fundamental rights, through acts or omissions that do not yet constitute violations of national criminal laws but of internationally recognised norms relating to human rights".* When we use this definition of victim in the context of the armed conflict, hundreds of thousands of Nepalese people are the conflict victims. Every day we are observing cases of gross human rights violation such as killings, disappearance, torture, rape, forced donations, threats of attack, arrest, etc.

The important question is: why do people engaged in armed conflict violate human rights? Is it not possible for them to respect basic human rights of people? Several causes can be present to answer this question. The people directly engaged in armed conflict (i.e., security forces and Maoists fighters) constantly fear from possible attack by other sides, they remember their family and relatives when they are far from their homes or active on war, as they are human beings. Often they are not getting enough rest, proper food and sleep. They are deprived of sexual satisfaction. If they are facing heat and cold, working on difficult terrain and seniors are not accompanying or consoling or even arrogant, the level of stress further increases (Upreti, 2005i). Consequently they become distraught. When they become distraught, they lose judgment of possible consequences of their actions on human rights violation. They just act on the basis of their immediate conscience. All these are the result of combat stress. For example, if they are fearful of possible attack from other side, they see all unfamiliar people as their enemy, deeply suspect and act accordingly. If they lose confidence, they lose judgment too. The result is human rights violations.

If and when the other side attacks their colleagues, they want revenge and act brutally once they meet the enemy. Even some fighters develop psudo-superiority complex when they have arms in their hand and act to demonstrate their superiority. Occasionally, they violate human rights with the hope of getting rewards (such as promotions, increment in benefits, medals, etc.) from their seniors.

Sexual violence is often the result of either infatuation, or sexual urge or separation from spouses for a long time. Sexual harassment, molestation and rape are common sexual violations. This happens within the fighting groups or between ordinary civilians and fighters. Another major cause of human rights violation is misinformation to the fighters, as they often act on limited information or no proper information.

When they feel severe risks or threat from other side, they always want to minimise that risk by either escaping or exposing ordinary people to risk. For example, human shield is one of the common strategies of the fighters if they are exposed to severe risk from other side. We sometimes hear that seniors often send juniors first on the roads with ambush or areas of landmines. These factors highly affect behaviour of combatants. It is often reported in the media that after the provision of operation of unified command under the army, armed and civilian polices have to go first, first exposed to risks, which cause a feeling of injustice and frustration.

7.3.1.2 Strategy of the warring parties

Warring parties often use fear, threat of violence or terror as a means of achieving their goal in the time of war. When examining the civil wars of different countries it can be said that there is always a trade-off between respecting human rights standards and weakening other side by creating terror and horror (Armon, and Carl, 1996; Lord, 2000; Lucima, 2002; McCartney, 1999; Armon, and Philipson, 1998; Armon, *et al.,* 1998; Armon *et al.,* 1997; Barnes, 2002; Carl, A. and Garasu, 2002; Conen, 1999; Crandall, 2004; Garcia- Duran, 2004; Hendrickson, 1998; Putnam, 1993; Stankovitch, 1999; Lode, 2002; Macrae, 2002; Misra, 2002; Senghaas, 2001; Susskind & Cruikshank 1987 and Upreti, 2004a; Abdullaev, and Barnes, 2001).

7.3.2. Ways of adherence to human rights standards

If the warring parties adhere to the international human rights and international humanitarian laws, they can drastically reduce the level of human rights violence. The following box provides some of the major human rights and humanitarian laws and instruments.

If the warring parties adhere to the above-mentioned human rights provisions they can create a favourable environment to initiate the dialogue and reach negotiated settlement through peace talks (Upreti, 2061BS).

7.3.3 Armed conflict, human rights situation, and international concerns

Since the escalation of the armed conflict in Nepal, the international

BOX 7.2 Relevant Human Rights/Humanitarian Law Instruments

- Universal Declaration of Human Rights
  - International Covenant on Economic, Social and Cultural Rights
  - International Covenant on Civil and Political Rights
- UN Charter
- Common Article 3 of the Geneva Conventions
- Protocols I & II to the Geneva Conventions
- Universal Declaration on the Rights of Indigenous Peoples (ILO)
- Convention on the Rights of the Child
- Convention on the Elimination of all Forms of Discrimination against Women
- Declaration on the Protection of Women and Children in Emergency and Armed Conflict
- Declaration on the Right of Peoples to Peace
- Declaration on the Prevention and Punishment of the Crime of Genocide
- Declaration on the Right to Development
- Declaration on the Rights of Persons Belonging to National or Ethnic, Religious and Linguistic Minorities
- Convention against Torture and other Cruel and Inhuman or Degrading Treatment or Punishment
- Convention on the Elimination of all Forms of Racial Discrimination
- UN Guiding Principles on Internal Displacement
- Vienna Declaration and Programme of Action, World Conference on Human Rights
- European Convention for the Protection of Human Rights and Fundamental Freedoms

community is repeatedly expressing its concern on the violation of human rights. Senior official of the UN, Samual Tamrat, special envoy of the Prime Minister of the United Kingdom Jeffrey James, high-level delegation of European Union 'Troika', representatives of the United Nations Commission on Human Rights and officials of other many government and international organisations are visiting Nepal, assessing the situation and coming up with the assessment of worsening situation in Nepal. Different meetings of the United Nations Commission on Human Rights at Geneva seriously expressed concern about the deteriorating human rights situation in Nepal. Again, the fifty-three member states of the United Nations Commission on Human Rights meet in Geneva from 14 March to 22 April 2005 came to the conclusion that to prevent human rights crisis in Nepal, monitoring by the OHCHR is imperative. Even Agenda Nine was discussed and with the full commitment from the government the Agenda-9 was stopped and Agenda

19 was passed with the agreement between the government of Nepal and the OHCHR to open its office in Nepal (see box 7.1). The Geneva meeting also scrutinised the commitment of the Nepalese government to implement the human rights provisions agreed upon by the government on 26 March 2004.

7.3.3.1 Concerns of the UN

Concerns of the UN Secretary General: The Secretary General of the UN is not only repeatedly expressing his deep concerns but also offering help from the UN if Nepal needs it to end the armed insurgency. The Spokesman for the Secretary-General issued a statement on 23 December regarding the deteriorating situation in Nepal. He stated, *'The Secretary-General is deeply troubled by reports of an escalation of fighting in Nepal and of continued grave human rights violations. The conflict is undermining democracy and human rights and seriously hindering development activities. Reports that human rights defenders in Nepal face grave threats to their safety and security are very disturbing. The safety and ability of the National Human Rights Commission and all human rights activists to carry out their essential work should be guaranteed. In that regard, the recent signing of a Memorandum of Understanding between His Majesty's Government of Nepal and the Office of the High Commissioner for Human Rights is a welcome step. The Secretary-General once again calls for an urgent cessation of fighting and the initiation of dialogue between the Government and the Communist Party of Nepal (Maoist) with the participation of all political and civil forces. He stands ready to assist such a national effort*". This statement clearly demonstrates the serious concerns of the UN about the deteriorating situation in Nepal. The secretary general has several times issued similar statements asking the warring parties to end violence and reach political settlement through peace talks. He also issued a strong statement after the first February royal takeover asking to return to democracy and to prevent further deterioration of the human rights situation and political crisis in Nepal.

Amnesty International in its statement of 19 December 2004 stated, *"The heightened threats occur as the international community reacts to the human rights situation with growing alarm. The UN Working Group on Enforced or Involuntary Disappearances (WGEID) concluded a visit to Nepal on Tuesday having received more reports of disappearance cases than from any other country in the world"*.

The UN Human Rights Commission watches the human rights violations in Nepal and exerts pressure to the warring parties. A team of the UN Working Group on Enforced or Involuntary Disappearance led by its chief Stephen J. Toope visited Nepal from 6 to 14 December 2004. The team asked the Nepalese government to respect the 25-point human rights commitment it made public on the 26th March 2004. Mr Toope appealed to the government to maintain an up-to-date accessible list of detainees, to allow access of the NHRC, families and lawyers of the persons detained. He said, *"No circumstance whatsoever, whether a threat of war, internal political insatiability or any other public emergency, may be invoked to justify enforced disappearance"*[1].

7.3.3.2 Concerns of the International Commission of Jurists (ICJ)

The ICJ team, which visited Nepal,[2] said on 30th November 2004 that the Government of Nepal and the Communist Party of Nepal (Maoist) must take urgent steps now to end the human rights crisis if any future political process and negotiations are to be successful. *"We are deeply concerned about the escalating and gross human rights abuses being committed by both sides of the conflict in Nepal. Addressing the breakdown of the rule of law cannot wait for a peace settlement. On the contrary, urgent steps can and must be taken to protect non-combatants, halt the spiralling descent into lawlessness and build the confidence for a political process. It is time for the Government and the Maoists, as an important confidence building measure, to sign the Human Rights Accord. It is tragic that so many of the abuses and the failure to obey the Nepali Constitution and laws, which the ICJ observed when it visited in 2003, persist or have worsened"* said Nicholas Howen, ICJ Secretary-General towards the end of the ICJ's nine-day mission to Nepal[3]. The ICJ delegation expressed its dissatisfaction with the armed forces saying, *"It saddens us that the Royal Nepalese Army (RNA), which has a reputation for professionalism and discipline in United Nations peacekeeping operations, must now face up to daily reports of unprofessional and undisciplined behaviour of soldiers in their own country. The army leadership must act to restore the confidence of the people in the military - starting with the documented killings in Doramba in August 2003"*. The ICJ claimed that it received reliable information about the secret, unlawful and arbitrary detention, extra judicial killings, enforced disappearances, and torture by the security forces are widespread.

Similarly, the ICJ delegation highlighted the gross violation of international humanitarian law by committing unlawful killings, using children in their operations and abducting civilians by the Maoists.

7.3.3.3 Concerns of Human Rights Watch

Human Rights Watch has played an instrumental role around the world and is protecting human rights and resolving conflict through human rights approach. The recent decision of the US Congress to tie its military assistance to Nepal with the human rights issue had resulted from the contribution of Human Right Watch. Human Rights Watch has played a crucial role in informing and sensitising the US towards the violation of human rights in Nepal. It is regularly monitoring the human rights situation and lobbying internationally for protecting human rights in Nepal. In every major event of human rights violation such as February royal takeover, Maoist attack in Pili and explosion on passenger bus in Madi, Chitwan, issuance of media ordinance by the government, etc., Human Rights Watch is issuing press statements and asking concerned parties to respect human rights.

7.3.3.4 Concern of EU

Considering the worsening situation of Nepal, a high-level European Union's delegation -- the Troika of Regional Directors led by Robert Milders, the Director, Department of Asia and Oceania of the Netherlands Foreign Ministry, who was representing the EU presidency visited Nepal from 13 to 15 December 2004. The delegation asked the conflicting parties to respect human rights and resolve the armed conflict through dialogue and negotiation. The Danish Embassy (current EU presidency in Nepal) issued a press statement, *"The EU calls upon all constitutional forces in Nepal to work closely together in support of a common strategy for achieving a comprehensive and inclusive settlement in the country, based upon multiparty democracy and constitutional monarchy*[4]*"*. Again, after the royal takeover, the Troika led by Mr. Tom Phillips, Director for South Asia and Afghanistan at the UK Foreign and Commonwealth Office came to visit Nepal and discussed the political situation. They came to the conclusion that returning to the path of democracy is the only viable option for Nepal to resolve its political crisis. This is a signal of international pressure for the resolution of the conflict.

7.3.3.5 Concern of the USA

Clarifying the position of the USA in the human rights situation in Nepal, US Ambassador Mr. James Moriarty said[5], "I want to be clear that we do not believe that the human rights situation with respect to the Nepali security services is satisfactory – and I think that both the Prime Minister and the King would agree with me on that. But I want to stress that all U.S. military-to-military assistance programs worldwide have an element that focuses on the critical importance of respect for human rights. Additionally, military-to-military engagement gives us opportunity to impress upon our military colleagues the importance of respecting human rights, and the importance of carrying out speedy and transparent investigations when credible claims of abuses are raised. We strongly and publicly condemn human rights violations by all sides in this conflict. Furthermore, the U.S. Government is also working together with the rest of the International Community to try to bring this conflict to an end: through support for the Peace Secretariat; through discussions with the government and civil society; and through public statements like the one released just over one week ago on November 11, when we along with the EU, the UN and key donors called on the Maoists to accept the government's invitation to begin peace talks". This can be observed in the US Department of State's document entitled 'Country Report on Human Right Practices for 2003' which was submitted to the US Congress and International Relations Committee of the US Senate. The USA has passed a bill conditioning military assistance on the government's compliance with its commitment to respect human rights and cooperate with the NHRC.

The USA is in a further difficult position after the royal takeover, as it provides military supports to state to defeat Maoists militarily. However, because of the pressure from the senators and congressmen to suspend its military aid as there is serious violation of human rights by the state after the 1st February royal takeover, the US government faces a unique dilemma.

On 28 October 2005, US Senator Tom Daschle vehemently opposed the government's attempts to control the media and the midnight raid on Kantipur FM radio station. Issuing a press statement he said, "The actions taken against the media in Nepal and most recent attacks against Kantipur FM undermine what is left of democracy in Nepal. Nepalis from all sectors of society, and members of the international community, including the US State Department, have spoken out strongly against last week's raid on Kantipur FM. I am saddened that the government has responded to these pleas by shutting down a radio station guilty of nothing more than broadcasting news." Likewise, US Ambassador Moriarty on 26 October 2005 said, "Imposing restrictions on media does not advance democracy. Clearly, such measures are at odds with the goal of promoting free and fair elections in Nepal. "Reacting to the forthcoming elections, ambassador said, "It is not too late to alter this course, however. We call on the King to begin good faith talks with the parties as a first step, because without their participation, the parliamentary elections are unlikely to have national or international legitimacy. In other words, if municipal elections next February and parliamentary elections in 2007 occur without the robust participation of the legitimate political parties, we fear that these elections will be a hollow exercise".

A strong statement was made by US Senator Patrick Leahy in the United States Senate on July 28, 2005 about the worsening human rights situations in Nepal. It states, "...Last year, after receiving disturbing reports of widespread human rights violations by the Royal Nepalese Army, including arrests, disappearances, torture and extrajudicial killings of civilians, the Congress imposed a number of conditions on our military aid to Nepal. Those conditions required the Nepalese Government to (1) comply with habeas corpus orders issued by the Supreme Court of Nepal; (2) cooperate with the National Human Rights Commission to identify and resolve all security related cases of individuals in government custody; (3) grant the National Human Rights Commission unimpeded access to all places of detention; and (4) take effective steps to end torture by security forces and prosecute members of such forces who are responsible for gross violations of human rights. Unfortunately, not only have those conditions not been met, the situation was made significantly worse on February 1st when King Gyanendra, with the backing of the security forces, dissolved the multiparty government, arrested and jailed political opponents, human rights activists and journalists, and declared a state of emergency. The state of emergency has since been lifted, but civil liberties, including freedom of the press and association, remain restricted, the former Prime Minister has been jailed for corruption by an extrajudicial, politically motivated anti-corruption commission, and arrests of journalists and democracy activists continue...". These statements and reactions from powerful politicians severely pressurised the US government and consequently the USA is suspending its military aids.

7.3.3.6 Concern of India

Indian concerns are more related to the effects of Maoists insurgency in India than in human rights violation in Nepal. These concerns are related to boarder issues as Nepal shares an 1800 kilometre-long open border with India, Maoists' shelter in the adjoining Indian states of West Bengal, Bihar and Uttar Pradesh, and their activities there. Further, the connection[6] between Nepali Maoists and the Indian Maoist groups like PWG and the MCC, formation of Coordination Committee of Maoist Parties and Organisations of South Asia (CCOMPOSA) on July 1st 2001)[7]. India suspects that if Nepal's Maoists capture power in Nepal, it could possibly trigger similar movements across the South Asian region and Indian Maoists will be encouraged. Indian Prime Minister Man Mohan Singh said that the Nepalese and Indian Maoists are becoming a serious threat to the India's internal security. In October 2004, Indian Ministry of Home Affairs organized a Chief Ministers' conference in Hyderabad to discuss and formulate a common and comprehensive strategy to deal with the increasing security threat posed by the growing Maoist activities. Therefore, India wants to avoid this situation. Hence, India has declared the Maoists as a terrorist group, heightened border surveillance and monitoring, proposed to construct a military training school at Salijhandi area in Rupandehi district for the RNA, arrested some of the top Maoist leaders earlier. India is the largest suppliers of arms and ammunitions to the Nepali security forces to control the Maoists' activities in Nepal (Bhattarai, 2004)[8].

In 5-6 December 2004, a retired senior military officer in close consultation with the Indian government organized a two-day track II conference in New Delhi inviting political leaders, former diplomats, academicians and political activists of India and Nepal to discuss the Maoist insurgency. Former Prime Minister Surya Bahadur Thapa in an interview expressed that if understanding could be reached between Nepal and India, the Maoists problem could be resolved' (*Kantipur Daily*, 20 August 2004). After the 1st February royal takeover, the position of India was unfavourable to the king, as India partly suspended military aids and opposed the takeover. Even the Indian Prime Minister once refused to attend the SAARC Submit to humiliate the King.

7.3.3.7 Concern of Amnesty International (AI)

Interim Program Director of Asia & Pacific Program of Amnesty

International Ms Ingrid Massag on 10th of January 2005 wrote an open letter to Maoist leader Prachanda[9] condemning abduction and killing of civilians and mass abductions of children by the CPN (Maoist). Amnesty International also issued a statement[10] on 19 December 2004 about the security of human rights defenders. The statement was entitled "Nepal: Human rights defenders under threat -- enhanced international protection urgently needed". It wrote, "Human rights defenders in Nepal face grave threats amid the country's deepening human rights crisis, Amnesty International, Human Rights Watch and the International Commission of Jurists said. The Nepalese government and the United Nations must begin effective implementation of an agreement signed for providing UN assistance to the National Human Rights Commission (NHRC) in monitoring human rights. Recently a number of human rights defenders, including journalists, lawyers, NHRC staff and local human rights activists, have faced increasing harassment from both security forces and the Communist Party of Nepal (Maoist). Human rights defenders have been killed, detained under anti-terrorist legislation, abducted, tortured and threatened, and the offices of human rights organisations have been raided". AI is constantly monitoring the human rights violation in Nepal and issuing press statements and lobbying internationally. It has played an instrumental role in forming opinion of 52 members of UN Human Rights Commission to pass Agenda 19 and force the government of Nepal to sign an agreement to open OHCHR in Nepal.

7.4 RESPECTING HUMAN RIGHTS AT THE TIME OF THE ARMED CONFLICT

In this section some programmatic actions in respecting human rights at the situation of escalated conflict and roles and responsibilities of different organizations have been discussed.

7.4.1 Collective and concerted actions

At the time of the conflict, all human rights activists, government, political parties, civil society and security forces have to work together to protect or at least minimize human rights violations. Massive human rights awareness at different levels (from centre to local) is essential. In addition, training security forces in basic human rights, creating pressure to the Maoists to respect human rights of the people, creating regional and local human rights monitoring networks, etc, can definitely help minimize human rights violations and consequently create a conducive environment for the peace talks.

7.4.2 Roles and responsibilities of different actors

7.4.2.1 Roles and responsibilities of the NHRC

The NHRC has a crucial role to safeguard the human rights. In the situation of escalated conflict, NHRC gets support and cooperation from international community to protect human rights. The Accord proposed by the National Human Rights Commission (NHRC) in 2003 is one of the important initiatives to create a conducive environment and prevent the human rights violations as it has outlined clear obligations on both sides and taken responsibilities of monitoring compliance throughout the country with the help of United Nations. If the warring parties continuously violate human rights, NHRC can internationalise it by putting tremendous pressure on them.

7.4.2.2 Roles and responsibilities of security forces

Security forces are the frontline fighters engaged in fighting with the insurgents. Experiences of international human rights organisations such as Amnesty International and Human Rights Watch around the world show that security forces have been engaged in violating human rights at the time of war. Therefore, security force needs to be alert in this aspect. They should not hold people secret and illegal detentions, provide list of all persons in custody to public, brief regularly to the public about the situation of detainees. Security forces have to provide access of lawyers to all detainees, family members, doctors and the NHRC. The security forces should not arrest people at night by using plainclothed commandos and blindfolding the victims. That will increase trust in security forces and create a positive environment.

Security forces need to cooperate with the NHRC, non-governmental human rights organizations and bar association. If and when security forces act immediately on cases of alleged human rights violations, people trust and support them. Therefore, the prime functions of the security forces are: to respect human rights of people, cooperate with the human rights organisations and work with civil society. Security forces are the state apparatus established to provide security to the country and its people. People are paying tax to operate the security force in the country. Therefore, people expect security from them. If it fails to provide security they criticise security forces too. Security force should not take the people's expectations and frustration otherwise. One of the best ways to win trust of the people is to transparently investigate and adequately punish those security forces responsible for extra-judicial killings, disappearances, torture and other human rights violations.

If security forces comply fully and faithfully with all judicial orders, including writs of habeas corpus, and end the practice of re-arresting those who are released following a court order and cooperate with human rights activists, lawyers, civil society leaders and journalists to perform their peace-related work openly and without fear, it develops trust, creates a conducive environment and contributes to negotiated settlement. However, there is still a lot to do by security forces. In the past few years, military and police organisations have established human rights office to protect human rights. They are also training their forces in the human rights issues by bringing external (national and international experts) resource persons both at central and local levels. These are good initiatives and need to be further strengthened.

7.4.2.3 Roles and responsibilities of insurgents

The insurgents are equally responsible to respect human rights. Even if they do not respect Nepalese constitution and laws, they should abide by international human rights and humanitarian laws and therefore they must respect human rights of individual. If they respect human rights, they have to change their current strategy by ending the practice of unlawful killing of civilians or captured combatants. If they increase abductions, the government will also increase security response, which virtually invites more fights, more killing and bloodshed. Therefore, the insurgents should avoid the abductions and forced recruitment of ordinary citizens. Another charge for the Maoists is the use of children in their war. They should stop using children (under 18) in combat or support operations. If they respect the international law, they should stop recruiting children. This will create a conducive national and international environment.

Another severe pressure realised by community is the forceful donations and extortion of money and demand for food by the insurgents. If they stop such activities, it will create a conducive environment and get public support. Another responsibility of the insurgents is to ensure the movement of people, journalists, etc. The insurgents are blaming as informers those whom they killed or severely tortured. Instead of such violation of human rights, if the insurgents give opportunity to improve the accused persons, this will not only improve their image but also create a favourable environment for political settlement. Therefore, if the insurgents allow the journalists, lawyers, human rights activities freely to accomplish their work in the insurgent held areas, it will help develop confidence among people in future negotiation and minimise human rights violations.

7.4.2.4 Roles and responsibilities of the government

The counter-insurgency strategy of the government very much influences the conflict dynamics either positively or negatively. If the government is determined to respect basic human rights of the people, committed to international human rights provisions and promotes activities that address the root causes of the conflict, it helps in conflict transformation. Instead, if the government only pays lip service, lies to international community, believes in violence as the means of resolving conflict, it contributes to protracting the civil war.

One of the major responsibilities of the government is to fulfil its national and international human rights obligations. If the government does not fulfil the international and national obligations, it erodes trust of the citizen and international community. The Nepalese government has lost trust of international community and Nepalese people because of repeatedly issuing of the Terrorist and Disruptive Activities Ordinance (TADO). It contradicts with the Constitution of the Kingdom of Nepal 1991 and international standards. The Nepalese government should translate the Memorandum of Understanding agreed with the UN Office of the High Commissioner for Human Rights (OHCHR) on 16 December 2004 into practice. It has to play a facilitating role to obtain international assistance to the National Human Rights Commission.

While examining the strategy and actions of the present government, it is difficult to find any genuine commitment to the peaceful resolution of the ongoing conflict. Some of the evidences of this conclusion include issuance of TADO, justification of the Prime Minister for hiking the price of petroleum products to meet the security expenses[11].

House arrest, detention and restriction on mobility, censorship in media, curtailing freedom of speech and writing were the main psychological factors used in the February first takeover to create fear and keep all silent. These activities are defined in the human rights discourses as violation of basic human rights of individuals.

7.4.2.5 Roles and responsibilities of judiciary

Judiciary is one of the pillars of democracy. It has great responsibilities to promote and strengthen democracy as well as protecting human rights violation at the time of civil war. In the present context of Nepal when there is no parliament (House of Representatives), the government has eroded its trust; the role of Supreme Court and other courts has become more prominent in protecting the rights of people. The judiciary must be able to make the government and the security forces accountable. Therefore, bold and courageous decisions from the judiciary to prevent human rights violations and the encroachment of democracy is utmost essential. If the judiciary escapes citing narrowly interpreted jurisdictions it may knowingly or unknowingly serve to worsen the situation.

7.4.2.6 Roles and responsibilities of political parties

Political parties need to demonstrate consistent, coherent and judgemental response to protect human rights and to end the armed conflict through a negotiated settlement. So far political parties and their leaders have not been able to demonstrate their ability to handle the present crisis. They are not able to work together with a common minimum agenda. Mistrust between the political parties is mounting. If political parties work together to protect human rights violation, it creates an enabling environment for them to work together and when they start to work together trust could build up. Therefore, engaging collectively to protect human rights violations is an opportunity to work together for political settlement. If all parliamentary political parties come together to settle the armed conflict, it is not difficult to reach the negotiated settlement.

After the royal takeover, they should have learnt lessons. However, they are still unclear on many issues such as position of the monarchy in the new constitution and political changes, restructuring of the stare (federal or decentralised or any other model). They have a strong hangover of the past and therefore they are stuck in restoration of the parliament. However, restoration of parliament will not solve problem at all. Rather it will complicate the problem and create a crisis.

7.4.2.7 Roles and responsibilities of non-governmental HR organizations and civil society

Non-governmental human rights organisations play a crucial role at the time of escalated conflict. If we see the roles of human rights community in Nepal they are not only engaged in defending human rights of the people but also facilitating between the government and the insurgents in many grievances (e.g., closures of educational institutions, industries, etc.). They are also exploring potential options for negotiation, preparing codes of conduct, keeping records of human rights violations, pressurising the warring parties to respect human rights of Nepalese people and internationalise the excess on human rights violations. At the time of escalated conflict, the roles and responsibilities of human rights organizations further increase and they need to work in a concerted and collective way. Human rights community in any war-torn countries play a crucial role (Lode, 2004; Adhikari, 2004; Lucima, 2002).

Role of civil society (business leaders, entrepreneurs, writers, researchers, teachers, leaders, artists, musicians, singers, actors and actress, etc.) is important not only to have solidarity with and support the human rights community but also to boldly and assertively raise human rights concerns and pressurise the warring parties to come to the negotiation table. Civil society has started some good initiatives but they are not enough. All civil society leaders should come together for the concerted action in addition to their own individual efforts (Upreti, 2003; 2004a).

7.4.3 International solidarity and commitment

Another important mechanism to ensure and respect human rights is to develop international solidarity and network as it creates international awareness to exert pressure over human rights violating warring party. If there is strong and persistent international pressure the warring parties cannot always ignore it. The role of international solidarity network was crucial in Guatemalan peace process (Crandall, 2004). There are some international networks established to pressurise the warring parties to respect human rights.

For example, there was a strong international solidarity while the king promulgated the media ordinance. International reputed organisations such as Committee to Protect Journalists (CPJ), International Federation of Journalists (IFJ), International Media Support (IMS), International Press Institute (IPI), Reporters sans Frontières (RSF), United Nations Educational, Scientific and Cultural Organization (UNESCO), World Association of Community Radio Broadcasters (AMARC), World Association of Newspapers (WAN) are extending solidarity to the media and exerting pressure on the government and the rebels.

7.5 CONCLUSION

Internationalisation of human rights violation pressurizes violators to reduce excesses. Whether Nepal likes it or not, international community will closely monitor the conflict situation of Nepal and internationalise if the state or the rebels continuously violate human rights. Past experiences have demonstrated that a large proportion of international community sincerely advocates the protection of human rights and peaceful resolution of the armed conflict in Nepal.

Peaceful settlement of the armed conflict in Nepal is pragmatically possible only by ensuring full respect of human rights. If human rights are not respected, the society develops a negative psyche and resolution of the conflict becomes extremely difficult as it assumes the syndrome of protracted war. Hence, the armed conflict in Nepal is turning into protracted war and becoming extremely complicated. If the major conflict actors do not respect human rights, the armed conflict could go beyond their control soon.

Human rights and conflict transformation are interdependent and intertwined in shaping negotiated settlement of conflict in a war-torn society. However, in Nepal none of the conflict actors are bothering about this relation. Conflict scholars such as Galtung (2000a and 2004a and b), Armond, Hendrickson and Vines (1998); Conen (1999); Armond, Sieder and Wilson (1997); McCartney (1999) and Stankovitch (1999) examining the conflict and peace process in different countries (Mozambique, Guatemala, Georgia, Cambodia, Mali, Sierra Leone, Northern Ireland and Philippines) conclude that there is a strong relationship between the human rights and peaceful negotiation of conflict. Where there is respect of human rights the reconciliation and reactivating democracy is relatively easy. Therefore, human rights, conflict transformation and democracy are strongly interrelated. Hence, respecting human rights helps in rebuilding trust and creates a conducive environment to initiate negotiated settlement and strengthens democracy.

NOTES

1. *See the Kathmandu Post*, 14 December 2004 for detail.
2. The ICJ delegation consists of Secretary-General Nicholas Howen, human rights jurist and journalist Periathamby Rajanayagam and ICJ Legal Adviser Ian Seiderman. The delegation met conflict victims, human rights activists, ministers, and senior officials of the government, senior judges and lawyers of Supreme Court. The delegation also visited Sindupalchok and Kavrepalanchowk districts.
3. See ICJ website: http://www.icj.org for the detail report and press release.
4. *See The Kathmandu Post* ,13 December 2004 for detail.
5. Address of Ambassador James F. Moriarty regarding the Support of U.S. Government in Protection of Human Rights and Conflict Transformation At the Kathmandu School of Law on November 22, 2004.
6. A prominent Indian fortnightl,*Frontline* reported in its May 2000 issue that the "growing coordination between the extremist groups" in Nepal and India have resulted in simultaneous attacks in both countries (Bhattarai, 2004).
7. Nepali Maoists have built linkages with the Indian insurgent groups like Kamtapur Liberation Organisation (KLO), United Liberation Front Assam (ULFA), NDFB, MCC, PWG etc. Rajan Bhattarai states that 'Indian intelligence report indicates that Maoist senior leader Mohan Baidhya was arrested in last March because of his connection with KLO of West Bengal, NDFB of Bodoland and ULFA of Assam and C.P. Gajurel's arrest August last year in Chennai Airport was because there was a suspicion that he was maintaining relations with LTTE of Sri Lanka' (Shrestha: 2004).
8. [1] Rajan Bhattarai (2004) in his paper quotes Indian daily 'The Times of India' reported that the Nepali government had made an official request that the activities of Nepali Maoists in Indian territory be checked, claiming that they were being trained in Bihar by members of the People's War Group (PWG) and Maoist Coordination Centre (MCC). Quoting Intelligence reports, the paper claimed that the PWG was planning to create a Compact Revolutionary Zone from Hyderabad to Kathmandu taking Madhya Pradesh, Bihar and Jharkhand into its area of influence with the help of other outfits (Mishra: 2001)".
9. Reference of her letter is: ref: T/ASA 31/CPN-Maoist/2005.1, Doc ref: ASA 31/003/2005, date 10 January 2004.
10. Reference: AI Index: ASA 31/190/2004 (Public), News Service No: 323, 19 December 2004. For detail see: http://web.amnesty.org/library/Index/ENGASA311902004?open&of=ENG-2AS

11. *The Kathmandu Post* of January 13th 2005 referring to the speech of the Prime Minister in the Capital quotes, "Security expense is increasing since the Maoist continue to resort to violence; therefore, the government has no other options but to increase petroleum prices to meet security and other expenses".

CHAPTER 8

Impacts of the Armed Conflict

8.1 INTRODUCTION

Armed conflicts and civil wars have an enormous impact on the host countries (Anderson, 1999; OECD, 2001; Leonhardt, 2000; Nyheim et al., 2001; OECD/DAC, 2002). This can be clearly observed in Nepal. The armed conflict in Nepal has had enormous impacts on politics, democracy, governing practices, state's security structures, demographic features, culture and tradition, national economy, social system, thinking and behavioural patterns of the Nepalese people, livelihoods of poor and marginalized groups, development interventions and international relations.

The impacts of conflict vary over the timeline of the conflict. There are different impacts of conflict at different time periods, i.e., before the State of Emergency (SoE) period (1996-2001 November), the period between the first ceasefire to announcement of second time ceasefire (November 2001 and January 2003), during the second ceasefire period (February 2003 to August 2003), after the second ceasefire (August 2003 to January 2005) and 1st February Royal takeover to date (February 2005 to February 2006).

This chapter discusses the impacts of the Maoist armed conflict on different dimensions of Nepalese society. The small rebellion that started ten years ago in the four western hill districts of Nepal is now having severe social, political, economic, psychological impacts in the country. Comprehensive assessment of impacts of the ongoing armed conflict in all sectors is beyond the scope of this chapter. Hence, only a glimpse of positive and negative impacts of the ongoing conflict in different aspects has been discussed here. Pragmatically, wider impacts of this conflict in all sectors of Nepalese society, economy, environment and resource management, development interventions, social services (e.g., health, education, drinking water, etc.) international relations, politics and party building process, deserves the scope of a separate book.

While talking about the impacts, the government's effective control is mainly limited to the district headquarters and the immediate areas of the deployment of security forces. Absence of local elected government has created a political vacuum in the Village Development Committees (VDCs), which the insurgents are filling. As a result, the continuity of development programmes in these areas entirely depends upon the decision and behaviour of the local leaders of Maoists.

After the breakdown of the 2001 first ceasefire, the Maoists had targeted larger development infrastructures such as telecommunication towers, hydro-electricity plants, roads, bridges, police posts, VDC buildings, forest range posts, etc. built either from the government resources or from the financial and technical supports of international community. Attacks on district headquarters and security bases by the Maoists sharply increased after the failure of peace talks both times.

In the following section, different impacts of the ongoing armed conflict are discussed.

8.2 SOCIAL IMPACTS

As the duration of the Maoist insurgency is getting prolonged in Nepal, new phenomena are developing and new characters are emerging. While examining the course of expansion of Maoist insurgency during the ten years of its existence, many different unanticipated and unexpected characters are customized and socialized. Though it is a new phenomenon to Nepal, if comparison to Nepal's civil war is made with other civil wars in Africa, Asia and South America, many similar characteristics can be found. Some of the emerging characteristics are outlined below:

The current conflict has not only eroded the social capital that existed in communities but has also severely altered community relationships. Indigenous forms of social networks and institutions, which glued the society together, are divided, causing the decline of both binding (relation within communities) and bridging (link between communities). New social relations are emerging.

In the following section, different social impacts of the ongoing armed conflict are discussed:

8.2.1 Criminalisation of society

Criminal activities sharply increase in war-torn societies. Such criminal actions are either supported by the parties in conflict, or ignored by them. Often the state security apparatus is not able to control crimes at the time of war or it is not their priority, as the existing security forces have to stretch to fight the war as well as to control the growing crimes in society. Occasionally, armed people of the warring parties themselves engage in committing social crimes and banditry. Criminals use messy security situations to retaliate against their enemies, to those who oppose their action. Robberies, rape, looting and gang fights are examples of such a situation.

After the escalation of the armed conflict in Nepal, criminalisation in society has increased. Many fake Maoists are active in the community and creating fear in people, involved in extortion, forced donation and other social anomalies (like sexual abuses, looting, etc.). Law-enforcing agencies (like police, Chief District Office, etc.) are concentrating either on preventing or controlling Maoists' activities in their areas or shifting themselves to safe places, which have created a vacuum and insecurity to people in the community. Several crimes - murder, rape, drug trafficking, smuggling, trafficking in women, vulgarism and hooliganism, looting and kidnapping are increasing. Once these context-specific characters become societial characters, resolution of the conflict becomes extremely difficult and it becomes a syndrome of protracted war. Another example is the emergence of *Madeshi Tiger* and its activities. When people do not get anticipated support from the state to contain criminal activities they accept it as an unwanted reality and socialize it. If the major conflict actors do not make sincere efforts to settle this conflict politically, it could go beyond their control.

As the conflict is protracting, robberies, land grabbing, petty thefts and abductions, social crimes are increasing as the police offices moved away from villages and a sense of insecurity and fear is mounting across the country. Appearance of fake Maoists involved in looting, violence and extortion and creating fear and terror in local people has increased. People's meaningful participation in development projects is affected by the restriction imposed by the rebels and security forces. *Bands* and strikes have severely disrupted civilian life.

8.2.2 Migration and internal displacement

The ongoing armed conflict has huge impacts on migration and displacement. Migration from rural to urban and hills to Terai areas has been a general demographic phenomenon in Nepal for the last 40 years, particularly after the eradication of malaria in Terai. Therefore, it is difficult to distinguish between conflict-induced (forced or obliged to leave) IDPs and voluntary migration (by their interests for a better life). In the coming years, the rate of migration will continuously increase because of two reasons.

Conflict-induced internal displacement is one of the main forms of migration observed in Nepal. India is the largest destination of migrants from Nepal. Because of accessibility (open border; similar religion, culture and language; relatives working there), very large proportions of Nepalese migrants go to India. The study of the Duijn (2003:13) states, *"Monitors at the border estimated that between November and December 2003 (the normal period of peak migration) over 1,200 people were crossing the border per day in Nepalgunj"*. This statement highlights the severity of conflict-induced migration. This displacement issue is dealt with in the following section:

Conflict-induced displacement in Nepal is becoming a major concern particularly after the breakdown of the peace talks in August 2003. The phenomenon of displacement has significantly increased with the increased intensity of conflict. For example, approximately 24000 people of 3500 households of Rajapur areas of Bardiya District recently left their village and entered the Baharaich and Bachhya areas of India[1].

A recent report of the Inter-Agency Internal Displacement Division (IDD) Mission to Nepal (11-22 April 2005)[2], based on the consultation with senior Government officials, donors, the UN Country Team, ICRC, international and national NGOs and representatives of IDPs and field visit to Kapilvastu, Banke and Kailali Districts, concludes that '*Nepal faces a very serious political, security and humanitarian situation in which preventive measures are urgently required to prevent further deterioration.*' It further states, '*While the full magnitude of population displacement is unknown, best reliable estimates suggest that up to 200,000*[3] *Nepalese may have been internally displaced by the conflict, with perhaps 2 million or more moving to India in recent years*' (IDD, 2005).

It is very hard to find clear data on IDPs. The situation of silent

IDPS is also unclear as they are not in the limelight. Some people even estimate the number of IDPs to be 600000[4]. This is a very worrying scenario and if the conflict continues, the number of IDPs will increase sharply. However, neither the state nor the international community is taking IDPs issue seriously. This is mainly because they fear long-term involvement in IDPs once they enter this area. Nevertheless, since 2004 the United Nations Office for the Coordination of Humanitarian Affairs (OCHA) has initiated some work in Nepal.

Karnali and Bheri Zones (especially Dailehk, Mugu, Jumla, Kalikot, Dolpa, Rolpa) have more severe problem of IDPs. It is extremely difficult to project the number of IDPs, as it is changing frequently. Different practices are adapted by IDPs for their living. First, staying in loosely organised camps (organised and supported by some (I)NGOs, e.g., in Rajhana of Nepalgunj and Birendranagar of Surkhet). Second, staying in public lands, melting in recipient society (with relatives, working as labourers, etc.) within Nepal and seasonally or temporarily migrated to India. Mainly, people move from rural and insecure areas of the conflict-affected districts to urban or relatively safe areas (e.g., district headquarters, town centres of nearby Terai and big cities like Nepalgunj, Kathmandu) and India. Some people go to the Gulf countries and a few others (especially rich, educated or powerful elite) go to Western or developed countries.

The main causes of the IDPs are: the perceived or actual security risks from the security forces and the Maoists[5], pressure from the Maoists to join them as 'Whole Timer' (WT) worker, painful family circumstance (e.g., killing or torture of family members), fear of being caught in crossfire, etc. The government recognises only those IDPs who have registered with Chief District Officers (CDOs). Therefore, the IDP record of the government is incomplete and biased. Victims of security forces (mainly supporters of the insurgents) do not register with CDOs because of security risks.

There is no reliable and neutral organisation responsible yet for registering IDPs. Therefore, it is very hard to track IDPs: where they originated, where they are now and in what conditions. A study conducted by Leonard van Duijn on IDP in 2003 presents different categories of people not registered as IDP. It states, *'It clearly excludes the following several important categories of IDP, including: families of security forces forced to flee by the Maoist; Ex-Maoists; those fleeing, conscription; people who are too frightened to register or see no benefit in doing so (*Duijn, 2003: 6*)'*.

The growing phenomenon of displacement has numerous economic and social implications for host communities. Pressure in the existing basic infrastructure (such as roads, water supplies, sanitation, waste management and housing infrastructures); increasing competition for unskilled labour market and irrational exploitation of scarce natural resources of the host areas and consequent mistrust and conflict are some of the immediate effects of the internal displacement.

It is realized that the government is not yet able to internalize the gravity of the IDPs problem. Donor community and big INGOs are also not proactive and say that Nepal is not in a situation of humanitarian intervention to address conflict-induced displacement. Based on experiences of other countries, they argue that IDPs are managing themselves (often illegally) settling around the east-west highway and other road heads with relatively safe location with some opportunities of survival, diffusing with host communities and staying with their relatives) and therefore there is no need to intervene. If humanitarian assistance is provided, influx of IDPs will further increase.

8.2.3 Acceptance of brutalisation of violence

Brutalisation of violence is one of the developing phenomena in Nepal, as inhumane violent actions are becoming regular events of society. Rape of wife in front of husband and family members, forceful eviction from home, murder and assassination of people after capture, torture and retaliation are frequent and society is forced to accept it as usual. Experiences around the world show that use of violence is one of the common means used by parties in armed conflict. The extreme example is Rwandan genocide in mid-1994. Brutalisation of violence occurs when certain principles of war and armed conflict are undermined or ignored, which often happens when the political process becomes weak and use of arm dominates course of action in the war.

8.2.4 Reutilization of negativity

In a situation of war and escalated armed conflict, society often develops a negative psyche, as everywhere they observe negative characters. The hope of ordinary people erodes, people visualize the future as deem and dark, they experience fear and hopelessness. They link all their failures and with the war and political situation; they do not make individual efforts to change the deteriorated situation. Often they blame others. Ultimately, they leave their areas or work and look for exit options. Individuals, families, social groups, community, political institutions all shape their behaviours and actions with a negative psyche. Even if there are some genuine efforts made by some people to contribute to changing the conflict dynamics into positive, people suspect and negatively characterize them. Negative psyche can be observed everywhere in Nepal, particularly in middle class intellectuals and urban elites.

8.2.5 Working with unpredictability

Unpredictability is a general character at the time of high intensity conflict. Therefore, course of actions of people are also unpredictable. Politicians frequently change their positions and opinions; civil society leaders change their opinions, and the state ignores standard governing practices, frequently changing or altering its public commitments. No one can be certain in forthcoming situations and acts on ad hoc basis.

8.2.6 Socialization of conflict triggers

Society unwontedly accepts the conflict-triggering activities as normal. For example, forced donation, forced information sharing, interception of telephonic conversations, blockade, restriction of public movement, transportation strike or *Nepal Bandh*, painting and chanting of unwanted slogans, disappearance and detention, closure of schools or security control of public places, excessive flow of state resources in the war, targeting those who do not support violent actions of the conflicting parties or strongly oppose them have been gradually socialised and accept as usual . People do not speak the truth and fear to bring any abuses in public. Communities do not help the victims of war simply because of fear of retaliation or threat by the abusers. So society accepts all these activities as a normal social phenomenon.

8.2.7 Distortion of information

Warring parties attempt to influence conflict dynamics in their favour and one of the frequently used means is distortion of information to harm the other side or to get strategic advantages. This results in misinformation, wrong information and actions of security forces and the insurgents based on the distorted or wrongly interpreted information.

The gross victims of such distorted information are local people. State Controlled Media are blatently abuse to undermine rebels.

8.3 ECONOMIC IMPACTS

Needless to say that the ongoing armed conflict has caused devastating economic consequences. Economic infrastructures are collapsing. The tourism sector is severely suffering. External investors are not willing to invest and even dropping the agreed projects (e.g., Norway withdrew from Melamchi Drinking Water Project). Existing factories and industries are closing down because of the fear of extortion and insecurity. Food insecurity has sharply increased. Politicians and their supporters have abused state's resources claiming ten times more compensation of their property damaged by the rebels (e.g. one former Home Minister said to have claimed nearly 10 million rupees from the state). The cost of armed conflict is immense and unaffordable.

One of the important indicators of the impacts of the armed conflict is the expenditure pattern of the state during the conflict period. Some economic indicators such as the proportion of security budget is invariably increased overtime, the disproportional increase in the amount of 'administrative cost' compared to the 'programme cost', decrease in proportion of resource allocation for basic social service sectors (e.g., health, education, drinking water, etc.). The Table 1 clearly shows the negative impacts of conflict based on these indicators.

8.3.1 Shift in budget allocation

Operating and maintaining the rapidly expanding Maoists ethnic and geographical wings, political commissars and fighting forces requires huge financial resources. It is estimated that it requires approximately 15 million rupees per day as the operational coast of the Maoists in addition to the cost of weapons and other strategic expenditures (such as attacking district headquarters). The state security forces are also rapidly expanding across the country and that demands huge increase in security expenditure. Nepal is obtaining huge military assistance from India, the USA and UK[6]. So the, available resources of the state to be invested in the social service sectors are diverted to the ongoing war (Rana & Sharma, 2004). The total number of security force has also been sharply increased during the period of the insurgency. The following table gives an indication of resource shifts.

TABLE 8.1 Comparative Expenditure in Nepal (Million rupees/Year) between 1996-2004

Fiscal Year	*Total*	*Royal Nepal Army*	*Police*	*Palace*	*General*	*Development*
1996/97	57566	2425	2235	70	24984	32581
	(100)	(4.21)	(3.88)	(0.12)	(43.40)	(56.60)
1997/98	62022	2629	2521	73	27983	34039
	(100)	(4.24)	(4.06)	(0.12)	(45.12)	(54.88)
1998/99	69693	3028	2922	83	31952	37741
	(100)	(4.34)	(4.19)	(0.12)	(45.85)	(54.15)
1999/00	77238	3511	3324	88	35686	41852
	(100)	(4.55)	(4.30)	(0.11)	(45.81)	(54.19)
2000/01	91621	3897	5271	93	43513	48108
	(100)	(4.25)	(5.75)	(0.10)	(47.50)	(52.50)
2001/02	99792	4521	5795	116	49322	50470
	(100)	(4.53)	(5.81)	(0.12)	(49.42)	(50.58)
2002/03	96125	7228	6304	388	57445	38680
	(100)	(7.52)	(6.56)	(0.40)	(59.76)	(40.24)
2003/04	102400	7179	6279	329	60555	41845
	(100)	(7.02)	(6.13)	(0.32)	(59.14)	(40.86)

Source: Pokharel (2004). Numbers in parenthesis are percentage.

The Table 8.1 demonstrates a harsh reality. Administrative cost of the country increased from 43.05 per cent in 1997/97 to 59.14 per cent in 2003/04. Similarly, the development cost drastically decreased from 1996/97 (56.60 per cent) to 2003/40 (40.86 per cent). Social expenditure is decreasing but the military expenditure is increasing from 4.21 per cent in 1996/97 to 7.02 per cent in 2003/04. A similar trend can be observed in police expenditure (Table 8.1). Such increase in security expenditures causes serious diversion and ramifications. The scarce resources to be invested in the critical social sectors (education, health, drinking water, local development) are going to fund the expanded security costs. This situation can be observed from the following Table 8.2.

TABLE 8.2 Decreasing budget pattern (percentage) in crucial service sector

Sector	*FY 2000/01*	*FY 2001/02*
Health	2.78	2.75
Education	1.97	1.87
Drinking water	2.40	1.74
Local development	4.62	4.15

Source: NPC (2003:24)

The Table 8.2 indicates the decreasing pattern of the development budget in all the four major service sectors, i.e., health, education, drinking water and local development. The High Commission for the Government Expenditure projects that 41 per cent of the administrative cost of the country will be defence expenditure[7] by 2014. Report of the same Commission reveals that 17 per cent of the total budget of the country is used in security expenditure. Similarly, 7 per cent of the total budget is allocated by the government to emergency fund, which is distributed by the government as 'financial assistance' but most of which is not properly used[8]. Annual growth rate of foreign loan is 7 per cent and the principal and interests of such loan reaches up to approximately 15 per cent of the total annual budget of the country. This has also direct impacts on the development sector. A study of Acharya (2005) shows that 'the development expenditure at 1994/95 price had increased by 0.7 per cent per year during 1990 to 2000, while such expenditure declined by 4.6 per cent per year during 2001-2005. The growth rate of defence expenditure (at 1994/95 price) was 4.8 per cent, whereas it increased sharply by 11.9 per cent during 2001 to 2005'.

8.3.2 Economic cost of the conflict

Economic cost of the ongoing armed conflict is quite complicated to measure precisely. Calculating indirect cost such as loss of life, losses caused due to mass displacement and social value thereof, erosion of trusts, etc. is not only extremely difficult but also highly controversial.

Acharya (2005:4) states that 'the average growth rate of Gross Domestic Products (GDP) during the eleven years period (1990-2000) was 4.8 percent, where it remained at 2.6 percent during 2001-2005. Therefore, the economy is losing on an average 2.2 percent GDP each year after 2001'. This is a worrying scenario.

The Table 8.3 provides a general scenario of cost of conflict in Nepal. This data is for only two years and it has increased even in higher proportion in the recent years. The state is also paying more than NRs one billion rupees as compensation for the loss of lives of people by the Maoists. Reduction of tourists, business losses due to strike, sanctions and regulations from rebels in their areas, displacement of economically productive workforce, centralisation of projects, reduction of foreign investment, closure of industries have serious negative impacts on the national economy. There are frequent reports about Maoists taxing tourists, which affects the tourism industry.

TABLE 8.3 Estimated cost of conflict in Nepal (2001/02 & 2002/03)

Expenditures/Loss	*Cost*
Direct cost	
Direct expenditure on security (Govt.)	39.63 Billion (10% of GDP at factor cost[9])
Maoist Army's Expense	1.94 – 2.13 Billion[10]
Damage on physical infrastructures and banks	25 Billion[11]
Sub total	66.63 Billion
Indirect cost	
Loss in business due to strike and *Bandh* (closure)	1 Billion
Loss due to decrease in the number of tourists inflow	11.05 Billion
Impact on the income due to damage in human resources	14.04 Billion
Loss in income due to displacement	8 billion[12]
Loss due to shift of development expenditure for defence	12.30 Billion
Impact on the direct foreign investment	6.05 Billion
Sub-total	52.44 Billion
Total	119.07 Billion

Source: Rana & Sharma (2004); Kumar, (2004).

Negative impacts are far wider and have long-term implications than the positive impacts of the ongoing armed conflict. However, it is extremely difficult to find authentic figures on the financial and economic cost of this war. Nevertheless, the crude estimate goes beyond billions of rupees, as several infrastructure projects have been destroyed. If the economic cost for two years goes beyond 119 billion rupees, how much it will cost for 10 years is predictable.

8.3.3 Impacts on market and employment

The insurgency has created wider market disruption. Local *hat-bazar* system has been severe disrupted. Black-marketing, shortage of goods and services are becoming common. Further, physical damage to goods and foodstuff is severe, as Maoists have destroyed hundreds of truckloads of goods; farmers are forced to throw away their agricultural products such as milk, vegetables on the road because of the frequent transport strikes and bandhs. This situation is forcing thousands of farmers towards bankruptcy.

Employment opportunities within the country are severely constrained due to scaling down of existing industries and there is no favourable environment for investing or establishing new enterprises. People engaged in self-employment, agriculture and small-scale cottage industries are leaving their villages/occupations due to insecurity. Mass migration to India and the Gulf countries is increasing with huge loss of human resources[13]. Because of the market disruption, uncertainties and insecurity (looting, rubbery, etc.) the role of banking sector is severely constrained. This has major impacts on productive investments and generating employment.

Smugglers are more strongly organised in border areas and transit points when the security posts moved to district headquarters and safe places due to the threat from Maoists. The Maoists have now filled this security vacuum and are regulating transit points. For example, security post of Byas VDC of Darchula district was an important commercial point but since the 1st State of Emergency 2001 security force was moved out and Maoists regulate it. This transit point is an important smuggling area for *Yarsagumba* (extremely high valued medical herb), other high value non-timber forest products and wild animal products. Maoists impose taxes and allow smugglers to continue their smuggling practices. Last year they had collected more than 30 million rupees as tax from this Byas transit point alone to operate their war[14]. Now they have established a formal tax collection office. Maoist domination can be observed in major transit points (e.g., Pancheshwor, Dimber, Baker and Dharmaghat) of Baitdi district, Kanchanpur district (e.g., Belauri, Parasan, Chandani and Barhmadev), Dadeldhura district (e.g., Tamalighat and Parsuramghat) and Kailali district (e.g..Fulbari, Khatraula, Lalbhauji, Dhansinghpur and Hasulia). Such a situation is causing enormous loss in revenue collection.

Some multinational companies are either reducing their activities or planning to shift to India. A Joint Venture Colgate Palmolive Nepal P. Ltd situated in Hetunda is scaling down its activities and planning to shift to Himachal Pradesh in India. The company has cited reasons of shifting as: failure of government to meet its commitment of exemption of income tax while establishing the industry, industrial insecurity, strikes and *bands* (blockades). Once Maoists have bombarded this industry and consequently it has scaled down its production. Now three other packaging industries are closed. As consequence more than 300 workers are now unemployed. In the 2nd week of August 2005 Maoists burnt Joti Spinning Mills in Sharlahi and caused more that

200 million damage. This had a direct impact on the workers.

8.3.4 Impacts on tourism

The tourism sector is one of the most hard-hit by the insurgency. The numbers of tourists visiting Nepal are decreasing and very negative publicity is mounting about Nepal around the world as a war-torn, insecure and highly risky country. Travel advisories of foreign ministry of developed countries are full of negative information about Nepal. Nepalese diplomats working in the developed countries have completely failed to promote tourism. The Maoist strategy of attack and 'sabotage' caused damage of infrastructures of large companies such as Uniliver Nepal, Surya Tobacco Company, Coca-Cola Company, distilleries, and even public infrastructures (e.g., police post, government office buildings, etc.). All these activities have negative effects on the employment of labourers as well as on the national economy. The Maoists' strategy of sabotaging infrastructures has great negative economic impacts. The following points are a summary of negative impacts of insurgency on the tourism sector:

- Forced to close some big hotels through labour strikes.
- Demanded huge donation with big business companies.
- Negative image (risks to visit Nepal) at international level about the Nepal's situation that is reducing numbers of tourists visit to Nepal.
- Forced donation and levy on tourist visiting the Maoist-influenced area.
- Rapid decrease in tourists.
- Travel movement of tourists visiting Nepal is restricted due to the uncertainties of strikes, bands and blockades.

8.4 POLITICAL IMPACTS

The gradually evolved political institutions like political parties are severely weakened, generally in the time of conflict and specifically in the period of political experiment after 4th Oct 2002. Political parties are breaking one after another and losing credibility and trust of the people. They are severely suffering from internal conflicts. Dissolution of the Parliament, a basic political institution, has virtually opened the windows of monopolising governance system (law, regulations, policies, etc.). The Constitutional crisis is mounting and fuelling the conflict.

Political culture of nominating executive body of local government is further weakening their legitimacy. Because of the absence of elected representatives in House of Parliament and local bodies there is a severe political vacuum. Political institutions are not functioning. The political process has been replaced by nomination. The country is being ruled through ordinances because of absence of parliament.

Another major setback to the conflict and political power struggle is the local governance structures. The Maoists want to make local bodies dysfunctional to create a political vacuum, which they want to fill by their local *janasarkar*. The then Deuba government greatly helped to meet this objective of the Maoists. He neither conducted local election nor extended the tenure of the existing elected bodies. Instead, he assigned responsibility of the elected representatives to government official that virtually took away the principle and spirit of local government. The Maoists emerged even more stronger in absence of the local government and maintain high degree of their control. Now most of the office-bearers of the government offices at local levels (except teachers and health workers) have withdrawn from the villages[15].

There are severe potential dangers of starting a separatist, ethnic or religious fight and war if this conflict is not resolved in time. Civil defence disasters have already been started (see *Kantipur Daily* of 12 December 2004 where the negative effects of Civil Defence Committee are reported). There is a potential danger of breaking of Maoists into different fractions, as the order of the high command is already being disobey by their cadres. Those who want to see Nepal as an unstable country (I firmly believe that there is a very strong invisible force active to escalate conflict and maintain war in this country) could also play role in a ethnic or separatist divide.

This conflict has turned governing system in Nepal dysfunctional. Whether it is in Afghanistan, Somalia, Angola, or East Timor, state-governing apparatus (institutions, laws and regulations, employees) does not work according to the state constitution and regulatory provisions. Government top ranking officials and employees either ignore or abuse these provisions and authorities. One of the examples in Nepal is the decision of the Cabinet to increase monthly house rent of the ministers at the time of food-to-mouth problem of ordinary people. People of Dolpa are even not getting 2 kg foodgrains per month form the State but the ministers are increasing their benefits from the poor taxpayers' money. If anyone observes the behaviour of government staff in District Revenue Office and District Survey Offices in Lalitpur, example of the dysfunctional governing system can easily be realised.

8.5 PSYCHOLOGICAL IMPACTS

Society is systematically forced to move towards developing a war mentality. Fear, mistrust, insecurity, brutality, etc. have influenced the psychology of the elderly, children, women, youth towards helplessness. Positive thinking is fast eroding and social psychology of the society is shaped by war, fights and killing. Small children, imitating from media, pick up toy guns and point to their colleagues or parents. Communal harmony, trusts and social bonds are severely eroded in the conflict-affected areas.

Personalization of achievements: In the situation of escalated armed conflict, all actors attempt to personalise if some positive things happen. They often compete to get credit of some initiative taken jointly or by someone else. Lying, twisting, or distorting facts and capitalising from someone else achievement is frequent. Blaming others for something wrong from own side or designing ill-intended activities to discredit others is common. Often this practice can be observed in Nepalese society.

Amplification of risks: When there is tension, fear and mistrust people suspect everyone. They have no trust in anyone. They do not share information or they exaggerate the situation. Writings, speeches, private conversations all are shaped by perceived risks and potential fears. So they link every present event with potential future risks and express accordingly. Social discourses in family, community, society and nation are shaped by risks and fear.

Extortion of resources: This is a very common characteristic in the time of conflict. All key players want to pull resources or use existing weaknesses to extort resources. Competition instead of collaboration, duplication instead of concerted action, repetition because of secrecy of one's own work, establishing especial networks and linkages with power centres and working for their interests, etc. are some of the frequently observed characteristics in Nepalese society.

8.6 SECURITY IMPACTS

It is reported that some resourceful and powerful people have started to establish private security mechanism, as in South American war-torn countries. Therefore, they have no faith over state security and that is bad in the long run. The government has initiated civil defence committees with training, and is distributing weapons that virtually lead to the fate of Angola and Guatemala, where thousands of innocent people were killed, thousands of women were raped, and many other thousands of ordinary civilians were tortured by the members of civil defence force simply because they had weapons in hand and supported by the state. No one is secure in this country. Disappearance, kidnapping, killing is common. INSEC Human Right Year Book 2004 states that in a single year 2003 a total of 2236 people were killed (646 by Maoists, 1217 by the state and remaining by others).

8.6.1 Landmines and proliferation of small arms and light weapons

Landmines are common practices of the Maoists and security forces to hurt the other side. Maoists are extensively placing landmines in the routes of security forces. Nobody knows how many landmines are placed but the effects are severe already. Similarly, small arms and light weapons have proliferated in Nepal. Illegal arm trading from India is becoming a lucrative business in these days.

It is needless to say that illicit trade and use of SALW is not only intensifying the ongoing civil wars and armed conflicts in different parts of the world but also severely hindering the post-war reconciliation and reconstruction efforts. The International Action Network on Small Arms (IANSA) describes that small arms are in fact the weapons of mass destruction. It is extremely difficult to find out the actual amount and types of small arms and light weapons illegally produced, traded and used in different countries. Furthermore, due to unwillingness of the state to actively participate in disarmament and controlling SALW in conflict-ridden countries, the situation is becoming more complicated.

It is estimated that each one out of 10 persons of the world population shares a gun. Although 8 hundred thousand guns are destroyed in the world each year, 10 guns are illegally manufactured in place of one destroyed. At present more than 640 million weapons are being trafficked around the world and 8 million are manufactured each year. In the same way, about 1 billion 400 million bullets are produced in the world. That means one person of the world population shares 2 bullets. At present, 1249 companies in 90 countries of the world manufacture arms and weapons (Upreti, 2005a).

According to a report (called Shattered Lives) of Control Arms Campaign the five permanent members of the UN Security Council,

France, Russia, China, UK, and the USA account for 88 per cent of the world's conventional arms exports. Arms Control and Disarmament Agency of USA highlights that Iraq alone imported armaments costing around 50 billion US dollars during the period of sever years (1983 to 1990) (Banerjee, 2000). It is interesting to note that 85 per cent of total import of arms in Middle East is shared by the five Permanent Members of the UN Security Council (Ibid).

In the process of advancing the Maoist armed conflict, Maoist and the state are collecting, using and abusing huge scale of SALW. The state is actively engaged in collecting SALW from different countries in the name of counter insurgency. When Unified Command under the RNA (armed police, Nepal Police, army and intelligence) came into existence, the demand for SALW increased.

Similarly, the Maoists are also collecting arms and weapons, mainly from three sources. They are, first, the arms collected from the locals (mainly Twelve-bore and home made guns). Second, the arms snatched from the police and army. They have collected 3 -0 -3 rifles, 22-point rifles, short guns, pistols/revolvers in the earlier stage and advance weapons at the later stage. Third, the SALW secretly imported arms from India (Shrestha, 2061BS). Maoists collected huge number of modern arms from the by attacking Royal Nepalese Army Barrack in Dang immediately after the breakdown of the first ceasefire in 2003 August and after the breakdown of the second ceasefire attack on army barrack in Beni, distrcut headquarters of Myagdi district (Upreti, 2005a).

One of the main purposes of their attacks is to collect arms and ammunitions from the RNA barracks. The Maoists have collected 265 units of different types of arms in total from Beni attack alone. They are 2" Mortar, L MG, SLR, INSAS, Magnum Rifles, AMG, Twelve-bore and short guns (Paudel, 2061BS). The government had announced a reward for those Maoists who surrender the specific weapons that were looted from the Dang and other barracks attack. The government announced reward for 81 mm Mortar was 2 hundred thousands; 40 mm mortar and GPMG was hundred thousand; LMG was 75 thousand; Base Set and M-16 Rifle was 50 thousand; SLR was 20 thousand; 2 inch Mortar, Galil and Insas rifle was 30 thousand; SMM Pistol was 15 thousand; 22 Magnum short gun, Twelve Bore, 22 bore guns, Browning pistol, loading gun, and air gun and SMG was 10 thousand; Chinese Pistol was 8 thousand; Revolver and pistol was 6 thousand; Very light pistol was 25 hundred; 66 no. Plastic hand grenade was 4 thousands[16]. Shrestha (2061 BS) argues that Maoists also obtain AK-47 rifles from

People's War Group and ULFA of India. Adhikary (2061BS) argues that the Maoists have, except armoured helicopter, all types of the arms that the RNA has. However, it is very difficult to independently verify.

As the armed conflict grows during 10 years in Nepal, more than 13 thousand people have lost their lives and hundreds of thousands have become impaired. Together with the increase of the armed conflict, the state or non-state secret agents or the stalwarts, organized criminals and international weapons traders have got involved in dealing SALW. It is also reported that Nepalese land has been used as a transit point for arms trafficking (Shrestha, 2061BS).

The legitimate users of the SALW in Nepal are the army, armed police, Nepal police and other licence holders. However, monopoly over SALW of ruling elites and privileged groups in Nepal had ended after the Maoist armed insurgency.

When strength of Maoists grew, the government mobilized established Armed Police Force, mobilised RNA and modernised security sector by equipping them with modern arms and weapons. After the Al Quada attack in Pentagon and World Trade Centre on 2001 September 11, the global security perspective has changed. The USA came with a heavy-handed approach against terrorists around the world and kept security as top priority to provide military support. Nepal has greatly benefited from this changing security perspective of the USA and got arms, military hard wares, training or instruction to Nepalese army (Thapa and Sijapati, 2003; Upreti, 2004a). As India and Britain were traditionally giving training, SALW to Nepalese army, the intensity increased after the September 11 attack in the USA. Nepal also imported arms and ammunitions from other different countries including china, Belgium. Khadka (20611 BS) argues that old SLR of military has been replaced by American M-16, as more than 15 thousand units M-16 have been imported from USA. Further, security forces use Belgian Minimi Machine Guns, Israeli Galil and Indian Insas rifles (Shrestha, 2061BS).

The rough estimate of the security forces, small arms and light weapons possessed by government at present has been presented as follows:[17]

TABLE 8.4 Rough Estimate of the Arms and Weapons with the Government of Nepal

S.N	*Organisation*	*Number of persons*	*Number of arms*
1	Royal Nepal Army	80 thousand*	1 Hundred thousand
2	Armed Police	16 thousand*	16 thousand
3	Nepal Police	47 thousand*	50 thousand
	Total	143 thousand	1 hundred 66 thousand

Source: Shrestha, 2061BS: P-6, Table 1.

* The number of all 3 forces is increasing and by now it may be reaching 150 thousand in total.

Table 8.4 reveals that approximately 166000 SALW exists with the government. However, it is extremely difficult to find real data on arms and weapons of the government due to lack of transparency and access to information. Hence, researches have calculated the total numbers of arms and weapons based on the total number of security personnel. The latest conservative estimate goes beyond 200 thousand SALW. It is reported in different newspapers and weekly and fortnightly magazines that SALW include muzzle loaders, rifles, magnum rifles, short guns, pistols, revolver, hornet, gas-gun, SMG, LMG, SLR, 2- Inch mortar, Sniper Rifle and grenades (Shrestha, 2061BS).

It is even more difficult to obtain actual data on the SALW with Maoists. It has to be estimated based on the number of Maoist 'Peoples' Army' and number of their Militia. According to Hirnaya Lal Shrestha, Maoists have provided arms to 25 thousand fighters and further planned to train other 50 thousand militia in using land mines, socket bombs, pipe bombs, ambush and other explosives due to lack of arms (Shrestha, 2061BS).

The major sources of SALW with Maoists are obtained from smugglers, snatched from landlords, robbers, looted from different police posts, and military barracks and fighting security forces in different parts of the country[18]. Maoists also produce small arms locally. They use improvised explosive devices (e.g., traps, pipes and socket bombs, pressure cooker bombs, etc.).

In the nongovernmental sectors, private security services and the Bank Guards take Twelve-bore and twenty-two bore guns. Many private security service companies have been established for the last some years. A preparation is being made to provide non-governmental security services to different private sectors including industrial security forces.

Arms were provided to some villagers' groups through a village defence program to counter the insurgents.

As discussed earlier, some elite, high class and privileged persons specially landlords, ex police and army officers, some ex National Panchayat Members, and some former MPs used to keep licensed arms and light weapons like Katuwa, Twelve-bore, Air gun, Short- gun, Rifle, pistol, etc. for hunting. But, as the armed conflict expanded either the Maoists took them from the owners or the District Administration Offices collected them. Still some of the retired security persons and other powerful ones have SALW. The ex-National Panchayat Members and ex- parliamentarians have also imported arms with license coming back from foreign visit[19].

Occasionally, international power centres have provided arms to the Tibetan refugees to conduct a campaign against Chinese Autonomous region of Tibet. It has been reported that Nepal is becoming a transit point for arms trafficking. South Asia is situated between the narcotic producers Golden Triangle[20] and Golden Crescent[21] where Nepal is a transit point for smuggling of arms together with the smuggle of narcotics (Shrestha, 2061BS). However, the Nepalese government is not able to control the illegal arm trading and smuggling of narcotics. Arms are being trafficked from one conflict-ridden region to another in South Asian countries.

The total number of security force has also been sharply increased during the period of the insurgency. A nearly 45 thousand army existed in 1990 and is now reaching hundred thousand. In mid 2005, RNA has 85 thousand army and according to the plan of Ministry of Defence is to reach number of Royal Nepal Army to hundred thousand within three years, new 7 thousand posts have been approved by the government and after the recruitment of these posts the total number of army will reach 92 thousand.[22].

Public perception on implications of SALW: A quick public perception assessment SALW was conducted with local communities of Doti, Dadeldhura, Achham, Kailali, Bardiya and Banke districts (one of the most conflictaffected areas of Nepal) from 13 to 22 September 2005. Responses of more than 200 people contacted during the perception assessment are summarised in the following points:

- Insecurity: fear, anxiety, suspension, intimidation, distrust and frustration
- Rapid displacement (physical, political and social) at both levels (forced and voluntary displacement)

- Deep polarisation of society (ethnic, political and other divide)
- Breaking of traditional bonds and social relations
- Erosion of trust and credibility of government because of its failure to provide security to local people
- Negative impacts in their livelihoods and earnings
- Restriction of exercising their religious, customary and social activities
- Increased level of understanding and familiarity with SALW
- Restriction on access to health, educations and other basic services
- Physical violence (abduction, physical injuries, killing, sexual abuses, etc.) and damage to properties
- Psychological effects (tension, shock and mental disability)
- Restriction on mobility
- Obstruction on social and economic development of their areas.

Implications of SALW on security: Almost 1800 km of porous border between India and Nepal is favouring insurgencies in both countries. Trespass of insurgents of one country to another and carrying insurgency related activities are posing security challenges to both countries. Free trans-border movement with weak border monitoring system is one of the major causes of illegal trading of SALW. The hijack of Indian Airlines flying form Kathmandu to New Delhi raised severe issue of security. There is a growing realisation among the defence analysts, conflict experts, scholars of international relations that the rapid proliferation of SALW is posing a severe threat to national security.

Implications of SALW on society: Human insecurity is the largest single impact of SALW. Though there is a common saying that 'arms do not kill people, but people do', thousands of people are killed and many more thousands of human rights violations are inflicted by the use of arms. Respondents from Banke, Bardiya and Kailali districts reported that crimes like robbery, looting, killing, abduction and kidnapping, smuggling, narcotics trafficking dacoity, oppression of children, persecution of women, rent-seeking, etc. are increasing due to such arms[23]. According to the respondents robbery has highly increased compared to the other crimes. Most of the respondents said that small arms are brought from across the southern border, used in election time to terrorize voters, threaten them and capture election booths. They are also used for the security of the election candidates.

The palace massacre of 1 June 2001 can be taken as the climax and unexpected consequence of the misuse of small arms and light weapons in Nepal. Further, one of the members of sitting parliament Mirja Dilsad Beg, alleged as leader of one criminal gang was assassinated by another gang in 1997 in Kathmandu. This case clearly reveals the link of organised crime in politics and society.

Suspicious foreigners by committing crimes in other countries often enter Nepal through southern open border to use it as their hiding place. Nepal has been used by the international criminals as a transit point due to which illegal dealing with small arms and light weapons is growing in Nepal (Shrestha, 2061BS). Criminals are now active in floating explosives, counterfeit foreign notes, narcotics, etc. in Nepal to earn lucrative profits.

The criminals are hunting rare animals, collecting important parts of musk deer, smuggling furry skin and tiger's bones in the northern region of Nepal by using arms. The bandits come with arms in the bordering districts of Nepalese Terai. The cross-border criminals are involved in trafficking arms along with narcotics. The later time crime with arms has been to kidnap rich family members and demand huge money as ransom.

In these days, the armed criminals are creating trouble for both the government and the Maoists. The fake Maoists with illegal arms are involved in looting, robbing and collecting money by force. Unregulated spread of arms has causing devastating effects on law and order.

Implications of SALW on economy: It is extremely difficult to calculate the economic cost of proliferation of SALW, as it involves several direct (damage of property, shift of budget from social and service sector to purchase arms, obstruction of economic activities, investment of resources in domestic production, transfer and possession of small arms; and indirect costs (such as increase violence and political instability, fuelling crimes, state repression and domestic abuses, militarization of society, disappearance, extra-judicial executions, and other cost associated with the breach of international human rights and humanitarian laws, etc.). Criminal activities and organised criminal gangs are emerging in Nepal and influencing country's economy. They are engaged in smuggling drugs, idols, narcotics, non-timber forest products, endangered animals and animal parts, and small arms and light weapons, which is helping to develop 'war economy'. It is widely suspected that arms smugglers are bringing arms all the way form Chechnya, Eastern Europe, Afghanistan to Nepal via different international routes (first arriving at Bangladesh and spread from there). The arms entered Afghanistan at the time when the USA supplied arms to *Mujahideen* (collective term used to several arms groups resisting USSR invasion) under the 'Afghan Pipeline Project' are now spreading across the south Asia including Nepal.

Implications of SALW on politics: Relationships between politics and arms proliferation is deepening and becoming disturbingly dangerous in Nepal (Shrestha, 2061BS). Political violence is becoming a common character in Nepal especially with the rise in possession of firearms by politicians. Use of lethal weapons in pursuing politics is a growing phenomenon in the Indian bordering districts of Nepal. Winning election, grabbing power and eliminating political influence of opponents is becoming a sole agenda of politicians and they use SALW-induced violence as effective means by mobilising hired thugs and hooligans, professional criminals and mercenaries. Politicians are widely using guns (even one Member of Parliament fired gunshots at Kathmandu discotheque) (Thapa and Shah, 2000). Gun culture is developing in political elites and use of arms as a means of influence is criminalising politics. Recurring cycle of political violence in Nepal is severely eroding political legitimacy and democratic viability. Politicians are also alleged to involve in illicit trade of small arms to generate financial resources to win election.

Implications of SALW on development: Proliferation of small arms and light weapons has severe negative impacts in development sector in Nepal. Extortion of resources from development sector by using or threat of using arms, shift of development budget in purchasing arms and weapons, interference in development activities by security forces and insurgents, etc are common. It is impossible to continue development free from fear and risks at the time of conflict where arms are determining everything. Proliferation of small arms is severely affecting business sector, tourism sector, education sector, service sector and hampering economic growth and overall development of country.

8.6.2 Privatisation of security

It is reported that some resourceful and powerful people have started to establish private security mechanism, as of South American war-torn countries. Therefore, they have no faith over state security and that is bad in the long run. The government has initiated civil defence committees with training, and distributing weapons that virtually lead to the fate of Angola and Guatemala, where thousands of innocent people were killed, thousands of women were raped, and many other thousands of ordinary civilians were tortured by the members of civil defence force simply because they have weapons in hand and supported by the state. No one is secured in this country. Disappearance, kidnapping, killing is common.

8.7 ENVIRONMENTAL IMPACTS

There are several environmental consequences of this armed conflict. Dead bodies have caused pollution in water sources. Security forces are burning forests suspecting the hiding of the Maoists. Smugglers are active and forests, medicinal plants, non-timber forest products and wild animals are smuggled. Illegal poaching and hunting has increased. Environmental concerns are not the priority of the state at the time of the war.

The armed conflict has direct impact on pollution. Evidences show that the dead bodies of the people killed in the attacks such as Pili, Beni, Solukhumbu, and Dang were thrown away in water sources, rivers and forests and the decomposed bodies are creating pollution around the deposed areas. Land mines are also polluting the areas. Security forces are firing in the forests suspecting hiding of insurgents. Such forest firing is not only damaging flora and fauna but also polluting the environment.

Impacts on genetic resources: So far we did not find empirical results of any in-depth studies on impacts of armed conflict on genetic resources. However, severe disruption of farming systems and seed flow mechanisms, disturbance on forests management, encroachment on and irrational exploitation of non timber forest products, rare species of flora and fauna in the war running areas, deforestation in specific areas security forces for the security reasons, over harvesting of some high value medicinal plants (e.g., Yarsagumba = *Cordyceps sinensis, Chiraito=Swertia Chiraita, Jatamasi = Nardostachys grandiflora, Kutki = Picrorhiza scrophulariiflora, Bikhama =Aconitum palmatum, Padamchal = Rheum emodi, Panchaunle = Gaiearis stracheyi, Sunpati = Rhododendron anthopogon, Sughandhawal (Valerina wallichii)*, etc. by rebels for the economic benefits have adversely affected genetic resources. On the other hand, works of conservation organizations working in the field of conservation of genetic resources have been disturbed by the armed conflict.

Impacts on land and water: Land is one of the most affected natural resources by the ongoing armed conflict. Land has been a symbol of power, prestige and social status in the villages for a long time. Reason being that power brokers and local elite captured valuable land resources by using their networks and connections with state power centres and traditional power structures. Therefore, land remained as one of the major means of exploitation. Hence, land became most prominent target of Maoists. Maoists evicted local landlords and village elites from their village and captured their lands. In some areas, especially in the Maoist-controlled areas, they distributed the lands of landlords to poor people but the poor people were not able to utilize them because of fear of security forces. Local landlords are not able to cultivate their lands and consequently the scarce land resource is under- utilized. Government has started a Land Bank programme to buy lands from landlords and sell to the landless. However, it is a game plan of the feudal government to serve the interests of feudal elites by buying their wasted lands.

Investment in water resource is severely disturbed because of the armed conflict. Exploitation of water resource for hydropower, irrigation, drinking water, recreation and industrial uses is limited because the political environment for the investors and entrepreneurs is not conducive at all. Similarly, water sources are polluted by the war and normal water supply systems are disturbed.

Impacts on protected areas: The ongoing armed conflict has direct impacts on the management of protected areas. The Royal Nepal Army deployed for the protection of the National Parks and Wildlife Resources has to be mobilized for the counter insurgency operation that resulted in lack of security protection. The weak security of the protected areas has been abused by the smugglers, poachers, hunters and other unauthorized persons. The insurgents are influential in some of the protected areas (for example, Khaptad National Park, Makalu Barun Conservation area, etc.) and therefore park authorities are not are able to manage and regulate parks[24]. The attention and priority of the state shifts from protected areas to manage the war. That ultimately leads to lack of resource to manage protected areas. On the other hand, because of the security restrictions, poor people who base their livelihood in forest resources are deprived. Five rhinos were killed at the time of state of emergency in 2001 in Bardya National Park. In Lantang National Park slaughtering of musk deer by poachers has been reported.[25]

8.8 GENDER IMPACTS OF THE ARMED CONFLICT

Gender roles and social relations in the villages have been drastically changed in the armed conflict affected areas (Upreti, 2061BS). Because of displacement of male people from the villages, the conventional roles of men and women have been changed. For example, women have started to plough land in absence of their male members of family, which is culturally forbidden. Women are also engaged in other functions performed by male members such as representing in meetings and discussions, attending funerals, dealing with outsiders (e.g., security forces or insurgents). This has changed the role and at the same time, added extra work burden to the women in the community.

Several cultural restrictions (e.g., unequal treatment and discrimination against women) have been forcefully changed by the Maoists in their areas of influence that virtually benefit women and children. The ongoing armed conflict has opened opportunity for women to be empowered. For example, there is changed responsibility and decision-making that single women took up in absence of husbands or other male members of the family. Women participating in the armed conflict found a new environment. In the Nepalese armed conflict, gender relations have been changed and they are developing their capacity to decide and act, which ultimately empowers them.

Gender violence is one of the major effects of armed conflict. There is then an increase in the incidence of rape, both by armed forces and insurgents. They also use rape sometimes as a deliberate tactic to intimidate the opposing side. Nepalese press has frequently reported that incidents of rape are becoming increasingly common. Reports of Amnesty International and other national human rights organizations have clearly stated that rape, intimidation are common characteristics of the armed conflict in Nepal.

There are also some reported cases in the Nepalese media that there is connection between the spread of AIDS and armed conflict as some female IDPs are directly or indirectly forced into the commercial sex sector.

Sexual violence against women has a negative effect on the social relations. Many female IDPs are forced to engage in prostitution. It is generally claimed that there is a high increase in the commercial sex sector in IDPs influx areas such as Nepaljung, Surkhet, Kathamndu, etc. Rape survivors have serious psychological effects and feelings of insecurity, retaliation and revenge. They are also socially ignored or neglected as living-dead people, refused to deal with humanly and treated as outcaste by community.

Numbers of single women are increasing because of the armed conflict. They have difficulty in securing access to government compensation, basic rights and resources such as land, public services, etc. Subordination and exploitation of women is common in the situation of civil war. However, Nepal's case is far worser than this. Women are also displaced along with their minors after the loss of their husband from either warring party due to forced cultural practices of society

In the case of Nepal, women are not just victims of conflict and sufferers of agony. They are also active participants in the armed conflict. Their roles are seen beyond supporters of insurgency, even working as combatants. In the Maoist army, approximately 30-35 per cent of the fighting forces are women. This case has proved that women are equally capable of fighting or taking on difficult work together with male members. As a consequence, Royal Nepal Army has started to recruit female soldiers.

In agriculture and resource management sectors in the conflict-affected areas, farming systems are very much depending upon women as their male members go out of the village to escape from the warring parties. The recent field research (September 2005) of the author in Achham and Doti reveals that women are taking responsibility of both households and agriculture such as crop production, livestock or horticulture, marketing of their agricultural products.

8.9 IMPACTS ON HUMAN RIGHTS

While visiting Nepal (23-26 January 2005), UN High Commissioner for Human Rights Louise Arbor issued a press statement highlighting the severe human rights crisis. The statement says, "*I would warn the leaders of the insurgency not to misread development in the wider world nor to believe that they can operate outside of the law*. Series of reports of Amnesty International (Nepal: Killing with Impunity, 20 January 2005; Nepal: State of Emergency Deepening Human Rights Crisis, 1st February 2005 and Nepal: A Long Ignored Human Rights Crisis Now on the Brink of Catastrophe, 18 February 2005) highlights the worsening human rights situation of Nepal.

The Secretary General of the UN issued several statements concerning the crisis. These statements amply demonstrate his worries about the deteriorating situation of Nepal.

Similarly, Amnesty International warned that the human rights situation of Nepal is deteriorating. The situation of enforced or involuntary disappearances is also alarming and Nepal was in the top list of countries having disappearance in 2004 (Upreti, 2005i).

The assessment of International Commission of Jurists (ICJ) is also alarming regarding the human rights situation. The ICJ team had visited Nepal to assess the situation and concluded that gross human rights abuses being committed by both sides of the conflict in Nepal are escalating. They were worried about the breakdown of the rule of law in the country and that lawlessness is expanding. According to the assessments of globally reputed organisations such as ICG, Amnesty International, the political and security situation is further worsening after the royal takeover (AI, 2005a and b; ICG, 2005a and b).

Research on Child Workers in Nepal reveals that more than 328 children have lost their lives, 250 children have been injured and 6698 children are joining Moist insurgency. This is a serious human rights concern. It is observed that conflict orphans have serious psychological problems, stress disorders and abnormalities. Anger, revenge and retaliation and suspicion are replacing love, affection and trust in the conflict victim children. They need psychological counselling but the state is not taking this issue seriously.

8.10 DEVELOPMENTAL IMPACTS

Earlier studies of Hogger (2001), Upreti, (2005g); Kievelitz and Polzer, (2002); Howel and Upreti (2005), Upreti et al., (2005) show that strategies of the Maoists towards donor-funded developments are contextual and inconsistent. But they are not firmly anti-donor. The credibility of the development projects and their benefits to the poor and marginalized people and background of the country determine their strategy towards particular projects. Community-based, quick impact-oriented projects directly benefiting marginalized people are less hampered. However, the Maoist responses towards particular projects entirely depend upon the judgement of the local in charges of the Maoist. If they judge a particular project as exploitative, capitalistic, imperialistic, religious or simply useless, then possibility for obstruction is high.

This conflict has also severe developmental impacts as big infrastructure projects are suffering from security risk and are likely to be closed (some have already closed). It is not possible to continue planned development work in the rural areas because of security risks.

NGOs are often not able to go and work. The recent policy of the Maoists to allow development work if such development activities are coordinated with them has added another complication as the government does not allow them to do so. Severe destructions of basic infrastructures have caused billions of damage cost and take these many years to develop.

Destruction of basic development infrastructures such as VDC buildings, range posts, bridges, roads, schools, electricity, drinking water, telephone, etc. is widespread. After August 2003 ceasefire breakdown, the Maoists in different districts informally announced, 'no development without political settlement'. Serious violation of human rights from the warring parties, used villagers as human shield and arbitrary arrests general public[26] are common across Nepal (AI, 2005a and b; INSEC, 2005).

Critical examination of the overall impacts of development programmes (Pandey, 1999; Shrestha, 1997; Upreti, 2004a and b) poses a fundamental question as to why development has failed to address poverty and social exclusion, major structural causes of the conflict. The question directly points towards the performance of the government and development administration and governing system.

Widening rural-urban inequalities, increasing internal displacement and migration, shifted priority of the government to security and fragile state of private sector are severely damaging the prospects of achieving the Millennium Development Goals by 2015. The Tenth Five-Year Plan is a major development response to address root causes of conflict. This plan offers comprehensive poverty reduction strategies and identifies priority areas. However, its effective implementation is severely questioned by the escalated conflict and mal-governance (weak, ineffective and corrupt governing practices) within development administration of Nepal.

There are not only negative impacts of conflict on development. But development projects could have negative effects on conflict (Upreti, 2061BS). These negative effects of development programmes funded by big INGOs/Donors are:

- Involuntary transfer of resources to rebels.
- Supporting ineffective government structures that resist change.
- Failure to address issues of social exclusion and poverty.
- Created high and unfulfilled expectations of people in the project areas.

- Created perception of inequality and grievances due to the use of expensive vehicles, computers, better pays and expensive life style of project staff, which provides evidences or at least feeling that international aid goes to serve the privileged group instead to needy poor.
- Created dependency and decreased government incentives to mobilise internal resources and distorting local production and exchange system.
- Sudden withdrawal of projects had created a vacuum that even fuelled conflict.
- Aids provided by the international community have contributed to conspicuous consumption of elites of Kathmandu and very little trickle-down effects to the rural poor.

Damage of physical infrastructures: Physical infrastructures are one of the main targets of the Maoists during their 'people's war'. They have even targeted infrastructures related to basic services such as health, education, drinking water, etc. Most of these offices are damaged while Maoists raided district headquarters, or scattered attack on the individual offices. It is extremely hard to get data on physical damage of the physical infrastructures from government offices as well as to find the actual cost of the damaged properties. However, conflict experts, economists and development professionals engaged in the conflict analysis and impact studies estimate that the cost of the damaged infrastructures goes beyond twenty billion rupees.

TABLE 8.5 Infrastructures damaged by Maoists (February 1996 to July 2005)

S.N	*Types of infrastructures*	*Number*
1	Police posts	579
2	District Police Offices	35
3	Post offices	641
4	Health posts	85
5	Roads	45
6	Forest office and range posts	290
7	Irrigation infrastructures	30
8	District Education Offices	34
9	Agricultural offices	149
10	Land Revenue offices	43
11	Land reform offices	9

S.N	*Types of infrastructures*	*Number*
12	Soil conservation offices	8
13	Livestock offices	24
14	Women development offices	18
15	Revenue offices/units	22
16	Airports	14
17	Jail	7
18	Courts	18
19	Radio station	2
20	National parks and reserves	8
21	Bridges	44
22	Dairy development units	9
23	Municipalities and wards	77
24	Village Development Committees	1621
25	Drinking water systems	22
26	Telecom towers	128
27	Powerhouses and electricity offices	96
28	Sajha transport (government transport company)	7
29	Food depots/stores	25
30	Schools	159
31	Treasury offices	5
32	Financial institutions	222
33	Land measurement offices	15
34	Family planning offices/units	38
35	Others	619
	Total	5138

Source: Samaya Weekly, Vol. 2, No 69, 28/4-2/5 2062(12-18 Aug 2005), P. 38

Targeting police posts or security stations is understandable but it is not clear why Maoists damage infrastructures that are directly providing basic services to poor people such as health posts, schools, suspension bridges, rural post offices, drinking water systems, as against their claim of working for the betterment of poor people. In terms of number of the damage, VDC buildings are the highest hit as they interpret functioning VDC as 'the presence of the old regime', which they don't want. Schools are comparatively less damaged. They have damaged many infrastructures in the capital, Kathmandu valley. The state is not able or willing to reconstruct most of the damaged infrastructures mainly because of resources required to sustain war and apprehension of repeated attack and damage by the insurgents.

The reasons for targeting physical infrastructures might be their orientation that 'destruction and reconstruction are integral parts of people's war', to demonstrate their capability and attract national and international attention. Hence, these infrastructures are becoming victims of Maoists' war propaganda. Otherwise, there is no justification for damaging these infrastructures. After the intense pressure from human rights activists, civil society and donors/international community, Maoist leader Prachanda issued statements asking his cadres to stop targeting infrastructures, but these statements are not always fully translating into practice.

At the operational level, some projects were threatened to be expelled from the working district/sites[27], or asked to leave[28], staff of some projects were abducted[29], attacked or bombing offices[30] and looting[31]. Many local NGOs were asked to stop their work. Some projects of the Creation of Creative Society (CCS) were forced to close in Kailali. CARE Nepal faced different conflict- related problems such as bombing of its office in Achham, emergency rescue of its staff at the time of 1st Accham attack, disturbances of irrigation part of the SAGUN project, shift of office of Bajhang Poverty Reduction Project and JIBIKA Project of Achham to Nepalgunj, distance management of some projects due to insecurity to manage projects on the site, etc. Some development agencies (both national and international) working in the conflict-affected areas to address structural causes were moved to less risky areas or stopped their work because of these threats and immediate security concerns.

8.11 IMPACTS ON INTERNATIONAL RELATIONS

This conflict has changed the image of Nepal from a peaceful mountainous country with peace-loving people to a corrupt and war-torn country with unprecedented human rights violence. It would be almost impossible to change that perception once it is cemented. Because of the conflict and extremely poor performance of the government, many international donors are even withdrawing support (e.g., the recent decision of the Dutch government). Arms supply is increasing and international arms traders are active and they want to keep the conflict going and therefore they will do whatever they can to maintain the civil war in Nepal.

8.12 IMPACTS ON FOREST AND AGRICULTURE

There are several environmental consequences because of this armed conflict. Dead bodies have caused pollution in water sources. Security forces are burning forests, suspecting the hiding of the Maoists. Smugglers are active and forests, medicinal plants, non-timber forest products and wild animals are smuggled. Illegal poaching and hunting has increased. Environmental concerns are not the priority of the state at the time of the war.

- The Maoist slogan 'land to tillers' has gained sympathy of tenants, poor farmers and marginalized people but the existing production relations in the rural areas is severely disrupted.
- In the recent study (Upreti, 2005c) key informants[32] explained that most of the big landholdings are either directly controlled by Maoists, or exerting pressure over tenants to stop paying contractual payments to landlords. The Maoists ask to pay the landlords' share to them. Collecting the landlords' share of the rent from the tenants is increasing. Such a situation has negative impacts on the productivity of land, as these productive lands are uncultivated or under-cultivated or cultivated with no/low investment.
- Some of the commercial farmers (e.g., tea growers in Ilam and Panchtahr, who are often medium to rich farmers or local elite with strong links with power centres) have been either controlled or disturbed by the Maoists. Such control has ultimately forced the commercial farmers to leave the area. Rich and medium commercial farmers are facing continuous pressure to pay them huge amounts of money. Such extortion is greatly affecting commercial farming: tea gardens, fruit gardens, livestock farming, cardamom growing, broom grass and ginger growing. Consequently, it is negatively affecting agriculture processing and distribution systems too.
- Investment in agriculture sector by the Agriculture Development Bank and other financial institutions has decreased. It became extremely difficult for Agriculture Development Bank staff to visit field, as the insurgents are very negative towards ADB loan and they have damaged several branches of the Bank and destroyed the documents.
- Many farmers are notable to take/repay bank loans due loss of their business. Big farmers and entrepreneurs are not ready to

investing in agriculture due to insecurity. In some cases farmers are not collecting money even after approval of the loan from the bank (Upreti, 2005g).

- The Maoists have recognised the importance of agricultural development in their 75-point Common Minimum Policy and Programme. The 31st point states, "*...Special attention shall be paid on the development of agricultural industries and proper arrangement shall be made for agricultural market...*". However, their sayings (or writings) and doing are often different, which has direct impacts on agriculture.
- The office buildings of agriculture and forestry (e.g, the Regional Agriculture Directorate in Biratnagar[33], Agriculture Development Office in Dhankuta, Forestry and agriculture offices in Khotang[34], etc) were damaged by bomb-blast by the insurgents,
- Several restrictive rules imposed by the government are directly hitting to farmers. For example, farmers need to get recommendations from VDC Secretary to sell their rice[35] but unavailability of the VDC secretaries in VDC due to insecurity,
- Selling timbers from community forestry was obstructed,
- Dual tax (to the government and the Maoists) on the non-timber forest products to be paid by community/local people.

8.13 IMPACTS ON PEOPLE'S LIVELIHOODS

The notion of livelihood is complex in its scope, nature and understanding. Generally, livelihood comprises the capabilities, assets (both material and social resources) and activities required for a means of living. Livelihood is sustainable when it can cope with and recover from stresses and shocks and maintain or enhance its capabilities and assets both now and in the future, while not undermining the natural resource base (Chambers and Conway, 1992). Livelihoods of Nepalese people become better when:

- They have access to basic rights established through international conventions. If they access to high-quality education, information, technologies and training and better nutrition and health;
- Supportive and cohesive social environment;
- Secure access to, and better management of, natural resources;

- Better access to basic and facilitating infrastructure, and financial resources; and
- A policy and institutional environment that supports multiple livelihood strategies and promotes equitable access to competitive markets for all (DFID, 1999).

If we examine the current livelihood situation of poor, marginalized and socially excluded people of Nepal based on these criteria, their livelihood is in vulnerable situation.

Employment generations, ensuring access to means of production and provisions of safety net measures are some of the main responsibilities of the state towards it's citizens, particularly to the poor, landless, marginalized, women, dalit, disables. However, despite the vulnerable state of poor and marginalized, the Table 3 shows that the state is refrained from these responsibilities.

TABLE 8.6 Number of households and food sufficiency situation

Household characteristics (food insufficiency situation)	*Total no of holdings*	*Number of land holding*
Total holdings	3364139 (100%)	26700 (100%)
Sufficient to feed household	1337965 (39.8%)	1728 (6.5%)
Not sufficient to feed household	2026174 (60.2%)	24972 (93.5%)
• 1-3 months insufficient	439592 (21.7%)	755 (3%)
• 4-6 months insufficient	877362 (43.3%)	2250 (9%)
• 7-9 months insufficient	342039 (16.9%)	2275 (9.1%)
• 10-12 months insufficient	357544 (16.6%)	19633 (78.6%)

Source: CBS 2004 (Table 2.32, pp-104-107)

If the state has failed to secure food for more than 60 per cent of households and more than 16 per cent households of Nepal have food insecurity all round the year, where is the responsibility of the state to secure livelihoods of its citizen and how they feel the ownership of state. When the state refrains from its responsibility, citizen will be further alienated that potentially leads to conflict.

Among the production resources, land is a fundamental means of livelihood of Nepalese people. It is also a basic means of social status, which further provides basis for securing other rights such as citizenships, loan from the banks, registration of childbirth, etc. If people are landless they not only lose means of their livelihoods but also deprived from enjoying other rights.

TABLE 8.7 Land distribution situation in Nepal

S.N.	*Category of people*	*% of total population*
1	Landless	24.44
2	Semi-landless (owing less than 0.20 acre or 0.08 ha)	6.98
3	Marginal cultivators (owing 0.21 to 1 acre or 0.084 to 0.4046 ha)	27.59
4	Small cultivators (1.01 to 2 acres or 0.4087 to 0.809 ha)	20.15
5	Semi-medium (2.01 to 4 acres or 0.809 to 1.618 ha)	13.42
6	Medium cultivators (4 to 10 acres or 1.659 to 4.05 ha)	6.25
7	Large cultivators (more than 10.01 acre or 4.06 ha)	1.17

Source: UNDP (2004: 176).

The Table 8.7 demonstrates a general landholding pattern prevalent in Nepal. More than 24 percent people are landless and another 6.98 percent people are semi-landless. When more than 30 percent of the population of an agricultural country is landless, they face livelihood insecurity and when state fails to provide means of their survival they frustrate with the state and take arms. The state should have addressed this problem to minimise their frustration, a source of conflict. Series of the rallies and mass protests (in Siraha, Saptari, Dang, Kailali, Chitwan) organised by tenants, dalits, landless, squatters and ex-kamaiyas is the evidence of their frustration. When they feel ignored, neglected, or victimised by the state, they get organised and start protest to demand their rights. This is one of the perennial sources of conflict and instability in Nepal. In addition to land, similar inequalities can be observed in access to and control over of forest (e.g., threat to forest-based livelihoods of poorest) and water resources (e.g., privatisation of water and higher user fees).

Previous studies (Upreti, 2001; Seddon and Hussein, 2002) show that in rural areas 20 percent people are wealthy landowners and peasants and remaining 80 percent people experiences livelihood insecurity and risks. The lives and livelihoods of women, girls and children are more threatened from the conflict, as they live in chronic poverty and social insecurity. Livelihoods of poor, marginalized and socially excluded people of Nepal involve a constant struggle for their survival because of lack of their control over and access to productive resources, weak social capital and networks, lack of stable or regular source of income, etc. (Seddon and Hussein, 2002). The extremely poor people entirely rely on casual or daily wage labour for their survival, which is also severely disturbed by the conflict. Exploitation and social discriminations are forcing poor people for deprivation and indebtedness. At present, livelihood insecurity of poor people is further aggravated by the armed conflict.

The study of the Seddon and Hussein, (2002) revels that security forces are restricting people from carrying more than one days food supply at a time to deny food supply to Maoists, as against the general practice of people to carry a months supply. In rural areas, people have to walk up to 3-4 days to reach market. Traditional livelihood opportunities of local poor are jeopardised by the conflict, as they are not allowed to go to forests by the security forces to collect forest based means of livelihoods (mushrooms, young sprouts of plants, medicinal herbs, non-timber forest products, fire-woods, etc.). And, if any one found in the forest is suspected as Maoist. Because of all these problems there are frequent famines in the Karnali region (ibid: 29) and other high-conflict areas.

8.14 IMPACTS ON PUBLIC SERVICES

Significant reduction of public services has been observed in the Maoist influenced areas mainly due to the fear and insecurity, reduction of transport of goods because of the blockade, *bands*, general and transport strikes, curfews, restriction on mobility. In this report public services include health, education, transport, market, employment and agriculture and forestry, which are briefly discussed in the following section:

8.14.1 Impacts on health

- Damage of ambulances, health posts and other health related infrastructures
- Restriction of supply of medicines in the Maoist influence areas by the security forces in the suspicion of use of medicines by insurgents,
- Increased unwillingness of medical professionals to go to remote areas for work and subsequent deficiency in health services
- Reduction of investment in the health sector
- Rapid brain drain from health sector (qualified doctors and nurses leaving country)

- Widening gap between rural and urban health facilities,
- Frequent disruption of water supply and blockade of water source.

8.14.2 Impacts on education

The ongoing armed conflict in Nepal is severely affecting the education sector particularly school education. Many schools are closed, teachers and students are kidnapped or forced to leave their residence. Several school buildings and buildings of educational institutions have been destroyed and the "Bandh" strikes and blockades hamper educational activities of schools, teachers and students. Consequently, teachers and students do not find a conducive teaching-learning environment in schools. Huge numbers of students, teachers and parents are displaced from their areas. Schools Management Committees (SMC) are under strong pressure from the insurgents and the government and therefore they are becoming helpless. Because of the armed conflict, utilisation of school resources is becoming imbalanced as some schools are overcrowded with less physical and human recourses and some others are under-utilized. Management of overcrowded schools and developing mechanisms to fully utilize under-utilized schools is a major challenge. Huge numbers of displaced children are lacking basic needs and not able to continue their educational activities. Students and teachers are also heavily traumatised and victimised but lack counselling services to resume their normal life. Following is the qualitative indication of impacts of armed conflict in education:

- Education is one of the most affected sectors. Conflict has created anarchy in the education sector and used it as ransom by warring parties. The evidences of this claim can be seen in the situation between 1996 and 2005. The data shows: Maoists have killed 60 teachers and 66 students, caused the disappearance of 151 teachers and abducted 516 students and 62 teachers. Similarly, the state has killed 44 teachers, 172 students, detained 158 teachers and 115 students; and 14 teachers disappeared (*Himalayan Times*, 10 July 2005).
- Mass abduction of students and teachers by Maoists and suspicion by security forces are causing great insecurity. As a consequence, teachers and students are leaving schools and colleges.
- Strike, bandhs and closures of schools have seriously obstructed

the school and university calendars and hindered teaching-learning environment.

- Schools are used as a battleground by the warring parties and as camps by security forces
- Great confusion and insecurities are created in schools because of pressure from Maoists to follow their curriculum.
- Teachers and students are also suffering from extortion and regular payment of levy.
- Performance of community schools of villages and remote areas is very poor, as shown by the SLC result of this year (2005). High percentage of failure in SLC creates frustration among the under-educated youth. They do not get employment and consequently become restless, angry and disconnected from society and some of them join the rebellion.

8.14.3 Impacts on transport

- Restriction/obstruction in physical mobility, travel and transportation of goods and services.
- Placement of landmines in major roads.
- Physical blockade of roads, damage of transport infrastructure (civil aviations towers, roads, suspension bridges, etc.).
- Physical damage to vehicles (burning or blasting of buses, loaded trucks, ambulances, motorbikes, etc.).
- Charging huge amounts of money to transport entrepreneurs by the insurgents.
- Deeply disturbing and humiliating security checks on roads.
- Insistence on transport companies to run their vehicles at the time of bandhs and strikes by the state.
- Many travel companies withdraw their services from conflict-affected areas.
- Maoists destruct bridges and roads to obstruct movements of security forces.
- Blockade of truckloads to supply food in district headquarters. This has severely disrupted market systems (rising prices; shortage of supply of basic foods; increasing black marketing, smuggling and carteling, etc.), which has direct and immediate impacts on the poor and marginalised people.
- Disruption of transport has slowed down economic activities, as big construction projects (e.g., Melamchi Drinking Water

Project, Kali Gandaki 'A' Hydro Power Project, different road construction projects, etc.) that require huge amounts of construction materials, are not able to continue their work smoothly. This has direct impact on the labourers' job.
- Furthermore, some ongoing road construction projects (e.g., Chhinchu Jajarkot road construction project) were stopped due to security risks and many other projects have slowed down.

8.15 SOME EXAMPLES OF POSITIVE IMPACTS

The insurgency in the earlier years has had some positive aspects. Until 2001, the Maoists had focused on the issues and concerns of people such as banning alcoholism, stopping polygamy, reducing extremely high interest rates imposed by the local moneylenders, etc.

The important issues sidelined by the state for more than 2 centuries, such as poverty; social exclusion; discriminations based on caste, class, ethnicity, religion and elite-centric political and governing system are now in the mainstream national debate because of the armed insurgency.

The Maoists brought issues and concerns of the poor, women, socially excluded and marginalized groups into national debate. They forced alteration of the feudal types of unequal patron-client social relations in rural areas, etc. Such practices were in fact contributing to required social change (Hogger, 2001, Upreti, 2002b; Goodhand, 2000). However, after 2001, they intensified targeting development infrastructures, obstructing development activities and multiplied human rights violations (killing, torture, abduction, etc.) (Raj, 2004; INSEC, 2005; ICG, 2005a and b). However, they claim that destruction and construction are integral parts of the revolution. As the Maoists established *'janasarkar'* (people's government) autonomous governments in the rural areas, they increase pressure on development projects and programmes to sever ties with the "old regime" and work by registering with them. Even in one of the statements after the 1st February political change, Maoist leader *Prachanda* exhorted international donors to discontinue support to the government (Howel and Upreti, 2005).

Various studies of Kievelitz and Polzer (2002) for GTZ, Upreti et al., (2005) for DANIDA, Meyer and Upreti (2004), Goodhand (2000) and Howel and Upreti (2005) for DFID, Upreti (2002b) and Hogger (2001) for SDC demonstrate that presence of Maoists in the project areas has contributed to promoting transparency and minimising corruption, as they closely scrutinise development activities at the local level. Direct entitlement of land and assets to certain households and poor people is increased in the Maoist stronghold areas. Awareness of and sensitisation to existing social problems have increased. It has helped to empower *dalit,* ethnic groups, women and marginalized people of the society. Gambling and alcohol abuse in Maoist-controlled villages has decreased. In the villages, moneylenders had lowered interest rates (some time from 60% to 8%); police harassment has decreased in villages.

Compared to the past, the state apparatus is becoming conflict-sensitive, particularly after the 2nd ceasefire breakdown. Now, government is sensitive at least in rhetoric but the translation of rhetoric into practice is extremely poor. The armed conflict forced the government to start some reform programmes. The government started and reforms, redefining women's property rights, regulation for sale and consumption of liquor, bills to regulate private schools, anti-corruption bill, etc. However, they were neither enough nor sincerely implemented. Grass-roots political awareness of the rural population has increased that could greatly contribute to democratisation process. Because of the armed conflict; exploitation by landlords and elite in the rural areas decreased. The Maoists also introduced various community decision-making mechanisms such as people's court, to deal with land issues, domestic violence, alcoholism, polygamy, etc. that have given a voice to socially excluded people, poor and rural women. Maoists' raised legitimate questions to the projects on amount of budget spent and types of people benefited, which forced donors to think on these issues. However, each of these impacts also has negative sides.

Conflict situation is also creating new opportunities to maximise local initiatives in project implementation and support local capacity building (civil society strengthening). As a consequence of conflict, many projects had adjusted their working style keeping a low profile, focused on transparency and flexibility. Security risk for project staff to work in the field has changed mode of operation from direct implementation to working through local organisations. This arrangement has further increased feeling of ownership of local people. It has also recognised and incorporated local knowledge and experiences and assisted to promote grass-roots democratic institutions like forest user groups.

8.16 EFFORTS OF DIFFERENT ACTORS IN MITIGATING NEGATIVE IMPACTS OF CONFLICT

8.16.1 HMG/N's efforts to mitigate negative impacts of conflict

The government has made some cosmetic and some real efforts in mitigating conflict. The government started initiatives to address some important causes of conflict. In addition, the government proposed 'forward-looking agenda on the reforms of the state system' in the Hapure peace talk. Summary of some of the main efforts of the government to mitigate conflict are as follows:

- Creation of Peace Secretariat, however this is in almost a dysfunctional situation at present.
- Integrated Security and Development Programme (April 2001), which became dysfunctional later.
- Kamaiya liberation (July 2000), they are still facing severe problem of finding shelter and employment.
- Establishment of National Human Rights Commission (2001), National Dalit Commission (March 2002), National Women Commission (2002), etc.
- Land reform legislation to lower the ceiling of land (August 2001).
- Legislation on women's inheritance right and 11th amendment on Civil Code.
- Anticorruption initiative by amending Commission on Investigation of Abuse of Authority Act to enhance its investigative and prosecutorial capacities.
- Investigation of wealth of high-ranking politicians and bureaucrats.
- Enactment of Local Self Governance Act (1999).
- Permission for ICRC to operate in Nepal,
- Establishment of Compensation Fund for Victims of Conflict (Prime Minister Relief Fund).
- Ganesh Man Singh Peace Campaign (suspended by 1st February royal takeover).
- Poverty Alleviation Fund and 10th Plan (deliberation on inclusion of socially excluded and poor).
- Established Human Rights Cells within the structures of the Security Forces.
- Mainly because of tremendous international pressure, Nepalese

government signed an agreement with UN High Commissioner for Human Rights to open Office of the UN High Commissioner for Human Rights in Nepal.

- Some minor initiatives taken for conflict victimss (e.g, rehabilitation programme for conflict victims[36]).
- The government had proposed a roadmap for the 'forward-looking reform agenda' at the time of the Hapure peace talks.
- Human rights cells created in royal Nepal army and police structures and trained military and police in human rights issues.

However, some initiatives such as Private Property Compensation Fund have been absurdly abused. For example, one of the Home Ministers is said to have claimed nearly Rs 10 million from the Private Property Compensation Fund by exaggerating the value of his property damaged by the rebels but ordinary civilians have not got compensation if they are not connected with political parties or other power centres. There is total lack of transparency in the distribution of Compensation Fund to Victims of Conflict.

8.16.2 Efforts of political parties

For a long time, political parties did not realize the complexity of the armed conflict and tried their best to gain narrow political interests from the conflict. However, after the 4 October 2002 royal takeover (18 Ashoj 2059), they gradually started to rethink their role in the peace process. Until 1st February 2005, they were not able to fully internalise the crisis. Instead, they were deeply engaged in power struggle instead of making concerted efforts to settle the crisis. On the positive side, some of the major political parties [for example, Communist party of Nepal-United Marxist Leninist CPN-UML)] formed special committees to propose ways and means of resolving the armed conflict[37]. CPN-UML proposed an eight-point roadmap[38], formed two committees to study the Maoists insurgency, *Janamorcha* Nepal and United Leftist Front also came up with some proposals for the negotiated settlement of the conflict. Now some leaders in each political party are specialising in conflict transformation and peace building. In a nutshell, their efforts and commitments were far too less than the expectations of the Nepali people. Later, when five of the political parties opposed the nominated government; they started agitation with an 18-point agenda of conflict resolution[39]. But this effort became feeble when the CPN

UML joined Nepali Congress Party-Democratic (NCP-D) government led by Deuba. But none of the major political parties who ruled the country made sincere and enough efforts to end the violence and restore democratic and permanent peace in Nepal.

8.16.3 Efforts of donors and INGOs

Donors and INGOs started to think seriously only when their development programmes and projects faced direct and indirect pressures from the insurgents and other many conflict-related problems. Among the 3 P's discourse (people, property and programme), donors and INGOs were not serious until warring parties targeted people and properties. Reconciling development and security became a major challenge for the development organisations after the 2001 State of Emergency. The immediate security concerns to the continuation of projects became a growing threat. Consequently, donors started to change their approaches, procedures, and practices to translate 'do-no-harm' principle into practice. However, Seddon and Hussein (2002) argue that it is difficult for donors to follow basic tenets of humanitarian aid and 'do-no-harm' principles. Examining the recent trend, Seddon and Hussein wrote, *"...several of the more influential bilateral development agencies are struggling with the position adopted by their governments and diplomatic representatives in Nepal encouraging a policy of security first, development second"* (Seddon and Hussein, 2002:7). It is very hard to see the present government's commitment to positively respond to donors' commitment to address structural causes of the conflict, democracy, human rights and civil and political freedom.

Development organisations implementing their programmes and projects in Nepal have mainly adopted three approaches ('working around conflict', 'working in conflict' and 'working on conflict'). Organisations 'working around conflict' approach are not directly engaged in conflict issues. They are either withdrawing their programme activities from the conflict-affected areas or shifting to low-risk areas. The majority of the development organisations working in Nepal are adopting a 'working in conflict' approach. They attempt to avoid 'doing harm' through their development activities, adopting a low profile while working in the conflict-affected areas, being alert to improve security management related to their projects, working through local partners, reducing high input programmes from the conflict-affected areas and focusing on poverty, etc. The concrete example of this type is the work of Association of INGOs in Nepal (AIN), which has developed operational guidelines and minimum working standards to ensure 'do-no-harm' principle in their project activities. Only some organisations are adopting a 'working on conflict' approach, which is supposed to be the highly desired approach in the conflict context. In this approach, development agencies engage in conflict analysis, make efforts to resolve it, seek opportunities to positively influence the dynamics of conflict. They revisit objectives, strategies, activities of their development programmes and projects to effectively address the root causes of the conflict. They focus on governance, poverty alleviation and social inclusion, providing incentives for peace and disincentives for violence, support for mediation and emphasis on protection of human rights and humanitarian assistance.

Some of the major donors were active in helping the government to establish the Peace Secretariat, offering political help if needed to reach negotiated settlement, training civil society, political leaders and government officials (both military and civil), assisting civil society to take a proactive role in conflict transformation and peace building. Many of them revisited their development assistance and its impacts and redesigned or reoriented the development priorities focusing on social inclusion, marginalized people, *Dalit* and women. Small-scale quick output project approaches (e.g., DFID Community Support Project) and explicitly conflict-mitigation focused approaches (e.g., UJYALO, a project funded by USAID and managed by a consortium of 5 big INGOs working in Nepal) emerged. UNDP and some other donors initiated a peace-focused intervention called Support for Peace and Development Initiatives (SPDI).

The USA, one of the main international players in Nepal's conflict and heavily supporting the military has tied its military aid to the Royal Nepal Army's response to respect human rights. The UN Congress passed a legislation in late 2004 that restricts military assistance to Nepal unless the Secretary of the State certifies that it is cooperating with NHRC to resolve all disappearance cases; granting the National Human Rights Commission unimpeded access to places of detention; and complying promptly with *habeas corpus* orders issued by Nepal's supreme court, including all outstanding orders (ICG, 2005a and b). This will have potentially big impacts.

8.16.4 Efforts of NGOs and civil society

Compared to the state, the roles of non-governmental sectors and civil society are strong towards conflict transformation. However, role of civil society in conflict transformation and addressing root causes of the conflict is always secondary. The government has to take the primary and leading role, of which political parties are an integral part. Nevertheless, NGOs and civil society are playing a useful role in bringing contested issues into public debate, exploring options and alternatives to reach negotiated settlement, collecting local peace agenda, etc. Some of the NGOs are actively working in addressing poverty and exclusion, empowerment of women, dalit, and marginalized people. The role of human rights organisations is crucial to defend basic rights of Nepalese people and to work as a 'watch dog' on the issues of human rights abuses.

8.17 DEVELOPMENT SCENARIOS

The development sector may face a difficult time in near future.

- Small, transparent, quick impact poverty focused infrastructure development projects/activities face less difficulties than social mobilisation focused and big projects. Big infrastructure projects may face difficulties because of transportation of construction materials, restriction on fetching of some materials like pipes blasting materials, etc. by security forces.
- High-sounding social inclusion and advocacy-related activities might face more problems.
- Software types of social mobilisation projects may face more difficulties in future.
- Reduced state budget in development.
- Weak capacity of the state to spend on development budget[40].
- Retardation in on-going development process.

Though it is difficult to predict, development in coming years will face significant changes in terms of its approach strategy, focus and activities. In the case of a strengthened autocracy development strategy and planning will be more centralised. on the contrary, if the political system is a democratic republic or co-existence of all forces, development will be redefined. However, it is not possible for any type of rule to ignore some of the issues to be addressed by development intervention such as regional disparity, economic inequalities, legal and social injustice, etc. Hence, in future development activities will focus on equity and poverty, reconciliation and rehabilitation.

8.18 NEED OF CONFLICT-SENSITIVE DEVELOPMENT RESPONSE

1. Social inclusion is a process of overcoming functional, institutional and policy barriers at macro and micro levels to increase the access of poor, marginalized and backward people to the development opportunities. Changes in incentive systems and improved capacity of the state and community are requisites of the social inclusion. Effective social inclusion leads to political, social and economic empowerment. Social inclusion must be a priority with a clear institutional mechanism and operational arrangement to ensure inclusion of excluded, to address poverty, inequality, injustice and discriminations, and employment generation in the project area. Social inclusion is far wider than the approach of social mobilisation. When tangible benefits to poorest, landless and marginalized people are assured, several risks related to social tensions and potential manipulations by insurgents can be minimised.
2. Development projects and programmes have to address concerns of landless, marginalized, indigenous and disadvantaged people. Projects not addressing these concerns could potentially face difficulties in the midst of implementation, as the insurgents often target those projects whose activities are not focused to these groups of people. In the current conflict situation, development projects and programmes have to strengthen and expand the initiatives to address issues and concerns of marginalized and disadvantaged groups.
3. Implementation staff needs to be selected locally from women, ethnic community, *dalit*, and poor. Similarly, engage community-level organisations, local clubs, and networks as local partners where appropriate. Employing local poor people in infrastructure project work helps to reduce poverty as they work as buffers between development projects and insurgents.
4. Flexibility is one of the fundamental principles in implementing projects in a situation of escalated conflict. Development projects and programmes need to be flexible in modus operandi and project management at local levels.

5. Conflict analysis (CA), conflict risks assessment (CRA), including peace and conflict impact assessment (PCIA) (CPN, 1999) need to be made compulsory provisions in regular project performance monitoring system, yearly reviews and periodic evaluations of any development project and programme. PCIA provides methodology and conceptual orientation to minimise negative effects of conflict, build harmony and provide opportunity to generate new prospects for peaceful coexistence in the changing political and security landscape within which the project has to operate. Periodic feedback mechanism into ongoing project management is essential. Train staff on Do-No-Harm principles (Anderson, 1999). It has to further intensify training on Do-No-Harm principles to all staff and implementing partners.
6. Any organisation working in conflict zones can influence the conflict dynamics positively or negatively. The positive or negative influence can be examined by the notion of connectors (those activities which positively influence the conflict dynamics, prevent fuelling the conflict) and dividers (those activities which negatively influence the conflict dynamics and consequently contribute to escalating conflict). For example, working with the poorest people in a transparent and accountable way helps to positively influence the conflict dynamics. On the other hand, resource capture by elites, concentration of development activities in accessible areas, biases towards certain power groups, manipulation or misuse of rules and regulations to justify ill intentions of power brokers, abuses of project resources and other malpractices are some examples of the dividers.
7. Development projects and programmes have to develop and implement operational guidelines (for example, Security Instructions for Guards, Security Procedure Manual, Travel Tips, Responding to Violence in the Operating Environment, Crisis Management Guidelines, etc.) to minimise conflict-related risks. Conflict dynamics is changing very fast and such guidelines need constant update, changes or adaptation. Project and programme should constantly monitor and adapt the guidelines according to the changing situation. One of the main operational problems in implementing development activities at local level is 'suspicion' and resultant risk from

security forces. Hence, development projects may need to proactively work to create a central level "Conflict Risk Management Committee" representing senior officials from Home Ministry, Defence Ministry, Royal Nepal Army, Armed Police Force, Nepal Police, NGO-Federations, Associations of DDCs and VDCs. This committee would make sure that implementing local organisations or staff working in the project do not face obstruction from security forces or help to overcome potential future difficulties. Donor agencies and development partners need to collectively work to establish similar mechanism at district level with the representation of security forces, civil society organisations, DDC, CDO, District Police Chief, and other appropriate institutions. This will minimise perceived and actual risks of project staff and partners to implement programme in field.

8. Basic Operating Guidelines of AIN, 14-point Basic Operational Guidelines of 10 donors, UN Operational Guidelines and Operating Guidelines of NGO Federation are some of the main guiding framework at operational levels to minimise conflict risks. These guidelines clearly state their position on conflict. Development project needs to practice regular conflict analysis, disclosure policy and distance monitoring systems.
9. Recruit local facilitators (male/female) from local NGOs and community-based organizations (CBOs), preferably from lower castes, ethnic groups, and women, to facilitate project activities. They can generally operate better than outsider staff, as they are familiar with the context and able to locally negotiate.
10. From the risk management perspective, considering increasingly unpredictable situation in the foreseeable future, risk-related information gathering, management and communication need more co-ordinated efforts. Make systematic efforts in coaching, orientating and training staff and partners in neutrality and operational risk management.
11. Create a flexible 'Rapid Response Mechanism' and make funds available to facilitate emergency response. In case of higher risk for project or its staff being direct target, resources are required for evacuation, trauma counselling, and other emergency measures.
12. Maintaining transparency at all levels (central level, project, implementing partners and users) is one of the main principles

in operating development intervention at the time of conflict. A transparent financial operation system accessible to social auditing and public scrutiny is essential to minimise the potential corruption/irregularities and threats from the insurgents. The experiences of different projects and INGOs and other projects working in the conflict zones have clearly demonstrated that if the projects are transparent, using public/social auditing[41] and geographical auditing[42], they are less affected. Hence, these lessons need to be replicated and institutionalised.

13. The political situation and conflict dynamics is changing so rapidly. Hence, it is not possible to predict a stable scenario. Therefore, development projects should develop scenario-based ('worst-case', 'best-case' and other scenarios) contingency plan both at operational and strategic levels.
14. Proper understanding of conflict and security situation, and appropriate skills of dealing with it are key factors for successful implementation of project in the conflict zones. Development projects have to further expand training project and partner staff in conflict and security risks assessment, conflict monitoring, risk mitigation, trauma counselling and evacuation, Do-No-Harm, peace building, dealing with insurgents and security forces and assessing security behaviour.
15. Development projects and programmes have to assist local communities. They have to provide them technical, financial or other supports to implement the need-based and quick impacting activities proposed by them. These activities should directly address root causes of the conflict.
16. The content of the development interventions should be focused on poor and marginalized groups to provide more and direct economic opportunities. The content also has to promote local people to be engaged in their self-employment activities that address poverty, one of the root causes of the present conflict in Nepal.
17. Capacity building of local communities and CBOs in coping with conflict should be part of the development projects and programmes. Local people have to be involved in mediating creatively, dynamically and locally to ensure the rights of communities.
18. Development intervention needs to focus on reducing power

imbalance. Addressing power imbalances requires strengthening weaker actors by providing new economic alternatives. Equipped with better information, new analytical skills and stronger network will enhance the actors' knowledge thereby gaining power. The powerful actors will realise that power abuse will not be tolerated any more. Under such conditions, stakeholders become increasingly prepared to negotiate and collaborate with others. Regardless of initial differences, stakeholders will be able to identify or build common ground for dialogue. Inclusion of excluded requires a process of selecting excluded from each area to support through development intervention. A process needs to be facilitated in favour of selecting the poor, marginalised and dalits to enhance the access of those categories in a formal decision-making body. With the active engagement of users in critical reflection and learning, existing elite domination in benefit sharing, representation and governance systems need to be re-examined. This will result in some mechanism for institutionalisation of inclusion of previously excluded sections of the communities especially poor, dalit and women. One of the important ways of addressing the root causes of the conflict is to ensure equity in benefit sharing. A process to create sensitivity among the poor, dalit and women is essential.

19. While working in the conflict-affected districts/areas development programme activities have to foster reconciliation, reintegration and rehabilitation through concerted action by the communities. In the situation of escalated conflict, need of reconstruction and rehabilitation of social and physical infrastructures is an often-expected activity, which requires concerted efforts of all actors (particularly donors). Hence, development programmes may need to be active to address this issue through a Multi-Donor Support Facility. There is a need to engage in a debate of addressing humanitarian crisis and rehabilitation and reconstruction of social and physical infrastructure. Development projects need to rebuild damaged infrastructure at local level.

NOTES

1. See Samaya Weekly (Year 2, No 63, Ashad 17-23, 2062/1-7 July 2005) for the detail story.
2. The mission was led by Dennis McNamara, accompanied by Carmen van Heese (IDD) and Romano Lasker (CRD).
3. *Source – Global IDP Database, Norwegian Refugee Council*
4. However, the official estimate of the government is 6000-7000 IDPs only.
5. The security forces suspect as supporter of the Maoists and Maoists suspect as informants.
6. Since 1st February 2005 all these three countries temporarily suspended the military assistance citing the reason of the royal takeover as a setback to democracy. However, their stand is now gradually changing over time and they have started to supply non-lethal weapons and equipment.
7. See *Samaya* Weekly, Year 2 Vol. 59, Jestha 20-26, 2062, Pp 37-38.
8. Ibid
9. Including foreign aid for security expenses (US Aid: 1.33 billion; UK: 780 million; India: 3.2 billion and additional 1.6 billion rupees)
10. With adjusted estimates of Rs. 2 billion for Maoist army expenses,
11. Loss due to damage in infrastructure construction: 20 billion,
12. Loss due to closure of agriculture production and cottage industries,
13. Though huge amount of remittance is earned, it is not a preferred option for people to leave country due to insecurity and conflict.
14. Samaya Weekly, 2005, Year 2, Vol 69, 12 August 2005, page 41.
15. For example, 39 police posts existed in Rolpa were reduced to 2 in 2000 and 23 police posts of Rukum were reduced to 2 in 2000 (Seddon and Hussein, 2002).
16. See Policy Paper of HMG/N on Surrender, 2061 BS for detail.
17. This estimate is based on : a. Hobaji Hatiyarko, Samaya Weekly, Kathmandu,Jesth 7, 2061. b. Shahi Senama Dui Pritana ra Panch Bahini Thapine, Space Time Daily, Kathmandu, Asar 25, 2061.
18. The supreme commander of the Maoist Prachanda in his interview to 'Jandesh Weekly, 17 Kartik 2055' said they have three sources of obtaining arms as: (a) snatched from enemies, (b) produced by the party' experience and (c) purchased.
19. Former MP Mr Hirandya Lal Shrestha has stated this situation in his research report (Shrestha, 2061BS).
20. The areas adjacent to the large quantity opium producers Myanmar, Thailand and Laos of South East Asia.
21. Iran, Afghanistan and Pakistan, where the largest quantity of opium is produced in the world.
22. See Kantipur Daily 22 Ashoj 2062 (8 October 2005) for details.
23. Interviewed with them on 13-22 September 2005.
24. See *Samaya Weekly*, *Nepal Weekly* and *Himal Fortnightly* for the detaiedl story on how Maoists are controlling the protected areas. These news

magazines have also reported that government staff are absent in some of the parks or reserves since 2 years.

25. Different issues of *Hakkahaki Partika* (an environmental magazine) report the terrible impacts of the ongoing armed conflict in environment, natural resource and protected areas.
26. United nations Working Group on Enforced and Involuntary Disappearance on 1st March 2005 said that in 2003-2004 Nepal scored highest in the world for new cases of disappearance.
27. e.g. LLINK project of HELVITAS,
28. United Mission to Nepal form Dailekh, and Jajarkot Poverty Reduction Project of CARE Nepal (in 1998),
29. e.g., Netherlands Development Organisation (SNV) in Karnali,
30. e.g., The Mountain Institute office in Sankhuwasawa, GTZ office in Bhojpur and CARE-Nepal offices in Achham and Bajura.
31. e.g., Rural Develop Programme- Gorkha
32. The respondents were ordinary farmers; small growers; traders and marketers as well as rural landlords and local elites who left their villages due to insecurity and staying in Kathmandu.
33. The incidence happened in 23 Baishakh 2061 BS (5 May 2004).
34. Maoists attacked district headquarters of Khotang on 21 June 2005 (11 Ashad 2062) where 11 government offices were damaged (Nepal Weekly, Year 5, No 64, 19 Ashad 2062 (3 July 2005).
35. See Nepal Weekly Year 5, No 45 (26 June 2005/12 Ashad 2062) for the detail story.
36. For example, in the "Peace Budget" of FY 2061/62, Deuba government allocated 0.5 billion rupees for the rehabilitation of conflict victim and expected to obtained 1.5 billion rupees from donors. However, public does not know the outcome of this programme.
37. CPN-UML had prepared a document entitled 'Proposal of National Consensus for a Progressive Way Out' which was endorsed by Central Committee of the CPN-UML held from April 21 to 27, 2003.
38. On - January 10, 2004, CPN-UML had prepared a Roadmap, which they called The Proposal for Resolution of National Problem.
39. Five major political parties - the CPN-UML, Nepali Congress, United People's Front, Nepal Peasant Worker's Party and Nepal Sadvawana Party (Anandidevi)- were leading a national people's movement in the country. They came out with 18 points *'Forward Looking Reform Agenda'* which address the current problems of the country. These 18 points were endorsed by a special session of the dissolved Parliament in July 2004. According to the parties, the present impasses of the country can only be resolved by implementing the 18 points *'Forward Looking Reform Agenda'*. Later CPN-UML joined the government leaving and remaining 4 parties continued this agitating until January 2005.
40. For example, in FY 2061/62 the government allocated Rs 32 billions out

of 115 billions for development but the actual development expenditure is less than 15 billions (*Samaya Weekly*, Year 2, No 64, 24-30 Ashar, 2062, page 33).

41. Making all financial provisions and programme activities, including staff and partners selection publicly available (by preparing small broachers, displaying these information on public notice boards in public places, wall magazine etc.),
42. Examining whether the programme activities are reached to remote, neglected and marginalized areas and poor, disadvantaged and socially excluded people and making sure that these programme activities and benefits reach to them.

CHAPTER 9

Requirements for Successful Negotiation of the Armed Conflict

9.1 INTRODUCTION

The 1st February 2005 Royal takeover virtually turned the already shaken infant democracy into an unprecedented political crisis. In the past the government did not take the insurrection seriously. Rather, the palace, the government and the parliamentary political parties used the insurrection as a means to grab power and minimize the political opponents (Karki and Kattel, 2005; Dahal, 2004; Upreti, 2004a; Karki and Seddon, 2003). This strategy ultimately backfired on the palace and the political parties and the Maoists became the absolute gainer. Even when the Maoists scaled up their activities, strengthened their military base, expanded their activities geographically and defeated the police force in several confrontations, the legitimate power centres did not realize the severity of the insurgency. The then governments constituted two commissions (i.e., Dhami Commission 1997 and Deuba Commission 2000) to advise the government to resolve the Maoist conflict; and both the commissions drew similar conclusions, i.e., the insurrection is of a political nature, therefore the governments should deal with it politically. These reports further stressed that this conflict cannot be solved without addressing the root causes of the conflict[1]. However, the subsequent governments did not properly follow the recommendations and continuously used the insurgency as a means of gaining and strengthening power. Further, after 4 October 2002, all the nominated royalist governments used the Maoist insurrection as the best means to weaken the nascent democracy.

After the failure of two negotiations (2001 and 2003), a debate on critical examination of the negotiation process, conditions of success and failure of such negotiation and basic requirements for a successful negotiation was started. This chapter sheds some light on the conditions for successful negotiation of the ongoing armed conflict and the structures required to achieve the desired results from the negotiation.

9.2 CONDITIONS FOR SUCCESSFUL NEGOTIATION OF THE NEPAL'S ARMED CONFLICT

9.2.1 Polarisation of existing power relations

A new polarisation is essential to resolve this conflict. The polarisation discussed here is the polarisation between those who want democratic peace and prosperity of the nation and those who want war and a strengthened autocracy. Democratic peace must be the mission as well as operational agenda of parliamentary parties and they must work to achieve this mission by concerted action for a peaceful resolution, refining their vision and perspective on reaching a negotiated settlement and promoting internal democracy. Achieving democratic peace requires a drastic change in their current approach, conceptual understanding and risk-bearing ability. If the polarisation sharpens between the above categories, it helps to tackle the main issue of contention (i.e., constituent assembly election), which ultimately address the major factors of Nepalese crisis (demands of the Maoists as well as new challenges posed by the first February 2005 royal takeover).

9.2.2 Trust building

Distrust is massively pervasive in the present Nepalese politics. It is destroying the political process and fuelling endemic conflict. Putnam (1993) in his book entitled 'Making Democracy Work' highlights the fundamental roles of trust in the democratisation process. Social capital is an important feature of society reflected in social network, norms, trusts, and faith. It is essential to promote civic engagement, public participation, mutual learning, concerted action to achieve negotiation and political stability (Upreti, 2004a). The current conflict between the king and the parliamentary parties proved that mistrust is detrimental to strengthening the democratic process. Trust is very fragile. Building trust takes considerable time and efforts. However, it can be eroded by a single mistake (e.g., royal takeover of February 2005) and in some cases; lost trust may never be rebuilt. Trust is a binding force of civil society building and functional democracy.

Now priority of all the actors must be to rebuild trust through collaboration, dialogue, and collective action. The Maoists must end violence and resume and sustain ceasefire that proves their commitment to peaceful negotiation. The palace must realise that it cannot solve the extremely complicated political crisis alone by undermining political parties, civil society and international community. It could greatly contribute to reaching a negotiated settlement if it agrees to establish supremacy and sovereignty of people, i.e., accept people's decisions on making a constitution through elected representatives of people. The civil society and most of the political parties have agreed to constitutional assembly election. If the palace continues with the current approach it will isolate Nepal from the international community, increase confrontation with civil society and political parties and ultimately worsen the political situation of Nepal.

Now three major actors are deeply suffering from perceived risk. The palace has perceived risk of possibility for republican state if the constituent assembly election is agreed to. Parliamentary political parties have developed a perceived risk of being undermined and sidelined by the Maoists or the palace. The Maoists have developed a perceived risk of possible suppression by the collective efforts of parliamentary parties and the palace. Consequently, they are not willing to enter into constructive dialogues to resolve the conflict. In this context, the parliamentary parties must initiate dialogue with the palace and the rebels.

9.2.3 People's participation in peace process

When public engagement in the peace process is ignored, success is rare (Barnes, 2002), Even if, by any chance, negotiated settlement of the ongoing armed conflict is achieved, it is temporary. The general public may not own elite-guided peace negotiation, if people are not participating in the peace process. If the peace talk is brought into the public sphere, it promotes transparency and accountability, enhances constructive dialogue, and gets public support and ownership. African examples in war and peace sufficiently tell us that peace in a war-torn society is seldom permanent when real civic engagement is not promoted. Achievement of viable and lasting peace is only possible when the capacity of local people is utilised and complemented by the efforts of government, parliamentary political parties, Maoists, human rights organisations, media, and other peace actors.

The important question is how to promote people's participation in Nepalese peace process. One of the potential answers would be to promote peace advocacy/lobbying and massive campaigns at local levels in a non-partisan way. If political parties are honest and sincere to peaceful settlement they can use their entire local party committee structures for collecting people's peace agenda and debating on it. There can be organisation of other civil society peace committees. People's Solidarity for Peace, *Shantimalika*-like national umbrella structures are already active in promoting peace and their work should be further expanded to organise civil society peace committees. Several civil society initiatives discussed in Chapter Five can be further promoted. Resources flow to community for peace campaigns would be more meaningful than fashionable, elite-biased, formality-focused, activities mainly concentrated in city centres.

Nepal should learn an important lesson from the role played by the civil societies and the people's participation in the settlement of the violent conflict in South Africa and Ireland. Peace committees should be formed in all villages, peace volunteers should be mobilized and different programs should be organized to help achieve peace. All the party structures or networks from the grass-roots to central committees of all political parties should work as peace committees and contribute to promoting peace. Since it is impossible to get success in peace talks without a conducive and congenial environment, initiative should be taken towards dialogue for the creation of such environment. The civil societies should unite to raise voices against the violent activities of both the state and the Maoists.

Similarly, talks or dialogues cannot be successful without the withering away of the environment of fear and terror of violence in villages. So, it is necessary to create positive pressure on both the Maoists and security forces. The media plays a crucial role in this regard. The media sector should bring different perspectives, theories, alternatives and experiences in debate to contribute to reaching a political settlement of the conflict and restoring peace.

Women's representatives must be members of the negotiating team in both parties to appropriately address the concerns and issues of women. Similarly, participation of dalit, ethnic group and socially excluded people in the negotiation team increases the level of acceptance of the agreement and appropriately incorporates the concerns and demands of these communities in the peace agreement.

9.2.4 Mobilization of external supports

As explained in preceding chapters, hundreds of armed conflicts and devastating wars have already taken place in the world in the 20th century and they have also been settled. The world has gained rich experiences in conflict settlement. Nepal must learn from these lessons and experiences. The UN has played very important roles in the settlement of conflict in different countries and gained great experience. So, Nepal should use experiences of the UN. There cannot be any other interest in the UN helping Nepal in the settlement of present conflict. Similarly, the European Community has a lot of experience in conflict settlement and it is also ready to help if Nepal wants it to. The 'International Crisis Group' also wishes to see peace in Nepal and to share its experience with Nepal. But the present government does not like to import and use such experiences by involving celebrated neutral international organizations like the UN, or the European Community or such others in conflict settlement. The main reason for this is the apprehension of the possibility of voices against the violation of human rights, or may not be acquired as desired and may need to abide by the internationally established values and norms. And the other reason is the objection of India.

9.2.5 Learning from experiences and mistakes

Nepal could learn from the experiences of successful conflict management in other countries. Both the conflicting parties of Nepal are not interested to learn from domestic and international experiences. They are not yet ready to show their flexibility and sincere commitment to peace and respect people's desire for peace as was the case in South Africa. F.W.D. Clerk from government side and leader Nelson Mandela from the rebels' in South Africa took a courageous decision to respect people's desire for peace. Different parties of South Africa showed extraordinary unity in the settlement of the conflict. The government and political parties had sent three representatives each from their part and formed a high-level peace committee. The committee formed different sub-committees. They prepared a comprehensive proposal and got it approved by National Peace Convention (Barnes, 2002).

This document became the main basis of the settlement of conflict. However, in Nepal political parties stayed indifferent at the time of 2003 negotiation period, saying, "Talks are held between the government and the rebels, we have nothing to give or take, what we can do, we can offer only good wishes". Similarly, government also did not make sincere efforts to bring political parties on board for the negotiation. Rather, the government while negotiating with the Maoists at that time was buying time and prolonging the process. Instead, the political parties, the Maoists and the government should have learned from South Africa.

In the process of conflict settlement in South Africa, 15 thousand peace volunteers were mobilized in villages, 11 regional and 260 local peace committees, church councils, businessmen and leading personalities of societies were active for peace in South Africa. The concerted efforts of all these actors finally achieved a durable peace and now this country is working for reconciliation and social development.

Similarly, in Guatemala the role of political parties and civil societies was very effective in the settlement of the 36 year-long conflict which had taken the life of more than 150 thousand and displaced more than 1 million people. Political parties and civil societies had formed 'Grand National Dialogue', 'National Consensus Forum' and 'Civil Society Assembly' (Armon, *et al.,* 1997) to facilitate peace process. The main issues of the conflict were settled through these structures. National Reconciliation Commission was formed and made active in the peace process. In Guatemala, civil societies and political leaders explored and agreed on a common agenda by organising several intercommunity meetings. They had played an instrumental role in the settlement of 1990-'96 conflict and in making the peace talks a success. The international nongovernmental organizations like Red Barna and UNDP had also helped in that peace process (Armon, *et al.,* 1997).

In Mali, peace talks had become successful due to the pressure and initiative of the people. After the settlement of the conflict, the Malian people had burnt the all the weapons used in the conflict by organizing a grand program naming it 'Flame of Peace' on March 27, 1997 (Barnes, 2002). But in Nepal, not much of such efforts have been seen. Why does not Nepal learn from such useful experiences?

A conflict started in Ireland since its independence in 1921 due to the decisions of six provinces to remain with Britain had taken in violent form by 1960. Civil societies and women communities had played a central role to bring the conflict to the Belfast Agreement (Good Friday Agreement) concluded in 1999 (McCartney, 1999). Different social groups such as 'Women Coalition, 'Civic Forum, etc. had not only created pressure for peace in Northern Ireland but also presented peace proposals for agreement. Why cannot a common consensus for peace be found in Nepal?

The conflict started in Mozambique after its independence from Portugal in 1974, was settled on October 4, 9192 through the understanding of political parties and initiatives of civil societies. Peace talks were held in Nairobi, Lusaka and Rome at different times by dint of pressure (Armon *et al.,* 1998).

Similarly, in the Philippines, citizens and civil society leaders including many social organizations had declared a 'Peace zone' and even forwarded 'Six ways for peace-program' in the efforts to settle the conflict, which was perpetrated by America in the Mindanao region of the Philippines. 'National Unification Commission Advisory Committee', 'My Civic Society', 'Peace Campaign Group', Peace Advocacy People's Group' were formed to create pressure on the warring parties to hold peace talks (Stankovitch, 1999). In the same way, in Liberia different groups such as 'Liberian Interfaith Mediation Committee', 'Ceasefire Monitoring Committee', Friends of Liberia', etc. are working for peace and settlement of the conflict that started in 1989 (Armon and Carl, 1996). But why should not a common single proposal be prepared from a consensus of all political parties, religious and civil society leaders, human rights activists, experts in Nepal to settle this crisis?

9.3 ENVISIONING SHORT-TERM, MEDIUM-TERM AND LONG-TERM STRATEGY

Conclusions of the structural, proximate and external causes of the Maoist insurgency have already been drawn from the explanations, analysis and discussions in different chapters of this book. Politicians, parliamentary parties, government, foreign diplomatic dignitaries, experts, civil societies, etc. have accepted the reality that the present state structure: governing processes, constitution and laws, rules and regulations cannot address the basic causes of the conflict and they need fundamental changes. Such change means, change in social, religious, economic, political and legal structures, which is not possible without national consensus and massive participation of the people.

So, short-term, mid-term and long-term strategies are necessary for such structural reforms. Proposals/ schema forwarded by the government to the Maoists at the previous talks, the proposals forwarded by the Maoists to the government, the 18-point proposal jointly prepared by the five parliamentary parties, 35-point proposal put forth by the CPN (UML), proposal of United Left Front, Proposal prepared by Nepali Congress and the proposals of other political parties have already included such strategies. But sufficient homework has not been done about how to implement them. So, all the proposals should be used as a basis of discussions to make common national agenda. As the role of political parties becomes crucial in multiparty system, they should take the lead to make durable and democratic peace by formulating short-term (ceasefire, peace talks and negotiation), medium-term (state restructuring process, formulating constitution, post-conflict reconstructions, etc.) and long-term strategies (economic and social reform) to restore peace, democracy and prosperity of Nepal.

9.4 DIFFERENT PHASES OF NEGOTIATION

Successful negotiation needs phase-wise specific tasks that have to be accomplished by the parties involved in the negotiation process (negotiators and their respective parties, facilitators or mediators, supporters, the state and other as appropriate). Negotiation is both an art and a science, which requires huge preparation, strong commitment, clear conceptual understanding and specific skills, as well as appropriate structures and arrangements. In this section tasks to be performed in different phases of negotiation have been discussed.

9.4.1 Preparation phase

In the situation of ongoing armed conflict, the urge of the general public is to hold peace talk in an environment of ceasefire, as it provides temporary peace to people and a favourable environment for the negotiators (however, negotiation can be continued without ceasefire). Therefore, the state should first withdraw the terrorist tag, cases and the red-corner notice issued against the Maoist leaders. Then the government, the Maoist party and the other parliamentary political parties should reach a consensus, ceasefire agreement and the government and the Maoist should jointly declare ceasefire in witness of some credible national or international organisations (such as NHRC,

OHCHR, ICRC, EU, UNDP, etc.). In the ceasefire agreement, a Code of Conduct to be abided by the warring sides should be included, which at least covers suspension of military activities of both sides, fair use of media, prohibition of abduction of people, stopping of extortion and cessation of violent activities. Besides, the ceasefire agreement has to ensure the constitution of 'Ceasefire and Code of Conduct Monitoring Committee' involving representatives of political parties, civil society and international experts and defining its modus operandi.

9.4.2 Ceasefire phase

Both the warring sides should abide by the aforementioned agreement. As there may appear different obstacles, 'Code of Conduct Monitoring Committee' should remain active to prevent or overcome them. A committee involving senior leaders of political parties, government authority, civil society leaders, human rights leaders and senior security officials should be formed to help the Monitoring Committee and facilitate to overcome any obstacles and deadlocks. This committee should take initiative to find a political solution in case any difficulty arises in the ceasefire situation. Since the rebels may get into crises of food, financial sources and daily necessities during the ceasefire period, arrangement should be made to supply such necessities through external assistance to rebels.

While looking into the history of the conflict-torn countries around the world, we find ceasefires have taken place in situations where:

- any change occurs within the ruling political circle,
- the head of state wants to change executive or government,
- the chief of rebels' side and the head of state or government reached any level of understanding with or without external pressure,
- differences widen within ruling party regarding its government and the party wanted to change the government,
- government or rebels came to the conclusion from internal assessment that stopping war would be strategically and operationally more beneficial to their side than continuing it,
- civil societies exert strong pressure,
- the conflicting sides realize the possibility of being isolated from general public and international community,
- any national festival or internal program approached or organized, and

- warring parties reach an understanding among themselves to have ceasefire.

Experiences of conflict-ridden countries such as Northern Ireland, Kosovo, Chechnya, Eastern Yugoslavia, Kuwait, Israel, Palestine, Vietnam, Cambodia, Sri Lanka, Nepal, Guatemala, Columbia, Peru, Nicaragua, Al Salvador, Mozambique, Congo, Sierra Leone, South Africa, Uganda, Burundi, Mali, Algeria, Sudan, Nigeria, East Timor, Ethiopia, Eritrea and Tazkistan show that most of the ceasefires (unilateral, bilateral, event-specific, whichever they are) have been declared for strategic reasons (Abdullaev, and Barnes, 2001; Armon, and Carl, 1996; Armon, and Philipson, 1998; Armon, *et al.,* 1998; Armon *et al.,* 1997; Barnes, 2002; Carl, A. and Garasu, 2002; Conen, 1999; Crandall, 2004; Garcia- Duran, 2004; Hendrickson, 1998; Lord, 2000; Lucima, 2002; McCartney, 1999; Putnam, 1993; Stankovitch, 1999; Lode, 2002; Macrae, 2002; Misra, 2002; Senghaas, 2001; Susskind & Cruikshank 1987 and Upreti, 2004a). Some of them have been used for peace talks and out of them only a few have become partially successful.

9.4.3 Preparatory Phase for Negotiation

The lessons of failed negotiations in Sri Lanka (Armon and Philipson, 1998), Guatemala (Armon *et al.*, 1997), Papua New Guinea (Carl and Garasu, 2002), Nepal (Upreti and Dhungana, 2004), Liberia (Armon and Carl, 1996) and Mozambique (Armon *et al.,* 1998) are that peace talks without full preparation and commitment can not be successful. So, full preparation with appropriate facilitation is essential to make the peace talk a success. The government should develop consensus with political parties and obtain support from civil society and international community. It should also involve National Human Rights Commission and international human rights organisations to monitor the human rights situation. Further, institutionalization of the negotiation process is extremely essential. A special negotiation facilitation committee composed of senior representatives of the government, leaders of civil society, negotiation and conflict management experts, leaders of political parties, needs to be formed. This committee will make all the necessary preparations for the success of the talk, take necessary caution, and provide necessary information to negotiators and co-ordinate with the government, the Maoist and other political parties as well as the international community. It works to create a congenial environment for the talks.

9.4.4 Negotiation Phase

Internationally recognized norms, values and principles established by the experiences of resolution of hundreds of conflicts were not used in the previous two negotiations in Nepal. Since the negotiation related to the settlement of armed conflict becomes very sensitive, it should not be media oriented. Only after having reached the conclusions of very complicated subjects through secret and informal talks, it should be taken to formal negotiating table. If negotiation is started discussing about 'position', it does not get success. The same happened in the past talks. So, negotiation should be based on 'need'. Informal talks greatly help in building confidential environment and to find mid-way solution (Curle, 1971; 1987; 1996).

The Maoist negotiators in 2002 peace talks repeatedly said to enter into political agenda, and if agreed on the issue of constituent assembly, other issues would be easily settled. However, this is not as simple as said and therefore it is not the right approach to reaching a negotiation according to negotiation principles. First, they have to be discussing other less complicated issues which could be relatively easy to agree and implement during the process of negotiation. By doing so, it will develop confidence. Even when they agree upon 'constituent assembly' election in principle, there are several contentious questions to be resolved by the negotiators like, 'how', by whom, when' and 'with whose help'. There would be several possible obstacles and social, economic and administrative issues to be dealt with at the negotiation table, which are equally tough and beyond constituent assembly questions. So, it would be naive of the Maoist negotiators to expect that all other issues will be settled if the constituent assembly election issue is settled.

Even after having political agreement in Mozambique, Liberia and Guatemala, the political agreement had not come into effect due to procedural complexity (Barnes, 2002; Armon *et al.,* 1997; Armon *et al.,* 1998). In Liberia, the 'Katonah' agreement was concluded in February 1994 for settlement of the conflict, but the conflict again flared up due to dispute over the question of participation in the transitional government (Armon and Carl, 1995). In Nepal also, political consensus was created in the 1990 democratic movement. But the present sorry state appeared due to the absence of clear process to lead the nation towards socio-economic transformation. Therefore, only political consensus cannot be sufficient. Political consensus and processes can be compared with the skeleton and muscles of our body respectively.

As the talk for the end of war and settlement of armed conflict becomes very complicated, fragile and lengthy, it needs meticulous efforts, sensitivity and commitment (Kleiboer, 1996 and 1998; Kriesberg, 1998; Miall, 1992 and 2001; Miall *et al.,* 1999; Reychler and Paffenholf 2001; Rose and Rothman, 1999; Rubin, 1980 and 1981; Sunders, 1996; Schmid, 1997; Wher, 1979; Wher *et al.,* 1994). Such efforts need to be held at both informal and formal levels. According to the strategy of shuttle diplomacy, it becomes necessary to held repeated talks at different levels. At first, informal talks are necessary to create a conducive environment, decrease differences and agree to procedural arrangements. Some important tasks to be carefully done during the negotiation phase are:

- To take help of experts by negotiators for alternatives/options,
- To address complexities if appeared in the negotiation,
- To use internationally recognized processes and procedures,
- To document and institutionalise decisions reached at the negotiation table by signing from the both sides of negotiators and witnessed by facilitators or mediators,
- Not to release all the decisions made to media (particularly if they are sensitive and fragile issues) forthwith while the negotiation is going on. If revealing sensitive and fragile issues agreed upon by the negotiators during the negotiation period could be detrimental in further proceeding with the negotiation process, particularly if media distrusts or disagree with the agreed points in negotiation.
- To inform public about the achievements about negotiation ensuring that it will get public support and create a positive environment,
- To appoint a spokesman for properly providing information to the media, to keep other negotiators and facilitators far from the media, and
- To implement the agreed upon points immediately to bring positive effects on the ongoing negotiation process.

In short, if a meaningful talk is to be held, consensus should be created on the political question and talks should be started conforming to the internationally recognized proceedings and processes. Successful negotiation means successful result in settling political crisis. So the priority of the king, Maoists, and political parties should be a successful negotiation. If the negotiation becomes successful with the agreement to bring about basic changes in the political/state structure, the 'retrogression' being voiced by the parliamentary parties will be addressed. So, all those who love the nation and those who are sensitive to the terrible situation that has already taken the life of more than 14 thousand Nepalese, should give top priority to peace talk and help to make the talk a success.

The deteriorating political and economic situation of the country has been intimately realised by all political forces of the country. However, they are not clear on how to get rid of this situation. They are confused, searching options for ways out by ensuring their positions and interests. If they are confused and searching for ways to resolve the crisis, it is a most opportune time for them (Maoists, king and political parties) to act for restoration of peace and democracy in the country.

If the government continues its conventional approach to bringing about peace through 'war', the crises will go on deepening and at that time the Nepalese will have to face an unexpected situation of foreign intervention. The present political crisis has developed into a critical situation. The Coalition government led by Deuba in 2004 continued the brutal approach of 'peace through war', which has greatly contributed to worsening the situation where CPN UML was a major coalition partner[2]. If the government continues the strategy to crush the Maoists by mobilizing security forces, it will get into unprecedented crises. Instead, if it could find a peaceful solution by taking civil society, security forces, Maoists and political parties in confidence, the government will reap a great political benefit. However, it is unlikely. The long-term existence of the monarchy depends on its relations with political parties and restoration of peace in the country.

The urge of the general public, civil society and a greater part of international community is for peace talks paired with ceasefire. But a very small invisible force linked with arm traders want to continue and escalate conflict. This invisible force has become an obstacle as well as challenge to peace.

The arm mafia has remained active to violate peace agreements. The violations of "Loma Agreement" on the settlement of Sierra Leone conflict reached on May 25, 1999 (Lord, 2000), the"Yomao-4 Agreement" reached on the settlement of Liberian conflict signed in

October–December were perpetrated by the network of arms traders (Ricigliano, 2005). It has always remained active against peace and for breach of agreements. The arms mafia has also used the governments of concerned countries, security forces, political parties and some persons of the international power centres.

9.5 ACTIONS NEEDED TO BE PERFORMED BY MAJOR FORCES TO REACH NEGOTIATED SETTLEMENT

In this section, a brief list of major activities to be performed by concerned actors is presented in a tabular form. Though this is not an exhaustive list of the works to be done by the important actors to change the conflict dynamics, the following table provides some important areas of intervention.

Concerned parties	To be done in the first phase (before formal peace talk)	To be done in the second phase (During peace talk to make it successful)
Palace	Change the current approach work as constitutional monarch Giving up power and collaborate with political parties Accept the role of political parties Prohibit activities of hard lincr monarchists which obstruct co-llaboration with political parties and restore peace	Agree to discuss all issues including the existence of monarchy subject to the decision of Nepalese people.
The govern-ment and security force	Create conducive environment for collaboration with political parties and work to reach negotiated settlement Take primary responsibility to make the talk a success Appointment of facilitators Withdrawal of terrorist tag and red corner notice, cases and security guarantee of the Maoists negotiators Making public the whereabouts of disappeared/arrested people Co-ordinate with civil society, international community	Full adherence to internationally accepted code of conduct of negotiation Involvement of the UN in negotiation process Full preparation and commitment Formation of an independent, powerful negotiation support committee and give responsi-bility of co-ordination of negotiation Holding both informal and formal talks together

		Suspension of mobilization of security forces
Maoist side	Suspend violent activities (killing, abduction, extortion, destruction of public properties) and express sincere commitment, Demonstrate genuine commitment to negotiated settlement Release of abducted, making public of the whereabouts of abducted Co-ordinate with civil society	Besides political agenda, acceptance of all the universally recognized processes and procedures of negotiation Full adherence to the code of conduct, suspension of all violent activities Be ready to discuss all possible options Suspend military activities
To be jointly done by government and Maoists	Full adherence to all the human rights-related provisions including Geneva Conventions. Implementation by signing the human rights accord prepared by NHRC Impose complete restriction on the military activities in educational institutions Form, sign and abide by code of conduct Form Code of Conduct Monitoring Committee involving civil society, political parties and international experts.	Accept help from UN or EU or any other reliable external force to facilitate negotiation and to act as guarantors Formation of a high-level coordination committee for negotiation involving representatives of political parties, Maoist, army, Human Rights activists, civil society to help make the talks success. Restriction on any activity adversely affecting the talks and inclusion of representatives of political parties in the negotiating team. Conducting the peace talks at both the informal and formal levels and taking the conclusion to the formal talk only after having agreed on the informal one
Political parties	Agree on common agenda and sincerely implement them Promote internal democracy in party structures and issue white paper on their past mistake and commit for not repeating the mistake they made in the past Creating all kinds of pressures for ceasefire and peace talks making 'peace' as their mission Formation of task forces to	Formation of Conflict Transformation Departments within their parties, capacity promotion of the leaders, keeping living contact and consultation with government, Maoists, army and civil society- holding talks Development of internal resource for conflict transformation

	support peace talk Participate in ceasefire monitoring committee, negotiation facilitation committee	Co-operate government with peace talks and send representatives to the negotiating team from their party's part.
Civil society	Creation of continuous pressure for negotiation Preparation of draft code of conduct of ceasefire and submission to the concerned parties Promote national-level civil initiative for peace process Co-coordinate with the government, political parties and the Maoists to create conducive environment for peace process	Finding different alternatives to the disputed subjects in the negotiation, submitting such alternatives as proposal to the concerned parties and holding discussions on the proposed alternatives Creation of positive pressure for peace by mobilizing people's participation, monitoring code of conduct and negotiation.
International community	Exchanges of international experiences Create continuous pressure for ceasefire Stop any kind activities affecting ceasefire and peace talks Suspend military aids and arms supply Stop interference in internal affairs other than human rights issues	Stop arms supply Maintain strategy of non-interference in internal affairs other than human rights issues Prepare and implement code of conduct of international community specifying the works to be done and not done during the period of peace talks, and abiding it Playing role of guarantor, Arrange resources needed for rebels to maintain ceasefire and continue negotiation,
Joint functions of the concerned parties	Form 'Peace Commission' to institutionalise peace process Declaring certain areas (schools, hospital, children parks, temples and public places) as 'Peace Zones' Form Code of Conducts Monitoring Committee involving political parties, civil society and international experts and assigning responsibilities and implement them Involve in preparation of ceasefire, create conducive environment for promotion of peace process.	Identify/explaining necessary expertise, skill, source and institutionalized structure for the success of peace talks, Making of Code Conduct for communication media specifying 'what can be done' and 'what must not be done' and implement it Keeping contact with the peace activities in districts and villages, coordinating with them and include all the concerns of the parties in talk process.

If peace talk is to be made meaningful by drawing a concrete conclusion, the negotiators should accept the 'universally recognized principles of peace talks' and should not repeat the past mistakes. Creating a consensus on only political questions does not suffice. Detailed discussions on the political questions, procedures and processes to be applied to get political consensus, possible obstacles on this way, their solutions, necessary structure for the implementation of political agreements, resource, manpower, time, alternatives, should be looked at.

9.6 SOME NECESSARY STRUCTURES FOR THE SETTLEMENT OF THE ARMED CONFLICT

It has been already 10 years since the nation was entrapped into armed conflict and now it is reeling in the throes of civil war. The efforts made in the past by the palace, the government, the Maoists and the political parties for the settlement of the conflict were complete fiascos. The situation gradually went on becoming complicated. The nation got into the crises of civil war. Tens of thousands of the Nepalese are losing their life for nothing. Therefore, this conflict must end. I have proposed some necessary structures for the transformation of the conflict and to achieve negotiated settlement of the ongoing armed conflict. If the concerned parties have no interest and no commitment to the settlement of this conflict, only the structures can do nothing. But, the experiences of the conflict settlement around the world have shown that despite the commitment of the concerned parties, there are several obstacles in the process of conflict settlement due to the absence of proper structures. The following structures are necessary for the settlement of the present armed conflict in Nepal:

9.6.1 National Peace Commission

A powerful and resourceful National Peace Commission should be constituted by involving representatives of all political forces, civil society and professional experts. The commission has to work to bring the conflicting parties together and hold formal and informal discussions on their fear, difficulties, desires and expectations to create a confidential environment. The commission has also to collect necessary experiences, expertise, and resources. It has to convene peace conference, or round table conference, or consultative conference to facilitate negotiated settlement. It has also to orderly document issues of the concerned people, prioritize and make necessary arrangements for debating at national level. It has also to explore possible structures (e.g., mode of powerful interim government) for their implementation of negotiated settlement.

9.6.2 Peace Secretariat

A separate Peace Secretariat of the level of HMG ministry should be constituted to regularize the negotiation process on behalf of HMG, to cooperate with the National Peace Commission and to provide information about the armed conflict from government's part. Leadership of the secretariat should be held by any HMG senior official and appoint necessary numbers of subject experts. The chief and the experts should not be transferred anywhere until the conflict is settled and the secretariat exists. This secretariat should be given every responsibility of the negotiation from the part of the state.

9.6.3 Ceasefire Monitoring Committee

One of the major causes of the disruption of negotiation and breaking of ceasefire is the lack of proper 'Ceasefire Agreement' and 'Ceasefire Monitoring'. So, if a meaningful conclusion is to be drawn from a negotiation, a 'Ceasefire Agreement' coupled with 'Ceasefire Code of Conduct' to be abided by both the conflicting sides should be signed by the government and the Maoists in presence of the representatives of parliamentary political parties, National Human Rights Commission, Civil Society, and international community. A ceasefire monitoring committee should be formed involving representatives of the aforesaid sides and human rights activists, peace and conflict transformation experts and other relevant people and experts given monitoring responsibility.

9.6.4 Negotiation Coordination Committee

A high-level Negotiation Coordination Committee should be formed to help find solutions to the problems, difficulties, disputes and unclear matters which may arise in the negotiation process and to implement the agreed upon points immediately. Decisive representatives of all the sides should be involved in this committee. Senior representatives of government, political parties, army, Maoists and civil society should be involved in this committee. The UN, EU, International Red Cross Society or any other experienced international forces supportive to negotiated settlement of Nepal's conflict should also be invited to advise the Committee. The main responsibilities of this committee are to prevent obstacles in the negotiation process, create a favourable environment for the success of the negotiation, to help negotiators and facilitators, and coordinate with the conflicting parties.

9.6.5 'Conflict Transformation Departments' within political parties

Now it has become urgent for the political parties to form conflict transformation departments or unit within their party structures and develop their capacity. Such departments should study and monitor the conflict, consult and coordinate with the National Peace Commission ,Government Peace Secretariat, Ceasefire Monitoring Committee, Negotiation Co-ordination Committee, Maoists, palace government, army, civil society, diplomatic missions and other concerned sides of the conflict; and bring out their party's approaches on conflict transformation, hold discussions and represent their party to different committees.

9.6.6 Reconciliation Commission

It is not only of the fighters', the psychology of the general public also has been terribly negatively affected by the destructive activities like killing of thousands of general public, impairing, internally displacing, raping, damaging personal properties, etc. The victims are going through conditions such as disappointment, revengeful feeling and involvement in social crimes. So, psychological remedy and reconciliatory approaches are necessary to arouse hope in them, return them to usual life and make them creative. A separate unit having special expertise is needed for such tasks.

The warring sides commit unimaginable violence of human rights during the conflict. So, a high level as well as powerful commission needs to take actions on the culprits as per the international law.

9.6.7 Donors' Nepal Conflict-Transformation Helping Group

According to the experiences so far, the international communities remain a very effective and strong outside force in the conflict-torn host countries. Therefore, they also directly or indirectly become active in conflict transformation and peace process. Those bilateral and multilateral donors and the international communities who wish for durable peace and functional democracy in Nepal should form 'Nepal Conflict Transformation Helping Group'. This group should stop any activity e.g. (arms sale) that may provoke war, coordinate with and help to civil society to formulate code of conduct and implement it, assist the structures such as National Peace Commission, High Level Negotiating Committee, create international environment in favour of peace talks, create pressure on conflicting sides to stop human right violation, assist civil society, collect necessary resources for the peace talks and post conflict transformation. Such donors' helping group is actively working in Columbia.

9.6.8 Judicial or Constitutional Court

A Judicial or Constitutional Court is necessary for finding solutions of constitutional and legal complications that may arise in the process of negotiation and constituent assembly election and for protecting the basic democratic principles, norms, values such as human rights, multiparty competition, periodical election system, etc. Such constitutional courts have played very important roles in South Africa.

9.6.9 Facilitator-Mediator Assistance Committee

The role of facilitators and mediators becomes very important to make the peace talk successful. But, it needs to make arrangements of rescores such as information, acquaintance, guarantee of their security, access to the palace, to the Maoists, etc. For this a 'Facilitator Assistance Committee' should be formed involving representatives of all concerned parties such as the palace, government, army, civil society, and other necessary experts. It should remain active in the process of peace talks.

9.6.10 Research and Resources Centre

The armed conflict in Nepal is a relatively new phenomenon. But there are many countries in the world, which have already undergone the situation of armed conflict. They have very important, useful theoretical and practical experiences, knowledge and skills in conflict management. We should use such experiences, knowledge and skills in our context.

We should do their comparative researches and study. Until now, our country lacks sufficient materials relating to the conflict transformation, peace talks, war, and security and so on. Therefore, it has become urgent to make arrangement for collecting such materials and utilize them in need. A recently established Nongovernmental organization named 'Friends for Peace' *(Shantika lagi Sahakarya)* has started a systematic works and arrangement towards this direction. This kind of service/work is necessary to widen more and more.

9.6.11 Human Rights Monitoring Committee

A Human Rights Monitoring Committee involving national and international human rights activists, torture victim experts and legal experts should be formed under the leadership of the National Human Right Commission. The state should help the human right monitoring teams in going to each conflict affected district and monitoring the human right situation.

9.6.12 Media Monitoring Committee

The role of media becomes very sensitive in the situation of armed conflict. False or sensitive news provokes conflict. So, a Media Monitoring Committee should be formed involving Federation of Nepalese Journalist, media experts, conflict experts and legal experts to monitor the communication media. This committee should make a code of conduct for the media to be abided by during the conflict and peace talks; and monitor its implementation.

9.6.13 Special Task Force

There are many sides concerned with the conflict. They are affiliated to either this or that organization. Besides the political parties, palace, security forces, Maoist; the national organizations such as Disables' Associations, Helpless Society, conflict victims' association, single women's association, association of handicapped people, dalit, indigenous people, women, students, religious groups, different professional groups etc. are the major concerned groups. Such organizations concerned with the conflict should form a special task force or unit to raise their concern voice, to specify their priority, to find alternatives for the settlement of the problems, and to co-ordinate with the above-mentioned commissions, committees and secretariats.

9.7 CONCLUSION

In short, complete restructuring of the state through a constituent assembly election is necessary to reach durable peace and functional democracy in Nepal. There is no basic difference in the questions like formulation of new constitution and an integrated solution of the problems of conflicting parties. However, the problem persisting against this direction is the psycho-fear of different power centres which are being haunted by the questions about their future status, right, power and privileges and their doubts whether there may arise any question mark even on their existence, if agreed to bring complete change in the state structure.

Monarchists are afraid by the Maoist statement that their ultimate aim is to bring 'People's Democratic Republic'. The Maoists seem to be willing to gor for a genuine negotiation. This has been indicated in the article written by the Maoist leader Baburam Bhattarai and published in Kantipur daily on Aasr 8, 2061. It is a nearly 10 year-old war. It has taken the life of more than 13 thousand people, devastated billions worth national and personal properties, impaired thousands of people. In such situation resoulution of the armed conflict through the election of Constitutional Assembly to formulate constitution through people's involvement.

If all the forces of the country have wanted democratic peace in Nepal, they should become active to create national consensus showing probity, flexibility and learning from the past weaknesses and avoiding to blame and counter blame. Similarly, if it is to truly accept people's sovereignty, election to constitutional assembly should be accepted as the proper way of conflict settlement. Different doubts and fears have been raised such as, 'if the Maoist did not lay down their arms, the result might go to the Maoist side due to fear and threatens, they might not accept if the result did not come in their favour and so on. Such doubts and fears should be correctly addressed by involving UN. Election can be held under monitoring and involvement of the UN, arms can be kept under the supervision of UN during the election period. Different arrangements can be made to deal on this issue. Both the conflicting sides should fully abide by the Geneva Conventions and violence should be stopped.

If violence, killing, blames, counter blames, attacks, counter attacks continue, if the days pass in the illusion that the Unified Command will solve the problems, if both sides remain engaged in conflict not learning from the past weaknesses and international experiences, if all the possible ways of conflict settlement are not utilized in an integrated manner, if all remained hankering after their vested interests, or remained feeling inferiority complex, and if a democratic solution is not to be dug out through national consensus, Nepal will turn into a failed state. At that time neither any power centre nor any force of this country will remain as now. The worst victim would be the monarchy.

Such problems have been solved in several countries including Cambodia and Namibia. So, the UN should be invited by creating a national consensus and given responsibilities to solve such practical problems.

NOTES

1. See Reports of Dhami Commission (1997) and Deuba Commission 2000 for detail.
2. CPN (UML) realised that its joining the four-party coalition before royal takeover was a great mistake, as the coalition government had amply prepared a basis for the king to take over.

CHAPTER 10

Nepal at the Crossroads

10.1 INTRODUCTION

At present Nepal is facing an unprecedented crisis. This crisis is the collective outcome of failure of the Nepalese governing system for more than two centuries, rapidly and unbelievably expanded Maoist armed insurgency, failure of democratic leadership and extraordinary ambition of the newly instituted king. The situation in Nepal is further complicating day by day and year by year. New problems and complications are arising. However, the mindset of major actors of this crisis has not changed. In this chapter, these issues are discussed.

10.2 THE ROYAL TAKEOVER AND CESSATION OF DEMOCRACY

The changing political dynamics of Nepal after Maoist insurgency has reached its peak from the royal takeover of the 1st February. The political context and conflict dynamics are changing very rapidly. The dissolution of the parliament as a result of an intense power struggle, unwillingness of the then government to conduct local elections or to extend the tenure of the elected representatives as per the provisions of the Local Self-Governance Act, the 4 October 2002 event (when the elected Prime Minister was removed by the king and the country was run by subsequent nominated governments) and finally the political takeover of the power on the 1st February 2005 have greatly contributed to the current political crisis in Nepal. The first February takeover was not a result of an overnight decision of the king. Rather, it was a cumulative product of long term, very well thought out, calculated and coordinated actions and planning.

The first February takeover includes the resumption of executive power by the King, removal of the nominated multi-party government, detention and arrest of political leaders, civil society members, journalists and human rights activists, censorship on media, and imposition of the State of Emergency and suspension of civil rights. Even after one year of the Royal takeover, the political and security situation did not improve. Rather, it is worsening. As an objection to the king's takeover, the USA, UK and India temporarily suspended military aids to Nepal. Denmark, Switzerland and a few other countries suspended their development aids to Nepal. Many other donors are still using a 'wait and see' strategy. Because of the royal takeover, Nepal seriously lost international support and presented bad image of the country.

At present, absence of an elected government accountable to the people at both central and local levels is creating a serious political vacuum in the country.

Since the 1st February Royal takeover, the security situation in is worst in rural areas. The overall political situation in the country is further worsening, as confrontation between the King-led government and the major political parties is increasing. The grievances within the political forces are mounting at the time of badly needed cooperation and conciliation to settle political crisis in Nepal. This is seriously weakening the newly established democracy in Nepal.

10.2.1 Arguments of the King for the 1st February takeover

The king made rigorous efforts and strong attempts to justify his takeover. In these attempts, he frequently argued that about the grand failure of the political parties to contain violence, to control corruption and improve economic situation of the country. In all his speeches, public comments and interviews, the king vehemently expressed his dismay and frustrations with political parties. Perhaps, the unique ambition-embedded personality of the king might be the main intrinsic reason of the royal takeover, as he wanted to rule the country as a executive head of the state. Time and again he had searched for his role in the Nepal's politics. However, political parties were either unaware or undermining the ambitions and intentions of the king.

In his assessment, the king neither indicated the legacy of panchayat and role of anti-democratic forces to make the democracy dysfunctional nor acknowledged the reality that monarchy is also a part of the democratic system since 1990. The following statement clearly indicates this denial. *"Nepal's bitter experiences over the past few years tend to show that democracy and progress contradict one another. Multiparty democracy was discredited by focusing solely on power politics. Parliament witnessed many aberrations in the name of retaining and ousting governments. Not a single House of Representatives was allowed to complete its tenure. Continuous confusion and disorder resulted in the obstruction of the democratic process.*[1] *The statement itself is correct to pitch the actual political situation of Nepal. However, it is not as simple as described by the king. If the political process is going wrong, as head of the state, he has the responsibility to make political parties aware, give advice and help to correct it through democratic procedure.*

Obviously, people's aspirations were shattered, they were frustrated, trust in the state was fast eroding and they were gradually alienated from the power centric politics. However, people were not opposing the multiparty democracy and demanding reform of political parties.

When the king took over on 1st February 2005, he was quite frustrated and angry towards political parties both in words and actions. The King, at the time of royal takeover in the 1st February, addressing the Nation said, '...today we have once again reached a juncture, where in keeping with popular aspirations, a historic decision must be taken to defend multiparty democracy by restoring peace for the nation and people. Even when bloodshed, violence and devastation has pushed the country on the brink of destruction, those engaged in politics in the name of country and people continue to shut their eyes to their welfare. Tussle for power, abuse on gaining authority on gaining power and unhealthy competition in fulfilling personal and communal interests at the expense of the nation and citizenry contributed further to deterioration in the situation. ...It is now time to bring to an end the ongoing act of terrorist violence and pledge, in earnest, to fulfil the people's aspirations with the restoration of peace and security in the country.... As it is our responsibility to preserve our nationalism, national unity and sovereignty, as well s to maintain peace and security in the country and ensure that the state of the nation does not deteriorate any further, we have, by virtue of the State Authority as exercised by us and in keeping with the spirit of the Constitution of the Kingdom of Nepal 1990, taking into consideration Article 27 (3) of the constitution, dissolved effective from today, the current Council of Ministers to fulfil to fulfil the people's desire for the restoration of peace and security and to activate soon the democratic dispensation[2]'.

However, one year's performance of the post-February government demonstrates that neither was peace restored and security situation improved nor were the civil rights of people respected. Anticorruption was another icon of the King's speech, but his first Vice Chairman severely weakened it, as he was blacklisted as Bank's defaulter. Further, the cabinet started to pay allowances not provisioned in existing laws of Nepal to its cabinet members. The performance and credibility of Royal Commission for Corruption Control was seriously questioned because of its ill-intention. The government's actions are contrary to what the King spoke on 1st February.

Time and again the king was highlighting the role of Shah Dynasty in nation building of Kingdom of Nepal since the foundations of the unification process was initiated by King Prithvi Narayan Shah. In his 1st February speech, he had vehemently highlighted this issue. He said, *"It is well known that to reign in accordance with the people's aspirations, our forefathers initiated revolutionary measures of historic importance, ensuring a bright future of the nation and her people. History is witness to the fact that both the Nepalese people and the King have, in unison, played decisive roles in each and every period of the Kingdom's process of unification, democratisation and modernisation*". Hence like his forefather, he wanted to play a more active role in Nepal's politics. This statement clearly reveals the difference in perception of the king and the role of the monarch defined by the 1990's constitution as a constitutional monarch. He wanted to establish active monarchy in Nepal again taking the foot-print of his father.

Another strong argument of the king in favour of 1st February takeover was the failure of the government to conduct the election. In this regard he said, *"After being incapable of holding elections, there were conspiracies to form undemocratic governments, which would be responsible to no one. There was also a written consensus amongst all political parties on vacuuming the people's representatives out but they could not see eye to eye when it came to working together in filling this void. The participation and concurrence of political parties in making way for a form of governance, which negated popular representation, was against the people's wishes and norms and spirit of multiparty democracy. ... In order to conduct the general elections in an environment of peace and security, opportunities were given to leaders of various political parties to constitute the Council of Ministers, with executive power. But the situation did not improve. National politics was plagued by not uniting in running the government but opposing it on being ousted from it"*. This seems quite good statement, but when we look at the reasons behind the failure of political parties to hold election the statement does not stand good. The subsequent governments since 2002 were unable to hold election and they were responsible for it. But deeper analysis reveals a different reality. None of the nominated governments was allowed to complete the time frame given by the king to them to hold election. Lokendra Bahadur Chand, Surya Bahadur Thapa and Ser Bahadur Deuba were sacked from the job before they started preparation for election. All of them were given a certain time by the king to complete election but none of them got a chance to complete the assigned responsibility and given time frame and the king changed the government. So, solely blaming political parties and their government for the failure of holding election is unfair and the king is also responsible for it. He wanted to continue the situation of non-election to consolidate his power and position.

On the 10th of October 2005 (Fulpati, the seventh day of the biggest festival of Nepal) the Election Commission declared February 8th for holding election of all 58 municipalities across the country. On his Dashain message to the nation on October 12th, King Gyanendra said that parliamentary elections would be conducted within one year to strength. But the 7-party alliance of political parties has decided to boycott the forthcoming election. The reasons cited for boycott are: (a) they do not want to recognise the illegal government (as there is no provision for chairpersonship and vice-chairpersonship of council of minister in the constitution) by participating in the election organised by this autocratic government, (b) The palace is simply using these elections (local and parliamentary elections) or rhetoric of commitment on democracy as an eye-wash to divert attention of international community from their demand to the king to hand over the state power to the people, and (c) the parties are suspecting the intention of the government to hold election after nominating regional and zonal administrators from the hard-line panchyati background, as they are not committed to multiparty democracy and want to establish autocracy. Hence, the election is just to confuse people and declare anti-democratic forces as elected representatives and change the constitution according to the desire of the king.

In his long speech on the first of February 2005, the king said, "*We also met a number of times with members of the general public, senior citizens, representatives of the civil society and leaders of political parties in our effort to gauze the popular mandate and try to convince them of the country's requirements and people's aspirations. We reminded them that the only wish of the Nepalese people and friends of Nepal was to bring to an end the ongoing violence and destructive activities and return peace and tranquillity to the country without any further delay*". Obviously, people were fed up with the continuous violence and insecurity and were very loudly requesting the king to restore peace in the country. All ordinary people were tired of violence and expected the king to end it. The Maoists were saying that they wanted to talk with the king to reach a political settlement of the conflict because the king has real power. In every civic reception, ordinary people were requesting the king for peace. While demanding peace from the king, they probably hoped that the king would agree to holding constituent assembly election. But, after the direct rule of the king there have been no peace talks and negotiation with the Maoists and no peace restored. If he had declared a ceasefire, invited Maoists to seat for peace talks, taken political parties into confidence and reached a negotiated settlement, ordinary people would have appreciated it. But this did not happen. The present government's loud claim about the 'improvement in security situation' is mainly because of the declaration of the three months' unilateral ceasefire by the Maoists, rather than the efforts of the state.

The king also put forward the argument that political parties and their governments made no serious efforts to control Maoists. He deliberately blamed political parties for not behaving with security forces in a responsive behaviour, aiming to worsen relationship between military and political parties. This is stated in his 1st February speech. He said, "*No serious efforts were made to attenuate the real threat posed against democracy by terrorism in the form of a single-party autocracy. The habit of passing carefree remarks on matters of national security continued. Political parties were unable to display responsible behaviour in augmenting the patriotic fervour of our dutiful security personnel, who are active round the clock in ensuring security of the nation and people. Multiparty democrats could not sincerely unite, with national interest as the focal point, to forever end the cycle of devastation being lashed out against the nation and people. Likewise, political parties also could not identify national priorities in keeping with the people's aspirations"*. It was true that there were not very cordial relations between the Royal Nepal Army (RNA) and the political parties and their government. But leaders of political parties were publicly saying that the security forces were not cooperating with the government. Girija Prasad Koirala had tendered his resignation earlier to the king citing the very same example of non cooperation from RNA. His home minister publicly expressed this issue. Earlier, while asked by the government to mobilise the military to control Maoists, Chief of the Army Staff publicly said that there should be unanimous decisions by all parties to mobilise the army (theoretically it is true but practically he was clear that there would be no consensus and no military would be mobilised). This case was taken by political parties as non cooperation from the security forces and they claimed that the palace was playing on security issues. Military was not happy with the political change of 1990 and marginalisation of the military compared to police in terms of providing resources by successive governments. Therefore, this issue seemed quite contentious for a long time.

In a nutshell, Nepal is facing an unprecedented crisis due to the Maoist insurgency and the unconstitutional act of the king. The present deep crisis is the cumulative effect of:

- Ambition of the King to be a visible and constructive monarch active in politics to rule the country.
- Intense power struggles.
- Rampant corruption and glaring malgovernance.
- Favouritism and nepotism (*afnomanchhe*).
- Discriminations based on gender, caste, class, ethnicity and geographical isolation.
- Political, social, economic and legal exclusions.
- Unequal distribution of resources.
- Monopoly and abuse of power and authority and distortion of rules and laws.
- Persistent and intense international interference in domestic policy (in the civilised world, raising concerns about the human rights violation in part of the world is an accepted norm but if there is external pressure on other than human rights issues, it is interference, which is immense in Nepal). Even change of director of a particular department, rising of price of a particular commodity, sending staff for higher study, or release of trimester budget are interfered in by donors.

Therefore, Nepal's polity seems to be leading towards a state failure. The king has not yet internalised this reality. Later it will be too costly for him if he does not return power to people.

Nepali identity is the systematic whole of ethnic identities and diversity of cultures, languages and dialects, scripts, literatures and religions (Ukayab and Adhikari, 2000). However, Nepalese polity failed to internalise this reality. The post-February government even undermined or neglected this reality. Despite the claim of the Nepalese governments, the concept of a multi-ethnic and multi-cultural Nepal is well understood and translated into governing practices. The freedom of expression, the notion of open society enshrined in the Constitution of the Kingdom of Nepal 1990 have provided ample opportunity to critically re-examine and brought forward these issues. The recent history of Nepal has demonstrated that the diverse nationalities existing in this country do not feel a true sense of self-recognition, belongingness, and representation (Khanal, 2005, Upreti, 2003c), as the state has failed to sincerely recognise the multi-ethnic, multi-lingual and multi-religious state (Upreti, 2003a and 2005h). The advocates of the 1st February takeover have seriously undermined this diversity of the nation.

Box 10.1 Ordinances issued between February and October 2005

1. Poverty Reduction Fund Ordinance, 2005
2. Private Investment on Construction and Operation of Basic Infrastructure Ordinance, 2005
3. Nepal Rastra Bank (First Amendment) Ordinance, 2005
4. Hydro-power Investment Ordinance, 2005
5. National Judicial Academy Ordinance, 2005
6. Nepal Treaty (First Amendment) Ordinance 2005
7. Local Administration (Fifth amendment) Ordinance 2005
8. Prison (Second Amendment) Ordinance , 2005
9. Land Management (Sixth Amendment) Ordinance, 2005
10. Terrorist and Destructive Activities (Control and Punishment) Ordinance, 2005
11. Nepal Drinking Water Corporation (Third Amendment) Ordinance, 2005
12. Drinking Water Management Board Ordinance, 2005
13. Drinking Water Tariff Fixation Ordinance, 2005
14. Royal Family Expenditure Management (First Amendment) Ordinance
15. National Academy of Medical Science Ordinance, 2005

16. National Human Rights Commission (First Amendment) Ordinance, 2005
17. Lumbini Buddhist University Ordinance, 2005
18. Information Technology Academy Ordinance, 2005
19. Local Self-governance (First Amendment) Ordinance, 2005
20. Social Welfare (First Amendment) Ordinance, 2005
21. Public Service (Second Amendment) Ordinance, 2005
22. Fiscal Ordinance, 2005
23. Disbursement Ordinance, 2005
24. Loan and Guarantee (Fifteenth Amendment) Ordinance, 2005
25. National Loan Reimbursement Ordinance, 2005
26. Education (eight amendment) Ordinance, 2005
27. Some Nepal Acts Related to Communication Ordinance (To amend Radio Act 1957, Press and Publication Act 1991, National Broadcasting Act 1992 and Defamation Act 1959), 2005

Nepali history reveals that very centralist; monolithic, autocratic governing practices have been inherited by rulers from rulers with few cosmetic changes since centuries. These changes are basically to strengthen the positions of the ruling elite rather than to address structural inequalities and exclusion. The current crisis of Nepal is the outcome of all these structural problems. The table (10.1) highlights the intentions, ambitions, strategies and actions of the major political forces in the country, particularly after the 1st February Royal takeover.

The post-February government took a George Bush approach, 'either with us or against us' to deal with Nepalese people (ordinary people, political parties, civil society and human rights activists, media, professionals, business community) as well as international community. This approach has severely divided the people, implanted disastrous mistrust and erosion of confidence. A unique situation developed in the country, which is explained in the following section as guided democracy, a new form of autocracy.

10.2.2 Basic characteristics of major political forces in the current context

The major four (three domestic and one external) power centres of Nepal have their own agenda, intensions, ambitions, strategies and action plans in reference to Nepal's crisis. There is a brief discussion of these power centres in this section.

10.2.2.1 Guided democracy as a pathway to full autocracy

Conceptually, the frameworks of guided democracy and authoritarian regimes used by the king at present are based on perceived risks, unfounded imagination and unrealistic ambitions. In the current context of Nepal, the King is using a framework of guided democracy similar to Malaysia or Pakistan. The establishment (the king with the post-1st February 2005 government and their supporters) wants to pacify and slow down the much-desired social and economic changes in Nepal that ensures direct benefits to ordinary citizens, especially poor, disadvantaged, marginalized people. Rather, the establishment wants to develop an authoritarian value system and to redefine the globally accepted democratic norms (civic liberty: free media, freedom of speech and movement; human rights, rule of law) to fit in the framework of controlled democracy. Despotic monarchists were extremely unhappy with the political change of 1990 and working in systematic and organised manner to weaken or destabilise the multiparty democratic system from the beginning and by the February royal takeover, they succeeded. Characteristics of the framework of 'guided democracy' in Nepal are:

- Regulation or control of civic liberty (e.g., media ordinance issued by the government, NGO Code of Conduct of Social Welfare Council, etc.),
- Always anticipates favourable behavioural response from citizen to the actions of rulers,
- Uses state power to control unfavourable civil behaviour towards them,
- Discourages socio-economic, political, cultural, religious freedom and rights that threaten their vested interests,
- Provides no space for political freedom other than defined by the regimes,
- Ignores multi-linguality, multi-ethnicity, multi-cultural and religious identities or wrongly interprets them,
- Ignores or wrongly interprets the concerns related to human rights and democracy raised by civil society, international community and opponents,
- Creates new institutions and supportive arrangements (e.g., new civil society organisations, new legal or semi-judicial provisions, new administrative arrangements. Recently issued Code of Conduct for I/NGOs and Media Ordinance are example

of such armaments[3]),

- Makes constant efforts of creating or maintaining fear, threat, insecurity to those who do not support the ruling class,
- Resists change and reform in the name of national unity or other similar sensitive issues.

TABLE 10.1 Summary of Basic Characteristics of Major Power Centre in the Present Political Context

Basic characteristics (governing intensions, ambitions, strategies and actions) of major power centres			
The King, his government, and the supporters of the 1st February takeover	*Parliamentary parties*	*Maoists*	*International community*
• Guided democracy (authoritarian rule), • Constructive and visible (controlling) role of monarch, • Awkward international alliance (e.g., Pakistan, North Korea, etc.), • Use of state resources (security forces, media and ordinances, etc.) to justify takeover.	• Functional democracy • Peaceful change, • Respect of human rights, free media, civic liberty • Slow and superficial change to maintain status quo	• Radical change, • Use of violence to change, • Centralised regime • Focus on poor, socially excluded and marginalised	• Supporting multi-party democracy, civic rights and stability • Maintaining influence • Isolating or marginalising Maoists

Source: Adapted from Upreti, 2005f.

Some scholars argue that 'guided democracy' is effective in disciplining the society and economic progress. However, this thought is incorrect. The authoritarian regime does not allow other ideologies, thinking and perspectives to grow. Authoritarian thinking now in Nepal is attempting to guide the actions and behaviour of people. Some characteristics of the guided democracy or new form of autocracy observed in Nepal are:

- Forces people to do according to the interests of regime (Box 10.1, list of ordinances clearly demonstrates the intention of the regime and how it wants to regulate behaviour of people),
- Controls or regulates media, economy, politics, and social life (see Box 10.2),

- Ignores individual freedom, restricts opposing thoughts, thinking and intellectuality,
- Does not provide political space for the opponents,
- Highlights economic prosperity at the cost of political diversity.

Box 10.2 Press statement of members of the 'International Press Freedom and Freedom of Expression Mission to Nepal[4]' on 17 October 2005

"We, as members of the 'International Press Freedom and Freedom of Expression Mission to Nepal', express our serious concern that HM King Gyanendra, together with the government and security forces, is seeking to further undermine Nepal's vibrant independent media, which has been opposing the actions of the authorities to curb press freedoms and freedom of expression since 1 February 2005. In specific, we condemn the 'Ordinance Amending some of the Nepal Act related to Media' promulgated on 9 October. This Ordinance contains a number of provisions to amend existing media laws, thereby introducing strict controls over the publication and broadcast of materials and ownership of the media, as well as introducing harsher penalties for those considered to be contravening the law. Penalties have increased dramatically, with journalists charged with defamation now facing fine ten-times higher than before, and a possible two-year jail term. The Ordinance also prohibits an organization or individual from receiving licenses to operate radio, television and newspapers. Those who have already been granted licenses to operate all three media are now limited to choosing any two forms within a year. Other provisions ban the importing of foreign publications that contain prohibited information and barring FM stations from broadcasting news-related programmes. These stations will be limited to airing "informative" programmes on health, education, weather, road and transport conditions and other similar development topics, whilst being banned from addressing, amongst others, "any subject matters with negative effects to political parties," "offensive matters," and "any matters against non-aligned foreign policy of Nepal". Under the Ordinance any news that "causes hatred or disrespect" to any member of the royal family will also be prohibited. We wish to reaffirm our solidarity with the media community and freedom of expression advocates in Nepal who continue to be the victims of intimidation, harassment, repression and violence. In this regard, we will continue to support the media community, without any intention to interfere in the editorial lines of the Nepali media. We praise the media community for its dynamism in defending media rights and freedom of expression and call on the authorities to reconsider the 'Ordinance Amending some of the Nepal Act related to Media', as well as end all forms of direct and indirect censorship, intimidation, harassment and attacks against the media community and freedom of expression advocates. In addition, we urge the international community to step up support for the independent media in order to help save one of the kingdom's last surviving democratic gains.

'Guided democracy' cannot satisfy the aspirations of Nepalese people, as it is not a right governing framework to address fundamental issues such as social exclusion, poverty, injustice and inequality in Nepal.

At present, functional democracy is replaced by the authoritarian regime. Though the 1st February proclamation of the King seriously charged the leadership of political parties and blamed them for political crisis and insecurity, the present rule clearly demonstrates that the establishment seriously lacks vision, commitment, understanding, responsibility and dynamic and qualified leaders in its circle to deal with the political crisis. The king has to rely on those people who are outdated, unaware of the global democratic spirit and aspirations, denying human rights, freedom and civil liberty. The strategy used in the 1st February takeover to control behaviour and action of people through fear, terror and military force has now proved counterproductive, as it got severe criticism and negative popularity within the country and abroad. The spirit and ambition of the 1st February takeover faded with the extremely poor and very controversial performance of the Cabinet to restore peace and security and resolve the armed conflict and anti-constitutional Royal Commission for Corruption Control (RCCC), failed to work in the principle of natural justice.

At the time of Royal takeover, some people, particularly the business community, some ordinary people, many ex-panchas and royalists groups were quite ambitious and hopeful of improvement in the security situation at the time of the King's direct rule. However, their expectations faded over time when there was no change in the political and security situation. Now, many of those who had actively or passively supported the takeover are frustrated and some of the diehard royalists are seriously opposing the king's government. Interestingly, their voice is also unheard and they are also marginalised. Another level of conflict is emerging between those who are in power and those who are not even within the group of the 1st February supporters.

The hardliner royalists have greatly helped to widen the gap between the king and political parties and that has ultimately contributed to developing opinion towards republican political system.

Former Chief of the army staff, who is said to be one of the very close advisors of the King, publicly asked the government to declare political parties as an antinationalist force. Even the Vice Chairman of the Cabinet, Dr Tulsi Giri clearly said that Nepal cannot go together with monarchy and democracy and therefore Nepalese people should choose either monarchy or democracy. In a television interview, he further said that sovereignty cannot be in two sources, it should be with the king. It is unlikely that he could speak on such a fundamental issue without the consent of the king. Based on the past experiences[5], it can be speculated that these issues are not coming without the consent of the King. This means that the King seems not ready to give up executive power and is not interested in reconciling with political parties. Consequently, Nepal's politics is heading towards republic set-up in Nepal. The Maoist demand of republican system is now in wider national debate. CPN-UML, which was strongly objecting to the demand of constituent assembly election of the Maoists earlier, has decided to go in for republican political system. Similarly, Nepali Congress, another strong supporter of the constitutional monarchy, changed its commitment by removing provision of constitutional monarchy from its constitution. Other leftist political parties were already in favour of a republican system. Youths, intellectuals, civil society leaders are also increasingly aligned in favour of a republican system. In this way, all influential forces earlier defending the constitutional monarchy are now distancing away and are inclined towards a republican political set-up. Hence the 1st February choice of king is paving way for the beginning of the end of the existence of the centuries old monarchy in Nepal.

10.2.2.2 Functional democracy

It would be too early for Nepal to anticipate a nearly perfect democracy as democracy is a self learning and self correcting system that requires longer exercise as well as commitment and sincerity of people. Therefore, 'functional democracy' is a working framework for Nepal as a first step towards a mature democracy. Some characteristics of functional democracy are:

- Respects and ensures rule of law, basic human rights, civil liberty,
- Acknowledges diversities in thinking, opinions, ideas and actions,

- Adopts self-correcting measures and learns from the mistakes and weaknesses,
- Explores unity within diversities (respects and promotes ethnic, cultural, lingual, religious diversities),
- Accepts criticisms, comments and queries and responds to them,
- Facilitates peaceful change process and discourages violent means of change.

Though the past democratic period (1990-2002) has observed several distortions, distractions and manipulations of democratic norms, values and practices and abuses of civic rights and violation of rule of in the country, the freedom of expression, exercise of civil liberties, accepting diversities were by and large existed. People were criticising the wrongdoings of political parties, importance of free media was accepted and human rights defenders and civil society leaders were not constrained. The political system was in the process of self-correction. Therefore, the political system was in essence working in a framework of operational democracy, a basic step for a functional democracy.

2.2.2.3 Situation of political parties

Political parties are gradually gaining lost trust. Because of the past performance of the political leaders, general people suspect politicians and therefore parties are struggling to take people in confidence. Therefore their morale is low at present. Further, the internal disputes and power struggle within major political parties are damaging their credibility. They are not yet able to break the legacy of past mistakes. They have not been able to maintain internal democracy. If they are not ready to democratise their party, they become morally weak to demand democracy. They are very much relying on external forces, particularly India. They are not able to come up with a 'white paper' embracing their past mistakes and committing to people to change their behaviour and actions. Because of all these reasons political parties are operationally weak at the moment.

The increased confrontation between the state and the Maoists has seriously threatened the basic human rights of Nepalese people and the post-February political change has severely constrained political space and consequently pushing the country towards a situation of 'state failure'. The assessment of the International Crisis Group states, "*the kings' actions have made any resolution of conflict less likely[6]"(ICG, 2005a and b). A similar conclusion was drawn from the international community. The INSEC record of killing of people during the ceasefire time of one month (3 September to 2 October 2005) shows that the state has killed 29 persons (per day 1 person) and 4 persons (per day 0.14person) by the Maoists[7].*

2.2.2.4 Situation of Maoists

The Maoist party has faced serious internal conflict between its two leaders Prachanda and Dr Babu Ram Bhattarai. Effects of this dispute have spread across the party. Blame and counterblame, character assassinations and groupism were widely growing between the two groups. This had a significant effect on the party life and Nepalese army was relatively successful in accessing internal information about the Maoists and they used it strategically to weaken the Maoists and became successful to some extent. However, Maoists became successful in managing this conflict and quickly recovered from the effects of the disputes. If they were not able to manage this conflict between the two leaders and if it had continued, there was a high chance of splitting of the Maoist party and an unimaginably serious setback to their 'people's war' (perhaps even its collapse).

The Maoists were quite successful in their strategy to widen the gap between the king and political parties as they were making all efforts from the beginning. The Maoists are the absolute gainer from the first February royal takeover and the palace is the absolute loser in the long term. Because of the first February takeover, the constituent assembly election, a long-standing demand of the Maoists, become a common demand of the political parties and Nepalese people, the relationship between the political parties and Maoists has improved and the tension between the palace and the constitutional political parties is increased, the government lost international support and faced tremendous pressure. The international community suspended military aid and consequently the government could face serious difficulties if it continued longer. Another important aspect of the first February takeover is the positive change in the Maoists' political orientation, as they have made a commitment to multiparty democracy and are showing their willingness to come to mainstream politics. This is an opportunity for the state and political parties to have negotiated settlement with them and resolve the crisis. If the state misses this opportunity and forces the Maoists to continue their violent approach, it would be too costly later.

Hence, at present, all three major forces have some serious problems and difficulties (Seddon, 2005a and b). Therefore, pragmatically, all three forces have no other option than to reach a negotiated settlement. However, their actions and behaviour are not indicating any realistic possibility for negotiation in the near future.

2.2.2.5 Roadmap of the king

The roadmap of the king is by far the most clear, straightforward and determined to fully establish autocracy and ultimately to follow the path of his father. In his roadmap, he stated, "*As it is our responsibility to preserve our nationalism, national unity and sovereignty, as well as to maintain peace and security in the country and ensure that the state of the nation does not deteriorate any further, we have, by virtue of the State Authority as exercised by us and in keeping with the spirit of the Constitution of the Kingdom of Nepal – 1990, taking into consideration Article 27 (3) of the Constitution, dissolved, effective from today, the current Council of Ministers to fulfil the people's desire for the restoration of peace and security and to activate soon the democratic dispensation. The Council of Ministers to be constituted will be under our Chairmanship. This Council of Ministers will give utmost priority to reactivating multiparty democracy in the country within three years with the implementation of effective reforms by restoring peace and security*". This roadmap has a 3-year time frame and to translate this roadmap into practice he has adopted a procedure which is entirely different from the globally accepted democratic norms, values and procedures.

His roadmap to resolve the Maoist conflict is also strange. He wants insurgents to surrender their arms and return to mainstream politics. Those who will accept this path will be pardoned by the state. Those who do not, will face military action. He said, "*We call upon all those who have gone astray, taking up arms against the nation and people, and those who are engaged in criminal activities against peace and democracy to return to the mainstream of national politics peacefully. Ensuring opportunities to freely express one's views with patriotism as the focal point, fulfilling one's aspirations and contributing to the welfare of the nation and people are the inherent features of multiparty democracy. We assure all those who avail of this opportunity to join the national mainstream that the state will give them opportunities and rights equal to those enjoyed by all our citizens, without any discrimination whatsoever; neither the people nor the law will tolerate any terrorist activities against the state or its citizens"*. It is quite unrealistic to expect the Maoists, who have control over more than 75 per cent of the territory of the country and total governing system is disrupted because of their activities, to surrender.

There is no mention about the peace talks with Maoists, ceasefire, negotiated settlement or any other agenda other than inviting them to surrender arms and join the mainstream. How can a rebel force join mainstream politics? It is either through compromise and negotiation or thorough establishing of their own rule. But, the king is not ready for negotiation.

The king is in no mood to negotiate with the insurgents and therefore, wants to continue a confrontational approach. He clearly revealed this intention while addressing the SAARC Summit at Dhaka on 12 November 2005. He said, *"It is ironical to note that the global war on terrorism is not matched by global action against it. The global war on terrorism has failed to reach every nook and corner of the world, especially in weak and vulnerable countries, as if they do not deserve justice and protection from terrorism. It is this double standard and selective approach that is assuming a dangerous character rather than terrorism itself. We cannot make a distinction between good and bad terrorism; terrorism is terrorism. In our region, the Declaration of the 11th SAARC Summit held in Kathmandu categorically stated that "terrorism, in all its forms and manifestations, is a challenge to all states and to all of humanity, and cannot be justified on ideological, political, religious or any other ground". We agreed that "terrorism violates the fundamental values of the United Nations and the SAARC Charter and constitutes one of the most serious threats to international peace and security in the Twenty-first century". Nepal has ratified the SAARC Convention on Suppression of Terrorism and its Additional Protocol with the belief that these instruments provide an effective tool to counter terrorism in the region. We call upon the SAARC member states to forge a strong partnership to eliminate terrorism from the region as well as spearhead a coordinated and earnest action against it"*. The king delivered a lengthy speech and urged the SAARC counties to unite for the collective fight against terrorism.

His statement was clear on how he deals with the Maoist insurgency. His statements were also targeted the powerful countries such as India, the USA, UK and EU who are constantly opposing the royal takeover and suspending their military aid to Nepal.

Economic reform and development was uttered in his roadmap. He said, "*Efforts at reforms in the utilisation of public expenditure and public service delivery will be made more effective. Banking discipline will be restored. Measures will be adopted towards the effective implementation of the poverty reduction strategy and the anti-corruption drive. Sustainable development is now our national agenda*". However, the economists, planners, bankers, investors and business communities are frequently warning against the deteriorating economic situation of the country. International investment is decreasing. So, it would be extremely difficult to translate this rhetoric of economic development into reality. Many donor countries have either stopped development projects or reduced their grant assistance to Nepal. If donors are not happy to provide aid in a country where more than 60 per cent of the development budget is coming from donors, how can he effectively implements poverty reduction projects and sustainable development? Further, the security expenditure has sharply increased and the budget in the social sector is decreasing. How will it be possible to improve the economic situation?

Another important agenda of his roadmap is corruption control. In this regard he said, "*Corruption, which has been continuously spreading its tentacles, has not only cast a shadow over politics and administration, but has also obstructed the nation's march towards progress. Corruption has struck at the very core of our society, the result of which the common man's confidence in the laws of the land has been shaken. Therefore, in keeping with the popular will and to fulfil the main criterion of good governance, effective measures will be adopted to curb corruption, while ensuring that the principles of justice are not infringed upon*". But the 2005 Report of Transparency International reveals that corruption has increased after 1st February 2005. The performance of high-sounding RCCC is limited to arrest and jail the former prime minister and his cabinet fellows and a few other officials. Its work is internationally and domestically criticised as biased and targeted to democratic leaders who oppose the royal takeover.

10.2.3 Responses to the 1st February takeover

10.2.3.1 Response of parliamentary political parties

The 1st February 2005 Royal takeover was a serious blow to the political parties, as the king blamed them for the corruption, insecurity, and violence and weakening of the national unity and sovereignty. Main leaders of the political parties were detained or arrested and jailed for several months. The distance between the king and the political parties has widened. Consequently, they realised that the King's move was to weaken political parties and multiparty democracy. Hence they united to fight against the King's takeover. Seven major parliamentary political parties have joined together and agreed on a six-points programme that contains restoration of the House of Representatives as an entry point and the election of constituent assembly as an exit point for resolution of the ongoing conflict. The behaviour and actions of the government is further alienating the political parties and forced to change their position from constitutional monarchy to democratic republic.

As a protest, the seven political parties have declared to boycott municipal election going to be held in February 2006. They are preparing different protest programmes. Likewise, they are trying to get more international support. Senior leaders of main political parties such as Girija Prasad Koirala (NCP), Bam Dev Gautam (CPN-UML), Gopal Man Shrestha (NCP-D) visited India and discussed Nepal's political crisis with Indian senior political leaders and the government. On 16 November 2005, CPN-UML leader Madhav Nepal with his party colleague Khadga Oli suddenly flew to New Delhi, only after 5 days of his return from there. Indian Ambassador met Mr Nepal the same day before departing to Delhi. Immediately after returning from Delhi, American Ambassador and British Ambassador also met and had talks with Madhav Nepal. Girija Prasad Koirala was also there for a week. American Ambassador J.F. Moriarty and Indian Ambassador also flew to New Delhi the same day. Maoist leaders were also said to be in New Delhi. There were important meetings between leaders of seven political parties and Maoists to resolve this crisis.

With all these efforts, the alliance of seven political parties was able to reach a 12 points understanding with the Maoists to end autocracy and restore democracy in Nepal. The 12 point understanding is as follows:

Letter of Understanding (Unofficial translation)

The long struggle between absolute monarchy and democracy in Nepal has now reached a very grave and new turn. Establishing peace by resolving the 10-year old armed conflict through a forward-looking political outlet has become the need of today. Therefore, implementing the concept of absolute democracy through a forward-looking restructuring of the state has become an inevitable need to solve the problems related to class, caste, gender, region etc of all sectors including political, economic, social and cultural, bringing autocratic monarchy to an end and establishing absolute democracy. We make public that, against this existing backdrop and reference in the country, the following understanding has been reached between the seven parliamentary parties and the CPN (Maoist) through different methods of talks.

Points of Understanding

1. Today, democracy, peace, prosperity, social advancement and a free and sovereign Nepal is the chief wish of all Nepalese. We completely agree that autocratic monarchy is the main hurdle in (realising) this. It is our clear view that without establishing absolute democracy by ending autocratic monarchy, there is no possibility of peace, progress and prosperity in the country. Therefore, an understanding has been reached to establish absolute democracy by ending autocratic monarchy, with all forces against the autocratic monarchy centralizing their assault against autocratic monarchy from their respective positions, thereby creating a nationwide storm of democratic protests.
2. The seven agitating parties are fully committed to the fact that only by establishing absolute democracy through the restoration of the Parliament with the force of agitation, forming an all-party government with complete authority, holding elections to a constituent assembly through dialogue and understanding with the Maoists, can the existing conflict in the country be resolved and sovereignty and state power completely transferred to the people. It is the view and commitment of the CPN (Maoist) that the above mentioned goal can be achieved by holding a national political conference of the agitating democratic forces, and through its decision, forming an interim government to hold constituent assembly elections. An understanding has been reached between the agitating seven parties and the CPN (Maoist) to continue dialogue on this procedural work-list and find a common understanding. It has been agreed that the force of people's movement is the only alternative to achieve this.
3. Today, the country has demanded the establishment of permanent peace along with a positive solution to the armed conflict. Therefore, we are committed to ending autocratic monarchy and the existing armed conflict,

and establishing permanent peace in the country through constituent assembly elections and forward-looking political outlet. The CPN (Maoist) expresses its commitment to move along the new peaceful political stream through this process. In this very context, an understanding has been reached to keep, during the holding of constituent assembly elections after ending autocratic monarchy, the armed Maoist force and the royal army under the supervision of the United Nations or any other reliable international supervision, to conclude the elections in a free and fair manner and accept the result of the elections. We expect reliable international mediation even during the dialogue process.

4. Expressing clearly and making public institutional commitment to the democratic norms and values like the competitive multiparty system of governance, civil liberties, human rights, the concept of the rule of law, fundamental rights etc, the CPN (Maoist) has expressed commitment to move forward its activities accordingly.
5. The CPN (Maoist) has expressed its commitment to create an environment allowing the political activists of other democratic parties displaced during the course of the armed conflict to return to their former localities and live there with dignity, return their home, land and property seized in an unjust manner and carry out their activities without let or hindrance.
6. Undertaking self criticism and self evaluation of past mistakes, the CPN (Maoist) has expressed commitment not to repeat such mistakes in future.
7. The seven political parties, undertaking self evaluation, have expressed commitment not to repeat the mistakes of the past which were committed while in parliament and in government.
8. In the context of moving the peace process forward, commitment has been expressed to fully respect the norms and values of human rights and press freedom and move ahead accordingly.
9. As the announcement of municipal polls pushed forward with the ill-motive of deluding the people and the international community and giving continuity to the autocratic and illegitimate rule of the King, and the talk of elections to Parliament are a crafty ploy, we announce to actively boycott them and call upon the general public to make such elections a failure.
10. The people and their representative political parties are the real guardians of nationality. Therefore, we are firmly committed to protecting the independence, sovereignty, geographical integrity of the country and national unity. Based on the principle of peaceful co-existence, it is our common obligation to maintain friendly relations with all countries of the world and good-neighbour relationship with neighbouring countries, especially India and China. But we request the patriotic masses to be cautious against the false attempt by the King and (his) loyalists to prolong his autocratic and illegitimate rule and delude the patriotic people

by projecting the illusory "Mandale" nationalism and questioning the patriotism of the political parties, and appeal to the international powers and the people to support, in every possible way, the democratic movement against autocratic monarchy in Nepal.

11. We call upon the civil society, professional organizations, various wings of parties, people of all communities and regions, press and intellectuals to actively participate in the peaceful movement launched on the basis of these understandings centered on democracy, peace, prosperity, forward-looking social change and the country's independence, sovereignty, and pride.
12. Regarding the inappropriate conducts that took place between the parties in the past, a common commitment has been expressed to investigate any objection raised by any party over such incidents, take action if found guilty, and to make the action public. An understanding has been reached to settle any problem emerging between the parties through peaceful dialogue at the concerned level or at the leadership level.

Roadmap of 7-Party Alliance[8]

For a long time with continuous discussion, meetings, and probably because of confusion, they were not able to come up with a common agenda. However, after long incubation of the contents of the discussion between the seven parties, they came up with a 'declaration for a united effort to resolve the national crisis' with the following points) as roadmap):

1. Take up the democratic road and not the one leading to extremism.
2. Today's need is to do away with the King's autocratic rule.
3. Reinstatement of the parliament for a people's representative government.
4. Some important points to resolve national crisis:
   a. The government shall be responsible for the parliament.
   b. Management of violent conflict and reinstatement of peace.
   c. Commitment toward the future progressive programmes.
   d. Constitution shall be adhere to the liberal multiparty democratic norms and values,
   e. Progressive movement to be based on the constitution of 1990.
   f. Plans to hold national elections.

Though this was a product of long discussions between the members of 7-party alliance, this roadmap has many confusions, complications and difficulties to translate into practice. The top priority to restore parliament is not only a confusing and weak agenda but also a source of conflict within the 7-party alliance members, if and when the parliament is restored. There is also a naive wish that the king will restore the parliament according to the wish of political parties. Another big confusion of the road map of 7-party alliance is its firm stand on the existing constitution. It is not possible to inter into constituent assembly election unless there is a change in the constitution, which needs full cooperation of the king. If there is a difference of opinion between the king and political parties in changing the constitution even by a two-third majority, there is a standstill. If this case inters into legal remedy, then it is less likely to get an outlet. Similarly, the roadmap is also not clear on the position of the king, whether they accept the constitutional monarchy or they opt for the ceremonial monarchy or no existence of the king at all. Further, though they have mentioned some aspects of what, the how part is completely missing in their roadmap and it will create enormous confusions and contradictions later if the procedure is not clarified and owned by all as their common approach. Hence, this roadmap of 7-party alliance is not strong enough and clear in dealing with the current crisis. Looking to the behaviour of the king in the past four years, he will not easily give up power. The only way to get it back would be to launch another 'people's movement' similar to that of 1990 and defeat him by people's power. The 12-point understanding between the seven party alliance and the Maoists has paved the path for massive people's movement. The only condition is to have strong collaboration between these two forces for the common cause.

10.2.3.2 Response of international community and donors' dilemma

The international response to the 1st February Royal takeover was not favourable to the King despite his rigorous efforts to justify his takeover as a response to crush the insurgency and restore peace in Nepal. Major international forces engaged in Nepal's politics expressed their deep dismay.

On 25 February 2005, Richard Boucher, Spokesperson of the US Department of State and strong supporter of RNA for military action against Maoists said, *"we think that the king needs to move quickly to reinstate and protect civil and human rights, to release those who are detained under the state of emergency, and to begin a dialogue with the political parties intended to restore multiparty democratic institutions under a constitutional monarchy".*

On his visit to Nepal (26-28 June 2005), Mr. Donald Camp (Assistant Secretary of the US Department of State), said that it is unacceptable for the USA and international community to return to pre-1990's political system. He further said that security is not above democracy and democracy is a system which wins over hate, divisions and violence. He also supported the unity of seven political parties and asked the king to address their concerns (Upreti, 2005f).

However, when the debate on the necessity of dialogue between Maoists and 7-party alliance was gaining momentum and leaders of political parties started a dialogue with the Maoists, the US Ambassador J.F. Moriarty on 4 November 2005 issued a statement warning political parties not to collaborate with the Maoists. The statement came after the CPN-UMP leaders Bam Dev Gautam and Yuba Raj Gyawali met senior Moaist leaders (said to be Prachanda, Baburam and Krishna Bahadur Mahar) in Rolpa. The Ambassador was insisting on political parties to work with the king instead of the Maoists. His statement almost thrilled major political parties and they clarified with him that they would not collaborate with the Maoists unless the Maoists suspend arms and express their sincere commitment to multi party democracy. However, the statement got severe criticism not only from civil society and intellectuals, but also from some of the leaders of political parties themselves[9].

On 15 November Mr Moriarty met with CPN-UML General Secretary Madav Nepal (who was in New Delhi for almost three weeks to discuss Nepal's political crisis with many senior Indian political leaders. He also met senior Maoists leaders and discussed the same issue) and discussed the political crisis as well as the possibility for collaboration between seven parties and Maoists. In his meeting with UML General Secretary, US Ambassador said that the USA is not against the political parties holding dialogue with the Maoists with the view to convincing them in rejoining the political mainstream. He also expressed strong support to the seven party alliance's assertion that it would not enter into an alliance with Maoists unless and until they renounced violence, put down their weapons and committed to supporting the democratic process[10]'.On the same day, the US President signed a bill that has imposed nine human rights and democracy related conditions to US military aids to Nepal[11].

Box 10.3 Reflection of comments about Nepal's crisis by international community

'We continue to urge the King to restore representative government and democratic freedoms. These are essential steps towards a sustainable peace process. We condemn the Maoists' violence and call on all parties to the conflict to respect and uphold the human rights of all people in Nepal. Following consultations in London, our Ambassador to Nepal has returned to Kathmandu to convey these messages directly to the Government of Nepal.'

—British Foreign Secretary, Jack Straw, 22 Feb. 2005

"We remain deeply troubled by developments in Nepal. King Gyanendra's dismissal of the government, declaration of a state of emergency, detention of politicians, human rights workers and students and the suspension of fundamental constitutional rights is a step away from Nepal's path toward democracy. The King needs to restore and protect civil and human rights, promptly release those detained under the state of emergency and move quickly toward the restoration of civil liberties and multi-party democratic institutions under a constitutional monarchy. The United States supports a peaceful, prosperous, and democratic Nepal. The protection of civil and human rights and strengthening of multi-party democracy are key components of Nepal's progressing along this path. We call on those in Nepal who are committed to the country's future to engage in meaningful political discussions leading to national elections. Those among the Maoists who wish to be a part of Nepal's future leadership must abandon their armed struggle and join the political mainstream through dialogue and peaceful means".

—Richard Boucher, Spokesman, Washington, DC, February 14, 2005

"In the last three months since my visit I have noted, with sadness and concern, the deterioration of the situation in Nepal. Of special concern are the recent government efforts to silence the independent news media. In early October the government of Nepal adopted an unfortunate media ordinance cementing the ban on FM radio news broadcasts and making criticism of the King or any member of the royal family illegal".

—US Senator Tom Daschle, 28 Oct 2005

"*We continue to urge the King to restore representative government and democratic freedom. These are essential steps towards sustainable peace process*[12]."

—Press statement of Foreign Secretary Jack Straw, 25 February 2005

"Imposing restrictions on media does not advance democracy. Clearly, such measures are at odds with the goal of promoting free and fair elections in Nepal."

—James F. Moriarty, US Ambassador to Nepal, 26 Oct 2005.

> "I will not take the time to discuss in detail the history of this tiny country wedged between China and India. Suffice it to say that not only is Nepal among the world's least developed countries, it is also facing a ruthless Maoist insurgency and a political crisis instigated by King Gyanendra which together threaten to turn Nepal into a failed state".
>
> —*US Senator Patrick Leahy in the United States Senate on 28 July 2005*
>
> "OHCHR is concerned that the 9 October 2005 Media Ordinance promulgated by His Majesty's Government violates international human rights standards, and that the 21 October seizure of broadcast equipment from an FM radio station without a judicial ruling shows lack of respect for the rule of law."
>
> —*OHCHR, 27 October 2005*
>
> ''Events in 2005 have darkened prospects for a resolution to the armed conflict and political crisis. We judge the changes of 1 February to have been self-defeating,'
>
> —*Tom Phillips, delegation of European Union (EU) Troika (6 Oct2005).*

Similarly, the UK government recalled the British Ambassador saying that "'*we strongly support constitutional monarchy and multi-party democracy in Nepal, and want to see a sustainable peace-process. We continue to call upon the Maoists to end their violence and for both sides to return to the negotiating table.*

'But we were very clear, when the King dismissed his Prime Minister, that we regarded this as a backward step which undermined Nepal's democratic institutions and risked further instability. 'In this serious moment, it is appropriate for us to recall our Ambassador so that we may reflect with him, and with our international partners, on the way forward[13]". After some time, by issuing a press statement the UK government also suspended its planned package of military aid (1.3 million-pound package of equipment announced in January includes vehicles, night-flying and communications improvements and bomb disposal equipment.) to Nepal. Foreign Secretary Jack Straw in a statement said, "*The British government has decided to suspend a planned package of military assistance to Nepal in the light of the disturbing situation there*[14]". He urged the king to restore democratic government immediately. These statements and opinions clearly reveal the strong objection of the UK government to the royal takeover.

On 9 February 2005, the Indian Ambassador met with the King and urged him to return to democratic processes, remove restrictions imposed to political leaders since 1st February and bring political party leaders into a broad national consensus.

On 25 February 2005, India decided to immediately suspend all

BOX 10.4 Indian Statement on the Royal takeover of 1st February 2005

The King of Nepal has dissolved the multiparty government led by Prime Minister Deuba, and has decided to constitute a Council of Ministers under his own Chairmanship. An emergency has been declared and fundamental rights have been suspended. These developments constitute a serious setback to the cause of democracy in Nepal and cannot but be a cause of grave concern to India.

There are also reports that several political leaders have been confined to their residences. The safety and welfare of the political leaders must be ensured and political parties must be allowed to exercise all the rights enjoyed by them under the Constitution.

India has consistently supported multiparty democracy and constitutional monarchy enshrined in Nepal's Constitution as the two pillars of political stability in Nepal. This principle has now been violated with the King forming a government under his Chairmanship.

We have always considered that in Nepal, it is imperative to evolve a broad national consensus, particularly between the monarchy and political parties, to deal with the political and economic challenges facing the country.

The latest developments in Nepal bring the monarchy and the mainstream political parties in direct confrontation with each other. This can only benefit the forces that not only wish to undermine democracy but the institution of monarchy as well.

India has a longstanding and unique relationship with Nepal, with which it shares an open border, a history of strong cultural and spiritual values and wide-ranging economic and commercial links. We will continue to support the restoration of political stability and economic prosperity in Nepal, a process which requires reliance on the forces of democracy and the support of the people of Nepal.

New Delhi, February 1, 2005

military aid (arms and ammunition for the RNA, helicopters, armoured vehicles, bullet proof-vests and helmets, besides a suspension of military training to Nepali soldiers) to Nepal. However, it said that military aid may be released if the king responded to the demand of international community for the release of detained leaders and members of civil society, restoration of civil and media rights and restoration of multi party democracy. Nevertheless, India said it continues economic cooperation in humanitarian support[15].

On the 4th of March 2005, Indian Foreign Minister Natwar Singh said in the Upper House of the Indian Parliament, "*The development in Nepal constitute a serious setback to democracy and bring the monarchy and mainstream political parties in direct confrontation with each other. This can only benefit the forces that not only wish to undermine democracy in Nepal but the institution of democracy as well*".

As an immediate response to the 1st February move, all major donors suspended their military aids and examined the development aids. They took a 'wait and see' strategy for the first 2-3 months, which is gradually changed. They had assembled in London to discuss the crisis brought by the royal takeover. They decided to put pressure on the king to restore democracy; release detained or arrested political leaders and civil activists. Likewise, on 8 March 2005, Kathmandu-based resident missions/representative of the major bilateral donors and the UN issued a statement concerning the royal takeover and its setback to democracy. The signatories of the statement were CIDA, DANIDA, FINIDA, DFID, SNV, GTZ, SDC, USAID, Norway, European Commission and UNDP. After the royal takeover, they have critically examined their development aids to Nepal. Some of them are very determined to tie their aid with the democracy and human rights and some of them are moderate.

The visiting delegation of European Union (EU) Troika had warned that there is a strong risk of political collapse in Nepal if there is no reconciliation. In a press meet at the end of their three-day visit to Nepal on 6 October 2005, Mr. Tom Phillips[16], leader of the EU Troika mission expressed the great concerns of EU as the country's situation is worsening. He said that there is a strong risk of political collapse in Nepal if political forces are not ready to quickly address the country's problems. The Troika mentioned that the Nepalese government should reach out to the political parties to develop a full return to multi-party democracy. The Troika said that the Maoist ceasefire, whatever the tactics behind it, offers an opportunity for a government response to create a much-needed truce. "*We believe there may be a role for third party support for brokering and monitoring the arrangements for a formal ceasefire agreement*". In the issue of the royal takeover of February 1, the Troika mission of EU was quite critical and said, "*Events in 2005 have darkened prospects for a resolution to the armed conflict and political crisis. We judge the changes of 1 February to have been self-defeating. The EU believes that the way forward has to be through an inclusive and comprehensive process to achieve a negotiated peace. The EU continues to believe that such a solution will require the assistance of an independent and credible external partner and the active support of the international community"*.

The Troika mission was supportive to the efforts of seven-party alliance to restore democracy. It mentions, *"We share your concern about the absence of a functioning multi-party democracy, and we see an effective multi-party democracy as the only sustainable solution to the problems of Nepal. We support your efforts to maintain and consolidate a common platform"*. But it was strongly against the violence of the Maoists. The leader of the troika said, *"should be under no illusions: the EU rejects the use of violence. We do not believe that Maoist ideology is the answer to the problems of Nepal or to the needs and wishes of the people of Nepal"*. The Troika mission also highlighted the urgency to settle the crisis. *"There is no time to waste. We believe that those in Nepal who want peace must act now,' the leader of the delegation said. It was also not in favour of election without political settlement. He mentioned, "In a country in a conflict situation, elections usually come at the end of a peace process*[17]".

In 22 April 2005, His Majesty the King Gyanendra and United Nations Secretary-General Kofi Annan discussed the political situation in Jakarta when they were attending the Afro-Asian Conference. During the meeting Kofi Annan emphasised the restoration of multiparty democracy in Nepal. A week after his discussion with King Gyanendra in the Afro-Asian Summit in Jakarta, UN Secretary General Kofi Annan on April 28 in New Delhi said that he wants to see the restoration of constitutional democracy in Nepal as soon as possible. In a press conference in New Delhi he said, *"We have been in touch with the King, and we discussed the issues"*. He further told to the audience, *"I think it's important that political parties are allowed to resume their activities as we have agreed during our discussions*[18]".

Some of the donors supporting military aids for Nepal are facing a major dilemma after the 1st February Royal takeover. The dilemma is whether to support the autocratic regime, which is curtailing civil liberty and violating basic rights of people (restriction of movement, freedom of expression etc.) or stop military aids to Nepal that ultimately help the Maoists. King Gyanendra never took any of these international concerns seriously and he never changed his behaviour from the international pressure. Instead, he continuously attempted to threaten as well as convinced them to support him.

At present, three schools of thoughts are prevalent in the donors' support to Nepal. One group of donors believes that supporting autocracy cannot restore peace and promote democracy and continuing their aids do not make any sense. Hence, either they stop giving new aids or reduce the volume of aid. They are more consistent in their position and their activities are more concentrated on human rights and democracy. In any case this group of donors was not providing military aids to Nepal earlier too. Another group of donors (both bilateral and multi lateral) does not seriously differ with the regime and therefore is almost indifferent in its response to the development assistance and continuing their support as usual. The third group of donors wants to engage more directly in the Nepal's crisis, mainly with the issues of military assistance. This group is providing both development and military aids. They want to continue their aids (including military assistance) but they are facing tremendous pressure from international human rights organisations and domestic ones to continue. The Amendment of 'Asian Security' bill in the American Senate and approved by the president (16 November 2005) is a prominent example of this kind.

The UN is quite concerned about the deteriorating political situation and the ongoing-armed conflict. The General Secretary of the UN Mr Kofi Anan sent his special envoy (Mr Samuel Tamrat, working in the Political Division) several times to discuss the conflict issues. The UN also offered any help Nepal needs to resolve the conflict. The Special Advisor of the General Secretary Mr Lakhdar Brahimi visited Nepal (10-15 July 2005) to assess the current political situation and conflict context in the country. He has performed similar tasks in other high-intensity conflict countries such as Lebanon, South Africa, Iraq, Afghanistan and Haiti. He met the King, representatives of the government, leaders of the political parties and members of civil society during his stay in Nepal. His appointment to assess situation in Nepal also clearly indicates the level of worry in the UN about Nepal.

The ongoing conflict has reached a dimension that can no longer be neglected by the international community, which exerts a disproportionate influence on Nepal's economic, political and social development. However, the establishment is not ready to compromise even with the international community. In private meetings and discussions with some of the diplomats, they are surprised at the gap between the saying and doing of the king. They seem more determined to act concertedly among the donors but it is not easy either.

India is emerging as an indispensable international force to deal with this conflict, as all forces of Nepal are overtly relying upon India. Maoist leader Dr Babu Ram Bhattarai, CPN-UML leader Mr Bam Dev Gautam, NC Leader Mr Girija Prasad Koirala, Janaskati Party leader Mr Surya Bahadur Thapa, Foreign Minister Mr Ramesh Nath Pandey, Madav Nepal, other many politicians and royalists visited India and met senior Indian leaders, government and discussed the Nepalese crisis. The UK and USA have also given a leading role to India to deal with the Nepalese conflict.

India has several stakes in the Nepal's crisis. They are:

- Increasing insecurity in the region in general and Indian states in particular due to expansion of the Maoist insurgency beyond Nepal.
- National security interest to keep Nepal into its security umbrella. Nepal's strategic geopolitical position, (situated between China and India) is one of the main reasons of India's continuous engagement, particularly in security-related issues (either referring to the 1950's Nepal-India Friendship Treaty, or relating to regional security). Nepal is using China-card to bargain with India by exploring possibility of purchasing arms from China, which India does not like at al.,
- Indian ambition to be a regional super-power/global power, which requires maintaining its heavy influence in other countries of the region.
- High expectations of the power centres of Nepal to India and relying on it for resolution of political crisis in Nepal.
- Economic interests of India, as Nepal is economically depending with India and many Indian industrialists and investors are major players of Nepalese economy.

Indian Foreign Secretary Shyam Saran, who was also Indian ambassador to Nepal and well familiar with the Nepalese politics and the monarchy, was expressing his opinion in New Delhi in a ceremony of releasing the book "Royal Nepalese Army - Meeting the Maoist challenge" written by Ashok Mehta, retired senior officer of Indian Army.. He said India would be keenly watching the current situation in Nepal which is 'not a happy one'. In the coming days, there could be optimistic or equally pessimistic scenario.... We will have to watch the situation extremely carefully, as stakes of India are very very high. India would be keenly watching how King Gyanendra's assurance on roadmap to restoration of multi-party democracy unfolds " .

- Emotional, cultural, religious and social attachments of people of the two countries.

Therefore, India may not allow Nepal to collapse or turn into a failed state, unless this situation favours Indian interests. However, major political forces of Nepal are primary actors and therefore, role of India depends upon their ability to utilise the tremendously high potentials of India to resolve the ongoing conflict and crisis.

10.2.3.3 Response of civil society and human rights organisations

Civil society was one of the hardest hit by the royal takeover. Rapidly increased human rights monitoring, peace and conflict transformation activities of the civil society before 1 February 2005 were severely restricted after the royal takeover. Movements of the civil society leaders were prohibited and some of them were detained. Blooming FM radio news were banned and journalists were severely threatened. Consequently, civil society, particularly journalists and lawyers, became very vocal against the royal move. Human rights community also protested the 1st February takeover.

After February 1st there are new state sponsored civil society organisations and actors emerged to support the royal takeover. They were allowed to organise rallies even in the time of the State of Emergency. The government security forces had provided escorts to them and they were using state-controlled media, public places (e.g., public places declared as sensitive areas and prohibited by government

Box 10.5 Concern of Human Rights Watch (HRW)

Issuing a press statement on 28 October 2005 at New York, Human Rights Watch said, *'The Nepali government should immediately reverse its decision to close the popular radio station Kantipur FM*[19] *and end censorship of the media'*. Reacting to the new media ordinance imposed by the government on 9 October, 2005, Brad Adams, Asia Director of Human Rights Watch said,, *"The new media ordinance takes unlawful censorship imposed since the King's coup and enshrines it into law. Press freedom in Nepal is moving from endangered to extinct. Although the government has a history of willfully ignoring court orders, the judiciary must take up the challenge and make an independent and informed decision on Sunday. The judiciary has now become the last best hope for the future of the free press in Nepal"*.

(Source: http://hrw.org/english/docs/2005/10/28/nepal11939.htm).

to organise meetings, rallies and public assemblies) and state resources. So, countering the mainstream civil society were their main activities. Though new civil society actors are created, their influence is virtually negligible, mainly because of their wrong footing.

Civil society is proactively engaged in protesting the royal takeover and organising mass rallies, debates, discussions and providing open support to 7 political parties to fight against the cessation of democracy. Civil society in Nepal is getting good international support (see Box 10.5 and 10.6). Initiatives of civil society to promote people's movement for democracy are helping political parties to develop confidence and revive the lost trust. Civil society has also mobilised its relatively strong international network against the royal coup. However, there is still lack of proper coordination between these two forces and to make concerted efforts in restoring democracy and peace in the country.

Box 10.6 Draft Resolution at the 113th Inter-Parliamentary Union Conference (October 14-19, 2005, Geneva)

Parliamentary Support to Reactivation of Democratic Institutions and Systems in Nepal

Concerned that after the lifting of the State of Emergency in Nepal on April 29, 2005, the situation in the country has not improved and rather worsened, and that civil liberties and fundamental human rights have not been restored;

Fully aware that a form of Royal Military Dictatorship without re-instating the Parliament of Nepal, which was dissolved on May 22, 2002, continues to implement the State of Emergency, resulting in the escalation of human rights violations such as illegal arrests and detentions, torture, enforced disappearances, censorship and bans on communication system such as newspaper, radio, and websites, and restrictions on movements, activities and assembly of human rights defenders including the members of the dissolved parliament;

Mindful of the Country Resolution on Nepal under Agenda Item 19 on Technical Cooperation and Advisory Services, passed in the 61st Session of the UN Commission on Human Rights, calling for full respect of all human rights for all;

Mindful of the Siracusa Principles on the Limitation and Derogation Provisions in the International Covenant on Civil and Political Rights[20], which asserts that "the burden is upon a state imposing limitations so qualified to demonstrate that the limitations do not impair the democratic functioning of the society;[21]

Recalling that such abrogation of civil liberties and freedoms are subject to "prompt and periodic independent review by the legislature, of the necessity for derogation measures"; "that effective remedies shall be available to persons claiming that derogation measures affecting them are not strictly required by the exigencies of the situation"; and that no state party shall, even in times of emergency threatening the life of the nation, derogate from the Covenant's guarantees of the right to life, freedom from torture, cruel, inhuman or degrading treatment or punishment, freedom of thought, conscience and religion[22];

Invoking IPU Resolutions on Strengthening National Structures, Institutions and Organizations of Society, which Play a Role in Promoting and Safeguarding Human Rights[23], as well as the Resolution on Ensuring Lasting Democracy by Forging Close Links between Parliament and the People[24];

Reaffirming the fundamental role played by parliaments in enacting laws and reviewing national policies to ensure their safe and positive impacts on the people;

Endeavoring to contribute to the task of seeking lasting solutions to the internal conflict in Nepal;

- Call upon the government in Nepal to restore the democratically established parliament at the earliest possible;
- Support any initiative for multi- stakeholders' dialogue, in particular, government, political parties, insurgents and civil society representatives, for peaceful and democratic resolution of the internal armed conflict;
- Call upon the government in Nepal to respect all human rights of people, in particularly human rights defenders, in accordance with international human rights obligations;
- Call upon the government in Nepal to ensure independent and effective functioning of the National Human Rights Commission of Nepal in addressing human rights violations and;
- Call upon all the world's parliament to contribute to the swift and effective return of democracy and peace in Nepal.

The first February takeover also provided ample opportunity to expose civil society leaders and politicians, as most of them took their position by either supporting the takeover or opposing it. Some of the renowned public faces were unexpectedly supporting the takeover and some of the people known to be close to the palace were opposing it.

10.2.3.4 Response of Maoists

The Maoists are strategically gaining much from the royal takeover. The attitude and behaviour of the king towards the parliamentary political parties has pushed them to change their commitment from constitutional monarchy to democratic republic. Earlier, they were a buffer between the King and the Maoists because of their commitment to the constitutional monarchy.. However, the extremely negative response of the king towards them, strong voices within the political parties are emerging within these parties on the relevance of monarchy and need of republic system. This is what the Maoists have been demanding for a long time. So, the political parties and the Maoists are coming closer to a common agenda of constituent assembly to decide the fate of the monarchy. Maoist leader Prachanda issued several statements against the royal takeover and expressed his commitment to support the struggle of political parties to restore democracy and return from royal takeover. CPN (Maoist) also sent its senior leaders (Dr Babu Ram Bhattarai and Mr Krishna Bahadur Mahara) to India to discuss the royal takeover and collaboration with political parties. It is said that they have discussed this issue with various Indian politicians too. It is said that there was a series of meeting between the Maoists and political parties at different levels at different times. The Moaists had discussed earlier with Girija Prasad Koirala and Bam Dev Gautam in addition to the leaders of seven parties staying in Delhi to garner support of India. As a result, mistrust between the Maoists and political parties decrease and decision of collaboration to a minimum common agenda are reached. In October, the 7-party alliance gave mandate to Madav Nepal and Girija Prasad Koirala to talk with the Maoists. After a series of discussions and meetings (see *Nepal Weekly*, Vol. 6, No. 15, 20 November, 2005 for detail on the talks between the Maoists and the political parties), they come closer in some of the issues. Political parties demanded that the Maoists suspend their arms at the moment. In response to the request of seven parties, Maoists announced that they would not attack any unarmed people, irrespective of background and activities. Maoists also repeatedly asked political parties to collaborate with them. Even Maoist chief asked political parties to form a talk committee. The Maoists also urged the international community to denounce the royal takeover and support constituent assembly election.

The Maoists declared a unilateral ceasefire for three months on 3 September and said that it was their step forward to collaborate with the political parties as political parties were demanding Maoists to declare ceasefire. This ceasefire was a very strategic choice of the Maoists to achieve the following:

1. They wanted to give the message across the world that they want peace and political settlement of the conflict.

2. They wanted to create a difficult position for the king, as the sole strategy of the king was to win international support on the ground of controlling 'terrorists'. The king had set his travel plan to attend the UN General Assembly where he could strongly argue to justify takeover as a bold step to control violence and restore peace. When they declared ceasefire, the government faced a very awkward situation. The government had to respond by declaring a ceasefire, in which it was not interested and therefore not ready to reciprocate. This situation raised serious questions on the intention of the government on peace. The king would be seriously criticised in the General Assembly of the UN. There was also a plan of different organisations and people to protest against the king. It was reported that the host country even did not invite him at welcome dinner to boycott him. All these incidences led him to cancel his plan to address UN General Assembly in September 2005.
3. The also gained sympathy from people and international community because of ceasefire. This ceasefire was declared at such a time when the Nepalese people were in the eve of national festivals Dashain and Tihar.
4. Strong pressure mounted over the government domestically and internationally to reciprocate by declaring ceasefire from the state side. When the government refused to reciprocate, Maoists and people opposing the 1st February takeover campaign against the king's real intentions (why he is not reciprocating if the rebel group has already declared a ceasefire, as the government must be more responsive to restore peace)
5. They organised political programmes, trained their cadres and fighters and accomplished organisational activities such as meetings and conventions, training and orientations, expansion of public relations, etc.

10.3 FUTURE SCENARIO OF THE CRISIS

As the present circumstance is changing rapidly and ambiguously, it is extremely difficult to draw clear and comprehensive scenarios of the ongoing conflict and the political crisis in Nepal. However scenario analysis is a part of the crisis management and contingency plan at the time of escalated conflict and political crisis. Based on the present course of actions of the main conflict actors, it is most likely that uncertainty, insecurity, instability and potential violence will persist in the country if the influential parties of the conflict are not ready to respond through a negotiated settlement. The following possible scenarios may help to think about the future situation of Nepal:

10.3.1 Immediate future scenarios

10.3.1.1 Scenario 1(best)

- Meaningful reconciliation starts between the major political forces,
- Meaningful dialogue starts with Maoists under the leadership of political parties backed by the King and military; interim government formed by representing political parties, Maoists and civil society; election of constituent assembly held and new constitution prepared and future of Monarchy is decided by people,
- The Maoists accept multiparty democracy and reach a negotiated settlement ensuring state restructuring, adapting inclusiveness of all stakeholders of Nepalese democracy (win-win situation),
- International community genuinely supports peace process and negotiated settlement (by providing required resources, knowledge and other political supports as and when required),
- Sincere implementation of the agreement of the negotiation (state restructuring-inclusive democracy, reconstruction, rehabilitation, reintegration, demobilisation, etc.).

This is the best-preferred option for ending the civil war and political crisis in Nepal. However, considering the behaviour and actions of the king at the current situation, this scenario is less likely to prevail soon.

10.3.1.2 Scenario 2

- Emergence of new alliances
  - o Maoists suspend arms and make alliance with political parties to pressurise the palace (need based approach for both parties but confrontational with the palace), their collective efforts prevail upon autocracy, or
  - o Palace reconciles with the political parties and prevents

seven parties-Maoists alliance (will fulfil expectation of international community but may not reach a full negotiated settlement), or

- o Palace collaborates with Maoists to undermine the political parties (ego-centric, and more threat to democracy) and reach a negotiation (but sustainability of negotiated settlement is in question),

- Passive role of international community but still some support to political parties and human rights areas,
- The King relies more on the military power and spirits/ideology of the Panchayat regime but no reconciliation (situation of stalemate),
- Some degree of democratic rights are selectively respected by the state to demonstrate to international community,
- The Maoists and government may decide to have ceasefire and peace talk. However, it will be used as strategic pause and strengthening their political and military bases (some progress but no full settlement),
- Weak political parties, weak palace and weak Maoists,
- Continue obstruction of development, social services and economic sectors.

Considering the King's three-year plan and his response so far, he may take a harder line and consolidate power by strengthening military, intelligence, police forces and other institutional mechanisms of the state and available resources. Suppression, curtailing of rights and freedom enjoyed by Nepalese people will increase. Political parties will be sidelined from the mainstream politics. The state may raise taxes to sustain required resources for some time. State will be more autocratic and dictatorial and people will be frustrated enough during the period of active ruling. This will lead to a strong people's movement for restoration of democracy starting in the leadership of political parties. It may result in a democratic republican system.

Role of international community in general (specifically the UK, USA and EU) and India in particular will be one of the determining factors in Nepal's political crisis. If the international community takes a Myanmar approach (more passive, superficial and ceremonial reactions), limits its concerns on human rights only or continues military assistance in the name of non-lethal support, autocracy will sustain longer. Another factor is relations of Maoists with India and its subsequent response to Nepal. If India is firmly against the Nepalese

Maoists, it would create extreme difficulty for Maoists and help autocracy. On the contrary, if India and Maoists make a trade-off, autocracy may face difficulty. The Maoists dispute within their party may help to strengthen autocracy. On the contrary, if Maoists reform themselves, settle the ongoing intra-party dispute smoothly and collaborate with political parties, suspend arms, the autocracy may fall.

10.3.1.3 Scenario 3

- The government holds election without participation of major political parties,
- Based on the experiment of the municipality's election (this is possibly a test case for the parliamentary election, if municipality election gives favourable results for the palace), parliamentary election will be held and royalists and anti-democrats will be declared elected parliamentarians,
- Parliament will change constitution to reinstate the active monarchy through an elected process and that will be claimed as democratic,
- Western world will recognise this process, as it did in Pakistan,
- Political parties will be weak,
- No ceasefire, no peace talks, fights, attacks and counter attacks continues,
- Obstruction of development projects and programmes (particularly implemented by NGOs) blaming that they are collaborating with the insurgents,
- International community divides and very few will support (e.g., Cuba, North Korea, Pakistan, some Arabian countries) the autocracy and many donors (who are mainly concerned with human rights and development of Nepalese people instead of military or political interests such as Norway, Switzerland, Denmark, etc.) will be determined on their stand and reduce their development aids (as they already started, e.g., Norway, Switzerland, Denmark have already reduced their volume of aid to Nepal, for example, Norway decided to reduce its aid to Nepal by 10 percent in 2006), may shift their assistance in humanitarian affairs and human rights activities. Countries with military and political interests such as the USA, UK and India will face a dilemma but find ways to continuously engage in both interests. India's role will increase in Nepal's politics

and international community may pore prominently back Indian approach.

10.3.1.4 Scenario 4 (worst)

- The king blames multi-party democracy for all misdeeds in the country and civil war.
- The Monarchy is presented as the only uniting force to stabilise the nation.
- Autocracy strengthens: civil rights, freedom of speech and movement curtails:
  - o Severely suppress and make parliamentary political parties dysfunctional, who oppose autocracy
  - o Ban on political parties,
  - o Military power dominates or (directly or indirectly) controls political course of actions,
  - o Militarisation of society: involvement of military in development, banking and social sectors, politics and rapid expansion of size of military[25] forces,
  - o Denial to negotiate with the rebels and therefore no peace talk.
- Humanitarian crisis mounts:
  - o Intense fight between the security forces and the insurgents causing grave violation of human rights,
  - o Massacre and mass displacement increase,
  - o Possibilities for external intervention increases (may be in the form of peace keeping forces).
- Maoists fail to effectively control insurgency:
  - o CPN (Maoist) splits
  - o Several uncontrolled factions emerge or several warlords start independent fights,
  - o Civil war spreads across the villages,
- Severe restriction on development:
  - o More damage of development infrastructures,
  - o Donor shift development funding to humanitarian support,
  - o Drastic shift of development budget to security budget,
  - o Root causes and structural conditions of the conflict remain unchanged

10.3.2 Scenarios for intermediate future

10.3.2.1 Active monarchy

If the autocracy sustains for the coming 3-5 years, it may expand further. This scenario is described as a situation where:

- The king with strong military back-up and expansion,
- Civil liberty and human rights are not respected,
- Parliamentary political parties opposing autocracy are banned,
- Militarisation of society: rapid expansion of military size, military controls politics, economy and social sectors, development, banking sector

There is less likely to be full autocracy for a longer period given the condition that international community, youths, young generation leaders of political parties, media and civil society will not tolerate full autocracy. Political parties will also fight against the active monarchy. Examining the behaviour of the king, it can be said that if autocracy prevails for some years, there will be a people's revolution that will end monarchy and establish democratic republican system in the country.

10.2.2.2 Maoists takeover

Maoists will take over and control the state and establish a People's Democratic System. They will claim to end all forms of exploitation - oppression of feudalism, bureaucratic capitalism and imperialism/ expansionism in the country and implement democracy for the people and dictatorship over the enemies of the people. They will form 'People's Council, a mechanism of revolutionary united front, which represents workers, peasants, people's army, petty bourgeoisie, national bourgeoisie, oppressed nations/nationalities, Dalit, women, expatriate Nepalese and various patriotic, democratic and leftist forces'.

- Suppression to 'anti-feudal and anti-imperialist/ anti-expansionist' elements in their words,
- International community will not support the new regime arguing that of the Maoists are 'authoritarian' (they said in their 75 point programme that 'democratic centralism shall be the fundamental principle of state organisation'),
- They will declare all laws; orders and judicial systems of old state as null and void and develop new laws and directives,

- They will establish centralized People's Army replacing RNA,
- Pro-palace people will continue fighting with the new communist state,
- Maoists will face scarcity of resources (they said, 'the principle of "Grasp revolution and promote production" shall be made the basic guiding policy for economic development'),
- They will seize the lands owned by landlords and *Guthis* (owned by social and religious institutions) and distribute to landless and poor peasants, and tillers,
- They will nationalise health and education sectors, natural resources such as forests, big irrigation projects, mines, grazing meadows, large uncultivated lands, rivers, lakes, places of historical/natural importance, arts and artefacts, industries, etc.
- They will face constraints of financial resources,
- They will nullify treaties and agreements blaming them as semi-colonial and neo-colonial and face problem in international relations,
- Communal type of development initiatives,
- Work of INGOs/NGOs will be regulated saying that they are part of imperialist financial penetration and influence.

However, it is less likely to happen because domestic politics as well as external forces such as India, the USA and UK are not favourable for this scenario to occur.

10.3.2.3 Democratic Republic system

- New coalition between parliamentary parties and Maoists forms to fight against autocracy. According to the guiding framework of 12 point understanding between the seven-party alliance and the Maoists.
- The fight between the autocratic force (palace and its supporters) and progressive force (coalition of parliamentary parties and Maoists) will lead to serious confrontation and virtually to the republican political system,
- Residual pro-palace force will continue their attempt to destabilise the newly established democratic republic system. Severe resistance from feudal elites,
- Formulation of new constitution through constituent assembly election,
- Power-sharing government will be formed by the representatives

of parliamentary political parties and the Maoists,

- International relations may be redefined in the new political change,
- New beginning and progress and prosperity with complete state restructuring.

10.3.2.4 Co-existence of all three major forces (Negotiated settlement)

- Reconciliation between the palace and political parties and they make collective efforts to reach negotiated settlement with the Maoists,
- An all-party government operates and holds elections for constituent assembly,
- New constitution, new political administration and social change process starts,
- Development gets high priority for the post-conflict arrangement (massive reconstruction, rehabilitation and economic reform programme, infrastructure development),
- Higher degree of international support arrives,

Pragmatically, potential of ending of the armed conflict exists in all scenarios. Even in the worst-case scenario, ending of armed conflict is possible when one party becomes disproportionably strong. However, in this scenario, cessation of armed conflict will be from the use of force. Ending armed conflict does not always mean that root causes and structural conditions of the conflict are addressed.

There is a reconciliatory scenario where co-existence is the guiding framework for the political forces to reach negotiation. Conversing points (popularly known in Nepalese language is *Milan Bindu*) for the negotiated settlement would be:

(a) Accepting sovereignty of people: constitution made by the people's representatives elected by constituent assembly and approved by people through referendum, and

(b) Monarchy subject to people's decision. However, expressions, behaviour and actions of the king so far do not confirm possibility for him to accept these conditions. In such a situation, only people's power can bring him down. Nepal needs similar people's revolution that had happened in the states of former USSR to defeat the autocracy. However, this possible only when progressive forces work together.

10.4 ENVISIONING THE FUTURE

10.4.1 Capitalise on the opportunity brought about by the crisis

This conflict has not only brought about a political crisis but also opened tremendous opportunities to initiate radical reform in the state structures towards achieving a more equitable and just society if the parliamentary political parties, the King and the Maoists genuinely want it. The state restructuring agenda put forward by the government, 18-point programme of the five parliamentary parties, reform agenda forwarded by all individual parties, time to time publicly expressed concerns of the King and the peace talk agenda put forward by the Maoists and the road maps proposed by the UML have clearly demonstrated that there is a common ground to reach negotiation and to initiate radical restructuring of the state.

International community is also supportive to resume peace talk and to address root causes of the conflict when Nepal initiates consensual reform process. The expressions from the EU, UN and other bilateral countries have clearly expressed their willingness to support Nepal in reaching negotiated settlement and post-conflict reconstructions. However, this effort needs consensus, which has to be started from breaking the present deadlock in mindset. If the present government gives way to form a broad-based interim government from a series of round-table conferences and genuinely commits to support interim government to reach negotiated settlement, the opportunity brought about by the conflict could be captured to start fresh negotiation process. However, looking to the expression, action and behaviour of the King, the negotiated settlement and reconciliation seems far way and confrontation is the consequent result.

The interim government should declare ceasefire, resume negotiation with the Maoists, and settle issues in a professional manner. This government should organise a series of mini round- table conferences to work further for constitutional change and socio-economic reform. While forming the interim government representatives from all parliamentary parties, Maoists and other stakeholders must be included. This government should hold the election for constitutional assembly. John Galtung (2004b:114) suggests four urgent tasks to be accomplished to restore peace in Nepal, i.e. first, to end the violence;

second, to address the root causes; third to build resource for peace; and fourth, to seek healing and reconciliation. If this concept is used as a guiding framework, the opportunities (the built-up opinion of people to go for the fundamental restructuring of the state to address centuries-old social exclusion, marginalisation, injustices, discrimination, poverty, etc., realisation of need of state restructuring by the rulers and international support) brought about by the armed conflict can turn this country into a prosperous, inclusive and democratic state.

10.4.2 Issues on state restructuring

10.4.2.1 Constitutional, social and administrative change

The current constitution did not envision three issues, i.e., insurgency types of violence in future, violation of constitution by the constitutional actors and potential anomalies while holding election by the majority or regular government[26]. Series of constitutional violations and encroachments happened from the constitutional force. The Article 27 (3) of the Constitution was one of the most abused articles in Nepal, as it was used to dissolve democratically elected government, and royal takeover. The judiciary has to have a great role in the growth and development of the constitution, but the judiciary did not provide timely rulings that prevented ill intentions of politicians. The constitution should ensure participation of all Nepalese people to create an environment for self-promotion and development (Khanal, 2005). Any constitution unable to address inequalities, discrimination, exploitation, and promoting the role of certain power centres cannot sustain (Khanal, 2003 and 2005). The constitution should promote national unity, territorial integrity, freedom of expression and speech; create opportunity for self-development of citizens, economic development, and harmony. The current constitution is not fully able to address many problems related to ethnic groups, women and dalit and political representation. A new constitution made by people needs to address all these issues.

Developing a new constitution from the election of the constituent assembly will be one of the best options. From the two rounds of failed negotiations, it became apparent that the best way to bring the Maoists into mainstream politics is to have unconditional constituent assembly election (means the future of monarchy subject to the decision of people). Certainly, there are some complications while making constitution through a constitutional assembly election. However, all these complications can be addressed through proper mechanisms and arrangements. The existing state governing system has been developed on the monarchy-centred framework for two centuries. However, this framework has not been changed to a people-centred system even after the multiparty system and it has created many governing confusions (Kumar and Sharma, 2005). It can be changed only through the election of constituent assembly.

One of the major reform agenda must be to eliminate the root causes of the conflict. This requires drastic shift from current perspective, regulatory and development frameworks, bureaucratic arrangements and practices. Such reforms could mean breaking vested interests of political and bureaucratic elites, which is not possible unless major constitutional and civil reforms are introduced. The main debate is whether to go for a federal system or to have complete devolution. Centralised administration, market mechanisms and agricultural institutions exclude large mass of rural people and contribute to develop feeling of injustice.

State restructuring in a federal system is becoming an important and one of the most debatable agenda. Some political scientists have proposed regions of full autonomy with the rights of self-determination and others have proposed mini self-governed structures under the decentralised governance system. The basic purpose of these structures or self-governed decentralised regions is to properly represent plural social and diverse ethnic issues in the governance systems. However, the opportunity should be given to decide these structures but that requires well-informed broad national debate first.

10.4.2.2 Political issues

The heart of the underlying causes of the crisis remains political. Therefore, the crisis should be addressed only through political process. Further, this crisis cannot be solved from within the current constitutional, legal and military frameworks. Political negotiation is the precondition for the conflict transformation and state restructuring. Likewise, social and economic reform process should go together with the political negotiation. This means, a comprehensive reform package must be developed, agreed and implemented. The reform agenda can be compared with human body, in which political framework through the negotiated settlement serves as skeleton and social and economic reform packages work as nerves, blood, flesh, etc. The reform process has to start with negotiating a state restructuring process which ensures more inclusive, decentralised and participatory democratic state enforced by new constitution and implemented by appropriate democratic institutions. So far there is no better alternative than multiparty democratic system. Hence, the political actors should think beyond the 'Westminster' model of winner takes all (Upreti, 2003a&b). What happens if the current conflict goes beyond the political control and warlords emerge? Therefore, this crisis must be solved politically.

10.4.2.3 Structural issues

With a new political and constitutional framework, the state has to implement a massive economic agenda that fully addresses rampant poverty and massive unemployment, severely skewed resource distribution patterns and centrally controlled planning and resource allocation system of development. The existing economic reform models devised and imposed by international financial institutions are widening the gap between rich and poor (Shreshta, 1997, Pandey, 1999), promoting conflict (Upreti, 2004a) and fuelling crisis (Kumar and Sharma, 2005; Misra, 2004). One of the thousands of examples is the abolition of the 'Food Depots' (so called economically unfeasible depots) by the government from the remote areas under the tremendous pressure and the conditions imposed by the Asian Development Bank to get the funding for the implementation of the Agricultural Perspective Plan (a failed plan in the history of agricultural development of Nepal). This has not only created food crisis but also fuelled the conflict in remote areas (Upreti, 2004a).

Likewise, the state restructuring must address centuries-old injustice, inequalities and discriminations based on class, caste, sex, ethnicity and geography. Without abolishing theses inhumane pathogenic characteristics of Nepalese society, thinking peaceful and harmonious society is meaningless. As we have sufficiently observed in the modern history of Nepal, attitudes, understandings, commitments and actions of politicians, social and economic leaders and rulers of this country is not enough to abolish injustices, inequalities and discrimination. Some cosmetic changes have been made either because of interest-based pressure from international community or to sustain own vested interests. Representation of ethnic minorities, women, marginalised communities, lower class people and dalit in the present economic, social, political and bureaucratic structures (their number in government, bureaucracy, social position, parties' decision-making structures) clearly indicate to what extend present polity addresses exclusionary issues (Thapa, 2003; Upreti, 2005h and 2003a).

10.4.2.4 Human rights issues

So far, human rights violation in Nepal is becoming a prime concern not only within the country but also around the world. Fundamental rights of Nepalese people are seriously undermined by the armed conflict. Furthermore, Nepalese rulers and the Maoists are either not able to internalise the global importance of human rights or they are deliberately ignoring it. However, human right is becoming a global principle of governance and those who will ignore it; will pay the price of human rights violence in the long run. Supreme military powers like the USA are to be ashamed in the case of human rights abuses in Iraq and Nepal. Human rights protection is one of the most pragmatic approaches in handling violent conflict, as other approaches do not effectively work in such a situation. Strengthening National Human Rights Commission and other human rights institutions at national and local levels, intensifying and expanding human rights protection work of Human Rights Cells of the RNA, Civil Police and Armed Police Force; training and orienting security forces to human rights, respecting the Geneva Conventions and other international human rights provisions, legal treatment to detainees and other arrested people are some of the major issues to be immediately dealt on by the state and other concern actors. The government and the Maoists must respect the basic human rights. The global conflict history, with the recent examples of the two tyrants Pinochet of Chile and Milosevic of Yugoslavia, has proved that the war criminals will not get immunity. The state restricting process should address human rights violations issues. Judicially punishing the human rights violators and giving justice to the victim as well as offering reconciliation must be package of the state restricting process.

10.4.2.5 Psychological issues

Unfortunately, the armed conflict and associated crisis has damaged at least two generations of Nepalese people. The Nepalese culture of peace and co-existence has now been replaced with violence, revenge and retaliation. The young generation, particularly children are the psychological victim of the armed conflict, as their young psychology is daily confronting with the scene of brutal killings, gun fights, disappearance, war and acts of incendiary, landmines, handling and abuses of arms and weapons. What do these scenes implant to the mind of young children? What to expect from the children struggling to survive in war zones, observing wars, revenges and retaliation? Anyone could easily imagine what children feel, perceive and learn when their parents, relatives, loved one are killed, raped, or detained by the warring factions.

Another danger symptom of social malfunctioning is the acceptance of 'culture of violence' by the society. Be it a blockade called by the Maoists, be it a student protest or a political agitation by political parties or even be it a 'Valley Band' called by insignificant or almost non-existent groups, Nepalese people accept it. Violence is becoming accepted as part of Nepalese culture. Violence, crime and fear are symptoms of dysfunctional societies. In this respect Nepalese society is gearing towards dysfunctional society and state.

Therefore, it is high time for the government, civil society, the Maoists and every member of society to seek the culture of co-existence, culture of harmony and finds ways to promote reconciliation. So far the government has not done enough in healing the individuals, families, communities and society victimised by the armed conflict. Rather, the government is financially supporting the families killed by the Maoists and discriminating against the families killed by security forces. It is unfair to assume that all family members of the persons killed by security forces are Maoists or their supporters. Such discriminatory treatments consequently strengthen feeling of injustice and contribute to escalate revenge and retaliation. There are no special programmes for psychological counselling, trauma healing and mental rehabilitation to the conflict victims, which is the responsibility of the state in any war-torn countries (Upreti, 2003a).

10.4.2.6 Human security issues

At the conceptual level, a new 'human security' paradigm is emerging to address the weaknesses of the dominant security system and meet the challenges of the twenty-first century while governing a nation state. This paradigm addresses poverty, inequality, environmental crisis, food security as well as national security concerns in a holistic and integrated manner. Hence the 'national security strategy' should be devised within the framework of 'human security'. The present security framework is not able to provide security to the Nepalese people. Instead, it is causing insecurity, as it shifts resources from social services (such as health, education, development projects and programme) to purchase arms, weapons and ammunitions, state invests huge amount of financial and human resources in unproductive activities which not only divide society but also implants hatred, fear, suspicion, revenge and retaliation.

10.4.2.7 Humanitarian assistance and issues of internally displaced people

Nepal is at a crossroads. Humanitarian crisis is looming in a severe scale. Thousands of people have been killed, hundreds of thousands of people are internally displaced, and millions of people are victims of the armed conflict. Many people have lost their homes, shelters, food, and property. Hundreds of thousands of children have lost their schools. Villages have been emptied due to the fear of the Maoists and security forces. But this humanitarian crisis is not getting attention from the donors and the government. There is an urgent need to start a humanitarian assistance programme to the worst victims of conflict irrespective of the families of the people killed or tortured by the Maoist or security forces. The government should immediately start a humanitarian assistance programme, a special programme for the internally displaced people to rehabilitate and reintegrate them in the community and rebuild their confidence and hope. The state restructuring package must contain the issues of IDP.

10.4.2.8 Foreign policy issues

The present international relation and foreign policy of Nepal in relation to the armed conflict and crisis is war focused (Pandey, 2005). It is conceptually and operationally outsider-reliant, guided by the notion of military might and working in a framework of 'peace through war' approach. However, it is a globally failed approach in restoring democratic peace and conflict transformation. The world's super power failed in its international relation and diplomacy in Iraq war because it had to face global resistance and failed to get active support of many nations. Further, it has to spend not only billions of dollars but also lives of many young men and women. Israel has failed in its power-based outsider reliance model of war diplomacy to defeat the Palestine independence movement. Israel is not yet able to achieve peace from the full military and diplomatic support of the USA, billions of dollars of investment in the war with Palestine people. Nepal is also adopting a similar diplomacy to implement a 'peace through war' approach.

Nepal is now increasingly seeking military support and depending upon military assistance from outsiders such as India, the USA and UK. But we did not learn from other war-torn countries that heavily suffered while relying on outsider military support. Maoists will also fail to achieve their aim by relying on their military strength instead of seeking political solution. Nowhere in the world have rebels been successful in winning by depending only upon their military power. Parliamentary political parties also need to change their current approach of international relations concentrating to peace diplomacy. Hence, all key actors have to change their current approach of international relation and must focus on diplomacy that ensures 'peace through peaceful means'.

10.4.3 Negotiated settlement-: pre-condition to revive political and democratic future

The political and democratic future of Nepal entirely depends upon the negotiated settlement of the armed conflict. Irrespective of the expansion of the Maoist-controlled territories through their violent approach, fear and terror, they will not be able to achieve their goal unless they agree for the negotiated settlement. They will not get success without winning the trust of the people, but the people's trust cannot be won through fear and terror.

Similarly, the state/government will not win over the Maoist problem with the current strategy of "peace through war" by mobilizing the Unified Security Command and forming Village Security Committees. The activities and expressions of the present king led government do not indicate any signs of commitment to negotiated settlement. The recent decision of the government to go for the election without taking political parties into confidence and negotiating with rebels is a glaring reflection of the lack of commitment of the government to negotiated settlement of the ongoing armed conflict.

If this nation is to survive politically as a democratic state, all political forces and social actors should be honest, give up their vested interests, party interests and agree on a negotiated settlement of the armed conflict. Collective and concerted efforts of all actors themselves to negotiated settlement ensure long-lasting consolidation of democratic process. Hundreds of armed conflicts and devastating wars have already taken place in the world in the 20th century and the world has experience in settling them. Nepal should learn lessons from these experiences. If peace talk is to be made meaningful, the negotiators should accept the 'universally recognized principles of peace talks' and should not repeat past mistakes. In the negotiated settlement Nepalese government, political parties and the insurgents should demonstrate full commitment for the just and sustainable peace and functional democracy in the country. That can be ensured through a negotiated settlement if both the parties agree on the following:

10.4.3.1 Guiding principles to resolve the present crisis

The present situation is becoming more complicated on economic, political, social and diplomatic fronts that it cannot be addressed by only a single force of the country. The guiding principles to resolve the present crisis of Nepal should be:

- The present crisis must be addressed peacefully, and all political forces of the country must realize their immense responsibility to resolve the crisis,
- The durable solution of this crisis is to accept multiparty democracy in behaviour and action. Appropriate constitutional and legal arrangements are essential to regulate violation of democratic values and norms,
- Sovereignty of people must be accepted and people should decide all controversial issues of national importance,
- Extremism of any type cannot address the national crisis but further accelerates it. Therefore, the best way to address this crisis is to have national consensus on inclusive democracy and governing the country by people's representatives through constitutional principles and procedures.

10.4.3.2 A framework for addressing the current political crisis

Establishment of an inclusive, participatory multiparty democracy is the need of the nation at present. However, it is not possible to flourish functional democracy without resolving the ongoing armed conflict. Therefore, political settlement of the Maoist insurgency is the precondition. The following conceptual framework provides a roadmap for the resolution of political crisis and the ongoing armed conflict as an integral package.

A. National Roundtable Conference

The national conference has to be organized by political parties representing all concerned stakeholders to discuss the future of the country. The national round-table conference should decide issues, procedures, mechanisms, time frame, representatives and mandate for the interim government. It has also to decide details of constituent-making process (constituent assembly election). International observers have also to be invited to the round-table conference.

B. Interim government to conduct election for constituent assembly

An interim government with full authority and responsibility has to form under the leadership of political parties by representing all relevant political forces of the country to accomplish election for the constituent assembly. Its main mandate is to successfully complete the constituent assembly election, as detailed by the national round table conference.

C. Procedure for developing a new constitution

A new constitution is indispensable to resolve the national crisis. However, the achievements of the popular movement of the 1990 must be protected. A new constitution must be drafted by exercising the sovereignty of people through the constituent assembly election, as outlined by the national round-table conference. The constitution prepared by the constituent assembly election will assure rule of law and sovereignty of people. It will also prevent emergence of unelected institutions in the politics. Until the new constitution is declared, the 1990 constitution with required amendment has to serve as an 'interim constitution'. The elected constituent assembly has to decide the future existence of the monarchy in this country.

D. Third-party involvement in monitoring of Constituent Assembly election

The deep mistrust and pervasive crisis of confidence in Nepal is hindering political resolution of the crisis. Therefore, involvement of experienced, neutral and credible international agencies is essential to monitor the election of constituent assembly. The frequently expressed concerns about the election of constituent assembly are dealing with arms and weapons of the warring parties and possibilities for not accepting the election result by either side if it is unfavourable to them. If the UN or any other credible international agencies are involved in election monitoring, making arrangement to keep the state security forces in barracks and rebels force in certain defined areas, handing over the weapons and arms to international monitors to conduct free and fair election, these concerns can be addressed. Therefore, Nepal needs to invite international community particularly the UN and EU, and get support from and confidence of India, the UK, USA and China to assist in resolving political crisis.

E. Management of arms, weapons and fighting force of Maoists

Management of arms and weapons and fighting force of Maoists is one of the major concerns in resolving the ongoing armed conflict. However, if the warring parties make a sincere commitment to the peaceful settlement of the conflict, it is not difficult. The able fighting force of Maoists who meet minimum requirement can join the state military force and remaining force can get opportunity of work on industrial security, infrastructure security, and other employment opportunities. In the new system, the existing security structures need to be changed and make more democratic.

F. Democratization and parliamentary oversight of military

Democratization and civilian or parliamentary oversight of the military would be the most contentious issue in future negotiation with the king, if there is any negotiation. The 1st February takeover proved that the source of power of the king is the army. One of the guiding principles of RNA is said to be 'service to the king and protection of the crown'. This means the army is the main power base of the king, which he does not want to relinquish. Therefore, the very first condition related to army is to dismantle this tie and keep it under the direct control and supervision of elected parliament. Security sector reform package should address this issue. The UN has vast amount of knowledge in this area and therefore its involvement in Nepal's crisis management will help a lot to deal with the parliamentary control of army.

G. Restructuring of the state

The new constitution-making process must address the state restructuring issues in an inclusive way. The restructuring of the state must address all social, political, economic, and geographical (regional), religious and linguistic concerns of marginalized and people below poverty line, women, Dalit, ethnic minorities, Madhesi communities of Nepal. It has also to ensure democratization of military and wider security sector reform. The constitutional provision of referendum must be there to settle all contending issues of national concern. Effective, efficient and transparent administrative mechanism, periodic election, redefinition of the constitutional bodies based on the changing context, are other areas of focus of state restructuring. The state restructuring is essential to change the present feudal social system, values and governing practices.

H. Existence of the monarchy: subject to decision of people

The existence of monarchy depends upon the decision of people. Whether the monarchy would be constitutional, ceremonial or active or the state would be republican depends upon the decision of the people. If the king accepts people verdicts, the people would agree to have monarchy as an institution. But if the king wants to rule as an active monarch, then people have to decide the fate of the monarchy and ultimately could pave the way for the republican set-up. If the king accepts sovereignty of people, he has to be ready to accept the decision of the people. Sovereign people have to finally decide the fate of Monarchy in Nepal.

10.5 CONCLUSIONS

The history of war and peace has shown that conflict transformation and maintaining peace require an active engagement of all sections of society, from ordinary citizens, security actors, and civil society to politicians (Armond and Carl, 1996; Hendrickson, 1998; Stankovitch, 1999; Upreti, 2004a; Conen, 1999; Armon et al., 1998; Barnes, 2002; Armon and Philipaon, 2002; Lord, 2000; Gracia-Durna, 2004; Lucima, 2002; McCartney, 1999; Carl, 2002; Misra, 2002). However, this dimension in conflict transformation and peace making in Nepal is not getting enough attention.

Conclusions of the basic, situational and external causes of the Maoist insurgency have already been drawn from the above explanations, analysis and discussions. Politicians, king, parliamentary parties, government, foreign diplomatic dignitaries, experts, civil societies, all have formally or informally accepted the reality that the present structural system of state governance, processes, laws, rules and regulations cannot address the basic causes of the conflict and they need fundamental changes. Such change means change in social, economic, political and legal structures, which is not possible without national consensus and massive participation of the people. So, short-term, mid-term and long-term strategies are necessary for such structural reforms.

In short, complete restructuring of the state is absolutely necessary to keep democratic the political system alive. There is no basic difference on the need of state reform. But, the persistent problem is the psycho-fear of different power centres, which are being haunted by the uncertainty about their future status and power as well as their doubts on their existence in the present form, if an agreement is made to bring complete change in the structure of the state power. It is natural for the monarchists to be worried by the Maoists' ultimate aim to bring 'People's Democratic Republic'. If there is a real negotiated settlement, the Maoists may compromise on their stand on republican demand, which is reflected in the article written by the Maoist leader Baburam Bhattarai published in the *Kantipur Daily* on 22 June 2004 (Aasr 8, 2061). It is nearly 10 years since the war started, it has taken the lives of more than 14 thousand people, devastated national and personal properties worth billions of rupees, maimed thousands of people. In such a situation, the Maoist leaders need a way for safe landing to justify the 'people's war' and satisfy their cadres. This safe landing is the election of constituent assembly to draft constitution through people's involvement.

If all the forces of the country want democratic peace in the country, they should become active to create a national consensus showing probity, flexibility and learning from the past weaknesses and avoiding blame and counter blame. Similarly, if it is to truly accept people's sovereignty, election to constituent assembly should be accepted as the proper way of conflict settlement. Different doubts and fears have been raised such as, 'if the Maoist did not lay down their arms, the result might go to the Maoist side due to fear and threats, they might not accept if the result did not come in their favour and so on. Such doubts and fears should be correctly addressed. For that election can be held under monitoring and involvement of the UN, arms can be kept under the control of the UN during the election period and arrangements can be made if they did not accept the result of the fair election, their arms would not be returned.

If violence, killing, blame, counter blame, attacks and counter attacks continue, if the days pass in the illusion that the Army Unified Command will solve the problems, if both sides remain engaged in conflict not learning from past weaknesses and international experiences, if all the possible ways of conflict settlement are not utilized in an integrated manner, if all remain hankering after their vested interests, or remain feeling an inferiority complex, and if a democratic solution is not sought through national consensus, Nepal's nascent democracy and multiparty political system will suffer permanent damage. Therefore, all political forces should realise the complexity of the problem and come to an agreement.

NOTES

1. Source: The King's address to the nation at the time of the Royal takeover on 1st February 2005. It was the morning of 1st February (10:50 am), security officials under the command of army were deployed in all strategic places such as media houses, party offices, security forces were sent to arrest or detain political leaders, human rights activists, telephone lines were cut and the king address to the nation for more than 34 minute to take the executive power. Prime minister and all other ministers were detained in their own office and residences. There was a meeting of the king with the security forces (all three forces military, police and armed police force in the evening of the 31 January. Even the king met the prime minister in the same day but the prime minister was not aware of the plan. Later, Mr Deuba acknowledged that when he met the king he felt that something could happen but he did not suspect such big step from the king.
2. See The Kathmandu Post. 2 February 2005 for the full text of the speech of the King.
3. The I/NGO Code of Conduct was promulgated on November 11, 2005, after the amendment of the Social Welfare Council Act-2049, which is vehemently opposed by the NGO Federation of Nepal, Donors and INGOs,

Civil Society and national and international human rights organisations.

4. The members of 'International Press Freedom and Freedom of Expression Mission to Nepal issuing the statement include ARTICLE 19; Committee to Protect Journalists (CPJ); International Federation of Journalists (IFJ); International Media Support (IMS); International Press Institute (IPI); Reporters sans Frontières (RSF); United Nations Educational, Scientific and Cultural Organization (UNESCO); World Association of Community Radio Broadcasters (AMARC) and World Association of Newspapers (WAN).
5. For example, Dr Mohamad Mohasin, Communication Minister in the *Deuba* government said to be representative of the king, repeatedly indicated in late 2004 and early 2005 about the forthcoming of 1st February event. Keshar Jung Rayamajhi had publicly asked the King to takeover. It happened after few weeks of these statements.
6. See ICG Asia Report No 94, 24 March 2005 entitled "Nepal Dealing with Human Rights Crisis, for detail.
7. *Source:* INSEC Report, One Month of Ceasefire: An Assessment of Human Rights Situation during the Unilateral Ceasefire by CPN (Maoist) in Nepal (September 03 – October 02, 2005).
8. Source: A Joint Declaration for a United Effort to Resolve the national Crisis, signed by the leaders of 7 parties and issued on 8 May 2005 (25 Baisak, 2062).
9. Narahari Achary, Bam Dev Gautam, Amik Serchan and many other leaders were not happy with what ambassador said and they openly disagree with him and insisted to continue dialogue, as it is the only right way to bring Maoists in mainstream politics.
10. See *The Himalayan Times*, 16 November 2005, p.5.
11. Some of the main conditions are related to respecting human rights (access to NHRC, OHCHR and international human rights organisations to detentions centres and related documents, stopping of extrajudicial killings, detentions and other human rights. violations, etc.) and related to the Royal Commission on Corruption Control (questioning on legality of this Commission and supporting the constitutionally constituted Commission on Investigation of Abuse of Authority).
12. *Bloomberg News* quoted this statement on 23 February 2005.
13. See press statement of the Foreign Secretary, Jack Straw on 14 Feb 2005, who called the British Ambassador in Kathmandu, Keith Bloomfield to London to discuss the royal takeover.
14. See press statement of Foreign Secretary, 25 February 2005.
15. See press release of Ministry of External Affairs of 25 Feb 2005.
16. Director for South Asia and Afghanistan at the UK Foreign and Commonwealth Office.
17. Source: nepalnews.com 6 October 2005.
18. *See The Kathmandu Post*, 29 April 2005.
19. Just before midnight on October 21, officials from the Ministry of

Information, accompanied by police force, arrived at Kantipur FM and demanded that the station abide by the media ordinance. Then police confiscated operating equipment of the station. Further, on October 27, the government ordered Kantipur FM to shut down entirely.

20. UN ECOSOC, Siracusa Principles on the Limitation and Derogation Provisions in the International Covenant on Civil and Political Rights [UN Document E/CN.4/1985/4, Annex (1985)]; University of Minnesota Human Rights Library
http://www1.umn.edu/humanrts/instree/siracusaprinciples.html
21. Ibid, Principle 20.
22. Ibid, principle 58.
23. Resolution adopted at the 92nd IPU Conference in Copenhagen, 17 September 1994.
24. Resolution adopted at the 98th IPU Conference in Cairo, 15 September 1997
25. Even at present, government is establishing *Pritana* in each development region, *Bahini* in each zone and *Gulma* in each district. Further army has started to produce small arms and light weapons (Chief of the Army said this in the occasion of 59th birth day of the king on 7 July 05). Military forces are engaged in constructing 13 roads in different parts of the country.
26. In discussion, Daman Nath Dhungan, one of the creators of the 1990 constitution expressed such opinion.

CHAPTER 11

Conclusions

In her modern history, Nepal is facing an unprecedented crisis and enshrined with enormous potentialiry. The instability created by the ten years of Maoist insurgency and failure of multi-party leadership has been further worsened by the unrealistic ambitions and subsequent actions of the king. Situation of the political, social, economic sectors and international relations is in a critical stage and it can turn to any direction depending on how the king will act and how the 12-point understanding reached between the seven-party alliance and the Maoist will translate into practice.

The current approach of the king cannot restore peace and cannot handle this crisis. Even in the past, efforts of the government, political parties, and international communities to resolve this conflict through dialogue and negotiation were not enough. All efforts should have focused on consensus building. Only genuine commitment from all key actors and building of national consensus could solve this problem. In the long term, the establishment of lasting peace in Nepal is possible only through addressing root causes of the crisis. In the immediate term a genuine commitment of all political parties, the king and the Maoists to solve this problem through dialogue and peace negotiation can pave the way for addressing root causes of the conflict. No one (neither Maoists nor the government) can win by confrontation and military might. A peaceful resolution of the present conflict is again possible only through meaningful preparation, genuine commitment to peace, clear vision for the future of the country and mutual trust and concerted action between the King, the rebels, the government, and all the political parties.

Nepal has to opt for alternative dispute resolution approaches (i.e., non-military option, by agreeing to rewrite the constitution through constituent assembly) if we want to fully resolve the Nepalese conflict. Military intervention is not an appropriate solution (it can only be an immediate option to minimize extreme escalation of bloodshed and violence). Similarly, the existing constitution cannot deal with this conflict as the context is going far beyond its scope. The only political option left is to settle the bloody conflict and the constitutional assembly is one of the best options, depending on all-party discussion on its various modalities and agreeing on one of them. The following points elaborate some ways to move ahead to resolve this conflict in Nepal:

Restoring peace in a conflict-ridden country is not easy. Examining the Sri Lankan peace process, Jayadeva Uyangoda concludes only after 19 years of conflict Sri Lanka is exploring new peace process. Uyangoda writes, "*Sri Lanka's new peace process has just begun and its future trajectories are still in a formative stage* (Uyangoda, 2003:27). This statement clearly indicates how complex the negotiation is.

While assessing the peace process in Nepal, though there was significance of having a formal face-to-face dialogue, the negotiation process did not advance correctly. The proper negotiation process starts with building trust and confidence, involving all stakeholders in the process, strong commitment from both sides; extensive informal consultation and exchange, open and constructive debate in all contested issues, etc. The six rounds of talks for the negotiation in the past were not accomplished according to the internationally accepted principles of negotiation. Proven negotiation procedures and steps were not followed. Both sides (the state and the Maoists) used the ceasefire as a 'strategic pause' to strengthen their military capabilities instead of making genuine efforts to make the talks successful. The warring parties must know that peace talks and negotiation is the only viable and lasting solution. Whatever may be their justifications, fighting, confrontation and war cannot be a solution.

One of the main reasons for the failure of negotiation in the past was perceived risk. All major political players of this country are severely suffering form 'fear for their existence' created by a risk perception. The supporters of the royal takeover perceive that a successful negotiation with the rebels agreeing on the constituent assembly might end the existence of the monarchy. They perceive that constituent assembly could result into a republican system. Most of the leaders of the major parties in power are deeply fearful about their involvement in corruption and irregularities that could jeopardise their political future, if and when the conflict is settled and a new political situation emerges. Some of the democratic leaders may be genuinely worried about the risk for multiparty democracy, as the Maoists are fighting for the establishment of a communist state. CPN-UML may be perceiving risks of replacing them by the Maoists as a mainstream communist party, as most of the social reform agenda of both parties are similar. The Maoists are fearful about loosing of their political existence from the collective efforts of the royal palace, parliamentary political parties and international forces even using external military force. Therefore, they are always trying to widen the gap between the parliamentary parties and the palace, and urging international community to stop external military intervention. Many bureaucrats might have perceived that they could face punishment for their wrongdoings and corruption in the past decades if there is a negotiated settlement and new political environment. Therefore, they are giving wrong advice to the government, parliamentary parties, and the King. All of the major actors of the conflict may also be worried about losing the privileges they are entertaining at present and therefore their efforts are to mint these privileges and benefits. In essence, the perceived risk is one of the main obstacles to politically resolve the ongoing crisis of Nepal.

The current approach of solving the Maoist conflict of Nepal needs a total change. The state should opt for a multi-track approach that includes negotiation efforts from all actors at different levels with different scales and mandate. The political parties, civil society, the palace and the government must start dialogue at different levels. An inclusive approach is essential. The crisis of confidence among and between the major actors of conflict is hindering political resolution of the crisis. The only way to overcome this problem is to sit together and work out the differences and come to a common understanding on how to restructure the state to address the root causes of the conflict that ensure durable and democratic peace in Nepal.

The government must start the state reform process and should not wait until the negotiation with rebels is made. Nepal must learn lessons for other conflict-ridden countries. The Maoists and security forces must stop violent approach. They should realise that violent actions produce a cycle of counter violence and retaliation that is counter-productive to themselves and the whole negotiation and peace process.

Both the government and the Maoists should realise that military solution of the conflict pushes the nation to militarization that cannot help democracy. It cannot strengthen rule of law, constitutional supremacy, and multiparty democracy. Militarization weakens the King, the parliamentary parties, the Maoists and civil society. It also pulls massive resources from the social development budget to spend in unproductive areas. Killing people, expelling them from village, creating terror cannot win genuine support of Nepalese people. If the Maoists and the government continue the current approach, their actions will soon lead to state failure, military rule, and foreign intervention. In this situation, both parties cannot achieve what now they are claiming to achieve. Therefore, it is time to rethink their military actions, stop terror, declare ceasefire, start dialogue, and reach a negotiated agreement.

The Maoist conflict is not difficult to resolve, if concerned actors are willing. This is not an ethnic conflict, this is not a separatist movement to break the nation and it is not a religious conflict, which are far more difficult to resolve. This conflict is political. If the main aims of the government, the political parties, the king and the Maoists are really to alleviate poverty, injustice, discrimination, to establish democratic governance procedures and practices, to make Nepalese people happy, prosperous and to develop equal and just Nepalese society, why do they not sit together and agree on the common and prosperous future of Nepal? The 12-point understanding reached between the 7 party alliance and the Maoists has given a good basis to start political process of settling the ongoing armed conflict. But if they are limited their 12-point understanding in paper and continue their old rhetoric and if the king continues the current autocratic practices and all the three major domestic actors of the conflict work only to fulfil their vested interests and achieve their unrealistic ambitions at the cost of human rights violations, isolation form international community and continue bloodshed, history will punish them.

If the key stakeholders do not sincerely commit to peaceful resolution of the conflict, repeated ceasefires and negotiations will not work. Creating a conducive environment is essential to resolve this conflict before proceeding to formal negotiations. A favourable environment can be created if the stakeholders come together to reach mutually acceptable principles and procedures for the future negotiations and state restructuring, facilitation of multi-track consultation at national and local levels engaging all political parties, ethnic groups, women, dalits, business community, students, etc.

Indigenous and traditional approaches, emerging civil society approaches and international approaches of conflict resolution can be combined in creating a conducive environment that would help to resolve armed conflict. It is not easy to successfully negotiate the complex conflict like the Maoist insurgency. It requires huge efforts, resources, vision and most importantly commitment form the key actors of conflict. The fundamental pre-condition of mediation for the negotiated settlement is the readiness of the conflicting parties. Negotiation through external mediation will not succeed if the parties in conflict are not ready to settle politically. The external mediators alone, irrespective of how powerful, skilful and experienced they are, cannot reach a negotiated settlement if the king, Maoists, and political parties are not willing.

Negotiation is a long-term process that demands sincere and continuous efforts, enabling environment and appropriate knowledge and skills to make it successful. In this process, there is a great prospect for external involvement in pre-negotiation and negotiation stages. Pre-negotiation is a set of tasks to begin prior to negotiation, sustain, and nourish peace process through changing relationships and paving ways for negotiation (Sunders, 1996). Essentially, pre-negotiation is a start of political processes that help change relationships and lead to end the conflict and to peace and reconciliations.

Nepal needs help from the international community in resolving this crisis. Who are appropriate and why, what models and approaches needs to be used, to what degree and duration of external involvement are genuine questions that need to be further debated and discussed before taking any decision. It has to be decided not by a single party or the government but by the whole nation unitedly. Considering the context, willingness, experiences and practicalities, Nepal should seek UN's help with full support of other well-wishers of Nepal. Nepal needs to request all well-wishers countries and intern-governmental organisations to form a Nepal Peace Support Group. This Group has to back the UN, it has to facilitate settling differences with the neighbouring countries, take them into confidence and help the UN in mediating in the armed conflict to reach a negotiated settlement and durable peace in the country.

The coming few syears will be an extremely important turning point in the history of Nepal, as it is now at a crossroads. This country will not remain the same but it may face even more crisis, confrontation and misery before transforming into a more democratic, liberal and inclusive state. It will be a hard time for Nepalese society in the near future to cope with mounting challenges of insecurity, fear, militarisation of society, abuses of civil liberty and human rights, suppression of opinion will be the cost of painful transformation process in Nepal.

All sections of society have realised that the 1st February royal takeover is a serious setback to democracy and it has greatly contributed to expanding the crisis and conflict in Nepal. Contrary to the formally expressed will of the king (to restore peace and strengthen democracy), the political situation is further deteriorating. Therefore, the very first step to restore peace and strengthen democracy is to hand over power to political parties, distancing from unrealistic and impractical ambition to rule the country by weakening or undermining major democratic forces. Imposing restrictions on media, civic liberties and human rights cannot strengthen democracy. Likewise, strengthening the military cannot restore durable and democratic peace. The present structures and processes of governance, and existing laws[1], rules and regulations cannot address the conflict and current crisis of Nepal. Therefore fundamental changes in social, economic, political and legal structures are required. That means a complete restructuring of the state is essential. However, persistent psycho-fear of different power centres, which are being haunted by the uncertainty about their future, is severely resisting bringing about complete restructuring of the state through a political settlement.

All the key actors of conflict and crisis should learn from their past weaknesses and mistakes as well as regional and international experiences. If they truly believe in people's sovereignty, election for constituent assembly should be accepted as one of the suitable ways of ending the political crisis in Nepal.

If violence, killing, blame, counter blame, attacks and counter attacks continue, and time passes in the illusion that the King alone (without working together with the political parties) will restore peace and end the political crisis, if the parliamentary political parties remain engaged in internal power struggle and do not form broad political visions; if the present government continues its derogatory approach (to control behaviour and actions of people though fear, terror and abuse of state authority and resources), if all hanker after their vested interests, or remain in an inferiority complex, and if a democratic solution is not sought through national consensus, Nepal's nascent democracy and multiparty political system will suffer more.

Though the current political situation is bleak, there are rays of hopes. In the past 15 years civil society is emerging as a powerful stakeholder committed to democracy and peace. It is collaborating with political parties and international community to restore democracy and peace in the country. Civil society alone cannot achieve this objective but it can greatly help political parties to restore peace and democracy in Nepal. The international community is supportive. Nepalese people are annoyed with violence and tired of the ongoing-armed conflict and they will pressurise the main actors to end the crisis conflict. Further, the commitment of CPN (M) on multiparty democracy & their willingness to come in open & competitive politics is not only positive but also great opportunity for this nation to turn from centraled feudal state to a modern porsporous state.

There are severe potential dangers of starting separatist, ethnic or religious fights and mini-wars if this conflict is not resolved in time. Civil defence disasters have already begun[2]. There is a potential danger of breaking of Maoists into different factions. If the conflict protracts, a situation of disobeying orders of the high command by their cadres is created. There is very strong invisible force active to escalate conflict and maintain war (mainly to earn commission from weapons trade) and they will continue to engage and play a role in the escalation of conflict. This force, willing to continue crisis and war in Nepal must be covertly engaged in a series of actions contributing to this end such as dissolving the parliament (the then prime minister was part of this process), removing elected government and starting the practice of nominating prime ministers, frequently changing governments, corruption and abuse of state authority and power implanting conflict between Maoist leaders.

The 1st February takeover has divided the country, curtailed basic human rights and civil liberties of Nepalese people, detained political leaders, civil society activists, journalists and human rights defenders, and imposed censorship on media. Consequently, the existing power structure is altered and a new form of power relations is developing. One power centre expanded after the 1st February takeover to resist change and another power centre to fight against autocracy. The first step in bringing all forces together to fight against autocracy was the formation of alliance of seven parties to restore full democracy, establish rights of people and to move the nation in a positive and peaceful direction. On 8 May 2005, the 'Seven Parties Alliance' came with a 'Joint Declaration for United Efforts to Resolve the National Crisis', which provides the framework for concerted action against the 1st

February royal takeover. However, this is not strong enough to achieve what the alliance has claimed to achieve. Parliamentary political parties need to review and acknowledge past weaknesses and mistakes, address shortcomings and refine and strengthen their ideological, political and organizational basis to win public support and to make the alliance more effective against the autocratic regime.

If political forces of the country opt for a confrontational approach, the one has to politically finish another party, which is obviously not easy and enormous human and other losses occur. Instead, if they opt for a reconciliatory approach, they need to change themselves and accept the following conditions:

1. Maoists without arms and weapons and committed to multiparty democracy.
2. Existance of Monarchy as an institution King subject to the decision of people.
3. Parties with internal democracy.

Some scholars argue that exploring weaknesses and negative aspects further fuels the crisis. This argument may be true. It is also difficult to ignore reality and hide truth. The Nepalese crisis needs to be critically examined. In this regard, it is my conclusion that the major political powers (the palace, political parties and Maoists) were knowingly and or unknowingly engaged to weaken nascent democracy, manipulate people and abuse their power and strengths. If the key actors of conflict are not ready to change their actions and behaviour urgently, Nepalese democracy would be dysfunctional because of:

- Erosion of trust: There is a severe erosion of public trust in political parties, the backbone of multiparty democracy. A study[3] of Krishna Hachhethu and his colleagues shows that 56 per cent of the population is unhappy with the functioning of democracy in Nepal, 94 per cent respondents feel political instability, 97 per cent feels politicians work for vested personal and political interests rather than national interests. However 62 per cent of the people see democracy better than any other political system. Almost similar a result was published by Himal Media[4], where 83.21 percent of the people are not satisfied and only 7 percent are satisfied with the present governing system.
- Fast and deep militarisation: By and large, the military controls civilian administration in districts under the provision of

unified command. Civil administration is almost dysfunctional. The state has increased military expenditure by more than 300 per cent within three years and most of the increased military costs are compensated for from the service sector budget (like, health, education, drinking water). The government is seeking more and more military help[5]. Militarisation of society is another worrying factor. Extra-judicial killings, detention, house-search, arbitrary arrests, intense fights, etc. are accepted by society as an integral part of their social system. Military action and counter actions are common.

- Absence of periodic election and elected representatives: Another building block of functional democracy is periodic election where people caste their vote to elect their representatives. However, in the last 4 years there is no elected body to govern the country. The House of Representatives, an elected supreme body, was dissolved and the country is now governed by the nominated people who are not responsible to the people. There is absence of elected leaders in all local government units (3915 village development committees, 75 District Development Committees and 58 municipalities). Ruling of political units by nominated people and civil servants who are not accountable to the people obviously work for the interests of their nominators. The Maoists are obstructing periodic election before settling the political conflict but there is no sign of any possibility to have a negotiated settlement.
- Breakdown of political parties: Almost all political parties have been breaking into splinters, mainly to grab power and for vested interests. There are serious undemocratic practices within political parties. Such a situation is contributing to further weakening the already threatened democracy.
- Prevalence of far-rightist authoritarianism: The interest of the king to be constructive, audible and visible[6] in Nepalese politics have encouraged the anti-democratic forces and despotic royalists to work against multiparty democratic system and partly they succeeded on the 1st of February. Before the 1st February Royal takeover, one-time established communist-turned noted royalist Keshar Jung Rayamajhi publicly suggested that the king has to chair the council of ministers, as the present system did not work. That happened precisely from 1st of February. One of the most powerful ministers, Dr

Mohamad Mohasin, said to be representing royalist interests in the Deuba coalition government some time before the royal takeover, said that Nepal needs to go in for autocratic systems as and when the democratic system is not able to address the crisis. He had also forecasted the imposition of autocratic system by the king if the democratic system does not function to deal with Maoists[7]. From the royal takeover, this turned out to be a reality. Now another royalist is saying that political parties have to be declared an antinationalist force and banned.

- Still there are no evidences that the state is committed to address the root causes. Without addressing the root causes of the crisis, it is meaningless to anticipate a stable and democratic political system.
- All these pulling and pushing factors are contributing to bringing about a collapse of the democratic political system established by the popular movement of 1990.
- The policies, strategies and practices adopted by the state in general & the king in particular so far in resolving conflict are not only insufficient but also irrelevant. They are adding further complexities and contributing to escalate the armed conflict.
- The Maoist state reform approach "change through violence" and the state's peace restoration approach "peace through war" are completely wrong, therefore they will not able to achieve their goals. No matter how much military aid Nepal gets from the USA, India, UK and other nations, no matter how many numbers increase in military structure, no matter how many battalions are expanded to every village and no matter how many Maoists are killed by the security forces, this conflict will not be solved unless the fundamental causes of the conflict (i.e., poverty, injustice, discrimination, and feeling of exclusion) are addressed. If the state does not address these causes and focus to finish the rebels though military support from outside, other extremist groups could emerge. Nepal must learn form Iraq, Afghanistan and other conflict-ridden countries that had adopted the "Peace through War approach".
- The best approach to address this crisis is to explore common ground, start with a common agenda, develop confidence and then entered into a deal on main issues.
- The government should start psychological counselling, special rehabilitation programme for internally displaced people and

reconciliation programme to the conflict victims.

- The government should work under the "conceptual framework of human security" , which not only deals with 'national security' issues but also incorporates 'livelihood and environmental securities' as an integral part of the 'holistic security'. The current 'security approach' is not enough to ensure security of Nepalese people. The government, Maoists, political parties and international community must realise the need for a 'human security approach'.
- The government should change its current mode of international relation and diplomacy in dealing with conflict. The 'peace diplomacy' should replace the existing "war diplomacy' practised by Nepal at present (focusing on obtaining arms, weapons and ammunitions to control the insurgency rather than addressing root causes of the conflict).

Despite all conflict trigger in king activities of the king led government some very positive developments are also happening. The 12 point understanding between the Maoists and the Seven Party Allience is generating hope, aspiration and future direction progressive forces coming together to fight autocracy and regressive force is giving strength to all people opposing autocracy. The Civil Society, Media, Lawyers, human rights activists, peace activists have demonstrated their commitment on democracy and willingnes to fight autocracy. All these positive aspects are indicating that autocracy will be defeated by the concerted action of civil society, Maoist and Political parties.

NOTES

1. For example, according to the legal experts 22 security-related acts are incompatible with the Constitution of Nepal 1990 and international human rights laws (see *The Himalayan Times*, 12 July 2005 for detail).
2. In *Kantipur Daily* of 12 December 2004, negative effects of Civil Defence Committee organised by the government are vividly illustrated.
3. Krishna Hacchethu, 'Jasnata Ke Bhanchan (What people say)', *Kantipur Daily*, 6 November 2004.
4. Rajendra Dahal, *Himal Khabar Patrika* 1-30 Kartik 2061, Pp 85-100
5. The USA, UK and India are major countries providing military assistance to deal with the Maoists. The justification of British government to provide military aid is to protect infrastructuale damage (on 2nd November at Dhankuta British Ambassador to Nepal Mr Keith Bloomfield said that "if the military capacity is increased, it will be able to protect infrastructure,

but even then our support is more in development areas" (*The Kathmandu Post,* 2004 November 3). In addition, countries like Belgium sold 5000 weapons to a country facing civil war. The latest country ready to provide military assistance to Nepal to crack the Maoists is Pakistan. On 2nd November, Pakistani Prime Minister Shaukat Aziz talking to the journalist in Kathmandu offered military assistance to Nepal. He said, "Pakistan is ready to provide military assistance if Nepal ask for it" (*The Kathmandu Post,* 2004 November 3). Inviting Pakistan for military assistance after India has severe long-term security implications.

6. These interests were expressed in the king's interview to the US-based *Time* Magazine's Alex Perry on 26 January 2004 and another interview to Nepal's fortnightly magazine *Tirtha Koirala*..
7. Explicit arguments of Minister Dr Mohasin, (an ideologue of the partyless autocratic political system, which was overthrown by the popular movement of 1990) to go for autocratic system are published in the *Kantipur Daily* on 11 November 2004.

Epilogue

When this book was in the process of printing, popular 'People's Movement' overthrown the despotic political regime and established people's sovereignty in Nepal. King Gyanendra surrendered with the People's Power on 23:30 hours of 24 April 2006, which will be remembered as 'April Revolution' in the history of Nepal. The content of this book therefore describes only until March 2006, right before the success of April Revolution.

Author

References

1. Abdullaev, K. and Barnes, C. (2001) (ed.), Politics of Compromise: The Tajikistan Peace Process. Accord issue 10/ 2001. London: Conciliation Resources.
2. Acharya, K. (2005), *An Assessment of Economic Cost of the Ongoing Armed Conflict in Nepal (An Empirical Examination of the Period 1990-2005).* A Paper presented in the NEFAS/FES Seminar on Cost of Armed Conflict in Nepal organized in Kathmandu on 29-30 September 2005.
3. Ackermann, A. (2000), *Making Peace Prevail: Preventing Violent Conflict in Macedonia.* Syracuse: Syracuse University Press.
4. Adhikari, B. (2004a), Kofi Anan Available to Help Search far a Solution to the Ongoing Conflict. Kathmandu: *Spotlight* Vol. 23, No 38, 9-15 April 2004, P28.
5. Adhikari, B. (ed.) (2004b), *Conflict, Human Rights and Peace Challenges Before Nepal.* Kathmandu: National Human Rights Commission.
6. Adhikary, S (2061BS), Hodbaji Hatiyarko, Smaya Rasriya Saptahik, Jeth,7,2061, Brikuti Prakashan, Kath. Page 29-31.
7. African Peace Forum, Centre for Conflict Resolution, Consortium of Humanitarian Agencies, Forum for Early Warning and Early Response, International Alert and Safer World (2004), *Conflict Sensitive Approaches to Development, Humanitarian Assistance and Peace Building: A Resource Book.* London.
8. Amnesty International (AI), (2005a), *Nepal: A Long Ignored Human Rights Crisis Now on the Brink of Catastrophe.* 18 February 2005, ASA 31/022/2005. London: Amnesty International.
9. Amnesty International (AI), (2005b), *Nepal: Killing with Impunity.* 20 January 2005, ASA31/001/2005. London: Amnesty International.
10. Amnesty International (AI), (2004), AI Index: ASA 31/190/2004 (Public), News Service No: 323, 19 December 2004 (http://web.amnesty.org/library/Index/ENGASA311902004?open&of=ENG-2AS)

11. Anderson, M. (1999), *Do No Harm: How Aid can Support Peace or War.* London: Lynne Rienner Publishers.
12. Armon, J. and Carl, A. (eds.), (1996) The Liberian Peace Process 1990-1996. Accord issue 1/1996. London: Conciliation Resources.
13. Armon, J. and Philipson, L. (eds.), (1998), Demanding Sacrifice: War and Negotiation in Sri Lanka, Accord Issue 4/August (1998). London: Conciliation Resources.
14. Armon, J., Hendrickson, D. and Vines, A. (eds.), (1998), The Mozambican Peace Process in Perspective. Accord Issue 3/1993. London, Conciliation Resources.
15. Armon, J., Sieder, R. and Wilson, R. (eds.), (1997), Negotiating Rights: The Guatemalan Peace Process. Accord Issue 2/1997. London. Conciliation Resources.
16. Axelrod, R. (1984), *The Evolution of Cooperation*, New York: Basic Books.
17. Azar, E. and John W. B. (1986), *International Conflict Resolution: Theory and Practice.* Boulder: Lynne Rienner and Wheatsheaf.
18. Azar, E. E. (1990), *The Management of Protracted Social Conflict*, Hampshire: Dartmouth.
19. Baechler, G. (eds.), (2002), *Promoting Peace: The Role of Civilian Conflict Resolution.* Bern: Staempfli Publisher Limited.
20. Bailey, S. (1993), *Peace is a Process.* Quaker Home Service and Woodbrooke College for the Swarthmore Lecture Committee.
21. Barnes, C. (2002) (ed.), Owning the Process. Public Participation in Peace Making. Featuring South Africa, Guatemala & Mali. Accord Issue 3/2002. London: Conciliation Resources.
22. Bell D., Raiffa, H. and Tversky, A. (eds.), (1989), *Decision Making: Descriptive, Normative and Prescriptive Interactions.* Cambridge: Cambridge University Press.
23. Bennett, D. Scott (1996), "Security, Bargaining and the End of Interstate Rivalry." *International Studies Quarterly* 40, 2: 157-184.
24. Banerjee, D. (eds.), (2000), *South Asia at Gun Point: Small Arms and Light Weapons Proliferation.* Colombo: Regional Centre for Strategic Studies.
25. Bercovitch, J. (1984), *Social Conflicts and Third Parties: Strategies of Conflict Resolution.* Boulder / CO: Westview.
26. Bercovitch, J. (ed.) (1996), Resolving International Conflicts: The Theory and Practice of Mediation, Boulder: Lynne Rienner.
27. Bercovitch, J. and Rubin, J. (eds.), (1992) *Mediation in International Relations. Multiple Approaches to Conflict Management.* London: St. Martin's Press.
28. Bercovitch, J. and Wells, R. (1993), Evaluating Mediation Strategies: A Theoretical and Empirical Analysis. *Peace and Change* 18: 3-25.
29. Bhandari, B and Pun, S. (2002) Local Level Conflict Mediation Systems in Kaski and Mustang: A Review. In: G. Shivakoti Chintan (ed.), *Human*

Rights and Legal Treatment. Kathamndu: Tribhuvan University Human Rights Centre. Pp 168-179 (in Nepali Language).

30. Bhattachan, K. B, (2003), Civil Society and Protection of Diversity in Nepal. In: D. B. Gurung (ed.), *Nepal Tomorrow: Voices and Vision*. Kathmandu: Koselee Prakashan. Pp. 32-62.
31. Bhattarai, B. R. (2003), *The Nature of Underdevelopment and Regional Structure of Nepal: A Marxist Analysis*. Delhi: Adroit Publishers.
32. Bhattarai, R. (2004), Geopolitical Specialties of Nepal and a Regional Approach to Conflict Transformation. Kathmandu: Friends for Peace.
33. BHCT (2003), Berghof Handbook for Conflict Transformation. Berghof Research Centre for Constructive Conflict Management: Budrich: Leske & Budrich
34. Bista D.B. (1991), *Fatalism and Development: Nepal's Struggle for Modernisation*. Calcutta: Orient Longman Ltd.
35. Bloomfield, D. (1997), *Peacemaking Strategies in Northern Ireland: Building Complementarity in Conflict Management Theory*, Basingstoke: Macmillan.
36. Bloomfield, D. and Reilly, B. (1998), The Changing Nature of Conflict and Conflict Management. *In:* Harris P. and Ben Reilly (eds.) 1998. *Democracy and Deep-rooted conflict*, Stockholm: Institute for Democracy and Electoral Assistance (IDEA).
37. Bottomore T. (1969), *Sociological Theory and the Study of Social conflict.* Publisher unknown.
38. Brams, S.J. (1990), *Negotiation Games: Applying Game Theory to Bargaining and Arbitration.* New York: Routledge.
39. Buckles D. (Ed.) (1999), *Cultivating Peace: Conflict and Collaboration in Natural Resource Management.* Ottawa/Washington: IDRC/ World Bank Institute.
40. Budathoki, P. (2003), A Category V protected Landscape Approach to Buffer Zone Management in Nepal. *Parks* 13(2), Pp 22-30.
41. Burgess, G and Burgees, H. (1996), *Constructive Confrontation: Theoretical Framework*. Colorado: Conflict Research Consortium.
42. Burton, J. (1987), *Resolving Deep-rooted Conflict: A Handbook.* Lanham, Maryland: University Press of America.
43. Burton, J. (eds.), (1990), *Conflict: Human Needs Theory*. London: Macmillan.
44. Burton, J. and Dukes, F. (eds.), (1990), *Conflict: Practices in Management, Settlement and Resolution*, Vol. 4 of the Conflict Series, London: Macmillan.
45. Busby, A. (1996), Report on Election Coverage Workshop, Mimeo for Conciliation Resources and the Sierra Leone Association of Journalists.
46. Bush R. A. (1995), Dispute Resolution- the Domestic Arena: A Survey of Methods, Applications and Critical Issues. In: John A. Vasquez, et. al., (Eds.). *Beyond Confrontation: Learning Conflict Resolution in the Post-Cold War Era*, Michigan: The University of Michigan Press.

47. Bush R. A. B. and Folger, J. P. (1994a), *The Promise of Mediation: Responding to Conflict through Empowerment and Recognition.* San Francisco: Jossey-Bass Publishers.
48. Bush R.A. B and Folger, J. P. (1994b), Ideology Orientation to Conflict and Mediation Discourse. In: Folger J. and Jones, T. (eds.). *New Directions in Mediation.* London: Sage Publications. Pp. 3-25.
49. Caplan P. (eds.), (1995), *Understanding Disputes: The Politics of Arguments.* Berg: Oxford Providence.
50. Carl, A. and Garasu, L. (eds.), (2002), Weaving Consensus: The Papua New Guinea-Bougainville Peace Process. *Accord* issue 12/2002. London: Conciliation Resources.
51. CBS (2004), *Statistical Pocket Book.* Kathmandu: Central Bureau of Statistics.
52. CIJ (Centre for Investigative Journalism) (2004), *People in the 'People's War'.* Himal Books, Kathmandu.
53. Chambers, R. and Conway, G. (1992), *Sustainable Rural Livelihoods: Practical Concepts for the 21st Century.* IDS Discussion Paper 296. Brighton: IDS.
54. Clark, H. (2000), *Civil Resistance in Kosovo*, London: Pluto.
55. Clements, K. (1998), A Field in Tension: From Alternative Dispute Resolution to Conflict Transformation. In: Rosemary du Pressis and Geoff Fougere (eds.) *Politics, Policy and Practice: Essays in Honour of Bill Willmott*, Christchurch / New Zealand: University of Canterbury. Pp. 129-148..
56. Clements, K. and Ward R. (1994), *Building International Community* (eds.). St. Leonard: Allen and Unwin.
57. Conen, J. (eds.), (1999), A Question of Sovereignty: The Georgia- Abkhazia Peace Process. Accord issue7/999. London, Conciliation Resources.
58. Coogan, T. (1995), *The Troubles: Ireland's Ordeal 1966-1995 and the search for peace'.* London: Hutchinson.
59. Corbin, J. (1994a), *Gaza First: the Secret Norway Channel to Peace Between Israel and the PLO.* London: Bloomsbury.
60. Corbin, J. (1994b), *The Norway Channel: The Secret Talks that Led to the Middle East Peace Accord.* New York: Atlantic Monthly Press.
61. CPN (Conflict Prevention Network) (1999), *Conflict Impact Assessment: A Practical Working Tool for Prioritising Development Assistance in Unstable Situation.* Brussels: Conflict Prevention Network.
62. CPN (Maoist) (2058), *Policy and Programme of URPC*, 2058 BS.
63. Crandall, J. (2004), Truth Commissions in Guatemala and Peru: Perpetual Impunity and Transitional Justice Compared. Conflict, Peace & Development, Issue 4, pp 1-19.
64. Crocker, C. (1996), Lessons on Intervention. In: *Managing Conflict in the Post Cold War World: The Role of Intervention.* Report of the Aspen Institute Conference, August 2-6, 1995. Colorado: Aspen Institute. Pp. 77-88.

65. Crocker, C., Hampson F. and All, P. (eds.), (1994), *Managing Global Chaos*. Washington DC: United State Institute of Peace.
66. Curle, A. (1987), *In the Middle: Non-official Mediation in Violent Situations*. New York: Berg.
67. Curle, A. (1996), *Another Way: Positive Responses to Violence*.
68. Curle, A. (1971). *Making Peace*. London: Tavistock Publications.
69. Dahal, D. R. (2003), *Conflict Resolution: A Note on Some Contending Approaches*. A paper prepared for the Seminar on Management of Conflicts in Nepal: A Preparation for Negotiation going to be organised by Centre for the Study of Democracy and Governance.
70. Dahal, D. R. (2004), *Conflict Situation in Nepal*. Kathmandu: Friedrich Ebert Stiftung.
71. Devetak, R. (1996), Critical Theory. In: Scott Burchill and Andrew Linklater *et. al.* (eds.), *Theories of International Relations*. London: Macmillan Press. Pp. 210-251.
72. DFID, (1999), *Sustainable Livelihoods Guidance Sheet*. London: Department for International Development of UK.
73. DFID, (2002), *Security and Risk Management Report For DFID Nepal*, Feb. 2002.
74. Diamond, L. and McDonald, J. (1996), *Multi-Track Diplomacy: A Systems Approach to Peace*. Washington DC: Kumarian Press.
75. Dougherty J. E. and Pfaltgraff, R. L. (1990), *Contending Theories of International Relations*. London: Harper Collins Publisher.
76. Duffield, M. (1997), Evaluating conflict resolution. In: Serbe G, Macrae J. and Wohlgemuth L. (eds.), *NGOs in Conflict - An Evaluation of International Alert*. Fantoft-Bergen, Norway: Christian Michelsen Institute, Pp 79-112.
77. Duijn L.V. (2003), Nepal IDP Research Initiative Findings. Kathmandu: Netherlands Development Organization (SNV).
78. EPCP (European Platform for Conflict Prevention) (1999), *Searching for Peace in Africa: An Overview of Conflict Prevention and Management Activities*. Utrectht: European Center for Conflict Prevention.
79. Felstiner W. L. F., Abel, R. L. and Sarat, A. (1981), The Emergence and Transformation of Conflicts: Naming, Blaming and Claiming. *Law and Society Review* 15.
80. Fetherston, A. B. (2000), *From Conflict Resolution to Transformative Peacebuilding: Reflections from Croatia. Working Paper 4 (April)*. Bradford: Centre for Conflict Resolution. Department of Peace Studies / University of Bradford.
81. Fisher, R. and Ury, W. (1981), *Getting to Yes: How to Negotiate Without Giving In*. London: Arrow Books.
82. Fisher, S., Abdi, D. I., Ludin, J. Smith, R., Williams S. and Willims, S. (2000), *Working with Conflict: Skills and Strategies for Action*. London: Zed Books and Responding to Conflict.

83. Fisher, R. J. (1983), Third Party Consultation as a Method of Conflict Resolution: A Review of Studies. *Journal of Conflict Resolution* 27, 2: 301-334.
84. Fisher, R. J. (1997), *Interactive Conflict Resolution*. Syracuse / NY: Syracuse University Press.
85. Fisher, R., and Keashly, L. (1991), The Potential Complementarity of Mediation and Consultation within a Contingency Model of Third-Party Intervention. *Journal of Peace Research*, Vol 28, No. 1, p. 29-42.
86. Fitzduff, M. (1999), Changing History - Peacebuilding in Northern Ireland, In: *People Building Peace*, Utrecht: European Centre for Conflict Prevention.
87. Folger J. P. and Jones, T. S. (eds.), (1994), *New Direction in Mediation: Communication Research and Perspectives*. London: Sage Publications.
88. Galtung J. (2004a), Conflict Transformation by Peaceful Means: The Transcend Method. United Nations Disaster Management Training Programme.
89. Galtung, J (2004b), Transformation of Conflict in Nepal: A Human Right Perspective. In: Bipin Adhikari (ed.), *Conflict, Human Rights and Peace Challenges Before Nepal*. Kathmandu: National Human Right Commission.
90. Galtung, J (2000a), *Peace by Peaceful Means: Peace and Conflict, Development and Civilisation*. London: Sage Publications.
91. Galtung, J. (2000b), *Conflict Transformation by Peaceful Means*. Participants' Manual, Trainers' Manual. Geneva: UN Disaster Management Training Programme.
92. Galtung, J. (1996), *Peace by Peaceful Means*. London, Sage.
93. Galtung, J. and Jacobsen, C. G. (2000), *Searching for Peace*. London, Pluto.
94. Garcia- Duran, M. (eds.), (2004), Alternative to War: Colombia's Peace Process. Accord Issue 14/2004. London: Conciliation Resources.
95. Gersony, R. (2003), *Sowing the Wind: History and Dynamics of the Maoist Revolt in Nepal's Rapti Hills*. Kathmadnu: USAID/Mercy Corps International.
96. Ghandi, M. K. (1950), *Satyagraha in South Africa*. Ahmedabad: Navajivan Publishing House.
97. Ghandi, M.K. (1938), *Hind Swaraj, or Indian Home Rule*. Ahmedabad: Navajivan Publishing House.
98. Goodhand, J. (2000), *DFID Nepal Conflict Assessment*. Kathmandu: DFID Nepal.
99. Gulliver P. (1979), *Conflicts and Negotiations: A Cross Cultural Perspective, Studies in Law and Social Control*. New York and London: Academic Press.
100. Gurung, D. B. (eds.), (2003), *Nepal Tomorrow: Voices and Vision*. Kathmandu: Koselee Prakashan.
101. Hachhethu, K (2003), The Question of Inclusion and exclusion in Nepal: Interface between State and Ethnicity, .Paper presented at 'The agenda of

transformation :Inclusion in Nepali Democracy' Organized by the Social Science Baha, Kathmandu 24-26 April, 2003.

102. Harris, P. and Reilly, B. (eds.), (1998), *Democracy and Deep Rooted Conflict: Options for Negotiators.* Stockholm: International Institute for Democracy and Electoral Assistance.
103. Hendrickson, D. (eds.), (1998), Safe Guarding Peace: Cambodia's Constitutional Change. *Accord Issue 5*, Nov. 1998, London Conciliation Resources.
104. Hill, B. (1982), An Analysis of Conflict Resolution Techniques: From Problem-Solving Workshops to Theory. *Journal of Conflict Resolution* 26, 1: 109-138.
105. Högger, H. (2001), *Contributing to New Strength: an Analysis of Threats and Opportunities in the Development Co-operation between Nepal and Switzerland.* Kathmandu: SDC.
106. Howel J. and Upreti, B. R. (2005), *Rural Access Programme: Mid-term, Output-to-Purpose Review 2005.* Kathmandu: Department for International Development, UKA
107. Hume, C. (1994), *Ending Mozambique's War.* Washington: United States Institute of Peace.
108. Hutt, M. (2004), *Himalayan 'People's War': Nepal's Maoist Rebellion.* London: Hurst and Company.
109. IANSA (International Action Network on Small Arms) (2003), *Implementing the Programme of Action 2003: Action by State and Civil Society.* London: IANSA, International Alert and Saferworld.
110. IDD (2005), *Report on the Inter-Agency Internal Displacement Division (IDD) Mission to Nepal* (11-22 April 2005).
111. INSEC (2003), *Nepal Human Rights Year Book 2003*. Kathmandu: INSEC.
112. INSEC (2004), *Nepal Human Rights Year Book 2004*. Kathmandu: INSEC.
113. INSEC (2005), *Human Rights Year Book, 2005*. Kathmandu: Informal Sector Service Centre.
114. International Alert (IA) (1996), *Resource Pack for Conflict Transformation*, London: International Alert.
115. International Crisis Group (ICG) (2003a), *Nepal Obstacle to Peace*. Brussels/ Kathmandu: ICG. No 57.
116. International Crisis Group (ICG) (2003b), *Nepal Backgrounder: Ceasefire-Soft Landing or Strategic Pause*, 10th April 2003 Brussels/Kathmandu: ICG. Research No 50.
117. International Crisis Group (ICG) (2003c), *Nepal Back to Gun ICG Asia Briefing Paper 22 October 2003*. Brussels/Kathmandu: ICG No 57.
118. International Crisis Group (ICG) (2005a), *Towards a Lasting Peace in Nepal: The Constitutional Issues. Asia Report No 99, 15 June*. Brussels/ Kathmandu: International Crisis Group.
119. International Crisis Group (ICG) (2005b), Asia Report No 94, 24 March 2005 entitled "Nepal Dealing with Human Rights Crisis. Kathmandu and

Brussels: International Crisis Group.

120. Jabri, V. (1996), *Discourses on Violence: Conflict Analysis Reconsidered*, Manchester: Manchester University Press.
121. Jandt F. E. and Pedersen, P. B. (eds.), (1996), *Constructive Conflict Management: Asia Pacific Cases.* London: Sage Publications.
122. Joongman, A. (2000), Mapping Dimensions of Contemporary Conflicts and Human Rights Violations. *World Conflicts and Human Rights MAP 2000.* PIOOM, Leiden: Leiden University.
123. Jwala, P. (2002), *Baicharik Bhumari ma Maobadi Andolon*. Kathmandu: Sangin-Madan Prakashan.
124. Karki, A, and Seddon, D. (2003), The people's war in historical context. (Eds.), *The People's War in Nepal: Left Perspectives*. Delhi: Adroit Publishers.
125. Karki, A. & Kattel, M. (eds.), (2005), Nepal: The Maoist Insurgency and Beyond. Hongkong: Asian Regional Exchange for New Initiative.
126. Kattel, B. K (2003), Exercise of Peace Accord in Nepal. *Informal.* Vol. 16. No. 3. Kathmandu: INSEC.
127. Khadka, R.J. (1997), *Sources of Conflict and Methods of Resolving them in Sindhuli, Nepal.* Proceedings of Conflict Management Workshop. Hawaii: East West Centre.
128. Khanal, K. (2003), *Ethnicity and Autonomy: Some Issues for Consideration in Remaking the Constitution.* Paper presented at 'The Agenda of Transformation: Inclusion in Nepali Democracy' organised by the Social Science Baha, Kathmandu, 24-26 April, 2003.
129. Khanal, K. (2005), Nepal's Discourse on Constituent Assembly: An Analysis. Kathmandu: Friends for Peace.
130. Khanna, D. D. and Kueck, G. (eds.), (2003), Conflict *Resolution, Human Rights and Democracy*. Delhi: Shipra Publications.
131. Kievelitz, U. and Polzer, T. (2002), *Nepal Country Study on Conflict Transformation and Peace Building.* Deutsche Gesellschaft fur Technische Zusammenarbeit (GTZ) GmbH.
132. King, M.L. (1963), *Why We Can't Wait*. New York: New American Library.
133. Kleiboer, M. (1994), Ripeness of Conflict. A Fruitful Negotiation? *Journal of Peace Research,* Vol. 31, No. 1 Pp 109-116.
134. Kleiboer, M. (1996), "Understanding the Success and Failure of International Mediation", *Journal of Conflict Resolution* 40, 2: 360-389.
135. Kleiboer, M. (1998), *Multiple Realities of International Mediation*. Boulder / CO and London: Rienner.
136. Kona, E. S.(1999), A Framework for Cross-Cultural Conflict Resolution Theory: Prospects for Cultural Contributions from Africa, Richardson Institute, Lancaster University: Unpublished thesis.
137. Kremenyuk V. (eds.), (1991), *International Negotiation: Analysis, Approaches, Issues.* Oxford: Jossey-Bass Publisher.

138. Kriesberg, L. (1998), *Constructive Conflicts: From Escalation to Resolution*. Lanham: Rowman and Littlefield.

139. Krippendorf, E. (1973), Peace Research and the Industrial Revolution, *Journal of Peace Research*, Vol 10, 185-201.

140. Kumar, D and Sharma, H. (2004), Security Sector Reform in Nepal: Challenges and Opportunities. Kathamdnu: Friends for Peace.

141. Kumar, D. (2004) P*roximate Causes of Nepal*. A Paper presented at International Workshop on Causes of Internal Conflicts and Means to Resolve Them: Case Study of Nepal organised in 22-24 February 2004.

142. Lawati, M. (2003), Inclusive Democratic Political Institutions for Nepal. Paper presented at 'The Agenda of Transformation: Inclusion in Nepali Democracy' organised by the Social Science Baha, Kathmandu, 24-26 April, 2003.

143. Lawoti, M. (2005), Towards a Democractic Nepal: Inclusive Political Institutions for a Multi-cultural Society. New Delhi : Sage Publications.

144. Lederach, J. P. (1997), *Building Peace. Sustainable Reconciliation in Divided Societies*. Washington, D.C.: United States Institute of Peace Press.

145. Lederach, J. P. (1999), Justpeace: The Challenges of the 21st Century. In *People Building Peace: 35 Inspiring Stories from around the World*, ed. European Centre for Conflict Prevention (in co-operation with the International Fellowship of Reconciliation (IFOR) and the Coexistence Initiative of State of the World Forum). Utrecht: European Centre for Conflict Prevention. Pp.27-36.

146. Lederach, J. P. (1995), *Preparing for Peace: Conflict Transformation Across Cultures*. New York: Syracuse University Press.

147. Leonhardt, M. (2000), *Conflict Impact Assessment of EU Development Co-operation with APC Countries: A Review of Literature and Practices*. London: International Alcrt and Saferworld.

148. Lode, K. (2002), *Mali Peace Process: Context Analysis and Evaluation*. Accord. Issue 13. 2002. London: Reconciliation Resources. Pp. 56-63.

149. Lord, D. (eds.), (2000), Paying the Price: The Sierra Leone Peace Process. Accord Issue 9/2000. London; Conciliation Resources.

150. Lund, M. (1996), *Preventing violent conflict: A Strategy for preventive Diplomacy*. Washington: United States Peace Institute.

151. Louise, D. and McDonald, J. (1996), *Multi-Track Diplomacy*. Connecticut: Kumarian Press.

152. Lucima, O. (eds.), (2002), Protractive Conflict, Elusive Peace: Initiatives to End the Violence in Northern Uganda. Accord Issue 11/2002. London: Conciliation Resources.

153. Mackinlay, J. and Upreti, B. R. (2003), The King and Mao. *The World Today*. London: Royal Institute of International Affairs. Pp. 26-27.

154. Macrae, J. (eds.), (2002), *The New Humanitarianisms: A review of treads in global humanitarian Action.* HPG Report 11 London, ODI

155. Mahat, R. S. (2005), *In Defence of Democracy: Dynamics and Fault Lines*

of Nepal's Political Economy. New Delhi: Adroit Publishers.

156. Mainali M, (2003), Development vs the Maobadies. In: Thapa, D. (2003). (Ed.), *Understanding the Maoist Movement in Nepal*. Kathmandu: MartinChautari. Pp. 125-127.
157. Maley, W. (1994), Peace making Diplomacy: United Nations Good Offices in Afghanistan. In: K. Clements and R. Ward (eds.), *Building International Community*. St. Leonard: Allen and Unwin, Pp. 250-254.
158. Martinelli D. P. and A. P. Almeida (1998), Negotiation, Management, and Systems Thinking. *Systemic Practice and Action Research*. 11 (3): 319-334.
159. McCarthy, R. M. and G. Sharp (1997), *Non-violent Action. A Research Guide*. New York and London: Garland Publishing, Inc.
160. McCartney, C. (1999), *Striking a Balance: The Northern Ireland Peace Process*. Accord Issue 8/1999 London: Conciliation Resources.
161. Mehrotra, L. (2003), The Role of United Nations: The Case of Cambodia. In: *Conflict Resolution, Human Rights and Democracy* (eds.) D. D. Khanna and Gert Kueck. Delhi: Shipra Publications, Pp. 156-174.
162. Meyer, W and Upreti, B. (2004), *Annual Review Report 2004 of Rural Access Programme (RAP) – Implementation Phase*. Kathmandu: Department for International Development (DFID), His Majesty's Government of Nepal (HMGN)
163. Miall, H. (1992), *The Peacemakers: Peaceful Settlements of Disputes Since 1945*. London: Macmillan.
164. Miall, H. (2001), *Conflict Transformation: A Multi-Dimensional Task*. Berghof Handbook for Conflict Transformation.
165. Miall, H., Rambotham, O. and Woodhouse, T. (1999), *Contemporary Conflict Resolution*. Cambridge: Polity Press.
166. Misra, A. (2002), Afghanistan: The Politics of Post War reconstruction. *Journal of Conflict security and Development*. 2:3, Pp. 5-57.
167. Misra, C. (2004), Locating the 'Causes' of the Maoist Struggle. A Paper presented at International Workshop on "Causes of Internal Conflicts and Means to Resolve Them: Case Study of Nepal organised in 22-24 February 2004.
168. Mitchell, C. R. (1981), *The Structure of International Conflict*. London, Macmillan.
169. Moscovici S. and Doise, W. (1994), *Conflict and Consensus: A Grand Theory of Collective Decision*. London: Sage Publications.
170. New Era (1988), *A Study of Legal System and Legal Situation in Rural Areas of the Kingdom of Nepal*. Kathmandu: Friedirich Naumann Foundation.
171. Nickson, R. A. (2003), Democratisation and Growth of Communism in Nepal. In: Thapa, D. (Ed.), *Understanding the Maoist Movement in Nepal*. Kathmandu: MartinChautari. Pp. 2-33.
172. NPC (2003), *The Cost of War in Nepal*. Kathmandu: National Peace

Campaign, P. 23.

173. Nyheim, D., Leonhardt, M. and Gaigals, C. (2001), *Development in Conflict: A Seven-Step Tool for Planners*. London: Forum for Early Warning and Early Response (FEWER), International Alert and Safeworld.
174. OECD (2001), T*he DAC Guidelines: Helping Prevent Violent Conflict.* Paris: Organisation for Economic Co-operation and Development.
175. OECD/DAC (2002), *Review of Development Partnership in Nepal: Review Team's Main Findings and Recommendations.* January 2002.
176. Oli K. P. (1998), *Conflict Resolution and Mediation in Natural Resource Management*. Kathmandu: IUCN-Nepal.
177. Onesto, L, (2005), *Dispatches from the People's War in Nepal.* London: Pluto Press and Chicago: Insight Press.
178. Paffenholz, T. (2002), *Designing Intervention Process: Conditions and Parameters for Conflict Transformation.* Berghof Handbook of Conflict Transformation. www.berghof-handbook.net
179. Paffenholz, T. (2003), *Getting Back to the Table: Why Two negotiation Processes have Failed, Recommendations towards Democratic Peace Building in Nepal.* Kathmandu: GTZ.
180. Pahari, A. (2003), *From Liberation to Insurgency: The Politics of Paradoxes in Nepal.* Paper presented at 'The Agenda of Transformation: Inclusion in Nepali Democracy' organised by the Social Science Baha, Kathmandu, 24-26 April, 2003.
181. Panday D.R. (1999), *Nepal's Failed Development: Reflections on the Mission and the Melodies.* Kathmandu: Nepal South Asia Centre.
182. Panday D.R. (2001), *Corruption, Governance and International Co-operation: Essays and Impressions on Nepal and South Asia.* Kathmandu: Transparency International Nepal.
183. Pandey, N. N. (2005), *Nepal's Maoist Movement and Implications for India and China*. Regional Centre for Strategic Studies (RCSS) Policy Studies, no. 27, RCCS (Colombo). New Delhi: Manohar Publishers and Distributors.
184. Panti, K (2004), *Kasari Chali Rahechha Maobadi Janasatta* (How Maoist Peoples Government is running)? Mulyankan Monthly Vol 126, Poush 2061 (December 2004) Pp 11 and 41-43.
185. Paudel M. (2061BS), Benibata lutiaka, hathatiyar gaun ma pradrashan,, Maobadi arko Bhishan akrman ko tayarima, , Box news,, Mulyankan Monthly,Jeth, 2061 Mulyangkan Prakasan prali. Kath. Page 10- 11 and 38 – 41
186. Pendzich C., Thomas, G. and Wohlgenant, T. (1994), *The Role of Alternative Conflict Management in Community Forestry.* Resolve Working Paper No 1, Forest Tree and People Programme. Phase II, FAO, Rome. Uppsala: Swedish University of Agricultural Sciences.
187. Philipson, L. (2002), *Conflict in Nepal: Perspectives on the Maoist Movement.* Kathmandu.

188. Phuong, C. N. (1991), 'Compassionate Action in the Midst of War', Karuna ,11, Spring.
189. Pokharel, B. (2004), *Cost of Conflict in Nepal*. A Paper Presented at the Seminar of "Cost of Conflict in Nepal" organised by Nepal Foundation for Advanced Studies, June 9, 2004. Kathmandu.
190. Pokharel, V. M. and Wagle, C. M. (2004) *Chure Fedima Khula Jail* (Open jail in the belt of Chure), Samaya Saptik, Year 1 No 35, 2061 (2004 December), Pp 36-37
191. Prein, H. (1994), A Contingency Approach for Conflict Intervention. *Group and Organisation Studies* 9, 1: 81-102.
192. Princen, T. (1992), *Intermediaries in International Conflict*. Princeton / NJ: Princeton University Press.
193. Pruitt D. J. and Carnevale, P. J. (1993), *Negotiations in Social Conflicts*. Buckingham: Open University Press.
194. Putnam, R. D. (1993), *Making Democracy Work: Civic Tradition in Modern Italy*. Princeton, NJ: Princeton University Press.
195. Raj, A. P (2004), *Maoists in the Land of Buddha: An Analytical Study of the Maoist Insurgency in Nepal*. Delhi: Nirala Publications.
196. Ramsbotham, O. and Woodhouse, T. (1996), *Humanitarian Intervention in Contemporary Conflict*, Cambridge: Polity.
197. Rana, R. S. and Sharma, S. (2004), *Development Cooperation and Conflict*. Paper presented at the workshop Causes of Internal Conflicts and Means to Resolve them: Case Study of Nepal, at Nagarkot, Feb 21-22, 2004.
198. Reychler, L. and Paffenholz, T. (2001), *Peace Building: A Field Guide*. London and Boulder: Lynne Rienner.
199. Ricigliano, R. (eds.), (2005), *Choosing to Engage: Armed Groups and Peace Processes*. London: Reconciliation Resources, Issue 16.
200. Ross, M. H. and Rothman, J. (eds.), (1999), *Theory and Practice in Ethnic Conflict Management: Theorizing Success and Failure*. London: Macmillan Press.
201. Ruane J and Todd, J., (1996), *The Dynamics of Conflict in Northern Ireland*, Cambridge: Cambridge University Press.
202. Rubenstein R. E. (1993), Analysing and Resolving Class Conflict. In: Dennis J., D. Sandole and H. v. d. Merwe, (Eds.) *Conflict Resolution Theory and Practice: Integration and Application*. Manchester: Manchester University Press. Pp. 146-57.
203. Rubin J. Z., Pruitt, D. G. and Kim S. H. (eds.), (1994), *Social Conflict: Escalation, Stalemate, and Settlement*. New York: McGraw-Hill, Inc.
204. Rubin, J. Z. (1980), Experimental Research on Third-Party Intervention in Conflict. *Psychological Bulletin* 87, 2: 379-391.
205. Rubin, J. Z., (eds.), (1981), *Dynamics of Third-Party Intervention: Kissinger in the Middle East*. New York: Praeger.
206. Rupensinghe, K. (ed.) (1995), *Conflict Transformation*, London: Macmillan.
207. Rupesinghe, K. (1998), *Civil Wars, Civil Peace*, London: Pluto.

208. Salla M, E. (2000), Conflict Resolution, Genetics and Alchemy-The Evolution of Conflict Transmutation. *The Online Journal of Peace and Conflict Resolution*, 3(3), June 2000.
209. Samaya Weekly, Vol. 2, No 69, 28 Shrawan-2 Bhadra 2062 (12-18 Aug 2005), Page 38.
210. Sanddelin R. (1997), *Interpersonal Relationships and Conflict Resolution. Community Resource Guide*. URL: http://www.infoteam.community/nonprofit/nica/resolution.html
211. Saunders, H. (1996), Pre-negotiation and circum-negotiation: Arenas of the peace process. In: C. Crocker, F. Hampson and P. All(eds.), *Managing Global Chaos* . Washington DC: United State Institute of Peace. Pp. 419-432.
212. Schmid, A. (eds.), (1997), *Violent Crime and Conflicts*, Milan: ISPAC (International Scientific and Professional Advisory Council of the UN Crime Prevention and Criminal Justice Programme).
213. Schmid, H. (1968), Peace Research and Politics. *Journal of Peace Research* 5, 3: 217-232.
214. Scimecca J.A. (1993), Theory and Alternative Conflict Resolution: A Contradiction in Terms? In: Sandole D. J. D and H. van der Merwe (Eds.) *Conflict Resolution: Theory and Practice: Integration and Application*. Manchester: Manchester University Press. Pp. 211-221.
215. Seddon, D. (2005a), 'The Maoist Insurgency: From Stalemate to Strategic Offensive'. Paper given at the Annual Conference of the Political Studies Association (PSA), University of Leeds, April 2005
216. Seddon, D. (2005b), *Armed Violence and Poverty in Nepal*. Case study for the Armed Violence and Poverty Initiative (AVPI), Centre for International Cooperation and Security, Department of Peace Studies, University of Bradford, January 2005.
217. Seddon, D. and Hussein, K. (2002), *The Consequence of Conflict: Livelihoods and Development in Nepal*. London: ODI Working Paper 185.
218. Senghaas, D (2001), *Civilizing Conflict: Constructive Pacifism as a Guiding Notion for Conflict Transformation*. Berghof Handbook of conflict Transformation, vol. I. Berlin: Bergh of Research Center for Construction Conflict Management.
219. Senghaas, D. (1973), Conflict Formations in Contemporary International Society. *Journal of Peace Research*, vol.10, 163-184.
220. Thapa, D. and Shah, A (2000), Small Arms and their increasing Proliferation in Nepal. IN: Deepankar Banarjee (ed.) *South Asia at Gun Point*. Colombo: Regional Centre for Strategic Studies, pages 97-103.
221. Sharma, P. R. (2004), The State and Society in Nepal: Historical Foundations and Contemporary Trends. Kathmandu: Himal Books.
222. Sharma, S. (2002), *The Ethnic Dimension of the Maoist Insurgency*. A Draft paper. Kathmandu
223. Sharma, S. (2003), The Maoist Movement: An Evolutionary perspective.

In: Thapa, D (ed.), *Understanding the Maoist Movement in Nepal*. Kathmandu: Martin Chautari. Pp. 362-380.

224. Sharp, G. (1973), *The politics of non-violent action* (3 vols.), Boston: Porter Sargent.
225. Shrestha N. R. (1997), *In the Name of Development: A Reflection in Nepal*. Kathmandu: Educational Enterprises.
226. Shrestha, S (2004), India's Possible Role in the Peace Process of Nepal', (preliminary draft paper in Nepali) Kathamndu: Friends for Peace).
227. Shrestha, H. L. (2061BS), Proliferation of Small Arms and Lights Weapons and problems caused by them: a Discussion (Nepal ma sana hatiya ra halka astra ko prashar ra aas bata srijit samasya: eka chalphal) (Nepali script). Kathmandu: Friends for Peace.
228. Sidaway R. (1996), *Outdoor Recreation and Nature Conservation: Conflicts and Their Solution*. Unpublished PhD Dissertation. The University of Edinburgh.
229. Smith P. (1997), Civil Society and Violence: Narrative Forms and the Regulation of Social Conflict. In: Turpin J. and L. R. Kurtz (Eds.) *The Web of Violence: From Interpersonal to Global*. Illinois: University of Illinois Press.
230. Stankovitch, M. (eds.), (1999), Compromising on Autonomy: Mindanao in Transition. Accord issue 6/1999. London: Conciliation Resources.
231. Stedman, S. J. (1991), *Peacemaking in Civil War: International Mediation in Zimbawe, 1974-1980*. Boulder / CO: Lynne Rienner.
232. Susskind, L.& J. Cruikshank (1987), *Breaking the Impasse: Consensual Approaches to Resolving Public Disputes*. New York: Basic Books
233. Tate, W (2004), No Room for Peace: United State's Policy in Columbia, In: *Alternatives to War: Columbia's Peace Process* (ed.) Mauricio Garcia-Duran. London: Conciliations Resources, Pp. 70-73.
234. Thapa, D. (eds.), (2003), Understanding The Maoist movement in Nepal. Kathmandu martin Chautari.
235. Thapa, D. and Sijapati, B. (2003), *A Kingdom Under Siege: Nepal's Maoist Insurgency, 1996 to 2003*. Kathmandu: The Printhouse.
236. Thapa, H. B. (2002), *Anatomy of Corruption*. Kathmandu: Published by Sangita Thapa.
237. Ukayab, T. and Adhikari, S. (2000), *The Nationalities of Nepal*. Kathmandu: National Committee for Development of Nationalities/Ministry of Local Development.
238. UNDP (2004), *Nepal Human Development Report: Empowerment and Poverty Reduction*. Kathmandu: UNDP Nepal.
239. Upreti B. R. (2005a), *Proliferation of Small Arms and Light Weapons: Security Implications and Policy concerns for Nepal*. A chapter prepared for the SASA-Net Nepal.
240. Upreti, B. (2005b), Conflict Resolution in Nepal: Traditional Approaches and the Question of Third Party Negotiation. In: Shrestha, Ananda Prasad

and Hari Upreti (eds.), *Critical barriers to the Negotiation of Armed Conflict in Nepal.* Kathmandu: Nepal Foundation for Advance Studies, PP.65-96.

241. Upreti, B. R. (2005c), *Armed Conflict, Political Crisis and Nepalese Media.* A paper presented at 'Media, Conflict Reporting and Human Rights' Conference organised by South Asian Free Media Association (SAFMA), Nepal in Hotel Annapurna, Kathmandu on 27-28 July 2005

242. Upreti, B. R. (2005d), Conflict Transformation and Peace Building: Choices of Approaches and Strategies for Nepal. In: *Readings on Governance and Development* (Vol. V) Mukti Rijal (Ed.). Kathmandu: Institute of Governance and Development. Pp. 24-33

243. Upreti, B. R. (2005e), Dialogue: only Recourse to Conflict. In: Good Governance (bi-monthly magazine) Vol 3, No 6, May-June 2005. Kathmandu: Propublic, Pp. 32-33.

244. Upreti, B. R. (2005f), *Changing Political Context and Conflict Dynamics in Nepal: A Quick Assessment.* Kathmandu: CARE Nepal.

245. Upreti, B. R. (2005g), Working on Conflict: Peace and Conflict Impact Assessment of Commercial Agriculture Development Project in Eastern Nepal. Final Report. Manila: Asian Development Bank.

246. Upreti, B. R. (2005h), *Intrusive Reality: Social Exclusion, Injustice and Conflict in Nepal.* A Paper submitted to SAP Nepal.

247. Upreti, B. R. (2005i), *Human Rights Approach to Conflict Transformation: Ensuring respect and fulfilment of human rights in peaceful settlement of the armed conflict in Nepal.* A paper presented at Human Rights and Peace Conference organised by National Human Rights Commission in Kathmandu on 24 – 25 January 2005.

248. Upreti, B. R. (2004a), *The Price of Neglect: From Resource Conflict to Maoist Insurgency in the Himalayan Kingdom.* Kathmandu: Bhrikuti Academic Publications. Pages 446.

249. Upreti, B. R. (2004b), Role of Civil Society in Conflict Transformation and Peace Building: Quick Reflections and Lessons from Nepal. A paper presented at the Regional Conference on "The Role of Civil Society in the Prevention of Armed Conflict in South Asia" organised by Regional Centre for Strategic Studies, in collaboration with Freidrich Ebert Stiftung and supported by UNDP, from 11-13 Sept. 2004 at Hotel Himalaya, Kathamndu.

250. Upreti, B. R. (2004c), *Causes and Consequences of the armed conflict in Nepal.* A paper presented at the seminar "Consequences of Maoist Movement: Role of HMG, United Nations and Stakeholders for the Protection and Assistance of Internally Displaced Persons " organized by CSWC Kathmandu, Nepal on 1st February 2004.

251. Upreti, B. R. (2004d). Land Conflict in Nepal: Peasants' Struggle to Change Unequal Agrarian Social Relations. *Journal of Community, Work and Family*, Vol. 7, No 3, Pp. 371-394.

252. Upreti, B. R. (2004e), Dynamics of Resource Governance, Resource Scarcity and Conflict in Nepal, *Journal of Forest and Livelihoods*, Vol. 4(1), July 2004.
253. Upreti, B. (2004f), Tiraskar ra Upechhya ko Parinam (Result of Hatred and Neglect), In: Mainali Mohan (ed.) *Samabesi Loktantrà Kathmandu Adharharu (Basis of Inclusive Democracy),* Kathmandu: Social Science Baha, Pp. 109-118 (in Nepali language).
254. Upreti, B. R. (2004g), Neglected Reality: Resource Governance and Conflict in Nepal. In: *Readings on Governance and Development* (Vol. III) Mukti Rijal (Ed.). Kathmandu: Institute of Governance and Development. Pp. 95-111.
255. Upreti, B. R (2004h), *Dundya Byabasthapanka Siddhanta ra Bidhiharu: Eak Parichayua* (Theories and Practices of Conflict Management: An Introduction). Kathmandu: Enabling State Programme. (Nepali)
256. Upreti, B. R (2004i), Dispute settlement at local level: Observations and Lessons from Nepal. A paper presented at the international workshop on "Local Democracy in South Asia" organized by Centre for Nepal and Asian Studies (CNAS) in collaboration with SNV Nepal from 30 Nov-1 December 2004 in Kathmandu.
257. Upreti, B. R. (2004j), Resource conflicts and their resolution practices in Nepal. *Mountain Research and Development Journal* Vol. 24.1 Pp. 60-66.
258. Upreti, B. R. (2004k), Conflict over biomass energy development in the United Kingdom: Some Observations and lessons from England and Wales. *Energy Policy* Volume 2, Issue 6, Pages-785-800.
259. Upreti, B. R. (2004l), *Nepal on Fire: A Tragedy of Triple Betrayal*. South Asian Journal Vol. 7 2004, December.
260. Upreti, B.R. (2004m), *Understanding the Dynamics of Conflict in Nepal*. A Background Paper prepared for the Human Development Report 2004 of UNDP Nepal.
261. Upreti, B. R. (2004n), *Sustainable Livelihoods, Environmental Security, and Conflict Mitigation in Protected Areas of Nepal: Trend and Challenges*. A preliminary draft report. Kathmandu: IUCN
262. Upreti B. R. (2003a), *Social Exclusion, Centralism and Conflict: Challenges for Conflict Transformation in Nepal*. A paper presented at the International Conference 'The Agenda of Transformation: Inclusion in Nepali Democracy' organised by Social Science Baha in Kathmandu from 24-26 April 2003.
263. Upreti, B. R. (2003b), Breaking the Barriers and Building a Bridge: A roadmap for structuring negotiation and peace process in Nepal. Paper presented at the Seminar on management of Conflict in Nepal: A preparation for Negotiation organized by Center of Democracy and Governance on 2 December, 2003, Kathmandu.
264. Upreti, B. R. (2003c), Interactive Conflict Management: An Alternative Methodology to Address Social Conflict at Local level. *International Journal of Development Issues,* No. 2, Vol. 2, Pp.77-90

265. Upreti B. R. (2002a), *Management of Social and Natural Resource Conflict in Nepal: Realities and Alternatives.* New Delhi: Adroit Publishers.
266. Upreti B. R. (2002b), *Nepal: A Nation in Search of Peace and Development. A Country Assessment Report.* Berne: Swiss Agency for Development and Co-operation.
267. Upreti, B. R. (2001), *Conflict Management in Natural Resources: A Study of Land, Water and Forest Conflict in Nepal.* Published PhD Dissertation. Wagenignen: Wageningen University.
268. Upreti, B. R. (2061BS), Nepal ma Maobadi Sashastra Dunda: karan, ashar ra samadhan ka prayash haru (Maoist Armed Conflict in Nepal: Causes, Effects and Efforts for Resolution). Kathmandu: Bhrikuti Academic Publications (Nepali)
269. Upreti, B. R. and Dhungana, D (2004*), Peace Process and Negotiation in Nepal: Revisiting the Past and Envisioning the Future.* Paper presented at the International Workshop "Causes of Internal Conflicts and Means to Resolve Them: Case Study of Nepal" organised by the Graduate Institute of International Studies, Geneva, Switzerland in Nagarkot, Kathmandu on 22-24 February 2004.
270. Upreti, B. R. and Van der Horst, D. (2003), National renewable energy policy and local opposition in the UK: the failed development of a biomass electricity plant. *Journal of Biomass and Bio-energy*. 26:1, Pp. 61-69.
271. Upreti, B. R., Timsina, N. P., Upreti, U, Shivakoti, I. C., Adhikari, K. P. and Upreti, S. (2005), *Searching for New Direction: Reorienting NARMSAP to Work on the Conflict Situation in Nepal (A report on conflict impact assessment of NARMSAP).* Kathmandu: Royal Danish Embassy.
272. Upreti, B.R. (1998), *Searching for an Alternate Approach for Community Level Natural Resource Management in Nepal: A Case Study on Natural Resource Use Negotiation -A Knowledge Systems Perspective*. MSc thesis submitted to the Wageningen Agricultural University, The Netherlands.
273. Ury W., J. Brett and Goldberg, S. (1989), *Getting Disputes Resolved.* San Francisco: Jossey-Bass Publishers.
274. Ury, W. (1991), *Getting Past "No": Negotiating with Difficult People.* New York: Bantam Books.
275. Ury, W. (1999), *Getting to Peace: Transforming Conflict at Home, at Work, and in the World,* New York: Viking.
276. Uyangoda, J. (2003), Beyond Mediation, Negotiation and Negative Peace: Towards Transformative Peace in Sri Lanka. Colombo: Programme for Alternative Learning.
277. Uyangoda, J. (eds.), (2000), Conflict Resolution and Peace Studies: An Introductory Handbook. Colombo: Centre for Policy Research and Analysis and FES.
278. Duijn, L (2003), *Nepal IDP Research Initiative Findings: An Initiative of Concerned Agencies in Nepal.* Kathmandu: GTZ, INFORMATION, SNV, UNDP/RUPP.
279. Vayrynen R. (ed.) (1991), *New Directions in Conflict Theory.* London:

Sage Publications.

280. Vayrynen, R (1991), New Directions in Conflict Theory: Conflict Resolution and Conflict Transformation. London: Sage Publications.
281. Wall, J. and Lynn, A. (1993), Mediation: A Current Review. *Journal of Conflict Resolution* 37, 1: 160-194.
282. Warner M. (2001), *Complex Problems-Negotiated Solutions: Strategies and Tools for Reducing Conflict as an Obstacle to Sustainable Rural Livelihoods.* London: Overseas Development Institute.
283. Weber, M. (1948), The Theory of Social and Economic Organization, Illinois: The Free Press.
284. Wehr, P. (1979), *Conflict Regulation.* Boulder, Colorado: Westview.
285. Wehr, P., Burgess, H. and Burgess, G. (eds.), (1994), *Justice Without Violence*, Boulder: Lynne Rienner.
286. Woodhouse, T. (eds.), (1991), *Peacemaking in a Troubled World.* Oxford: Berg Books.
287. Zartman, I. W. (1987), *Positive Sum: Improving North-South Negotiations.* New York: Transaction Publishers.
288. Zartman, I. W., (1985), *Ripe for Resolution: Conflict and Intervention in Africa.* New York: Oxford University Press.
289. Zartman, W, (1995), *Elusive Peace: Negotiating an End to Civil Wars.* Washington / DC: The Brookings Institution.
290. Zartman, W. and Berman, M. (1982), *The Practical Negotiator*. New Haven: Yale University Press.
291. Zartman, W. and Touval, S. (1996), International mediation in Post Cold War Era, In: *Managing Global Chaos* (eds.) C. Crocker, F. Hampson and P. All. Washington DC: United State Institute of Peace. Pp. 445-461.
292. Zartman, W. I. (1989), *Ripe for Resolution: Conflict Intervention in Africa.* New York: Oxford.

Index